ollins

AF662433

Dimensions 5

A Mathematics Textbook based on ELPSA Approach

Name : ....

Grade : .... Section : ....

I am in Hyderabad. I am a square-shaped monument with four pillars, one on each side. I have used the number four (or char) and its multiples in at least 22 spots in the design of my structure. What am I? ....

Series Editor | Sangeeta Yadav

HarperCollins*Publishers*

Publishing operations in 17 countries and 120+ imprints globally

William Collins' dream of knowledge for all began with the publication of his first book in 1819. A self-educated mill worker, he not only enriched millions of lives, but also founded a flourishing publishing house. Today, staying true to this spirit, Collins books are packed with inspiration, innovation and practical expertise. They place you at the centre of a world of possibility and give you exactly what you need to explore it.

Published by Collins Learning
An imprint of HarperCollins*Publishers* India
Building No. 10, Tower A, 4th Floor, DLF Cyber City, Gurugram, Haryana 122002, India

First edition: 2024
Reprint edition: 2024
ISBN: 9789362132369

Artwork, typesetting and layout by **GNZE Interactions**
Printed and bound in India by Shiv Shakti Printing & Trading Co.
Content developed by **Excelsoft Technologies Pvt Ltd.**

ACKNOWLEDGEMENTS
Title page: Created by Swasti Verma; **6:** Qvasimodo"; **7:** SiberianArt; filo; **25:** VectorUp; **40:** Macrovector, gomez77; **46:** Judyjump; **56:** non-exclusive; **57:** Turac Novruzova, texturis; **62:** pijama61, ankomando, DmitriyKazitsyn; **64:** prahprah, matheesaengkaew; **78:** Kharlamova; **83:** insemar, Siede Preis; **85:** Kusni ah; **86:** isoon kawsuk; **89:** Elena Chernykh; **90:** Flavio Coelho, Pakin Songmor; **91:** MaksimYremenko; **93:** SherSor; **94:** Hubei territory Network Technology Co., Ltd/ 500px; **97:** t_kimura, Lew Robertson, Siede Preis"; **105:** Natoushe, Suraj Raheja, wongmbatuloyo; **115:** klyaksun;**119:** Vectorig, Yana Shadurskaya; **121:** KAMURAN AĞBABA, msonick; **122:** Victor_Brave; **123:** SpicyTruffel; **125:** newannyart; **126:** petrroudny, sldesign78; **129:** kennykiernan, undefined undefined, Blueastro; **132:** Evgeniy Skripnichenko, CreativeDesignArt; **135:** Alfadanz; **138:** siridhata, TiktaAlik, Nandalal Sarkar; **142:** wakila, Witthaya Prasongsin, Peter Dazeley, alxpin, wwing; **145:** Vadim Rozov; **146:** IconicBestiary, Tetiana Garkusha; **147:** kyoshino; **154:** pialhovik; **155:** verdateo; **161:** VectorHot, Logorilla; **163:** graphic-bee; **166:** im a photographer and an artist; **172:** rhoon; **174:** Irina Karbainova, o-che, o-che; **180:** ninian; **193:** aekikuis, leremy; **195:** alexangel21, Mariya Palkina; **196:** Hammad Khan, Turac Novruzova, bgblue, Redlio Designs; **197:** amtitus; **199:** Bigmouse108; **200:** djmilic; **207:** Anastasiia_New; **208:** yongyut Chanthaboot; **210:** perori 00; **212:** Jc_Dh, aqabiz, Irina Cheremisinova; **216:** Dmytro Bosnak; **225:** Sana Farzouli; **227:** Veronika Oliinyk; **230:** Elena Emchuk, Mironov Konstantin, Sonya_illustration, MuchMania; **244:** Sheng Li; **244:** Mikhail Seleznev; **245:** jojoo64, alexsl RUSSELLTATEdotCOM, Mohamed Rasik; **246:** rambo182; **248:** Serhii Sereda, Salamatik, Arafat Uddin; **251:** eliflamra; **252:** Catur Nurhadi, ved007; **259:** Pavel Naumov, Irina Marchenko, Yuliya Nikolaeva

Browse the complete Collins catalogue at www.collins.in.
For any queries/feedback, please write to us at SCHOOLSUPPORT@harpercollins.co.in.

PREFACE

Dimensions is an eight-book series designed for classes 1 to 8, aligned with the **National Education Policy (NEP) 2020** and the **National Curriculum Framework (NCF) 2023**. This series aims to promote *proficiency* and *mastery* in mathematics through the innovative **ELPSA approach**.

This series focuses on a comprehensive learning experience, emphasising five essential components: **Experience**, **Language**, **Pictorial**, **Symbols** and **Application** (ELPSA). Students are introduced to concepts through concrete objects and experiences, followed by pictorial representations and finally, abstract concepts are introduced. This approach helps students visualise and comprehend complex mathematical problems with ease.

Moreover, the series encourages interdisciplinary projects, fostering scientific temper, vocational skills and sensitivities. It also places special emphasis on raising awareness about Indian knowledge systems and the invaluable contributions of Indian mathematicians.

Aligned with the NCF 2023, the chapters in ***Dimensions*** are thoughtfully designed to achieve curricular goals and develop essential competencies. Each concept receives ample instructional support, ensuring a strong understanding among students.

To engage students further, the series adopts an application-based approach, connecting mathematics to real-life experiences. This approach makes learning enjoyable and helps students understand the relevance of mathematics in their day-to-day lives.

For grades 1 and 2, the books follow a workbook style, tailor-made for young learners. Enriched with colourful pictures and extended activities, these books foster meaningful and joyful learning experiences.

We would like to take this opportunity to thank all the teachers and educationists who generously reviewed our books and offered their invaluable feedback. Their contributions have been instrumental in elevating the quality of the content and enhancing the overall learning experience for students.

Feedback, invaluable comments and suggestions from users are welcome.

Authors

About the Series Editor

Dr Sangeeta Yadav is an experienced Educator, Consultant and Author, with over 25 years of teaching experience. She has authored 27 books, including titles on mental maths and activity books. She has created Quiz Master editions for Collins Learning. Her work aims to inspire and inform, helping students develop strong mathematical concepts.

KEY FEATURES

Dimensions is a cutting-edge mathematics series that nurtures a profound understanding of mathematical concepts, promotes interdisciplinary learning and fosters a sense of pride in Indian knowledge heritage. With its engaging and comprehensive ELPSA approach (*the holistic learning circle*), this series empowers students to excel in their mathematical journey and appreciate the beauty of mathematics in the world around them.

Experience

Evoking out-of-school experience to build on understanding, reinforcing existing understandings to new concepts, providing physical experiences, if possible, for new concepts

Language

Reinforcing mathematics terminology throughout the lesson, fostering conversations that link experiences with language, encouraging students' own language while modelling precise terminology

Application

Applying symbolic reasoning to real-life situations, applying symbolic reasoning to related mathematics concepts, applying mathematics concepts outside the classroom

Pictorial

Including concrete manipulatives, external representations and students' encoded understandings, ensuring multiple representations including non-prototypical representations

Symbols

Introducing symbolic expressions alongside pictorial representations, encouraging multiple appropriate symbolic representations

How can Proficiency and Mastery be achieved?

By following the 5-step Learning Process through the key features given in the book.

Introduction → Conceptual Understanding → Practice → Application → Expansion

- Introduction
  - Why This Topic?
  - Are You Ready?
- Conceptual Understanding
  - ELPSA integrated content
  - Activities
  - Concept Map
- Practice
  - Exercise
  - Revision Exercise
  - Did You Master?
- Application
  - Word Problems
  - Application-based Questions
- Expansion
  - Projects
  - Financial Literacy

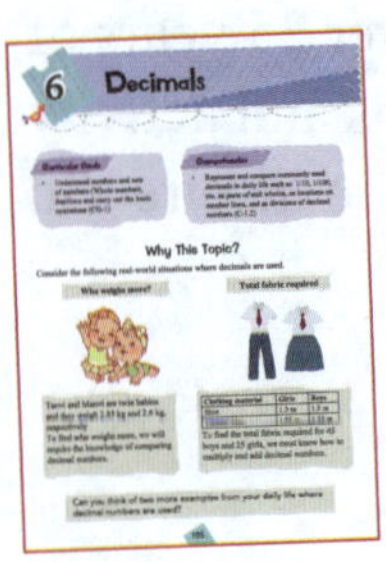

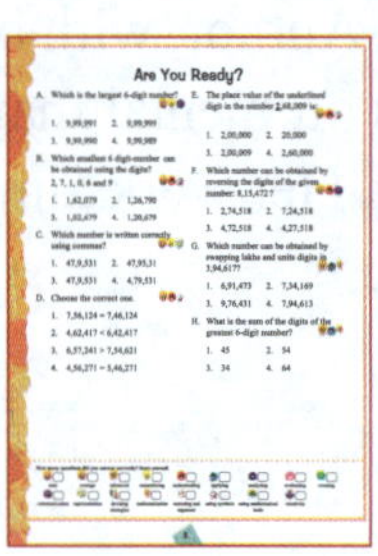

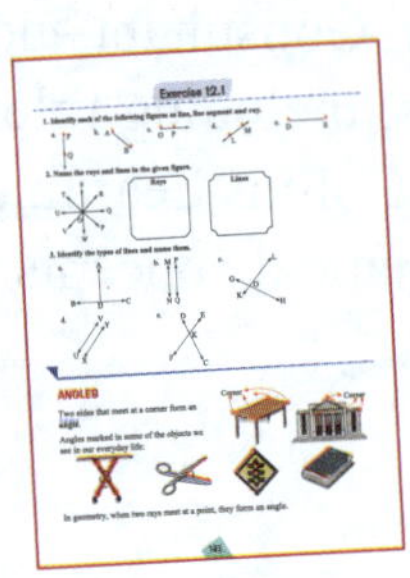
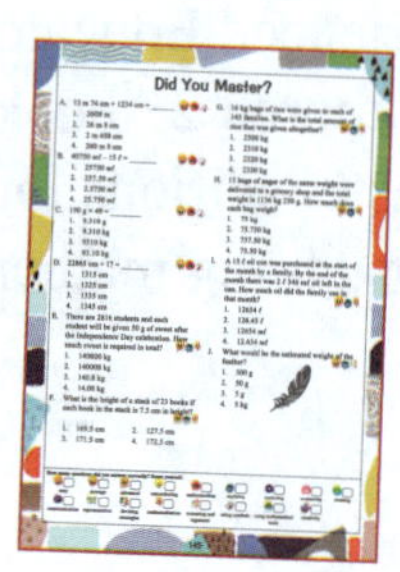

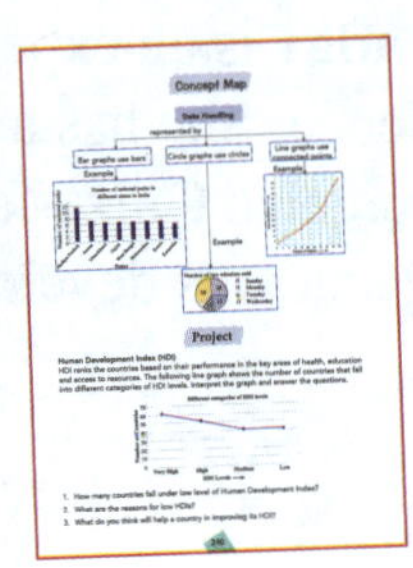

COMPREHENSIVE PRE- AND POST-ASSESSMENTS

These pre- and post-assessments employ MCQs tagged with icons to indicate competencies such as Difficulty Levels, Bloom's Taxonomy and Maths Learning Skills. Each assessment comes along with a scorecard for self-assessment.

Given for each chapter!

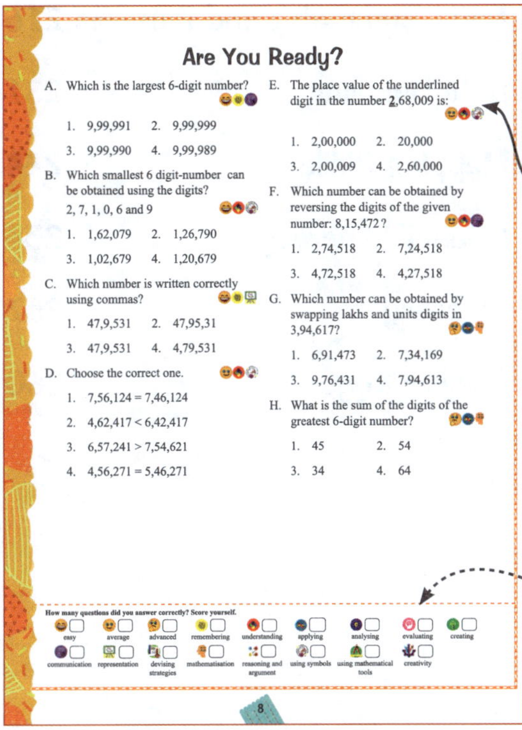

Icons

Scorecard

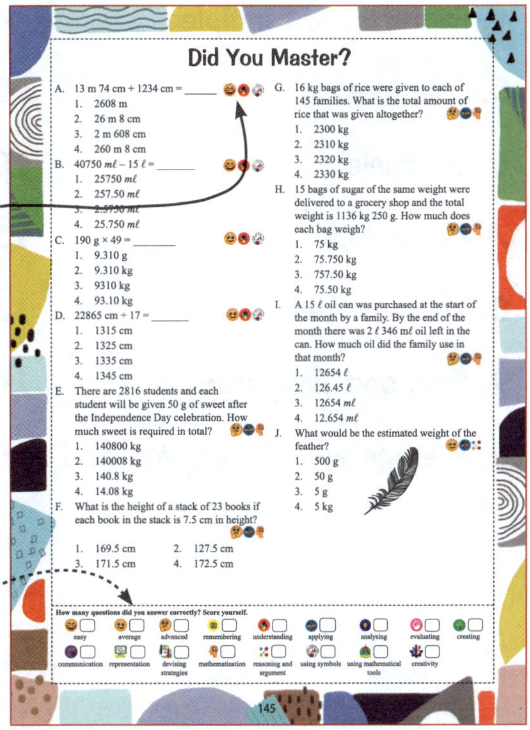

Competencies and Icons in Are You Ready? and Did You Master?

Difficulty Levels

Easy

Average

Advanced

Bloom's Taxonomy

Remembering

Understanding

Applying

Analysing

Evaluating

Creating

Maths Learning Skills

Communication

Reasoning and argument

Representation

Using symbols

Devising strategies

Using mathematical tools

Mathematisation

Creativity

CONTENTS

Learning Maths is easy and fun through Experience
Language
Pictures
Symbols
Application

1 Large Numbers

Curricular Goals

- Understand and represent counting numbers using the Indian place value system, discover and recognize patterns in number sequences (CG-1)

Competencies

- Represent numbers using the place value structure of the Indian number system, compare whole numbers, and know and read the names of very large numbers (C-1.1)

Why This Topic?

How do we read so many numbers at a time? To understand this, we may use Indian and international number system.

Population of India

According to the Indian census 2011, the least populated state of India is Sikkim.

Its population is 6,10,577.

The most populated state of India is Uttar Pradesh.

Its population is 199,812,341.

How do you read this number?

Distance between Sun and Earth

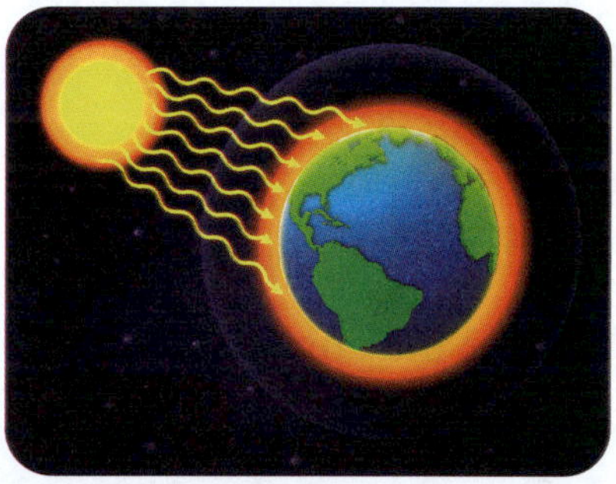

The distance between the Sun and the Earth is about 150,970,000 kilometres.

Can you write the number in word form?

List two examples from daily life where we use 8- or 9- digit numbers.

Are You Ready?

A. Which is the largest 6-digit number?

1. 9,99,991 2. 9,99,999
3. 9,99,990 4. 9,99,989

B. Which smallest 6 digit-number can be obtained using the digits?
2, 7, 1, 0, 6 and 9

1. 1,62,079
2. 1,26,790
3. 1,02,679
4. 1,20,679

C. Which number is written correctly using commas?

1. 47,9,531
2. 47,95,31
3. 4,795,31
4. 4,79,531

D. Choose the correct one.

1. 7,56,124 = 7,46,124
2. 4,62,417 < 6,42,417
3. 6,57,241 > 7,54,621
4. 4,56,271 = 5,46,271

E. The place value of the underlined digit in the number <u>2</u>,68,009 is:

1. 2,00,000 2. 20,000
3. 2,00,009 4. 2,60,000

F. Which number can be obtained by reversing the digits of the given number: 8,15,472 ?

1. 2,74,518
2. 7,24,518
3. 4,72,518
4. 4,27,518

G. Which number can be obtained by swapping lakhs and units digits in 3,94,617?

1. 6,91,473
2. 7,34,169
3. 9,76,431
4. 7,94,613

H. What is the sum of the digits of the greatest 6-digit number?

1. 45 2. 54
3. 34 4. 64

How many questions did you answer correctly? Score yourself.

easy ☐ average ☐ advanced ☐ remembering ☐ understanding ☐ applying ☐ analysing ☐ evaluating ☐ creating ☐

communication ☐ representation ☐ devising strategies ☐ mathematisation ☐ reasoning and argument ☐ using symbols ☐ using mathematical tools ☐ creativity ☐

INTRODUCTION TO 7-DIGIT NUMBERS

Observe the addition pattern and guess the number.

The number that you get on adding 1 to the greatest 6-digit number (9,99,999) is 10,00,000.

Note that it has seven digits. The seventh digit's position is known as **Ten Lakhs** and it is written as **TL**.

TL	L	TTh	Th	H	T	O
1	0	0	0	0	0	0

9 + 1 = 10

99 + 1 = 100

999 + 1 = 1000

9999 + 1 = 10,000

99,999 + 1 = 1,00,000

9,99,999 + 1 = ______

Ten lakhs and lakhs are together under the **period of lakhs** just like ten thousands and thousands are together under the period of thousands.

TL	L	TTh	Th	H	T	O
Lakhs period		Thousands period		Ones period		

Reading 7-Digit Numbers

Read the digits in the lakhs period first, then in the thousands period and finally in the ones period.

Example 1: Write the given number in the table alongside.

Solution: Thirty-eight lakh forty-one thousand two hundred seventy-six.

TL	L	TTh	Th	H	T	O
3	8	4	1	2	7	6

Use of Commas

Commas are used to distinguish the periods in a number. A comma is placed after the lakhs and the thousands periods to distinguish them from each other.

Example 2: Use commas to write the following numbers.

a. 3841276 b. 8239457

Solution:

	Number	Use of commas
a.	3841276	38,41,276
b.	8239457	82,39,457

Expanded Form

Expanding every digit as per its place in a number, is the **expanded form** of a number.

Place value of a number is the product of the digit and its place.

Face value of a digit is the digit itself.

Example 3: Write the expanded form for the following numbers. Also, write the place value and face value of the underlined digits:

a. 38,41,276   b. 82,39,457

Solution:

	Number	Expanded Form
a.	38,41,276	30,00,000 + 8,00,000 + 40,000 + 1000 + 200 + 70 + 6
b.	82,39,457	80,00,000 + 2,00,000 + 30,000 + 9000 + 400 + 50 + 7

Place value:

a. 38,41,276

$3 \times 10,00,000 = 30,00,000$

b. 82,39,457

$2 \times 1,00,000 = 2,00,000$

Face value:

a. 38,41,276: 3

b. 82,39,457: 2

8-DIGIT NUMBERS

We know that the largest 7-digit number is 99,99,999.

Ⓒ	TL	L	TTh	Th	H	T	O
1	0	0	0	0	0	0	0

What number would you get if you add 1 to it?

99,99,999 + 1 = 1,00,00,000

This place is known as **Crore** and it is written as **C**.

The number 1,00,00,000 is read as **one crore**.

<table>
<tr><td>C</td><td>TL</td><td>L</td><td>TTh</td><td>Th</td><td>H</td><td>T</td><td>O</td></tr>
<tr><td>Crore</td><td colspan="2">Lakhs period</td><td colspan="2">Thousands period</td><td colspan="3">Ones period</td></tr>
</table>

Note that 10 ten lakhs is equal to 1 crore.
Also, **1 crore = 100 lakhs.**

Reading 8-Digit Numbers

Read the digits of the crores period first, then the lakhs period, then the thousands period and finally, the ones period.

C	TL	L	TTh	Th	H	T	O
4	3	8	4	1	2	7	6

Use of Commas

A comma is placed after the crores, the lakhs and the thousands periods to distinguish them from each other.

Example 4: Use commas to write the following numbers: a. 43841276 b. 98239457 and write the expanded form of given numbers.

Solution:

	Number	Use of commas	Expanded Form
a.	43841276	4,38,41,276	4,00,00,000 + 30,00,000 + 8,00,000 + 40,000 + 1000 + 200 + 70 + 6
b.	98239457	9,82,39,457	9,00,00,000 + 80,00,000 + 2,00,000 + 30,000 + 9000 + 400 + 50 + 7

9-DIGIT NUMBERS

a

The population figures of three states in India are: Bihar (104099452), Maharashtra (112374333), and Uttar Pradesh (199812341). Among all the states in India, Uttar Pradesh has the largest population.

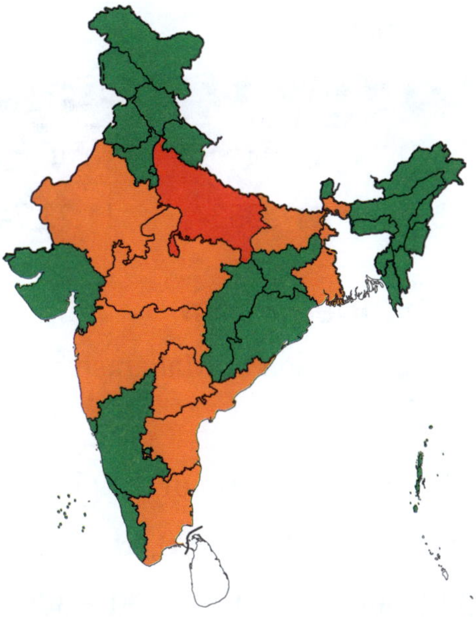

How do you read the given number: 199812341?

Note that the number 199812341 has nine digits. The position of the ninth digit is the ten crores.

Just like the lakhs and the ten lakhs together form a period, the crores and the ten crores are grouped into one period, that is, the crores period.

Ten crore is written as **10,00,00,000.**

INDIAN SYSTEM OF NUMERATION

Indian Place Value Chart								
CRORES		LAKHS		THOUSANDS		ONES		
Ten Crores	Crores	Ten Lakhs	Lakhs	Ten Thousands	Thousands	Hundreds	Tens	Ones
10,00,00,000	1,00,00,000	10,00,000	1,00,000	10,000	1000	100	10	1

1 ten	=	10
1 hundred	=	100
1 thousand	=	1000
1 ten thousand	=	10,000
1 lakh	=	1,00,000
1 ten lakh	=	10,00,000
1 crore	=	1,00,00,000
1 ten crore	=	10,00,00,000

10 tens = one hundred: $10 \times 10 = 100$

10 hundreds = 1 thousand: $10 \times 100 = 1000$

100 thousands = 1 lakh: $100 \times 1000 = 1,00,000$

Use of Commas

Place commas after the crores, the lakhs and the thousands periods. Then, read the number accordingly.

Example 5: Use commas for the following numbers: a. 104099452 b. 112374333

Solution:

	Number	Use of commas
a.	104099452	10,40,99,452
b.	112374333	11,23,74,333

Expanded Form

The population of Maharashtra is 11,23,74,333.

The expanded form of the given number is 10,00,00,000 + 1,00,00,000 + 20,00,000 + 3,00,000 + 70,000 + 4000 + 300 + 30 + 3.

TC	C	TL	L	TTh	Th	H	T	O
Crores period		Lakhs period		Thousands period		Ones period		

Example 6: Write the expanded form of the population of Uttar Pradesh and Bihar.

Solution: The population of Uttar Pradesh is 199812341 and Bihar is 104099452.

Population	Expanded form
199812341	10,00,00,000 + 9,00,00,000 + 90,00,000 + 8,00,000 + 10,000 + 2000 + 300 + 40 + 1
104099452	10,00,00,000 + 40,00,000 + 90,000 + 9,000 + 9000 + 400 + 50 + 2

Exercise 1.1

ia

1. Use commas and write the number names of the following numbers.

a. 2415786 b. 821600009 c. 12436205 d. 58042513 e. 34561897

2. Write the numbers corresponding to the following number names and expanded forms.

a. Ninety-five lakh sixty-three thousand forty-nine

b. 10,00,00,000 + 20,000 + 90 + 1

c. Seven crore two hundred one

d. Forty-seven crore forty-seven lakh forty-seven thousand four hundred forty-seven

e. 8,00,00,000 + 50,00,000 + 40,000 + 300 + 90 + 3

3. Fill in the blanks.

a. 28,45,32,156 = 20,00,00,000 + ________ + 40,00,000 + ________ + 30,000 + ________ + 100 + 50 + ________

b. 30,18,982 = 30,00,000 + ________ + 8000 + ________ + ________ + ________

c. 7,12,05,001 = ________ + ________ + 2,00,000 + ________ + 1

d. 80,00,00,000 + 7,00,00,000 + 5,00,000 + 6000 + 400 + 5 = ________

e. One crore one = ________

4. Write the missing numbers.

a. 10,000 = ________ thousands = ________ hundreds = ________ tens

b. 1,00,000 = ________ ten-thousands = ________ thousands = ________ hundreds = ________ tens

c. 10,00,000 = ________ lakhs = ________ ten-thousands = ________ thousands = ________ hundreds = ________ tens

d. 1,00,00,000 = ________ ten lakhs = ________ lakhs = ________ ten-thousands = ________ thousands = ________ hundreds = ________ tens

e. 10,00,00,000 = ________ ten lakhs = ________ lakhs = ________ ten-thousands = ________ thousands = ________ hundreds = ________ tens

COMPARISON OF NUMBERS

a

Two or more numbers can be compared by comparing the digits in the respective places (crores, lakhs, thousands, hundreds, ones) of the two or more numbers.

Example 7: Arrange the five states in the decreasing order of their populations.

State	Population
Andhra Pradesh	8,45,80,777
Odisha	4,19,74,218
Bihar	10,40,99,452
Maharashtra	11,23,74,333
Tamil Nadu	7,21,47,030

Solution:

	TC	C	TL	L	TTh	Th	H	T	O
Andhra Pradesh		8	4	5	8	0	7	7	7
Odisha		4	1	9	7	4	2	1	8
Bihar	1	0	4	0	9	9	4	5	2
Maharashtra	1	1	2	3	7	4	3	3	3
Tamil Nadu		7	2	1	4	7	0	3	0

Note that the population of Maharashtra and Bihar is more than ten crores. The digits at the ten crores place are the same. So, compare the digits at the crores place.

Bihar	1	0	4	0	9	9	4	5	2
		0 < 1							
Maharashtra	1	1	2	3	7	4	3	3	3

Therefore, 10,40,99,452 < 11,23,74,333

Compare the other digits of the three states:

8,45,80,777; 7,21,47,030; 4,19,74,218

The five states in their decreasing order of population are:

Maharashtra > Bihar > Andhra Pradesh > Tamil Nadu > Odisha

11,23,74,333 > 10,40,99,452 > 8,45,80,777 > 7,21,47,030 > 4,19,74,218

Exercise 1.2

1. Write the following states in the increasing order of their female population.

State	Female Population
Karnataka	3,01,28,640
West Bengal	4,44,67,088
Rajasthan	3,29,97,440
Tamil Nadu	3,60,09,055
Bihar	4,98,21,295

2. Add commas and fill in the blanks using the correct symbol (>/</=).

a. 27856145 ____ 278405614 b. 789999 ____ 789999 c. 1002540 ____ 6002504

d. 1000001 ____ 10000001 e. 68200547 ____ 68200527

INTERNATIONAL SYSTEM OF NUMERATION

The following table shows the **international place value** system and the periods corresponding to each group of three numbers. Notice that in the international place value system, after thousands, there are millions and billions instead of lakhs and crores.

International Place Value Chart											
BILLIONS			MILLIONS			THOUSANDS			ONES		
Hundred Billions	Ten Billions	Billions	Hundred Millions	Ten Millions	Millions	Hundred Thousands	Ten Thousands	Thousands	Hundreds	Tens	Ones
100,000,000,000	10,000,000,000	1,000,000,000	1,000,000,00	10,000,000	1,000,000	100,000	10,000	1000	100	10	1

Let us study the method of reading numbers in the international place value system. Consider the examples given below. Read the three digits in the thousands place together, followed by the three digits in the ones place.

THOUSANDS			ONES		
Hundred Thousands	Ten Thousands	Thousands	Hundreds	Tens	Ones
7	8	6	3	4	5

Example 8: Write the number names: a. 786,345 b. 561,296

Solution: a. Seven hundred eighty-six thousand three hundred forty-five

b. Five hundred sixty-one thousand two hundred ninety-six

READING MILLIONS

Let us read the number 560,687,797. Read the digits in the millions period, then the digits in the thousands period and finally, the digits in the ones period.

MILLIONS			THOUSANDS			ONES		
Hundred Millions	Ten Millions	Millions	Hundred Thousands	Ten Thousands	Thousands	Hundreds	Tens	Ones
5	6	0	6	8	7	7	9	7

Five hundred sixty million six hundred eighty-seven thousand seven hundred ninety-seven

Example 9: Write the number names: a. 336,533,716 b. 138,319,176

Solution: a. Three hundred thirty-six million five hundred thirty-three thousand seven hundred sixteen

b. One hundred thirty-eight million three hundred nineteen thousand one hundred seventy-six

Let us write the number corresponding to eighty-five million eight hundred thirty-four thousand nine hundred five.

Follow the given steps:

Step 1: Identify the periods. Here, there are three periods, namely, millions, thousands and ones.

Step 2: Write the given digits in each period.

MILLIONS			THOUSANDS			ONES		
Hundred Millions	**Ten Millions**	**Millions**	**Hundred Thousands**	**Ten Thousands**	**Thousands**	**Hundreds**	**Tens**	**Ones**
	8	5	8	3	4	9	0	5

Step 3: Place the commas after each period: 85,834,905

Example 10: Write the numbers corresponding to the given number names:

a. Nine hundred forty million three hundred seventy-three thousand nine hundred twenty-four

b. Nineteen million two hundred six thousand twenty-four

Solution: a. 940,373,924 b. 19,206,024

ROUNDING OFF NUMBERS

Read the following facts and find the meanings of the underlined words.

- As per 2011 census, there are roughly 56 crore literate people in India out of an estimated 120 crore people.
- There are about 300 million male literates in India whereas there are only about 200 million female literates.

Let us understand the method of rounding off numbers to different places.

Rounding off to the Lakhs Place

Step 1: In the given number, identify the digit at the ten thousands place. For example, 2,76,462

Step 2: If the digit is less than 5, then make the digits at all places except in the lakhs place 0. Otherwise add 1 to the digit at the lakhs place and make the other digits 0. In this case, $7 > 5$, so, add 1 to the digit at the lakhs place and make the other digits 0. i.e. 3,00,000.

Therefore, you get the number 3,00,000 after rounding off the number 2,76,462 to the nearest lakhs place.

Example 11: Round off these numbers:

a. 8,35,415 b. 5,52,089

Solution:

a. Since the digit at the ten thousands place is 3 and $3 < 5$.

Therefore, the rounded off number to the nearest lakhs place is 8,00,000.

b. Since the digit at the ten thousands place is 5 and 5 = 5.

Therefore, the rounded off number to the nearest lakhs place is 6,00,000.

Rounding off to the Ten Lakhs Place

Similar to the method followed in rounding off to the lakhs place, numbers can be rounded off to the nearest ten lakhs place as well. In this case, you need to find whether the digit at the lakhs place is less than 5 or not.

Example 12: Round off these numbers:

a. 72,14,560 b. 48,62,204

Solution: As the digits at lakhs place is 2 and 8 respectively and 2 < 5; 8 > 5.

Therefore, the rounded off numbers are:

a. 70,00,000 b. 50,00,000

Rounding off to the Crores

Look for the digit at the ten lakhs place and compare it with 5.

If it is greater than or equal to 5, then add 1 to the digit at the crores place and make the rest of the digits 0.

If the digit is less than 5, then make all the other digits 0 except the digit at the crores place.

Example 13: Round off the numbers:

a. 4,72,14,250 b. 4,32,14,250

Solution: As the digits at ten lakhs place is 7 and 3 respectively and 7 > 5; 3 < 5.

Therefore, the rounded off numbers are:

a. 5,00,00,000 b. 4,00,00,000

Rounding off to the Ten Crores Places

Look for the digit at the crores place and compare it with 5. If it is greater than or equal to 5, then add 1 to the digit at the ten crores place and make the rest of the digits 0.

If the digit is less than 5, then make all the other digits 0 except the digit at the ten crores place.

Example 14: Round off the numbers:

a. 55,72,14,250 b. 52,82,14,250

Solution: As the digits at crores place is 5 and 2 respectively and 5 = 5; 2 < 5.

Therefore, the rounded off numbers are:

a. 60,00,00,000 b. 50,00,00,000

Exercise 1.3

1. Write the numbers corresponding to the given number names. Also, write the number names of the given numbers.

a.	Five hundred forty-six million eight hundred ninety-six thousand four hundred fifteen	
b.	Six hundred seventy million four hundred six	
c.	Seventy-six million nine thousand nine hundred eighty-five	
d.		900,467,999
e.		735,084,206

2. Place commas as per the Indian place value system and compare the numbers. Put the correct symbols in the blanks (</>/=).

a. 124054 ____ 2140589   b. 24456122 ____ 34547892   c. 9000001 ____ 9000000

d. 5789456 ____ 50891243   e. 52214561 ____ 768741321

3. Write the following numbers in both the Indian and the international place value systems by using commas.

Number	Indian Place Value System	International Place Value System
a. 24587916		
b. 312458		
c. 748657136		
d. 50060090		
e. 9264906		

4. Write the numbers corresponding to the following number names.

a. Three crore forty-seven lakh fifty-five thousand two

b. Nine hundred sixteen million four hundred forty-five thousand two hundred ninety-one

c. Eighty-one lakh sixty thousand forty-five

d. Two million ten thousand four hundred six

e. Three hundred forty-five million seven hundred forty-five thousand six hundred twenty-one

5. Round off the following numbers to the underlined place.

a. 45,36,708   b. 2,76,36,708   c. 78,56,372   d. 54,30,36,708   e. 7,08,114

6. How many 7-digit numbers are there? Also, how many 8-digit and 9-digit numbers are there? How do you know?

7. Write at least three possible numbers if the digits 1 to 9 are used only once in the following number.

40,00,00,000 + ________ + 20,00,000 + 8,00,000 + 50,000 + 6000 + ________ + 90 + ________ = ________

ROMAN NUMERALS

The ancient Romans used letters to write numbers.

Look at this table of Roman numerals and their values.

I	II	III	IV	V	VI	VII	VIII	IX	X
1	2	3	4	5	6	7	8	9	10
V	X	XV	XX	XXV	XXX	XXXV	XL	XLV	L
5	10	15	20	25	30	35	40	45	50
X	XX	XXX	XL	L	LX	LXX	LXXX	XC	C
10	20	30	40	50	60	70	80	90	100
C	CC	CCC	CD	D	DC	DCC	DCCC	CM	M
100	200	300	400	500	600	700	800	900	1000

- There is no symbol for 0 in the Roman numeral system.
- A letter is never repeated more than 3 times.

Rule 1:

Repetition of letter denotes addition. Letter (I X C M) can be repeated up to 3 times, unlike V L and D, which are never repeated.

III = 1 + 1 + 1 = 3

XXX = 10 + 10 + 10 = 30 VV = Wrong!

CCC = 100 + 100 + 100 = 300

MMM = 1000 + 1000 + 1000 = 3000

Rule 2:

One or more numerals placed after a numeral of a greater value implies addition.

XI = 10 + 1 = 11

CLX = 100 + 50 + 10 = 160

MC = 1000 + 100 = 1100

Example 15: Write the Hindu-Arabic numbers for the following Roman numbers:

a. II b. III c. XXX

d. CC e. MMM

Solution: a. II = 1 + 1 = 2

b. III = 1 + 1 + 1 = 3

c. XXX = 10 + 10 + 10 = 30

d. CC = 100 + 100 = 200

e. MMM = 1000 + 1000 + 1000 = 3000

Symbol	Value in Hindu-Arabic Number System
I	1
V	5
X	10
L	50
C	100
D	500
M	1000

Rule 3: If a smaller number is written to the left of a bigger number, then it must be subtracted from the bigger number. The symbol 'I' can only be written to the left of V and X. The symbols V, L and D are never written to the left of a bigger number. Also, the symbol X can be subtracted from L and C only. Similarly, C can be subtracted from D and M only.

VX = Wrong!; IL = Wrong!; DM = Wrong!

Example 16: Write the Hindu-Arabic numbers for the following Roman numerals.

a. IV b. XL c. CD d. CM

Solution: a. IV = 5 – 1 = 4 b. XL = 50 – 10 = 40

c. CD = 500 – 100 = 400 d. CM = 1000 – 100 = 900

Rule 4: If a smaller number is written to the right of a bigger number, then it must be added to the bigger number.

Example 17: Write the Hindu-Arabic numbers for the following Roman Numerals:

a. XV b. LV c. CL d. DC

Solution: a. XV = 10 + 5 = 15 b. LV = 50 + 5 = 55

c. CL = 100 + 50 = 150 d. DC = 500 + 100 = 600

Rule 5: If a smaller number is written in between two greater values, then it is always subtracted from the greater number immediately following it.

Example 18: Write the Hindu-Arabic numbers for the following Roman numerals:

a. XXXIV b. MCIX

Solution: a. XXXIV = 10 + 10 + 10 + (5 – 1) = 30 + 4 = 34

b. MCIX = 1000 + 100 + (10 – 1) = 1109

Writing Hindu–Arabic Numbers In Roman Numerals

To write a given Hindu–Arabic number in Roman numerals, first write it in a suitable expanded form. Then, use the symbols to write each individual number.

Example 19: Write the Roman numerals for the following Hindu-Arabic numbers:

a. 256 b. 927

Solution: a. 256 = 200 + 50 + 6 = 100 + 100 + 50 + 5 + 1 = CCLVI

b. 927 = 900 + 20 + 7 = (1000 – 100) + 10 + 10 + 5 + 1 + 1 = CMXXVII

Exercise 1.4

ia

1. Write the following as Hindu-Arabic numbers.

a. XXXIV b. CCLXX c. MVII

d. DCCXC e. LV f. XCIX

g. DXXI h. MMCLI i. MCCLVI

j. MMDCCCIII k. CXLV l. MDCCLXXXV

m. MDCCXCI n. MDCCCXLV

2. Write the Roman numerals corresponding to the following Hindu-Arabic numbers.

a. 888 b. 348 c. 577

d. 799 e. 434 f. 287

g. 2765 h. 1449

Concept Map

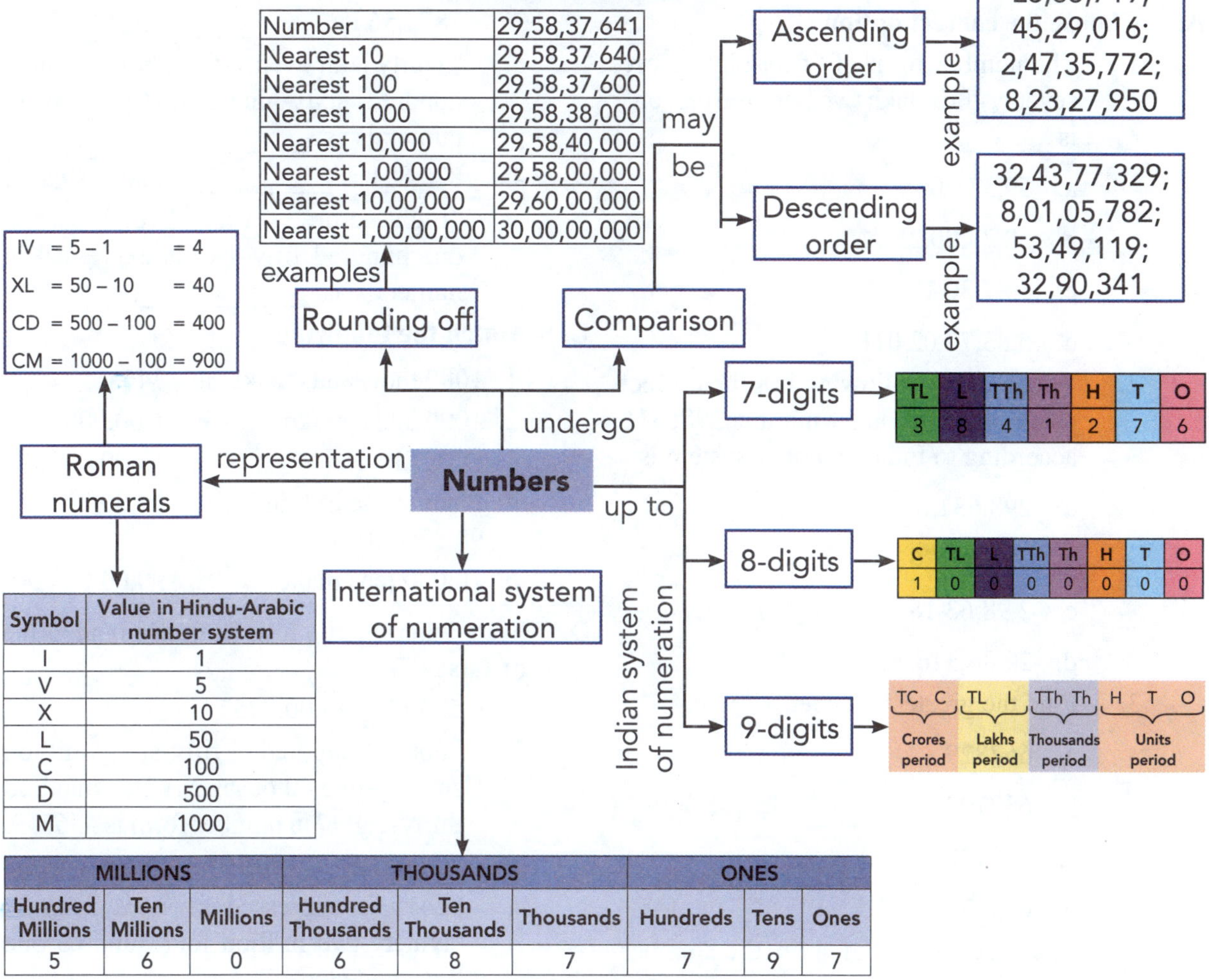

Number	29,58,37,641
Nearest 10	29,58,37,640
Nearest 100	29,58,37,600
Nearest 1000	29,58,38,000
Nearest 10,000	29,58,40,000
Nearest 1,00,000	29,58,00,000
Nearest 10,00,000	29,60,00,000
Nearest 1,00,00,000	30,00,00,000

Symbol	Value in Hindu-Arabic number system
I	1
V	5
X	10
L	50
C	100
D	500
M	1000

MILLIONS			THOUSANDS			ONES		
Hundred Millions	Ten Millions	Millions	Hundred Thousands	Ten Thousands	Thousands	Hundreds	Tens	Ones
5	6	0	6	8	7	7	9	7

Projects

A. Maths with matchsticks

Make a chart representing the Hindu–Arabic numbers in Roman numerals using matchsticks. The chart should have a minimum of 10 representations.

Also, represent the basic symbols of the Roman numerals.

B. Maths in Different Languages

Find the names of the words "ones", "thousands", "lakhs" and "crores" in your mother tongue. Try to find out the names in other languages as well. Make a language chart based on your findings.

Revision Exercise

W

A. Choose the correct option.

1. The number form of "fifty-eight crore seventy-three lakh two hundred eleven" is ______.
   a. 59,37,201
   b. 58,73,00,211
   c. 5,87,30,201
   d. 5,83,70,02,011
2. Which of the following has the correct usage of comma in the number 2986316 according to Indian number system is:
   a. 298,631,6
   b. 29,86,31,6
   c. 2,98,63,16
   d. 29,86,316
3. Find the greatest number.
   a. 667829
   b. 639792
   c. 619920
   d. 689123
4. The place value of 4 in the number 5049281 is ________.
   a. Ten thousand
   b. Hundred
   c. Thousand
   d. Lakh
5. The Roman form of 436 is ________.
   a. DCXXXXVI
   b. CDXXXXV
   c. CDXXXVI
   d. DCXXXV

B. Fill in the blanks.

1. "Forty-seven crore ninety-one lakh two hundred sixteen" is expressed in numerals as ___________.
2. 187,256 is __________ than 1,89,256.
3. "Thirty lakh twenty-four thousand nine hundred sixty-nine" is expressed in numerals as ___________.
4. 879,891 is ___________ than 789,897.
5. "Eight crore seventy-five thousand one hundred fifty-six" is expressed in numerals as ____________.

C. Match the following.

1. 1000 thousands make	a. 746
2. 1000 lakhs make	b. 1,00,000
3. DCCXLVI	c. 10,00,000
4. Place value of 9 in 98,32,15,024	d. 10,00,00,000
5. 10,000 tens make	e. 90,00,00,000

D. State whether the following are true (T) or false (F).

1. 500,825 = 5,00,825
2. "Four hundred fifty-six million seventy-one thousand nine hundred thirty-eight" in number form is 456719.
3. 704,021,045 > 508,021,036
4. 92411 is expressed in word form as "Ninety-two million four hundred one thousand eleven"
5. 9,11,14,523 > 9,21,55,025

E. Solve the following.

1. Use commas according to the Indian and the International place value systems for the number 50786124.
2. Write the place value of the underlined digit in the number 6<u>4</u>5,102,069.
3. Write the following numbers in ascending order.
   7,55,67,890; 17,55,76,980;
   7,55,76,890 and 7,55,76,980
4. Round off the number 86,10,593 to the nearest lakhs place.
5. Write the Roman numeral corresponding to the Hindu-Arabic number 220.

F. Application-based questions.

1. Sahana went to buy a toy, the price of which was written in Roman numerals as ₹CCXV. What is the price of the toy in Hindu-Arabic system?
2. Raju and Rekha played a video game, and their scores were 456782 and 489569 respectively. Who won the game?
3. Naveen got his ATM card from the bank. The card number is 781343 and the pin of the card is the number in thousand's and hundred's place. What is the pin of the card?
4. A factory manufactures 46,782 cookies in the month of May and 46,823 cookies in the month of June. In which month are the least cookies produced?
5. The cost of a car in the showroom is written in words as eighty-five lakh three hundred twenty-six. What is the cost of the car in the number form?

Space for rough work

Did You Master?

A. Which is the smallest 7-digit number?

1. 10,00,000
2. 11,00,000
3. 99,99,890
4. 23,56,901

B. Which of the following expressed as "Three crore five lakhs thirty-four thousand two hundred seventy-one" in numerical form?

1. 3,79,20,61
2. 3,05,34,271
3. 3,50,45,721
4. 3,05,34,371

C. Which is the largest 9 digit-number that can be obtained using the digits 3, 0, 1, 6, 4, 9, 8, 7, 5?

1. 13,45,67,890
2. 10,34,56,789
3. 98,07,65,431
4. 98,76,54,310

D. Which of these is the correct way to write 105 in Roman Numerals?

1. CV
2. CIIIII
3. C1V
4. CCCCDV

E. Which of the following is correct?

1. 1,87,56,124 > 1,87,56,134
2. 1,46,62,417 < 1,45,62,417
3. 10,63,57,241 = 10,63,57,241
4. 8,14,56,271 = 9,14,56,271

F. Find the place value of the underlined digit in the number 1<u>2</u>,37,68,416.

1. 2,00,00,000
2. 2,00,000
3. 20,00,000
4. 21,00,000

G. Which number can be obtained by reversing the digits of the number 1,68,15,478?

1. 8,47,51,861
2. 8,74,15,861
3. 8,74,51,816
4. 8,74,51,861

H. Which number can be obtained by swapping crores and lakhs digits in 1,21,94,617?

1. 1,12,94,617
2. 2,11,94,617
3. 1,21,94,617
4. 1,21,49,617

I. What is the smallest 9-digit number having 9 in the thousands place?

1. 10,00,09,000
2. 1,00,00,000
3. 10,00,00,009
4. 10,00,00,900

J. Which is the greatest 8-digit number with 6 in the tens digit?

1. 9,99,99,989
2. 9,99,99,969
3. 9,99,99,999
4. 8,88,88,868

How many questions did you answer correctly? Score yourself.

easy ☐ average ☐ advanced ☐ remembering ☐ understanding ☐ applying ☐ analysing ☐ evaluating ☐ creating ☐

communication ☐ representation ☐ devising strategies ☐ mathematisation ☐ reasoning and argument ☐ using symbols ☐ using mathematical tools ☐ creativity ☐

2 Addition and Subtraction

Curricular Goals

- Understand counting numbers and carry out the four basic operations with whole numbers (CG-1)

Competencies

- Understand and visualise arithmetic operations and the relationships among them, knows addition and apply the four basic operations on numbers to solve daily life problems (C-1.3)

Why This Topic?

Numbers with more than 6 digits are called large numbers. These numbers are used in various aspects of our lives, so the knowledge of their addition and subtraction is also important.

Cost of a villa

Raj and his family are buying a villa that costs ₹1,15,75,000.

An additional cost of ₹26,85,000 is to be paid for renovation.

Total cost of villa = ₹1,15,75,000 + ₹26,85,000

Profit earned by a company

Cost of cars manufactured by a company in a year = ₹35,12,79,600

Amount received on selling all the cars per annum = ₹59,18,54,300

Profit earned by the company in a year = ₹59,18,54,300 – ₹35,12,79,600

Can you think of two more examples where addition and subtraction of large numbers is used?

Are You Ready?

A. 30,864 + 65,135 = ________

1. 99,959 2. 99,599
3. 59,999 4. 95,999

B. 5,92,984 – 4,21,852 = ________

1. 1,17,132 2. 1,61,132
3. 1,71,132 4. 7,11,132

C. 97,125 + 23,705 = ________

1. 1,20,830 2. 1,02,830
3. 2,10,830 4. 1,02,380

D. 4,31,180 + 2,67,030 = ________

1. 6,98,120 2. 6,89,210
3. 6,98,210 4. 6,99,210

E. How much should be added to 6,54,321 to make it 7,00,000?

1. 55,679 2. 10,000
3. 55,680 4. 45,679

F. What should be subtracted from 1,04,187 to get 89,565?

1. 14,622
2. 41,622
3. 61,422
4. 64,122

G. 93,428 people watch a TV series every day in one city. The same TV series is watched by 24,785 people in a different city. Find the total number of people who watch the TV series.

1. 1,80,213 2. 1,08,213
3. 1,18,213 4. 1,81,213

H. A printing press printed 23,528, 24,673 and 26,782 notebooks in 3 consecutive years. Find the total number of notebooks printed in 3 years.

1. 74,893 2. 74,983
3. 74,389 4. 74,398

I. A poultry farm supplied 72,184 eggs to different stores in a market out of a total of 83,392 eggs. How many eggs are left in the poultry farm?

1. 12,180 2. 12,108
3. 11,280 4. 11,208

J. Stadium X has the capacity of housing 5,19,458 spectators. Stadium Y has the capacity of housing 2,78,375 spectators. How many more spectators can stadium X accommodate as compared to stadium Y?

1. 2,41,083 2. 2,41,380
3. 2,41,803 4. 2,41,830

How many questions did you answer correctly? Score yourself.

easy ☐ average ☐ advanced ☐ remembering ☐ understanding ☐ applying ☐ analysing ☐ evaluating ☐ creating ☐

communication ☐ representation ☐ devising strategies ☐ mathematisation ☐ reasoning and argument ☐ using symbols ☐ using mathematical tools ☐ creativity ☐

ADDITION OF LARGE NUMBERS

a

Large numbers are usually the numbers having more than 6 digits. In this chapter, we will study about 7-digit, 8-digit and 9-digit numbers.

The method of adding large numbers is similar to that of adding small numbers. You need to add the digits at different places, starting from the ones place and moving towards the left. Carry forward, if required.

Following are the general steps for adding 7-digit numbers, with and without regrouping. (Similar steps are followed for 8-digit and 9-digit numbers.)

- Add digits in ones place

  Regroup the ones to tens, if required, and carry forward to the tens place
- Add digits in tens place

  Regroup the tens to hundreds, if required, and carry forward to the hundreds place
- Add digits in hundreds place

  Regroup the hundreds to thousands, if required, and carry forward to the thousands place
- Add digits in thousands place

  Regroup the thousands to ten thousands, if required, and carry forward to the ten thousands place
- Add digits in ten thousands place

  Regroup the ten thousands to lakhs, if required, and carry forward to the lakhs place.
- Add digits in lakhs place

  Regroup the lakhs to ten lakhs, if required, and carry forward to the ten lakhs place.
- Add digits in ten-lakhs place

NUMBER FACTS

- 10 ones = 1 ten
- 10 tens = 1 hundred
- 10 hundreds = 1 thousand
- 10 thousands = 1 ten thousand
- 10 ten thousands = 1 lakh
- 10 lakhs = 1 ten lakh
- 10 ten lakhs = 1 crore

Example 1: A company pays ₹72,45,506 as salary to its employees in 1 month and ₹10,68,297 towards other expenses, such as electricity and water. What is the total expenditure of the company in 1 month?

Solution: Total expenditure of the company = ₹72,45,506 + ₹10,68,297

- Write 72,45,506 and 10,68,297 one below the other based on their places.
- Add digits in each place one by one. (Regroup, if required)

	Step 1	Step 2	Step 3	Step 4	Step 5	Step 6	Step 7
Carry	1 (tens)	1 (hundreds)		1 (ten thousands)	1 (lakhs)		
	7245506	7245506	7245506	7245506	7245506	7245506	7245506
+	1068297	1068297	1068297	1068297	1068297	1068297	1068297
	3	03	803	3803	13803	313803	8313803

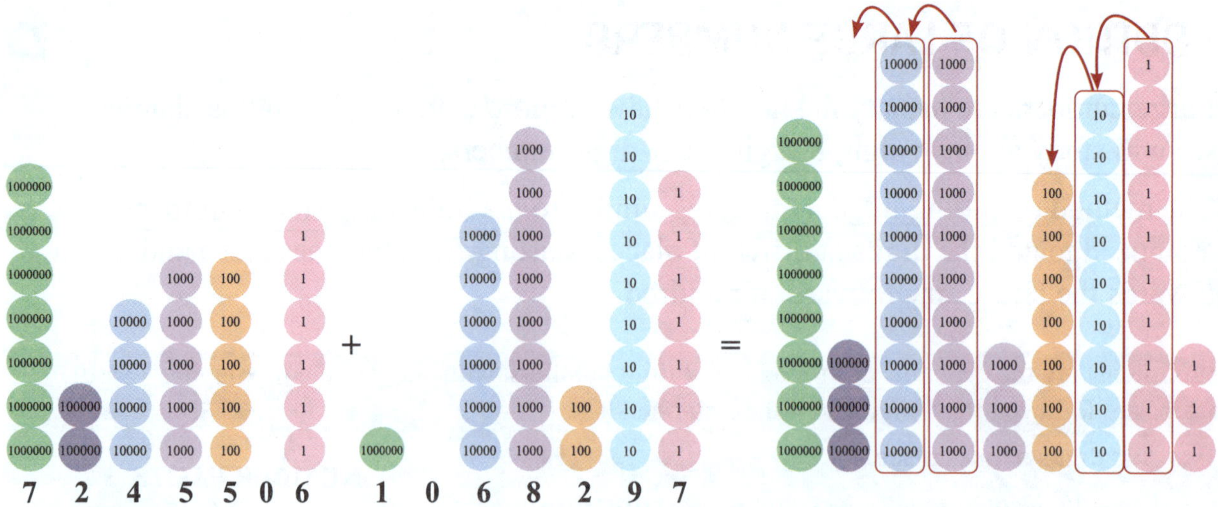

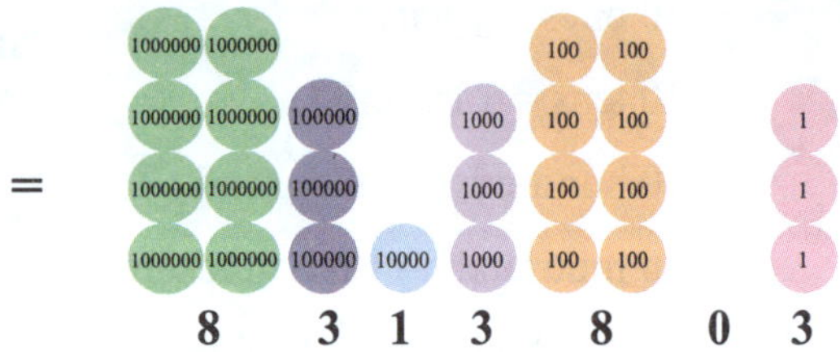

		1	1		1	1	
	7	2	4	5	5	0	6
+	1	0	6	8	2	9	7
	8	3	1	3	8	0	3

Therefore, the total expenditure of the company in 1 month is ₹83,13,803.

Example 2: Add 10,34,267 and 10,34,267.

Solution: Let us add 10,34,267 and 10,34,267.

Step 1

						1	
	1	0	3	4	2	6	7
+	1	0	3	4	2	6	7
							4

Step 2

					1		
	1	0	3	4	2	6	7
+	1	0	3	4	2	6	7
						3	4

Step 3

	1	0	3	4	2	6	7
+	1	0	3	4	2	6	7
					5	3	4

Step 4

	1	0	3	4	2	6	7
+	1	0	3	4	2	6	7
				8	5	3	4

Step 5

	1	0	3	4	2	6	7
+	1	0	3	4	2	6	7
			6	8	5	3	4

Step 6

	1	0	3	4	2	6	7
+	1	0	3	4	2	6	7
		0	6	8	5	3	4

Step 7

	1	0	3	4	2	6	7
+	1	0	3	4	2	6	7
	2	0	6	8	5	3	4

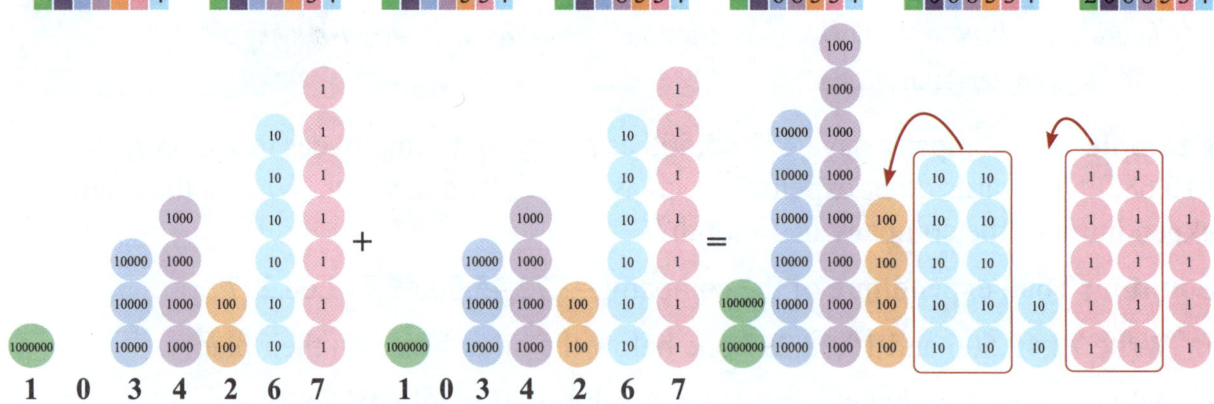

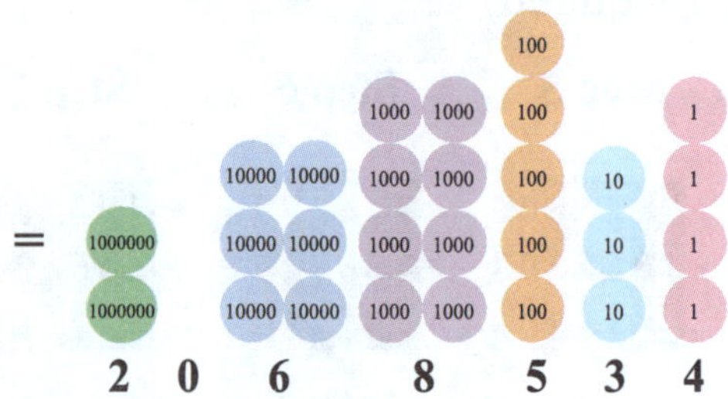

					1	1	
	1	0	3	4	2	6	7
+	1	0	3	4	2	6	7
	2	0	6	8	5	3	4

Therefore, 10,34,267 + 10,34,267 = 20,68,534.

Example 3: The approximate population of different states/union territories is given in the table. Find the total approximate population of Kerala and Jharkhand.

State/Union Territory	Population (Approx.)
Kerala	3,46,98,876
Gujarat	6,04,39,692
Bihar	10,40,99,452
Haryana	2,89,00,667
Lakshadweep	66,001
Jharkhand	3,29,41,000

Solution: Total population of Kerala and Jharkhand

= 3,46,98,876 + 3,29,41,000

Step 1

$$\begin{array}{r} 34698876 \\ +\,32941000 \\ \hline 6 \end{array}$$

Step 2

$$\begin{array}{r} 34698876 \\ +\,32941000 \\ \hline 76 \end{array}$$

Step 3

$$\begin{array}{r} 34698876 \\ +\,32941000 \\ \hline 876 \end{array}$$

Step 4

$$\begin{array}{r} 34698876 \\ +\,32941000 \\ \hline 9876 \end{array}$$

Step 5

$$\begin{array}{r} 1 \\ 34698876 \\ +\,32941000 \\ \hline 39876 \end{array}$$

Step 6

$$\begin{array}{r} 11 \\ 34698876 \\ +\,32941000 \\ \hline 639876 \end{array}$$

Step 7

$$\begin{array}{r} 34698876 \\ +\,32941000 \\ \hline 7639876 \end{array}$$

Step 8

$$\begin{array}{r} 34698876 \\ +\,32941000 \\ \hline 67639876 \end{array}$$

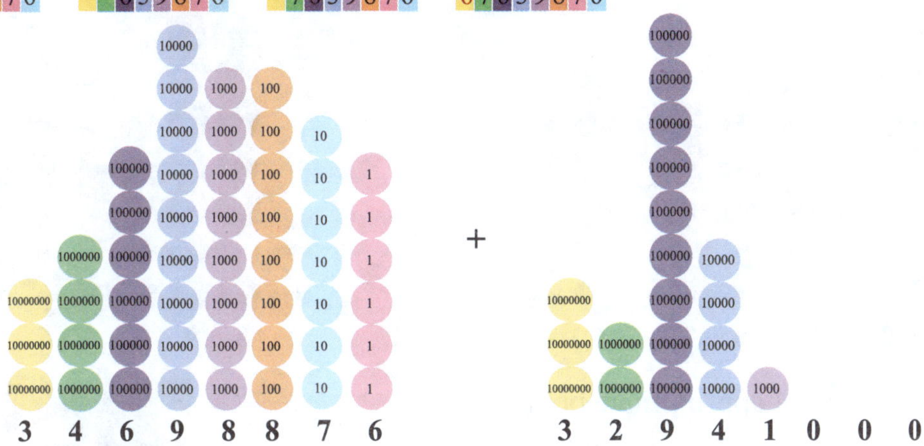

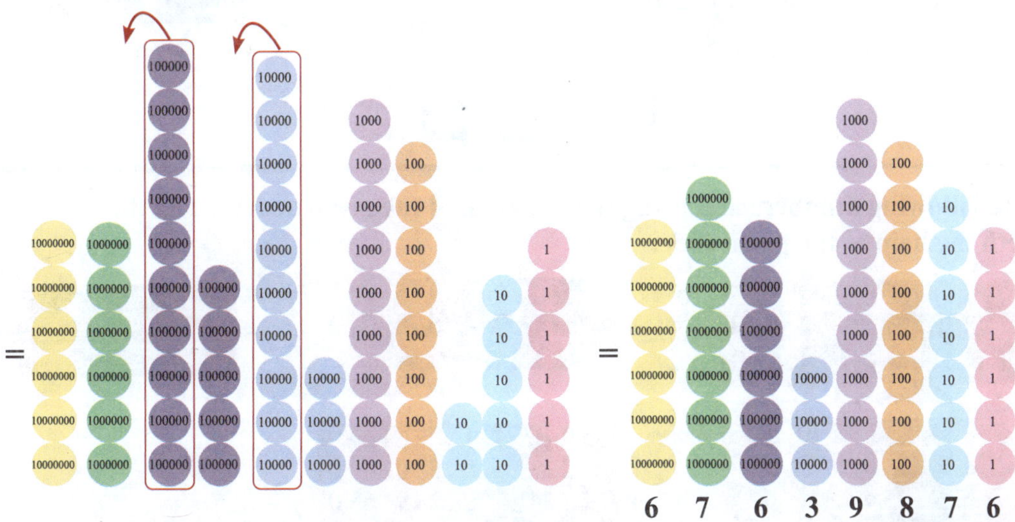

Therefore, the total approximate population of Kerala and Jharkhand is 6,76,39,876.

$$\begin{array}{r} 11 \\ 34698876 \\ +\,32941000 \\ \hline 67639876 \end{array}$$

Example 4: From the table given in the previous question, find the total approximate population of Haryana and Lakshadweep.

Solution: Total population of Haryana and Lakshadweep = 66,001 + 2,89,00,667

Step 1

	2	8	9	0	0	6	6	7
+				6	6	0	0	1
								8

Step 2

	2	8	9	0	0	6	6	7
+				6	6	0	0	1
							6	8

Step 3

	2	8	9	0	0	6	6	7
+				6	6	0	0	1
						6	6	8

Step 4

	2	8	9	0	0	6	6	7
+				6	6	0	0	1
					6	6	6	8

Step 5

	2	8	9	0	0	6	6	7
+				6	6	0	0	1
				6	6	6	6	8

Step 6

	2	8	9	0	0	6	6	7
+				6	6	0	0	1
			9	6	6	6	6	8

Step 7

	2	8	9	0	0	6	6	7
+				6	6	0	0	1
		8	9	6	6	6	6	8

Step 8

	2	8	9	0	0	6	6	7
+				6	6	0	0	1
	2	8	9	6	6	6	6	8

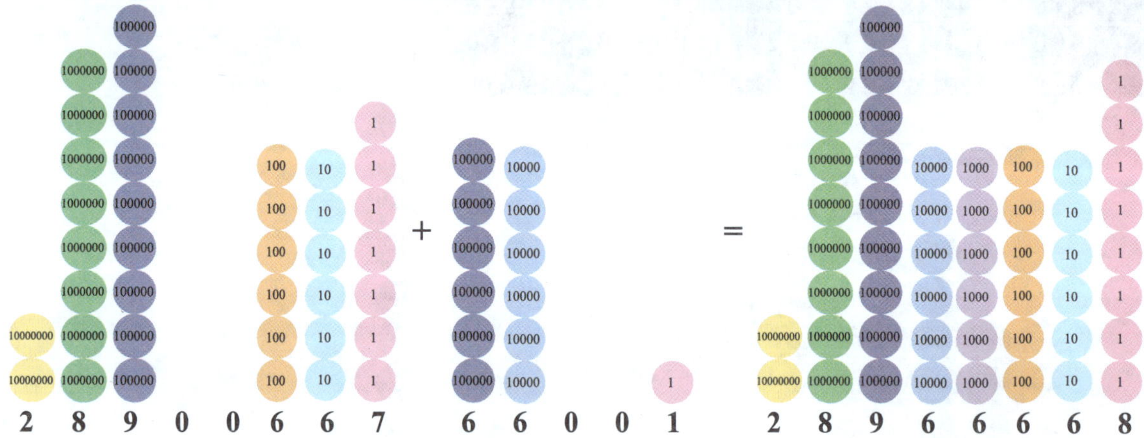

Therefore, the total approximate population of Haryana and Lakshadweep is 2,89,66,668.

	2	8	9	0	0	6	6	7
+				6	6	0	0	1
	2	8	9	6	6	6	6	8

Exercise 2.1

1. Add the following numbers and using the answers, in the given order, write the name of the city with the help of the given code.

a.

	7	5	1	0	6	5	2	9	5
		8	8	9	2	3	4	7	8
+		2	1	2	6	9	1	0	4

b.

		4	5	5	4	1	9	6	0
+			6	0	0	4	6	8	7

c.

	9	6	0	5	3	5	3	3	7
+		1	3	5	8	6	9	4	2

d.

	5	8	4	9	2	2	0	5	6
	2	8	3	0	8	9	7	8	9
		8	9	9	8	5	1	8	8
+			9	1	2	5	2	4	6

e.

	5	9	6	0	1	0	6	6	9
		2	5	5	0	8	0	4	0
+		2	4	4	9	1	9	6	0

I	F	L	E	M	H	D
64,60,10,669	87,41,22,279	97,41,22,279	5,15,46,647	5,15,06,647	96,71,22,279	86,12,57,877

State/Union Territory Capital City: ____________________

2. Add the following numbers and write the name of the city with the help of the given code.

a.

	3	6	3	8	7	7	5	1
+		2	6	0	4	0	0	6

b.

	8	3	3	0	4	6	3	9	0
		9	9	9	2	0	0	9	9
+			2	4	7	7	8	0	3

c.

	2	4	4	6	0	3	4	5
+	1	4	5	3	1	4	1	2

d.

	3	6	3	8	7	7	5
+			4	0	0	6	0

e.

	6	4	0	4	7	5	9
+	5	8	6	9	4	2	2

f.

	1	0	8	4	0	4	7	5	9
		4	6	9	7	2	7	8	0
+			1	5	6	2	5	5	7

I	U	A	H	D	B	M
15,69,40,096	93,54,44,292	1,22,74,181	36,08,835	15,69,00,096	36,78,835	3,89,91,757

State/Union Territory Capital City: ______________________

SUBTRACTION OF LARGE NUMBERS

Recall that to subtract a smaller number from a bigger number, the smaller number is written below the bigger number and subtraction is done from right to the left. Borrow, if required.

Following are the general steps for subtracting 7-digit numbers, with and without borrowing. (Similar steps are followed for 8-digit and 9-digit numbers)

- Subtract digits in ones place
  Borrow a ten from the tens place, if required
- Subtract digit in tens place
  Borrow a hundred from the hundreds place, if required
- Subtract digit in hundreds place
  Borrow a thousand from the thousands place, if required
- Subtract digit in thousands place
  Borrow a ten thousand from the ten thousands place, if required
- Subtract digit in ten thousands place
  Borrow a lakh from the lakhs place, if required
- Subtract digits in lakhs place
  Borrow a ten lakh from the ten lakhs place, if required
- Subtract digit in ten lakhs place

Example 5: A company manufactures two-wheelers and four-wheelers. It manufactured 15,46,824 units of vehicles in a year, out of which 12,18,452 were two-wheelers. Find the number of four-wheelers manufactured.

Solution: Number of four-wheelers manufactured

=15,46,824 – 12,18,452

- Write 12,18,452 below 15,46,824 based on their places.
- Subtract digits in each place one by one. (Borrow, if required)

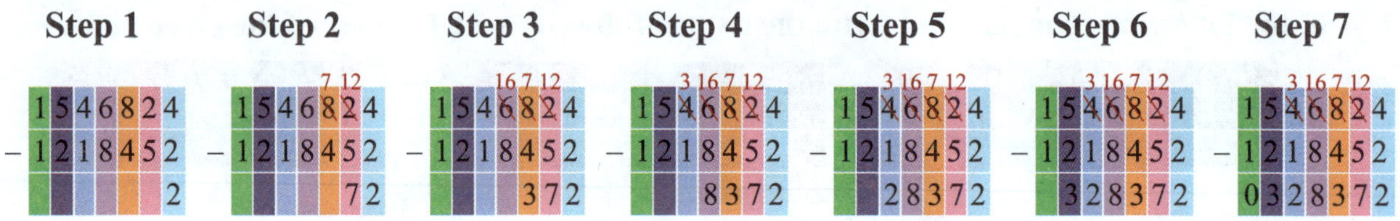

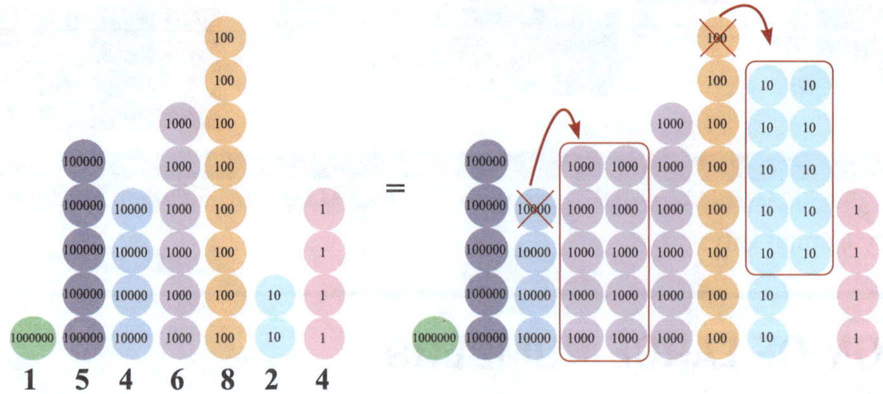

Now subtract 12,18,452 from 15,46,824, we get

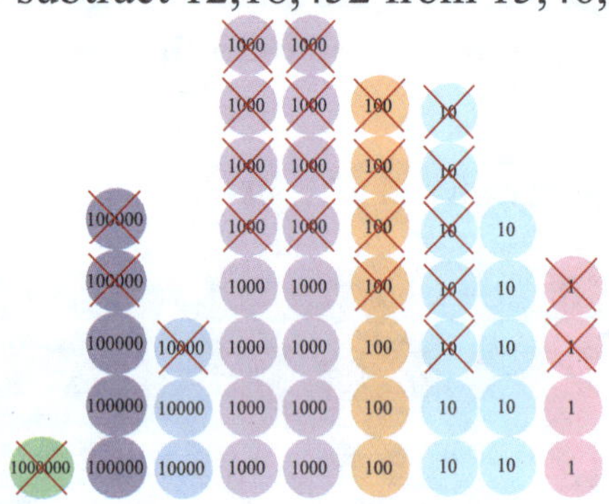

			3	16	7	12	
	1	5	4	6	8	2	4
−	1	2	1	8	4	5	2
		3	2	8	3	7	2

Therefore, the total number of four-wheelers manufactured is 3,28,372.

Verification of subtraction using addition

The sum of units of 2-wheelers and 4-wheelers should be equal to the total number of vehicles manufactured by the company.

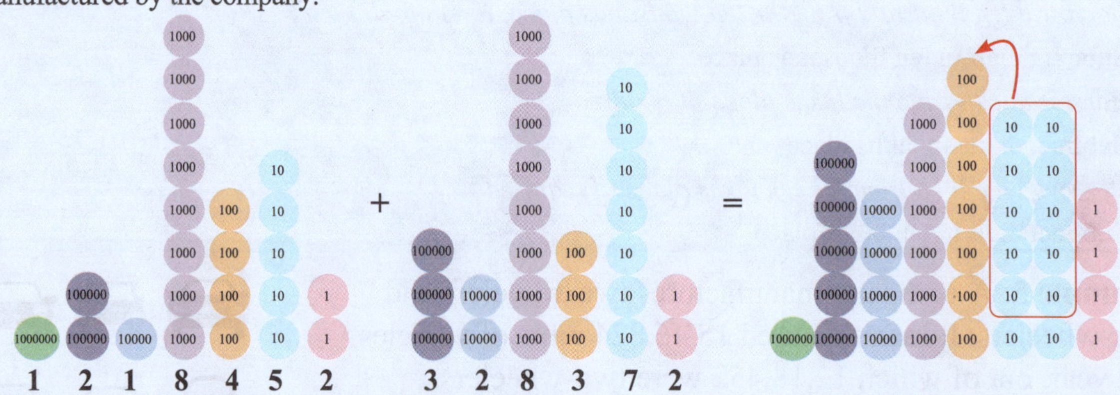

=

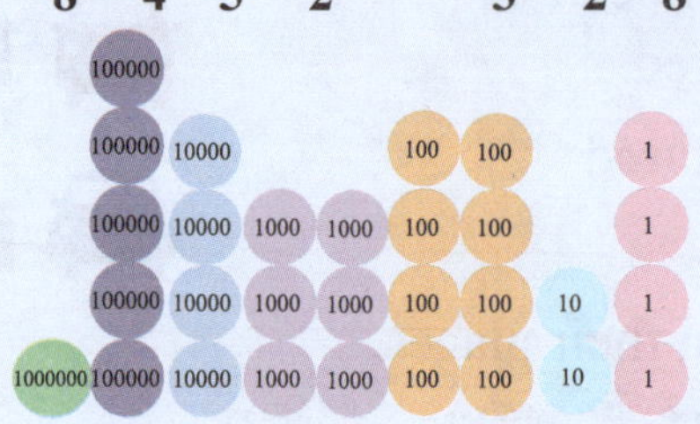

			1		1		
	1	2	1	8	4	5	2
+		3	2	8	3	7	2
	1	5	4	6	8	2	4

Example 6: Subtract 3,69,73,024 from 7,28,40,556.

Solution:

Step 1

	7	2	8	4	0	5	5	6
−	3	6	9	7	3	0	2	4
								2

Step 2

	7	2	8	4	0	5	5	6
−	3	6	9	7	3	0	2	4
							3	**2**

Step 3

	7	2	8	4	0	5	5	6
−	3	6	9	7	3	0	2	4
						5	**3**	**2**

Step 4

	7	2	8	~~4~~ 3	~~0~~ 10	5	5	6
−	3	6	9	7	3	0	2	4
					7	**5**	**3**	**2**

Step 5

	7	~~2~~ 1	~~8~~ 7	~~4~~ 13	~~0~~ 10	5	5	6
−	3	6	9	7	3	0	2	4
				6	**7**	**5**	**3**	**2**

Step 6

	~~7~~ 6	~~2~~ 1	~~8~~ 17	~~4~~ 13	~~0~~ 10	5	5	6
−	3	6	9	7	3	0	2	4
			8	**6**	**7**	**5**	**3**	**2**

Step 7

	~~7~~ 6	~~2~~ 11	~~8~~ 17	~~4~~ 13	~~0~~ 10	5	5	6
−	3	6	9	7	3	0	2	4
		5	**8**	**6**	**7**	**5**	**3**	**2**

Step 8

	~~7~~ 6	~~2~~ 11	~~8~~ 17	~~4~~ 13	~~0~~ 10	5	5	6
−	3	6	9	7	3	0	2	4
	3	**5**	**8**	**6**	**7**	**5**	**3**	**2**

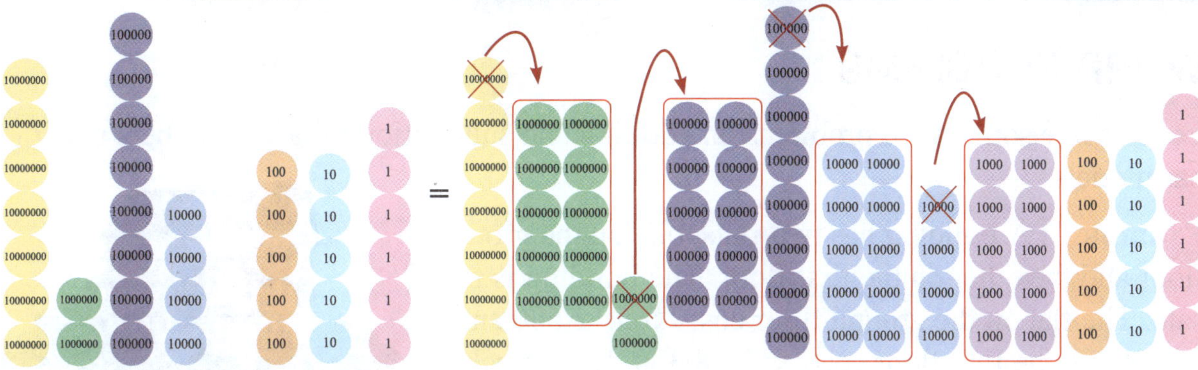

7 2 8 4 0 5 5 6

Subtracting 3,69,73,024 from 7,28,40,556, we get

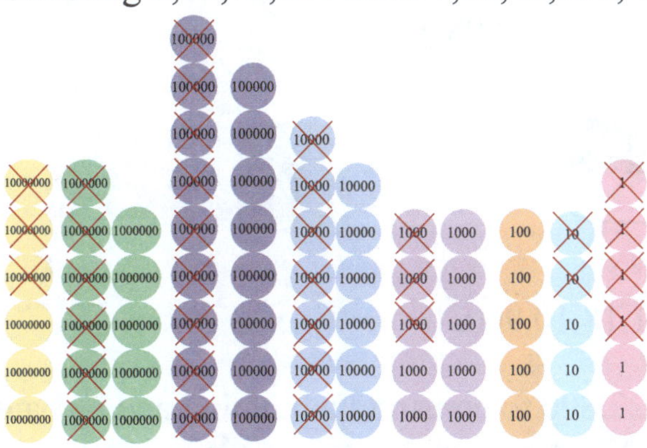

3 5 8 6 7 5 3 2

	~~7~~ 6	~~2~~ 11	~~8~~ 17	~~4~~ 13	~~0~~ 10	5	5	6
−	3	6	9	7	3	0	2	4
	3	5	8	6	7	5	3	2

Verification: The sum of 3,69,73,024 and 3,58,67,532 should be equal to 7,28,40,556.

	[1] 3	[1] 6	[1] 9	[1] 7	3	0	2	4
+	3	5	8	6	7	5	3	2
	7	2	8	4	0	5	5	6

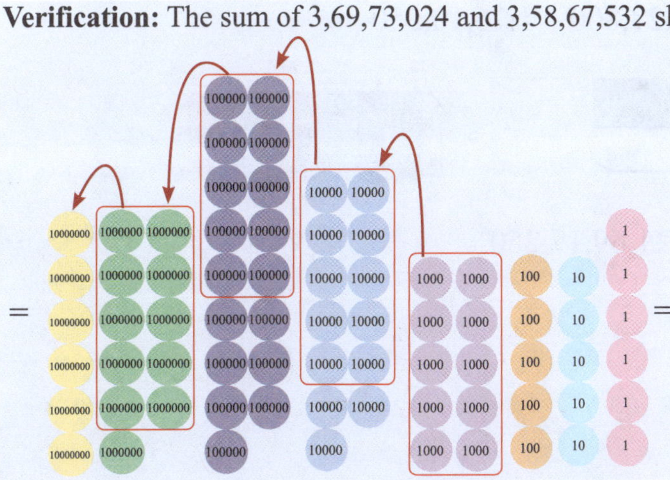

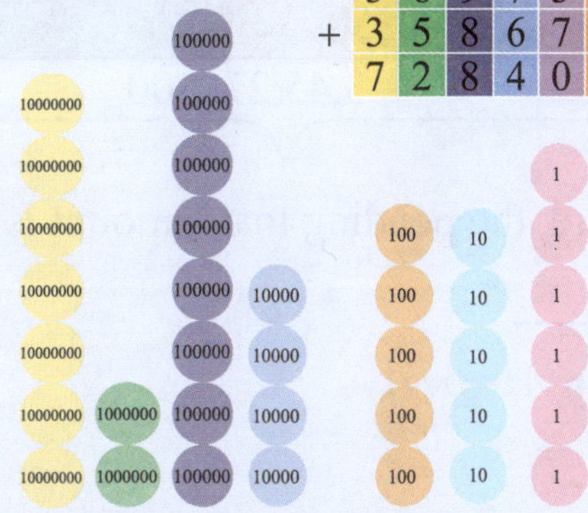

7 2 8 4 0 5 5 6

Exercise 2.2

Subtract the following numbers.

1.

	3	8	5	0	8	2	9	1
–	2	5	4	1	3	2	0	0

2.

	8	6	3	4	9	0	3	2	1
–	7	9	3	4	3	8	1	0	5

3.

	9	8	4	6	2	5	3	2	0
–	4	5	6	3	8	7	9	7	6

4.

	8	6	3	4	9	0	3	2
–	7	0	0	5	2	2	1	6

5.

	1	9	0	0	1	2	0	0	0
–		8	3	5	6	8	9	9	2

6.

	7	5	4	3	5	4	5	6	9
–		6	8	9	7	9	2	9	1

WORD PROBLEMS

Let us solve some word problems on addition and subtraction of large numbers using bar models.

Example 7: A building has two flats, one on the ground floor and the other on the first floor. The building is for sale. The flat on the ground floor costs ₹65,12,600 and the one on the first floor costs ₹52,98,300. How much will both the flats cost together?

Solution: Total cost of the building = 65,12,600 + 52,98,300

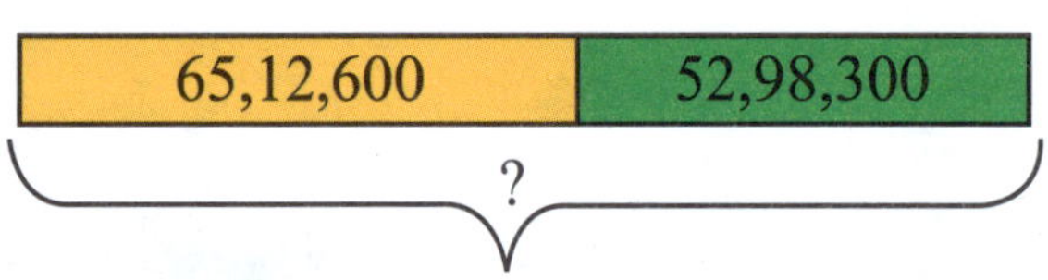

	1		1	1				
		6	5	1	2	6	0	0
+		5	2	9	8	3	0	0
	1	1	8	1	0	9	0	0

Therefore, the total cost of the building is ₹1,18,10,900.

Example 8: A builder took a loan of ₹3,45,27,800 to construct a building and he paid back ₹1,76,10,550 to the bank. Find the pending loan amount.

Solution: Pending loan amount = 3,45,27,800 – 1,76,10,550

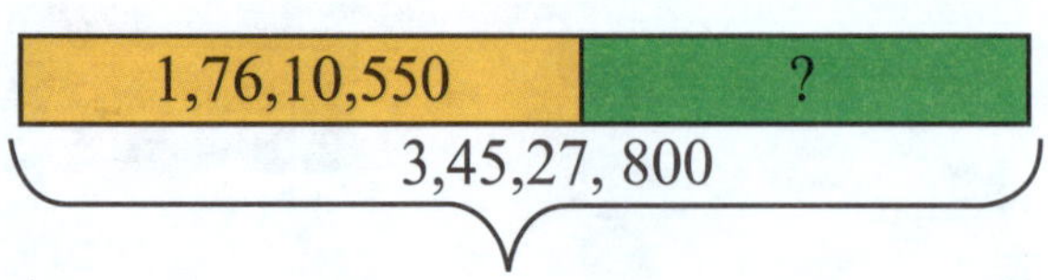

		13						
	2	~~3~~	15			7	10	
	~~3~~	~~4~~	~~5~~	2	7	~~8~~	~~0~~	0
–	1	7	6	1	0	5	5	0
	1	6	9	1	7	2	5	0

Therefore, the pending loan amount is ₹1,69,17,250.

Exercise 2.3

1. Solve the following word problems.

a. The following table shows the number of mobiles manufactured by a company in 3 consecutive years. Find the total number of mobiles manufactured by the company in 3 years?

Year	2020	2021	2022
Mobiles manufactured	9,04,983	9,24,196	9,74,291

b. Approximately 3,85,000 babies are born everyday in the world. Find the total number of newborns in 3 days?

c. According to a survey, there are 90 crore cricket fans in India today. If 22,85,45,675 people were added to the fans club in the present year, then what was the number of fans in the last year?

d. The given table shows the number of people who watched movies in a multiplex every month. Find the difference in the number of people between the 1st month and the 5th month.

Month	1st month	2nd month	3rd month	4th month	5th month	6th month
Number of people	1,11,50,975	1,11,80,642	1,12,30,758	1,12,42,350	1,13,56,264	1,13,75,670

e. An industrialist spent ₹18,64,53,880 to construct a house. He took a loan of ₹11,30,75,315 from a bank and withdrew the remaining amount from his savings account. What is the amount he withdrew from his account?

f. 1,24,97,420 people visited a zoo every year. If the number of men and women who visited is 56,23,456 and 45,18,998, respectively, find the number of children.

g. Write at least two different addition problems whose sum is 15,40,687.

h. Write at least two different subtraction problems whose difference is 15,40,687.

2. Find out the missing numbers.

a.

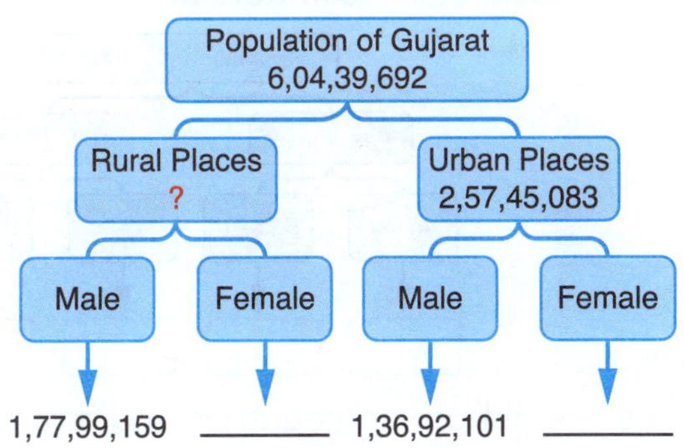

b.

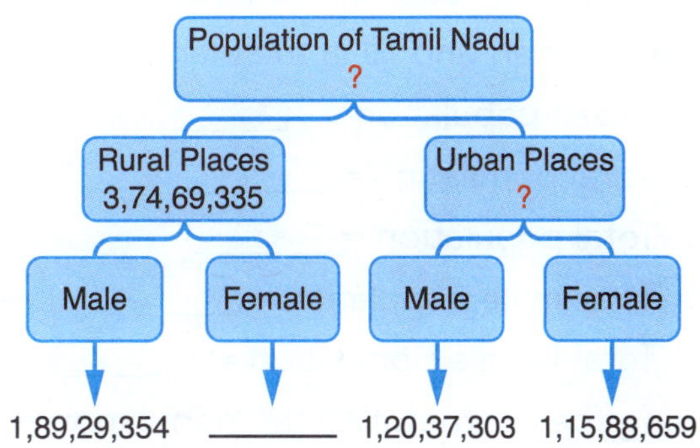

Concept Map

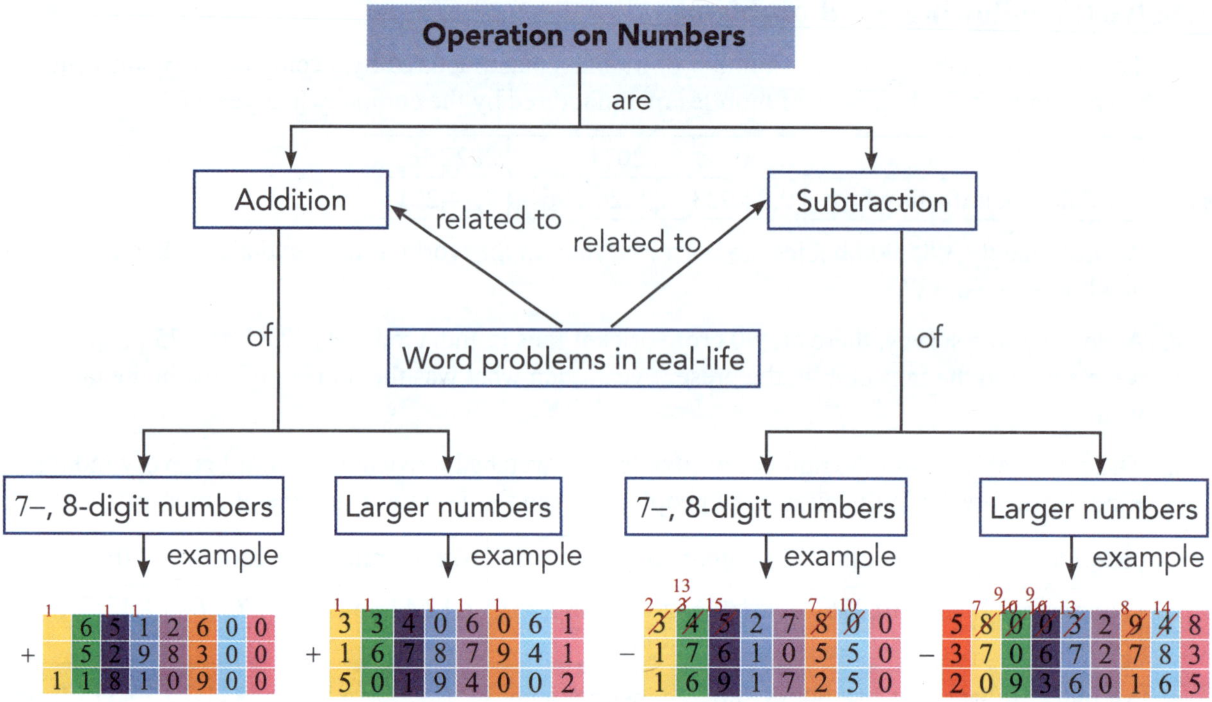

Project

Maths in Population

Find the population of males and females in rural and urban places in Kerala.

Use the chart and fill in the blanks.

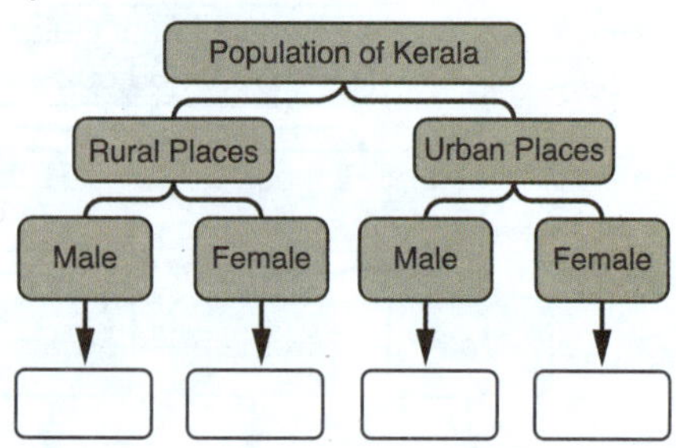

1. Urban population = _______
2. Rural population = _______
3. Total population = _______
4. Total male population = _______
5. Total female population = _______

Using the Internet, find the population of five of our neighbouring countries and arrange them in descending order.

Revision Exercise

A. Choose the correct option.

1. What is the sum of 23,07,890 and 21,09,871?
   a. 44,71,761
   b. 44,17,716
   c. 44,17,671
   d. 44,17,761
2. What is the difference between 87,548,910 and 6,59,78,056?
   a. 2,51,70,854
   b. 2,15,70,854
   c. 2,17,50,854
   d. 2,71,50,854
3. What should be added to 4,86,70,120 to get 5,00,00,000?
   a. 13,29,880
   b. 12,39,880
   c. 13,28,980
   d. 12,30,889
4. What should be subtracted from 70,00,050 to get 57,54,370?
   a. 15,24,680
   b. 12,45,860
   c. 12,45,680
   d. 14,25,680
5. What is the difference between the greatest 8-digit number and the smallest 7-digit number?
   a. 9,99,89,999
   b. 9,98,99,999
   c. 9,89,99,999
   d. 8,99,99,999

B. Fill in the blanks. Use symbols (+/–).

1. 15,08,794 ____ 2,71,09,126 ____ 70,00,05,678 = 72,86,23,598
2. 43,45,67,890 ____ 34,56,789 = 43,11,11,101
3. 25,10,13,705 ____ 2,34,56,789 = 22,75,56,916
4. 19,50,00,780 ____ 11,15,24,234 ____ 13,14,25,378 = 21,49,01,924
5. 5,23,78,807 ____ 93,45,678 ____ 2,20,15,000 = 3,97,09,485

C. Match the following.

1.	65,24,378 + 8,26,49,974	a.	20,59,376
2.	94,86,431 – 24,24,187	b.	58,73,898
3.	2,10,18,129 + 53,74,869	c.	8,91,74,352
4.	45,60,810 – 25,01,434	d.	70,62,244
5.	34,86,431 + 23,87,467	e.	2,63,92,998

D. State whether the following statements are true (T) or false (F).

1. The sum of 7,65,87,419 and 30,35,118 is 7,96,22,537.
2. The difference between 24,54,63,801 and 1,48,27,254 is 53,36,600.
3. The sum of 39,72,390 and 29,42,741 is 26,02,91,055.
4. The difference between 70,24,503 and 44,25,651 is 25,25,987.
5. The sum of the smallest 8-digit number and the greatest 9-digit number is 9,99,99,999.

E. Solve the following.

1. 1,19,59,552 – 37,46,985
2. 95,42,364 + 37,45,127 – 1,04,22,698
3. 18,32,305 – 10,32,903 + 43,61,724 – 35,14,001
4. 46,20,100 + 10,08,055 + 71,95,661 + 5,86,94,234
5. 9,89,23,519 – 9,65,48,705

F. Application-based questions.

1. Nisha and her family travelled 9,50,000 km to visit different places all over the world in 5 years. Their goal now is to visit a few more countries by flying 1,54,360 km more. Find the total distance Nisha's family would have travelled.
2. The total population of a city is 2,14,99,450. Out of them 95,19,590 are women and 42,14,800 are men. Find the population of children.
3. Find the total population of a town if there are 2,10,26,125 males and 2,13,89,745 females.
4. A company manufactured 17,26,34,700 shirt buttons. If 10,15,28,650 buttons have been sold, how many buttons are left unsold?
5. A factory produced 3,27,89,586 sofa sets in 1 year and sold 2,18,64,758 in the same year. How many sofa sets are left with the factory?

Space for rough work

Did You Master?

A. Find the value of 65,89,423 + 24,67,814.

1. 80,52,377 2. 90,75,237
3. 90,52,737 4. 90,57,237

B. 2,78,94,351 – 1,23,54,125 = ______

1. 1,55,24,026
2. 1,55,04,226
3. 1,55,40,226
4. 1,54,52,026

C. What is the sum of 10,84,04,759, 4,69,72,780 and 15,62,557?

1. 15,69,40,096
2. 65,14,09,096
3. 56,41,09,096
4. 16,59,40,096

D. Fill in the box with (+/–) to make one of the given options correct.

87,06,02,540 ☐ 5,42,10,748

1. 81,36,91,792
2. 18,63,91,792
3. 81,63,91,792
4. 81,63,97,192

E. A total of 89,75,325 people watched a movie on 1st day of its release and 95,24,765 people watched the same movie on the 2nd day. Find the number of people who watched the movie in these 2 days.

1. 1,58,00,090 2. 1,85,00,009
3. 1,58,00,009 4. 1,85,00,090

F. Which of the following will give the difference as 10,31,17,599?

1. 76,54,32,100 – 66,23,14,519
2. 76,54,32,109 – 66,23,14,510
3. 76,54,32,108 – 66,23,14,519
4. 76,54,32,199 – 66,23,14,510

G. A factory manufactured 67,84,57,519 pairs of shoes in 3 years, out of which 60,56,89,431 were sold. Find the number of pairs left with the company.

1. 7,72,68,088
2. 2,77,68,088
3. 7,27,68,088
4. 7,72,86,088

H. If the number of tourists who visited the Gateway of India in a span of 2 years is 33,92,274 and 67,84,548, what is the total number of tourists who visited in these 2 years?

1. 1,10,76,822
2. 1,70,16,822
3. 1,07,18,622
4. 1,01,76,822

I. A plant nursery sold 1,36,15,525 saplings out of 1,70,00,000 saplings in a month. How many saplings are left unsold?

1. 33,84,475
2. 33,87,445
3. 33,84,745
4. 38,34,475

How many questions did you answer correctly? Score yourself.

easy ☐ average ☐ advanced ☐ remembering ☐ understanding ☐ applying ☐ analysing ☐ evaluating ☐ creating ☐

communication ☐ representation ☐ devising strategies ☐ mathematisation ☐ reasoning and argument ☐ using symbols ☐ using mathematical tools ☐ creativity ☐

3 Multiplication and Division

Curricular Goals

- Understand counting numbers and carry out the four basic operations with whole numbers and discover and recognise patterns in number sequences (CG-1)
- Develop problem-solving skills with procedural fluency, to solve mathematical puzzles as well as daily life problems, and as a step towards developing computational thinking (CG-4)

Competencies

- Understand and visualise arithmetic operations and the relationships among them and apply the four basic operations on whole numbers to solve daily life problems (C-1.3)
- Select appropriate methods and tools for computing with whole numbers, such as mental computation, estimation, or paper pencil calculation, in accordance with the context (C-4.3)

Why This Topic?

In real life, we come across many situations of multiplying numbers.

Number of tyres manufactured in a production unit

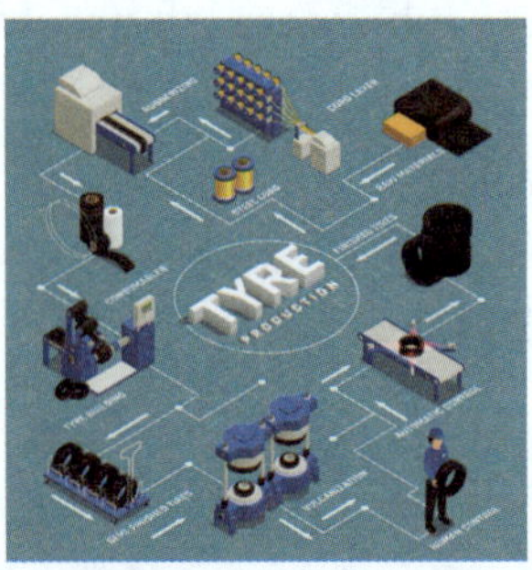

Tyres manufactured in a day: 6350

Tyres manufactured in a month:

6350 × days in a month can be 30/31/28/29.

Finding equal number of people allowed to enter a gate

Total capacity of the stadium: 1,32,000

Number of entry gates: 3

Number of people who can enter in each gate: 1,32,000 ÷ 3

List two more examples of multiplication and division from your daily life.

Are You Ready?

A. If 5630 ÷ 22, the remainder is ______.

1. 8
2. 20
3. 12
4. 9

B. Find the product of 122 × 32.

1. 3784
2. 4024
3. 3864
4. 3904

C. If 6745 ÷ 1000, the remainder is ______.

1. 45
2. 6000
3. 745
4. 5

D. The product of 4733 × 23 is______.

1. 3,45,618
2. 1,08,859
3. 2,34,162
4. 1,02,367

E If a shopkeeper packs 1080 sweets in 24 boxes, how many sweets are there in each box?

1. 25
2. 83
3. 24
4. 45

F. If there are 12 fruits in each box, find the total number of fruits in 25 boxes.

1. 250
2. 123
3. 300
4. 400

G. A number is divided by 18, the quotient is 126 and the remainder is 16. What is the number?

1. 1268
2. 2284
3. 3456
4. 2316

H. Mary sold 9 boxes of cookies, having 12 cookies in each box. She had 3 boxes left having 3 cookies in each box. Match the numbers.

a. cookies baked	i. 108
b. cookies sold	ii. 117
c. cookies left	iii. 9

1. a – i, b – ii, c - iii
2. a – ii, b – i, c - iii
3. a – i, b – iii, c - ii
4. a – ii, b – iii, c - i

I. There are 38 half-sleeve shirts and 12 full-sleeve shirts in each box. Find the total number of shirts in 742 boxes.

1. 45,670
2. 37,100
3. 45,623
4. 32,679

How many questions did you answer correctly? Score yourself.

easy ☐ average ☐ advanced ☐ remembering ☐ understanding ☐ applying ☐ analysing ☐ evaluating ☐ creating ☐

communication ☐ representation ☐ devising strategies ☐ mathematisation ☐ reasoning and argument ☐ using symbols ☐ using mathematical tools ☐ creativity ☐

PROPERTIES OF MULTIPLICATION

Following rules are used while multiplying numbers.

- **Commutative property of multiplication:** Product remains the same even after changing the order of given numbers in multiplication.

  Example: $152 \times 35 = 35 \times 152$

- **Associative property of multiplication:** Change in the grouping of numbers, do not change the product of the numbers.

  Example: $254 \times (45 \times 141) = (254 \times 45) \times 141$

- **Property of zero:** Product of any number and zero is always zero.

  Example: $547 \times 0 = 0$

- **Property of one:** Product of any number and one is the number itself.

  Example: $485 \times 1 = 485$

- **Distributive property of multiplication:** The product of the sum or the difference of any two numbers and third number is same as the sum or difference of the product of two numbers individually.

  Example: $(135 + 248) \times 32 = 135 \times 32 + 248 \times 32$

MULTIPLICATION OF 4-DIGIT NUMBERS

Example 1: Multiply 6524 and 432.

Solution: Multiply 6524 by each digit of 432 one by one and then add the products.

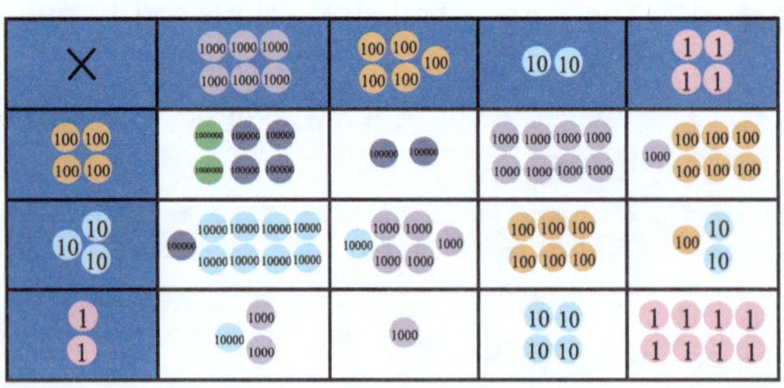

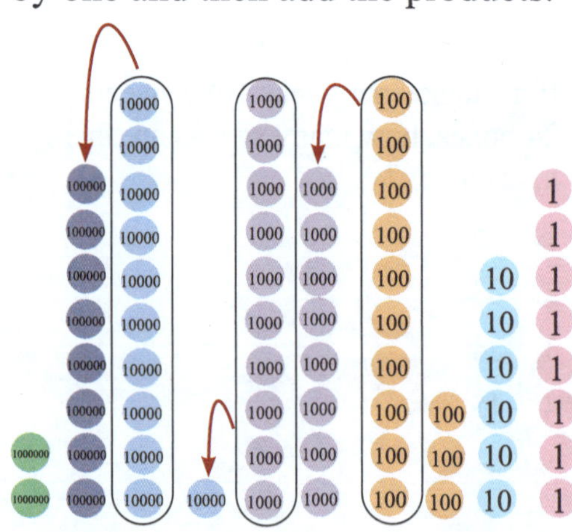

Step 1: Multiply ones.

6524 × 2

	6	5	2	4
	×	4	3	2
1	3	0	4	8

Step 2: Multiply tens.

6524 × 30

		6	5	2	4
		×	4	3	2
	1	3	0	4	8
1	9	5	7	2	0

Step 3: Multiply hundreds.

6524 × 400

Add the products

			6	5	2	4
			×	4	3	2
		1	3	0	4	8
	1	9	5	7	2	0
2	6	0	9	6	0	0
2	8	1	8	3	6	8

Therefore, 6524 × 432 = 28,18,368.

Example 2: Multiply 4312 and 2031.

Solution: Multiply 4312 by each digit of 2031 one by one and then add the products.

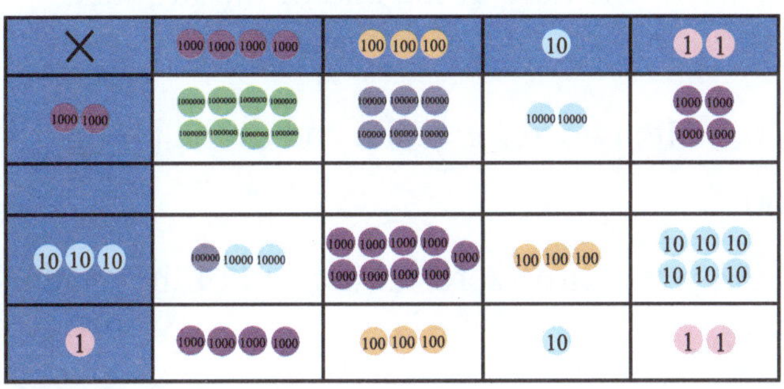

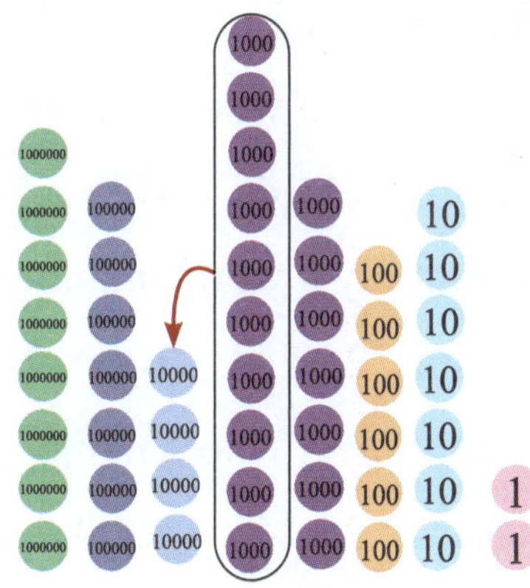

Step 1: 4312 × 1

	4	3	1	2
×	2	0	3	1
	4	3	1	2

Step 2: 4312 × 30

		4	3	1	2
	×	2	0	3	1
		4	3	1	2
1	2	9	3	6	0

Step 3: 4312 × 0

			4	3	1	2
		×	2	0	3	1
			4	3	1	2
	1	2	9	3	6	0
0	0	0	0	0	0	0

Step 4: 4312 × 2000

Add the products

			4	3	1	2
		×	2	0	3	1
			4	3	1	2
	1	2	9	3	6	0
0	0	0	0	0	0	0
8	6	2	4	0	0	0
8	7	5	7	6	7	2

Therefore, 4312 × 2031 = 87,57,672.

MULTIPLICATION OF 5-DIGIT NUMBERS

Example 3: Multiply 31421 × 5.

Solution: Multiply the number by 5 ones, we get

Therefore, 31421 × 5 = 1,57,105.

	1		1	1		
		3	1	4	2	1
×						5
	1	5	7	1	0	5

Example 4: Find the product: 24,312 × 23

Solution: Multiply 24,312 by each digit of 23 one by one.

Step 1: 24,312 × 3

2	4	3	1	2
		×	2	3
7	2	9	3	6

Step 2: 24,312 × 20 and add the products

	2	4	3	1	2
			×	2	3
	7	2	9	3	6
4	8	6	2	4	0
5	5	9	1	7	6

Therefore, 24,312 × 23 = 5,59,176.

Multiplication of 4-Digit or 5-Digit Numbers by 10, 100 and 1000

If any 4-digit or 5-digit number are multiplied by 10, 100 or 0, then respective numbers of zeros are added in the product.

- To multiply a whole number by 10, write one zero at the end of the product.
  Example: 25,143 × 10 = 2,51,430
- To multiply a whole number by 100, write two zeros at the end of the product.
  Example: 25,143 × 100 = 25,14,300
- To multiply a whole number by 1000, write three zeros at the end of the product.
  Example: 25,143 × 1000 = 2,51,43,000

Multiplication Techniques

Multiplication by 11

Step 1: Write the rightmost digit in the ones place.

Step 2: Add the digits from the right, (if needed carry forward the digit to the next place)

Step 3: Continue adding the digits

Step 4: Write the leftmost digit.

Example: 59 × 11

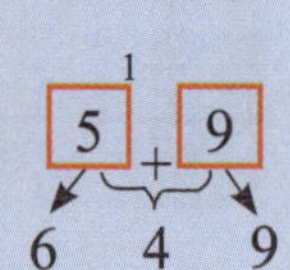

Step 1: Write 9 in the ones place.

Step 2: 9 + 5 = 14

Write 4 in the tens place, carry forward 1.

Step 3: 5 + 1 = 6.

Therefore, 59 × 11 = 649.

Multiplication by 15

The number 15 can be written as 10 + 5. Also, 5 is half of 10. So, in order to, multiply a number by 15, first multiply the number by 10 and then halve it. Add both the numbers to get the answer.

Example: 178 × 15

178 × 15 = (178 × 10) + (178 × 5)

(178 × 5 is half of 178 × 10)

Step 1: 178 × 10 = 1780

Step 2: 1780 ÷ 2 = 890

Step 3: 1780 + 890 = 2670

Therefore, 178 × 15 = 2670

Example: 265 × 11.

Step 1: Write 5 in the ones place.

Step 2: 5 + 6 = 11.

Write 1 in tens place, carry forward 1.

Step 3: 6 + 2 + 1 = 9.

Write 9 in the hundreds place.

Step 4: Write 2 in the thousands place.

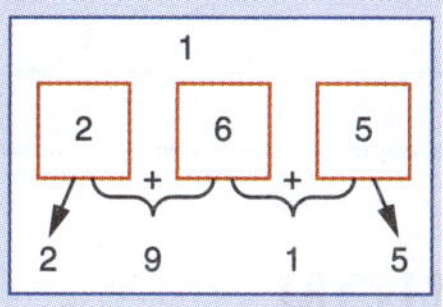

Therefore, 265 × 11 = 2915

Example: 896 × 15

896 × 15 = (896 × 10) + (896 × 5)

Step 1: 896 × 10 = 8,960

Step 2: 8960 ÷ 2 = 4,480

Step 3: 8960 + 4480 = 13,440

Therefore, 896 × 15 = 13,440

Exercise 3.1

1. State whether the following are true or false. ia

a. Product remains the same even after changing the order of given numbers in multiplication.

b. 0 × 3894 is equal to 3894.

c. (23 – 17) × 8 = (23 × 8) – (17 × 8), this property is called distributive property.

d. 1 × 4792 is 4798.

e. (234 × 28) × 456 is same as 234 × (28 + 456).

2. Multiply the following 4-digit numbers by 2-digit numbers.

a. 7968 × 56 b. 3564 × 16 c. 6723 × 22 d. 1085 × 43 e. 9741 × 18

3. Multiply the following 4-digit numbers by 3-digit numbers.

a. 9011 × 193 b. 2497 × 335 c. 6412 × 535 d. 6879 × 124 e. 9371 × 647

4. Find the products.

a. 2005 × 6662 b. 1111 × 1101 c. 1560 × 9047 d. 4523 × 7861 e. 1261 × 3981

5. Choose the correct answer.

a. 12,485 × 7	77395	87395	87305
b. 20,497 × 3	61491	60491	61498
c. 82,765 × 5	414825	413925	413825
d. 61,560 × 9	554050	554540	554040
e. 53,128 × 8	425124	425024	435024

6. Multiply the following 5-digit numbers by 2-digit numbers.

a. 87,405 × 19 b. 14,572 × 24 c. 52,065 × 81 d. 50,001 × 15 e. 86,189 × 4

7. Complete the table.

Number	Multiplied by 10	Multiplied by 100	Multiplied by 1000
a. 3459			
b. 1600			
c. 57,109			
d. 49,287			
e. 20,912			

APPLICATION OF MULTIPLICATION

Sometimes, we use more than one operation to solve problems. Identify the operations and carry them out in order to solve a problem.

Example 5: A shopkeeper bought the following groceries from a wholesale shop. Find out the total cost.

Item	Price (₹)	Quantity
Basmati rice	142	4250 kg
Cooking oil	75	100 ℓ
Sugar	52	1500 kg
Pigeon peas (*Toor dal*)	86	89 kg

Solution:

- Cost of 1 kg of basmati rice = ₹142

  The cost of 4250 kg of basmati rice = 4250 × 142

  The cost of 4250 kg of basmati rice is ₹6,03,500.

		4	2	5	0
		×	1	4	2
		8	5	0	0
1	7	0	0	0	0
4	2	5	0	0	
6	0	3	5	0	0

- The cost of 1 *l* cooking oil = ₹75

  The cost of 100 *l* cooking oil = 75 × 100 = ₹7500

- The cost of 1 kg of sugar = ₹52

  The cost of 1500 kg of sugar = 52 × 1500 = ₹78,000

- The cost of 1 kg of toor dal = ₹86

  The cost of 89 kg of toor dal = 89 × 86 = ₹7654

		8	9
	×	8	6
	5	3	4
7	1	2	0
7	6	5	4

Therefore, the total cost of all the items is
₹6,03,500 + ₹7500 + ₹78,000 + ₹7654, that is, ₹6,96,654.

Example 6: Kiran took a loan from a bank to buy a car worth ₹2,00,000. She paid ₹30,750 per month for a period of 9 months. Find the extra amount she paid to the bank.

Solution:

The price of the car = ₹2,00,000

The amount to be paid every month = ₹30,750

The amount to be paid for 9 months = ₹30,750 × 9 = ₹2,76,750

	3	0	7	5	0
				×	9
2	7	6	7	5	0

Therefore, the extra amount to be paid = ₹2,76,750 – ₹2,00,000
= ₹76,750

Exercise 3.2

Solve the following word problems.

1. A farmer sold 5450 kg of wheat on a particular day. How much would he sell in 248 days?
2. Find the cost of 265 toy cars, if each one costs ₹1490.
3. A retail store has 4352 bags of rice, each weighing 125 kg.
   Find the total weight of the bags in the store.
4. Rakesh paid a house loan of ₹9860 in the form of monthly instalments for 144 months. He also spent ₹ 2,45,800 towards the insurance of the house. Find out the total amount spent by him. (*Hint*: Find the total house loan and add the insurance amount to it).
5. The annual salary of Ram is ₹ 3,75,000, and his monthly expenditure is ₹ 14850. What is the amount left with Ram after a year?

DIVISION OF 5-DIGIT NUMBERS

a

If 29,064 litres of water are shared equally among 7 tankers, then find the amount of water in each tank. Will there be some water left?

Let us find the amount of water in each tank, by dividing 29,064 by 7 through an activity.

Activity

Aim: To divide a 5-digit number by a 1-digit number using counters

Material Required: Counters representing different places

Procedure: Follow the given steps below to divide 29,064 by 7 using counters.

1. Represent 29,064 using counters.
2. Here, 2 ten thousands cannot be divided by 7, thus regroup 2 ten thousand as 20 thousands. Now, there are 28 thousands.
3. Divide 28 thousands into 7 equal groups; each group has **4 thousands**. Now, the remaining is 1064.
4. Here, 1 thousand cannot be divided by 7, thus regroup 1 thousand as 10 hundreds.
5. Divide 10 hundreds into 7 equal groups; each group has **1 hundred**. Now, the remaining is 364.
6. Here, 3 hundreds cannot be divided by 7, thus regroup 3 hundred as 30 tens. Now, there are 36 tens.
7. Divide 36 tens into 7 equal groups; each group has **5 tens**. Now, the remaining is 14.
8. Here, 1 ten cannot be divided by 7, thus regroup 1 ten as 10 ones. Now, there are 14 tens.
9. Divide 14 ones into 7 equal groups; each group has **2 ones**. Now, the remaining is 0.

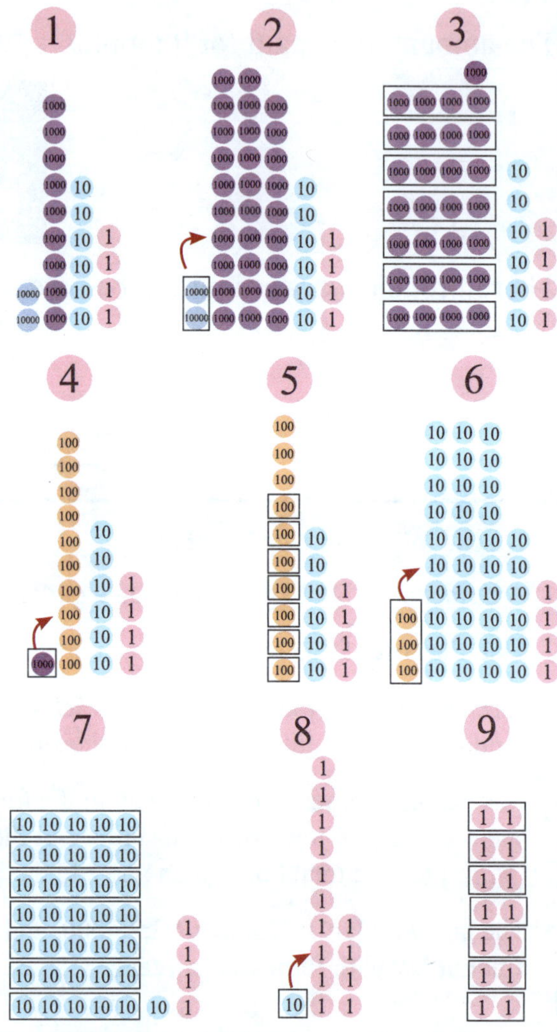

Conclusion: A 5-digit number is divided by a single digit number using counters.

Each tanker will have 4152 litres of water, and no water will be left.

Example 7: Divide 58,465 by 5.

Solution: 58,465 ÷ 5

Step 1: Write 58,465 (dividend) and 5 (divisor) as shown in the column.

Step 2: Divide 5 by 5. Quotient will be 1 and remainder is 0.

Step 3: Bring down 8, divide 8 by 5. Quotient will be 1 and remainder is 3.

Step 4: Bring down 4, divide 34 by 5. Quotient will be 6 and remainder is 4.

Step 5: Bring down 6, divide 46 by 5. Quotient will be 9 and remainder is 1.

Step 6: Bring down 5, divide 15 by 5. The quotient will be 3 and the remainder is 0.

Step 7: Verify the answer using the formula.

Dividend = (Divisor × Quotient) + Remainder

58465 = (5 × 11693) + 0

Therefore, quotient of 58465 ÷ 5 is 11693 with remainder 0.

```
Quotient →   1 1 6 9 3
Divisor ← 5 ) 5 8 4 6 5  → Dividend
            − 5
              0 8
            −   5
                3 4
              − 3 0
                  4 6
                − 4 5
                    1 5
                  − 1 5
Remainder ←             0
```

Example 8: Divide 64871 by 9.

Solution: 64871 ÷ 9

Step 1: 6 ÷ 9

```
     0
9 ) 6 4 8 7 1
  − 0
    6
```

Step 2: Bring down 4, 64 ÷ 9

```
     0 7
9 ) 6 4 8 7 1
  − 0
    6 4
  − 6 3
      1
```

Step 3: Bring down 8, 18 ÷ 9

```
     0 7 2
9 ) 6 4 8 7 1
  − 0
    6 4
  − 6 3
      1 8
    − 1 8
        0
```

Step 4: Bring down 7, 7 ÷ 9

```
     0 7 2 0
9 ) 6 4 8 7 1
  − 0
    6 4
  − 6 3
      1 8
    − 1 8
        0 7
      −   0
          7
```

Step 5: Bring down 1, 71 ÷ 9

```
     0 7 2 0 7
9 ) 6 4 8 7 1
  − 0
    6 4
  − 6 3
      1 8
    − 1 8
        0 7
      −   0
          7 1
        − 6 3
            8
```

Verification: (9 × 7207) + 8 = 64871

Therefore, quotient is 7207 and remainder is 8.

Example 9: Divide 17,460 by 12.

Solution: 17460 ÷ 12

Step 1: 1 can not be divided by 12.

```
       0
1 2 ) 1 7 4 6 0
    − 0
      1
```

Step 2: Bring down 7, 17 ÷ 12

```
       0 1
1 2 ) 1 7 4 6 0
    − 0
      1 7
    − 1 2
        5
```

Step 3: Bring down 4, 54 ÷ 12

```
       0 1 4
1 2 ) 1 7 4 6 0
    − 0
      1 7
    − 1 2
        5 4
      − 4 8
          6
```

Step 4:

Bring down 6, 66 ÷ 12

```
       0 1 4 5
    ___________
1 2 ) 1 7 4 6 0
    - 0
      1 7
    - 1 2
        5 4
      - 4 8
          6 6
        - 6 0
            6
```

Step 5:

Bring down 0, 60 ÷ 12

```
       0 1 4 5 5
    ___________
1 2 ) 1 7 4 6 0
    - 0
      1 7
    - 1 2
        5 4
      - 4 8
          6 6
        - 6 0
            6 0
          - 6 0
              0
```

Verification: (12 × 1455) + 0 = 17460

Therefore, quotient is 1455 and remainder is 0.

Example 10: Divide 55448 by 16.

Solution: 55448 ÷ 16

Step 1:

5 ÷ 16

```
      0
    ___________
1 6 ) 5 5 4 4 8
    - 0
      5
```

Step 2:

Bring down 5, 55 ÷ 16

```
      0 3
    ___________
1 6 ) 5 5 4 4 8
    - 0
      5 5
    - 4 8
        7
```

Step 3:

Bring down 4, 74 ÷ 16

```
      0 3 4
    ___________
1 6 ) 5 5 4 4 8
    - 0
      5 5
    - 4 8
        7 4
      - 6 4
        1 0
```

Step 4:

Bring down 4, 104 ÷ 16

```
      0 3 4 6
    ___________
1 6 ) 5 5 4 4 8
    - 0
      5 5
    - 4 8
        7 4
      - 6 4
        1 0 4
    -     9 6
            8
```

Step 5:

Bring down 8, 88 ÷ 16

```
      0 3 4 6 5
    ___________
1 6 ) 5 5 4 4 8
    - 0
      5 5
    - 4 8
        7 4
      - 6 4
        1 0 4
    -     9 6
            8 8
          - 8 0
              8
```

Verification: (16 × 3465) + 8 = 55448

Therefore, quotient is 3465 and remainder is 8.

DIVISION OF 6-DIGIT NUMBERS

Example 11: Divide 5,48,864 by 4.

Solution: 548864 ÷ 4

Step 1: 5 ÷ 4

```
   1
4)5 4 8 8 6 4
 -4
  1
```

Step 2: Bring down 4, 14 ÷ 4

```
   1 3
4)5 4 8 8 6 4
 -4
  1 4
 -1 2
    2
```

Step 3: Bring down 8, 28 ÷ 4

```
   1 3 7
4)5 4 8 8 6 4
 -4
  1 4
 -1 2
    2 8
   -2 8
      0
```

Step 4: Bring down 8, 8 ÷ 4

```
   1 3 7 2
4)5 4 8 8 6 4
 -4
  1 4
 -1 2
    2 8
   -2 8
      0 8
   -    8
        0
```

Step 5: Bring down 6, 6 ÷ 4

```
   1 3 7 2 1
4)5 4 8 8 6 4
 -4
  1 4
 -1 2
    2 8
   -2 8
      0 8
   -    8
        0 6
   -      4
          2
```

Step 6: Bring down 4, 24 ÷ 4

```
   1 3 7 2 1 6
4)5 4 8 8 6 4
 -4
  1 4
 -1 2
    2 8
   -2 8
      0 8
   -    8
        0 6
   -      4
          2 4
         -2 4
            0
```

Verification: (4 × 137216) + 0 = 548864

Therefore, quotient is 137216 and remainder is 0.

Example 12: Divide 640247 by 9.

Solution: Divide 640247 ÷ 9

Step 1: 6 ÷ 9

```
   0
9)6 4 0 2 4 7
 -0
  6
```

Step 2: Bring down 4, 64 ÷ 9

```
   0 7
9)6 4 0 2 4 7
 -0
  6 4
 -6 3
    1
```

Step 3: Bring down 0, 10 ÷ 9

```
   0 7 1
9)6 4 0 2 4 7
 -0
  6 4
 -6 3
    1 0
   -  9
      1
```

Step 4:

Bring down 2, 12 ÷ 9

```
    0 7 1 1
9)6 4 0 2 4 7
 - 0
   6 4
 - 6 3
     1 0
   -   9
       1 2
     -   9
         3
```

Step 5:

Bring down 4, 34 ÷ 9

```
    0 7 1 1 3
9)6 4 0 2 4 7
 - 0
   6 4
 - 6 3
     1 0
   -   9
       1 2
     -   9
         3 4
       - 2 7
           7
```

Step 6:

Bring down 7, 77 ÷ 9

```
    0 7 1 1 3 8
9)6 4 0 2 4 7
 - 0
   6 4
 - 6 3
     1 0
   -   9
       1 2
     -   9
         3 4
       - 2 7
           7 7
         - 7 2
             5
```

Verification: (9 × 71138) + 5 = 640247

Therefore, quotient is 71138 and remainder is 5.

Example 13: Divide 504516 by 12.

Solution: Divide 504516 ÷ 12

Step 1:

5 ÷ 12

```
     0
1 2)5 0 4 5 1 6
  - 0
    5
```

Step 2:

Bring down 0, 50 ÷ 12

```
     0 4
1 2)5 0 4 5 1 6
  - 0
    5 0
  - 4 8
      2
```

Step 3:

Bring down 4, 24 ÷ 12

```
     0 4 2
1 2)5 0 4 5 1 6
  - 0
    5 0
  - 4 8
      2 4
    - 2 4
        0
```

Step 4:

Bring down 5, 5 ÷ 12

```
     0 4 2 0
1 2)5 0 4 5 1 6
  - 0
    5 0
  - 4 8
      2 4
    - 2 4
        0 5
      -   0
          5
```

Step 5:

Bring down 1, 51 ÷ 12

```
     0 4 2 0 4
1 2)5 0 4 5 1 6
  - 0
    5 0
  - 4 8
      2 4
    - 2 4
        0 5
      -   0
          5 1
        - 4 8
            3
```

Step 6:

Bring down 6, 36 ÷ 12

```
     0 4 2 0 4 3
1 2)5 0 4 5 1 6
  - 0
    5 0
  - 4 8
      2 4
    - 2 4
        0 5
      -   0
          5 1
        - 4 8
            3 6
          - 3 6
              0
```

Verification: (12 × 42043) + 0 = 504516

Therefore, quotient is 42043 and remainder is 0.

Example 14: Divide 418272 by 18.

Solution: Divide 418272 ÷ 18

Step 1:

4 ÷ 18

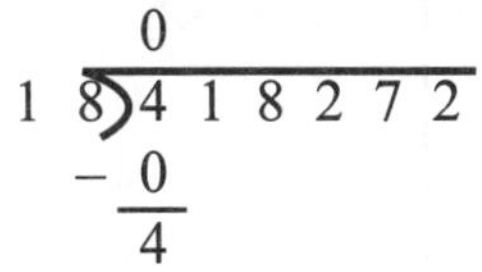

Step 2:

Bring down 1,
41 ÷ 18

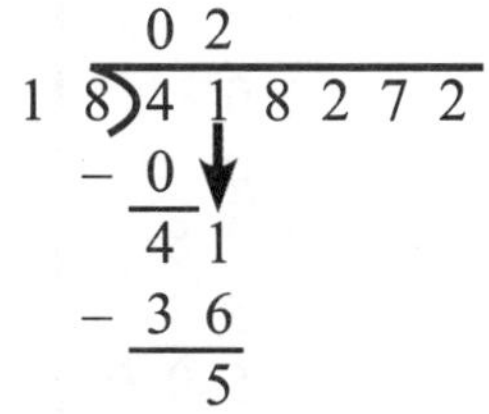

Step 3:

Bring down 8,
58 ÷ 18

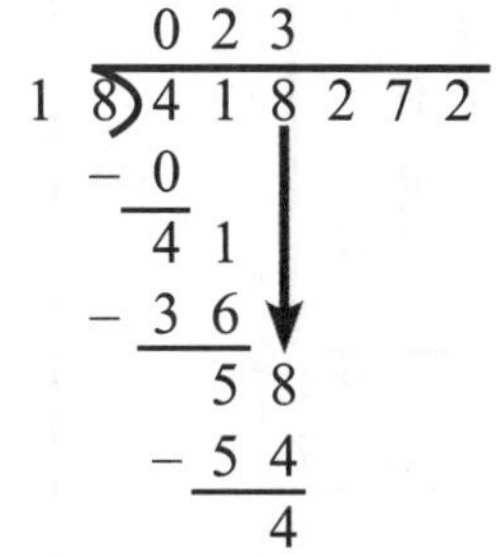

Step 4:

Bring down 2,
42 ÷ 18

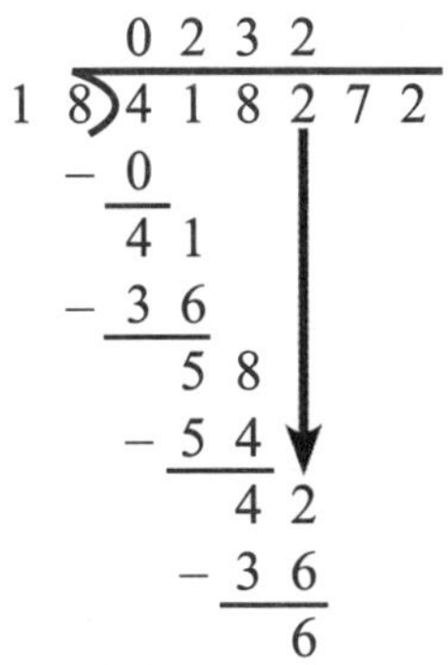

Step 5:

Bring down 7,
67 ÷ 18

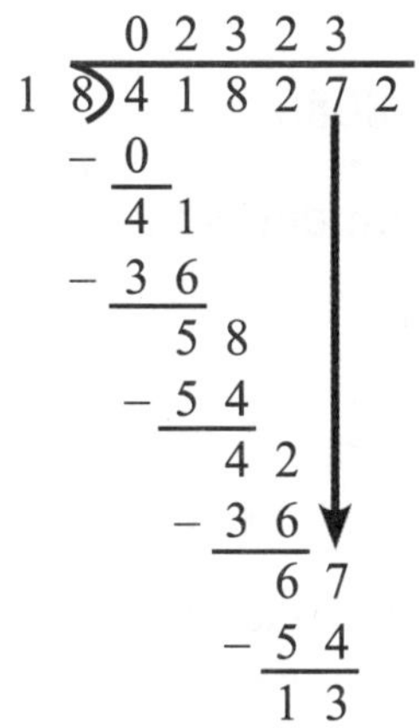

Step 6:

Bring down 2,
132 ÷ 18

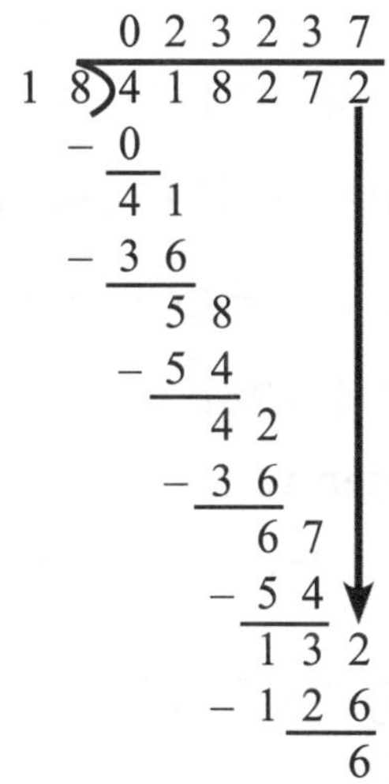

Verification: (18 × 23237) + 6 = 418272

Therefore, quotient is 23237 and remainder is 6.

Example 15: Divide 208086 by 158.

Solution: Divide 208086 ÷ 158

Step 1:

2 ÷ 158

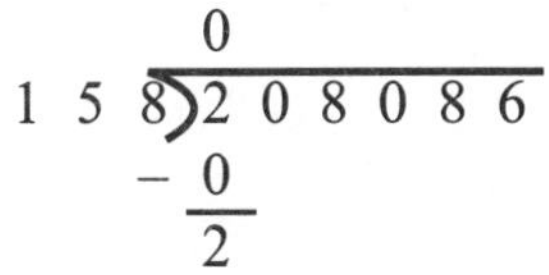

Step 2:

Bring down 0,
20 ÷ 158

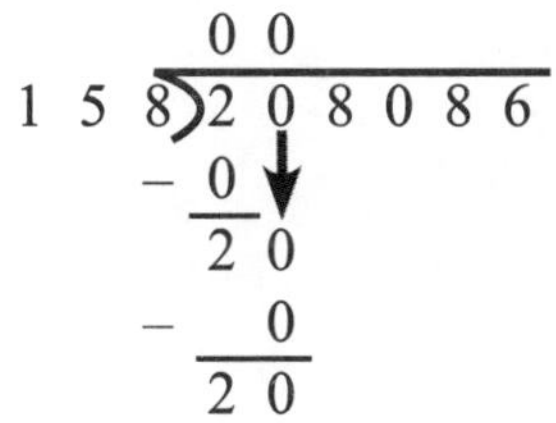

Step 3:

Bring down 8,
208 ÷ 158

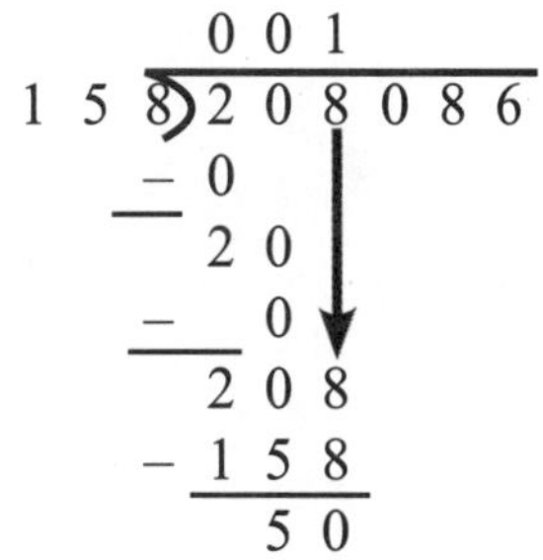

Step 4:

Bring down 0,
500 ÷ 158

```
         0 0 1 3
1 5 8 ) 2 0 8 0 8 6
      - 0
        2 0
      -   0
        2 0 8
      - 1 5 8
          5 0 0
        - 4 7 4
            2 6
```

Step 5:

Bring down 8,
268 ÷ 158

```
         0 0 1 3 1
1 5 8 ) 2 0 8 0 8 6
      - 0
        2 0
      -   0
        2 0 8
      - 1 5 8
          5 0 0
        - 4 7 4
            2 6 8
          - 1 5 8
            1 1 0
```

Step 6:

Bring down 6,
1106 ÷ 158

```
         0 0 1 3 1 7
1 5 8 ) 2 0 8 0 8 6
      - 0
        2 0
      -   0
        2 0 8
      - 1 5 8
          5 0 0
        - 4 7 4
            2 6 8
          - 1 5 8
            1 1 0 6
          - 1 1 0 6
                  0
```

Verification: (158 × 1317) + 0 = 208086

Therefore, quotient is 1317 and remainder is 0.

Example 16: Divide 685794 by 251.

Solution: 685794 ÷ 251

Step 1:

6 ÷ 251

```
         0
2 5 1 ) 6 8 5 7 9 4
      - 0
        6
```

Step 2:

Bring down 8,
68 ÷ 251

```
         0 0
2 5 1 ) 6 8 5 7 9 4
      - 0
        6 8
      -   0
        6 8
```

Step 3:

Bring down 5,
685 ÷ 251

```
         0 0 2
2 5 1 ) 6 8 5 7 9 4
      - 0
        6 8
      -   0
        6 8 5
      - 5 0 2
        1 8 3
```

Step 4:

Bring down 7,
1837 ÷ 251

```
          0 0 2 7
2 5 1 ) 6 8 5 7 9 4
      - 0
        6 8
      -   0
        6 8 5
      - 5 0 2
        1 8 3 7
      - 1 7 5 7
            8 0
```

Step 5:

Bring down 9,
809 ÷ 251

```
          0 0 2 7 3
2 5 1 ) 6 8 5 7 9 4
      - 0
        6 8
      -   0
        6 8 5
      - 5 0 2
        1 8 3 7
      - 1 7 5 7
            8 0 9
          - 7 5 3
              5 6
```

Step 6:

Bring down 4,
564 ÷ 251

```
          0 0 2 7 3 2
2 5 1 ) 6 8 5 7 9 4
      - 0
        6 8
      -   0
        6 8 5
      - 5 0 2
        1 8 3 7
      - 1 7 5 7
            8 0 9
          - 7 5 3
              5 6 4
            - 5 0 2
                6 2
```

Verification: (251 × 2732) + 62 = 685794

Therefore, quotient is 2732 and remainder is 62.

Exercise 3.3

1. Divide the following 5-digit numbers by 1-digit numbers.

a. 56895 ÷ 5 b. 24564 ÷ 6 c. 67543 ÷ 2 d. 97584 ÷ 4 e. 56743 ÷ 7

2. Divide the following 5-digit numbers by 2-digit numbers.

a. 87072 ÷ 16 b. 69800 ÷ 48 c. 59197 ÷ 19 d. 70050 ÷ 34 e. 31928 ÷ 13

3. Divide the following numbers and choose the correct quotients.

a. 567330 ÷ 6	94545	84555	94555
b. 857469 ÷ 3	285823	275823	285820
c. 789612 ÷ 4	197403	197413	198413
d. 236548 ÷ 7	33782	33792	23792
e. 100100 ÷ 5	2020	20020	2002

4. Divide the following and write the quotients.

a. 982432 ÷ 32 b. 456723 ÷ 13 c. 123458 ÷ 27 d. 574678 ÷ 13 e. 977200 ÷ 56

f. 871584 ÷ 185 g. 647640 ÷ 420 h. 897654 ÷ 456 i. 752252 ÷ 122 j. 994565 ÷ 25

PATTERNS IN DIVIDING BY 1000, 10000, 100000

If any 5-digit or 6-digit number is divided by 1000, 10000 or 100000, the following number of digits become the remainder.

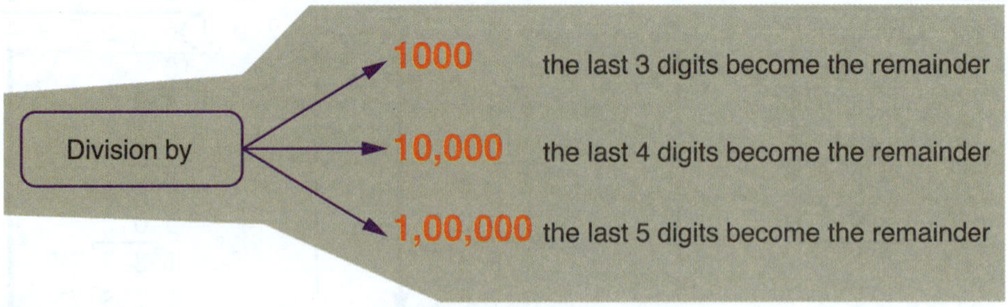

For example, 254824 ÷ 1000 or 10000 or 100000

- When 254824 is divided by 1000, quotient = 254 and remainder = 824
- When 254824 is divided by 10,000, quotient = 25 and remainder = 4824
- When 254824 is divided by 1,00,000, quotient = 2 and remainder = 54,824

WORD PROBLEMS ON DIVISION

In some cases, we use more than one operation in order to solve a given problem. In such cases, we have to identify the operations to be performed and carry out the operations.

Example 17: A rocket travelled a distance of 3,45,609 km in 13 hours. It travelled equal distances in the first 12 hours and some additional distance in the thirteenth hour. Find out the distance covered by the rocket in the thirteenth hour.

Solution:

The total distance travelled by the rocket = 3,45,609 km

For the first 12 hours, the rocket travelled the same distance in each hour.

The distance covered in each hour except in the thirteenth hour is the quotient of 3,45,609 ÷ 12. The remainder will be equal to the distance covered in the thirteenth hour.

Therefore, the distance travelled by the rocket in each hour for 12 hours = 28,800 km, and in thirteenth hour is 9 km.

```
       2 8 8 0 0
12 ) 3 4 5 6 0 9
   - 2 4
     1 0 5
   -   9 6
         9 6
       - 9 6
           0 0
           - 0
             0 9
             - 0
               9
```

Example 18: A company recruited 23 employees with ₹12,456 as monthly salary for each. The company offered ₹28,750 as bonus for these 23 employees. Find the salary of each employee for 12 months including the bonus.
Also, find the total salary of all the employees including the bonus.

Solution:

Salary of 1 employee for 1 month = ₹12,456

So, the salary of 1 employee for 12 months

= 12,456 × 12 = ₹1,49,472

	1	2	4	5	6
			×	1	2
	2	4	9	1	2
1	2	4	5	6	0
1	4	9	4	7	2

```
       0 1 2 5 0
  23 ) 2 8 7 5 0
     - 0
       2 8
     - 2 3
         5 7
       - 4 6
         1 1 5
       - 1 1 5
             0 0
           -   0
               0
```

The bonus amount for 23 employees = ₹28,750.

So, the bonus amount for 1 employee
= ₹28,750 ÷ 23 = ₹1250

The total salary of 1 employee for a year including bonus
= ₹149472 + ₹1250 = ₹1,50,722

The total salary of 23 employees including bonus
= ₹1,50,722 × 23 = ₹34,66,606.

Exercise 3.4

Solve the following word problems.

1. Each student in a hostel requires 24 litres of water for bathing. How many students can take bath with 38,550 litres of water? Will there be some water left?
2. Find the smallest number that should be added to 8,14,563 so that the result is completely divisible by 56. Also, what should be subtracted from 8,14,563 so that the result is completely divisible by 56? (*Hint*: Increase the quotient by 1, multiply by 56 and subtract it from the dividend to find the number to be added.)
3. A farmer produced 58,456 kg of wheat and packed it into bags each weighing 18 kg. How many bags are required to pack the wheat? Will there be some wheat left?

4. A ship had 27 containers of equal weight and some additional weight. The total weight on the ship was 3,19,213 kg. Find the weight of each container and the additional weight. (*Hint*: Divide total weight by the number of containers. Remainder is the additional weight.)
5. A factory produced 8,55,984 biscuits in 34 hours. Find out the number of biscuits produced by the factory in 1 hour. Also, find out the number of biscuits produced in 17 hours.

Concept Map

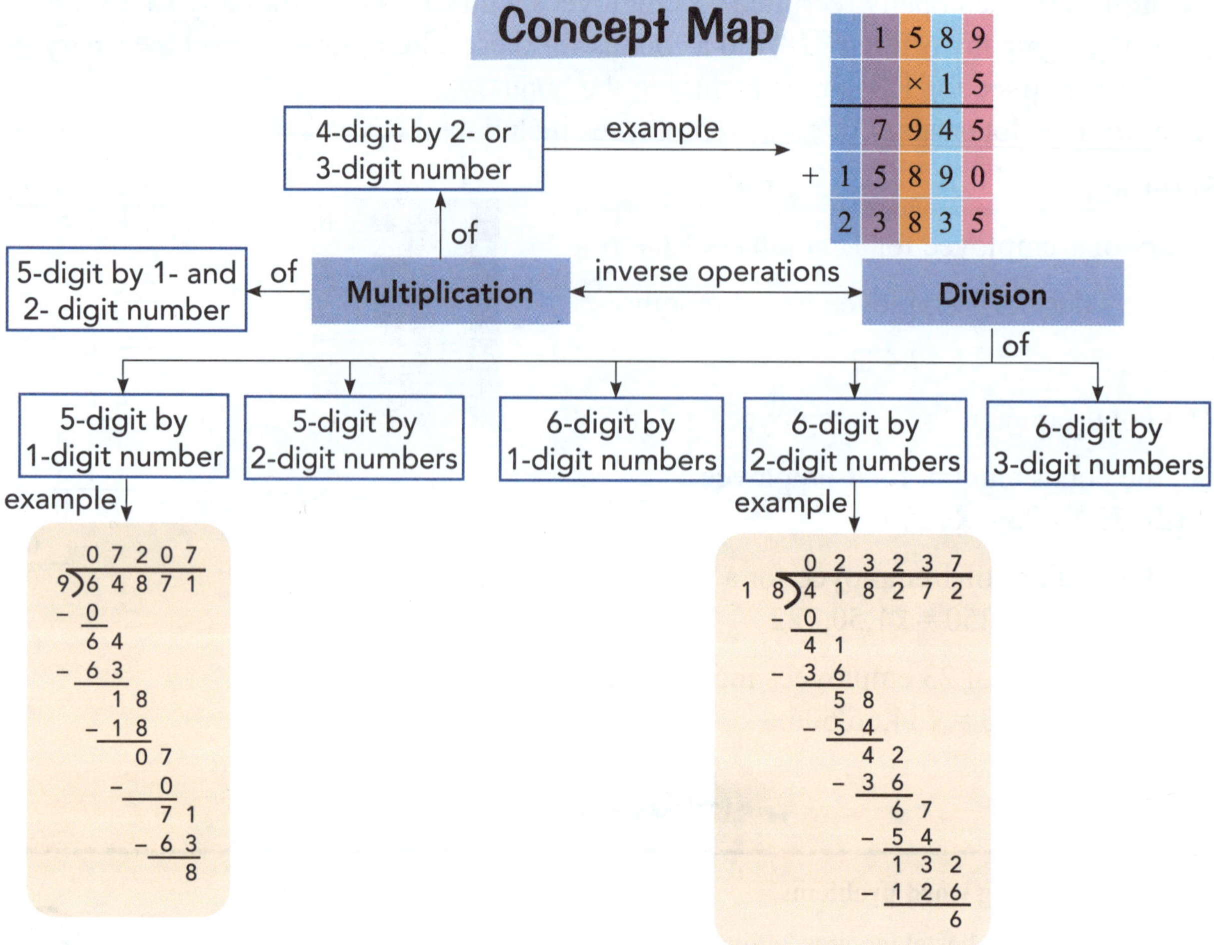

Project

Series of 9s

There are different methods of multiplying numbers. The shortcut method of multiplying the numbers with a series of 9s is given below.

Multiply a given number with an equal number of 9s:	Multiply a given number with a lower number of 9s:	Multiply a given number with a greater number of 9s:
Example: 42386 × 99999 **Step 1:** 42386 – 1 = 42385. **Step 2:** 99999 – 42385 = 57614. **Step 3:** Write the answer of Step 1 followed by the answer of Step 2. Therefore, 42386 × 99999 = 4,23,85,57,614.	Example: 42386 × 999 **Step 1:** Rewrite 42386 as 42386000. **Step 2:** 42386000 – 42386 = 42343614. Therefore, 42386 × 999 = 4,23,43,614.	Example: 42386 × 999999 **Step 1:** Rewrite 42386 as 042386. **Step 2:** 42386 – 1 = 42385. **Step 3:** 999999 – 042385 = 957614. **Step 4:** Write the answer of Step 1 followed by the answer of Step 2. Therefore, 42386 × 999999 = 42,38,59,57,614.

Prepare a chart solving random problems under each case and verify the answers using standard method.

Revision Exercise

A. Choose the correct option.

1. The product of 34863 × 4 is _______.
   a. 167542
   b. 139452
   c. 786541
   d. 209127
2. The remainder obtained when 398126 is divided by 21 is__________.
   a. 3
   b. 21
   c. 18
   d. 8
3. What is the quotient obtained when 34125 is divided by 25?
   a. 1365
   b. 2345
   c. 9812
   d. 2015
4. There are 29831 folders. In each folder, there are 125 pages. How many pages are there altogether?
   a. 290451
   b. 410723
   c. 3728875
   d. 407127
5. In an art exhibition, 376740 exhibits were displayed in 345 stalls. If each stall had an equal number of exhibits, how many exhibits were there in each stall?
   a. 2145
   b. 6712
   c. 4192
   d. 1092

B. Fill in the blanks.

1. 11 × 4532 = ______
2. 765 ÷ 100 = ______
3. 99 × 12000 = ______
4. 125 × 1231 = ______
5. 45,523 ÷ 1000 =_______

C. Match the following.

1. 34676 ÷ 4	a. 4202
2. 109252 ÷ 26	b. 3535
3. 677970 ÷ 18	c. 814
4. 894355 ÷ 253	d. 8669
5. 78958 ÷ 97	e. 37665

D. State whether the following are true (T) or false (F).

1. The product of 34856 × 23 is 79488.
2. The remainder obtained when 78965 ÷ 355 is 155.
3. 99,999 × 99 = 9,89,901
4. The highest product of a 4-digit number and a 2-digit number is 97,854.
5. If a number is not completely divisible by 10, then the last digit of the number is the remainder.

E. Find the product of the following numbers.

1. 54562 × 23
2. 109842 × 12
3. 901247 × 6
4. 78123 × 231
5. 87123 × 1072

F. Divide the following numbers.

1. 45671 ÷ 54
2. 78912 ÷ 36
3. 901233 ÷ 27
4. 890123 ÷ 7
5. 761022 ÷ 102

G. Application-based questions.

1. Rekha bought 46 grams of gold for ₹1,37,080. How much would it cost her if she bought 22 grams more? (*Hint*: Find the cost of one gram, and then add the cost of 22 grams to the cost of 46 grams.)
2. A builder bought iron worth ₹8,10,216 at ₹18 per kilogram. Find the quantity of iron bought.

3. A company has 37 employees and the company paid ₹4,60,650 as bonus to all the employees. Find the bonus paid to each employee.
4. What number should be subtracted from 63,700 in order to make it exactly divisible by 18? (*Hint*: Find the remainder.)
5. 46 sacks of rice cost ₹2,68,962, and 74 sacks of jaggery cost ₹2,11,566. Find out the price of 1 sack of rice and 1 sack of jaggery. Which is costlier, rice or jaggery, by how much?
6. Seven ticket agents sold 4662 tickets. Each agent sold the same number of tickets. How many tickets were sold by each agent?
7. There were 12,744 people who attended the 6 performances of a play presented by a theater group. If an equal number of people attended each of the performances, then how many people attended each performance?

Space for rough work

Did You Master?

A. Find the product of 45672 × 23.

1. 67,81,936
2. 10,50,456
3. 11,23,450
4. 67,81,203

B. If 291457 ÷ 14, then the remainder is __________.

1. 12
2. 3
3. 8
4. 5

C. If 59450 ÷ 58, then the quotient is __________.

1. 3-digit number
2. 2-digit number
3. 4-digit number
4. 5-digit number

D. Find the least product of a 6-digit number by a single-digit number other than 0 and 1.

1. 2,00,002
2. 2,00,202
3. 2,00,000
4. 2,00,020

E. Find the product of the smallest 6-digit number and the greatest 2-digit number.

1. 20,00,000
2. 10,00,000
3. 89,00,000
4. 99,00,000

F. The annual salary of an employee is ₹341400. How much money will the employee earn in a month?

1. ₹ 34,560
2. ₹ 24,518
3. ₹ 32,186
4. ₹ 28,450

G. A farmer cultivated 46,580 kg of rice and sold the rice at the rate of ₹39 per kg. He deposited the profit money of ₹3,78,900 in a bank. How much amount did he keep with himself?

1. ₹6,78,123
2. ₹14,37,720
3. ₹56,78,120
4. ₹4,56,721

H. In a showroom, the number of vehicles sold in a month and the price of each vehicle is given in the table.

Vehicle	Price per unit (₹)	Number of vehicles sold
Tractor	3,45,870	12
Car	8,36,100	38
Bike	1,75,560	75

Find the total amount received by the showroom.

1. ₹4,15,04,404
2. ₹4,90,85,312
3. ₹4,18,90,342
4. ₹4,90,89,240

How many questions did you answer correctly? Score yourself.

easy	average	advanced	remembering	understanding	applying	analysing	evaluating	creating

communication	representation	devising strategies	mathematisation	reasoning and argument	using symbols	using mathematical tools	creativity

4 Factors and Multiples

Curricular Goals

- Understand numbers and discover and recognise patterns in number sequences (CG-1)

Competencies

- Recognise, describe, and extend simple number patterns such as odd numbers, even numbers, etc (C-1.4)

Why This Topic?

In real life, we come across the concept of factors and multiples in many situations.

Arranging people in equal groups

Number of students in section A: 24

Number of students in section B: 28

We can make equal groups of students by finding the highest common multiple of 24 and 28.

Cutting a fabric into equal square pieces

We can make a fixed number of square napkins from a piece of fabric with a specific length and width by finding the highest common factor (without wasting any fabric).

List two more examples where factors and multiples are used in your daily life.

Are You Ready?

A. What is the 8th multiple of 6?

1. 64
2. 32
3. 15
4. 48

B. What are the factors of 24?

1. 2, 3, 5, 6, 8, 12, 24
2. 1, 2, 4, 6, 8, 12, 30
3. 1, 2, 3, 4, 6, 8, 12, 24
4. 2, 4, 8, 10, 24

C. Which of the following is an even prime number?

1. 0
2. 2
3. 1
4. 4

D. Which of the following is divisible by 2, 5 and 10?

1. 24567
2. 30982
3. 54365
4. 41780

E. What are the first 4 common multiples of 3 and 6?

1. 3, 6, 12, 18
2. 1, 3, 6, 9
3. 3, 6, 9, 24
4. 6, 12, 18, 24

F. 5 and 10 are common factors of 30 and ________.

1. 15
2. 60
3. 45
4. 25

G. What is the LCM of 14 and 23?

1. 234
2. 312
3. 123
4. 322

H. What is the HCF of 17 and 68?

1. 7
2. 68
3. 17
4. 9

I. Which of the following expresses 57 as a product of its prime factors?

1. $3 \times 3 \times 3 \times 3$
2. 3×19
3. $2 \times 3 \times 3$
4. $2 \times 2 \times 7$

J. Which of the following expresses 91 as a product of its prime factors?

1. $3 \times 3 \times 3 \times 7$
2. $3 \times 7 \times 7$
3. $13 \times 3 \times 3$
4. 7×13

How many questions did you answer correctly? Score yourself.

easy ☐ average ☐ advanced ☐ remembering ☐ understanding ☐ applying ☐ analysing ☐ evaluating ☐ creating ☐

communication ☐ representation ☐ devising strategies ☐ mathematisation ☐ reasoning and argument ☐ using symbols ☐ using mathematical tools ☐ creativity ☐

DIVISIBILITY RULES

Raju, a baker, made 85 pista cookies. He has sachets of different sizes that can hold 2, 5 and 10 cookies respectively.

Which sachet can be used to pack all the cookies equally without leaving any cookies?

We can find the solution to this by using the divisibility rule.

Divisibility rules or **Divisibility tests** are short calculations that help us to find if a particular number is divisible by the given number, without actual division.

Let's recall all the divisibility rules learnt.

Number	Divisibility rule
2	The digit in the ones place of the number should end with 0, 2, 4, 6, or 8.
3	The sum of the digits of the number should be divisible by 3.
5	The digit in the ones place of the number should end with 0 or 5.
6	The number is divisible by both 2 and 3.
9	The sum of the digits of the number should be divisible by 9.
10	The digit in the ones place of the number should end with 0.

Now let us check which number, 2 or 5 or 10 divides 85 completely?

- 85 is not divisible by 2, since the digit in ones place is odd.
- 85 is divisible by 5, since the digit in ones place is 5.
- 85 is not divisible by 10, since the digit in ones place is not zero.

Example 1: Apply the divisibility rules and check whether 56874 is divisible by the numbers 2, 3, 5, 6, 9 and 10.

Solution:

- 56874 is divisible by 2 since the digit in its ones place is an even number.
- $5 + 6 + 8 + 7 + 4 = 30$

  56874 is divisible by 3 since the sum of the digits is divisible by 3.

- 56874 is not divisible by 5 since the digit in its ones place is not 5 or 10.
- 56874 is divisible by 6 since it is divisible by both 2 and 3.
- 5 + 6 + 8 + 7 + 4 = 30

56874 is not divisible by 9 since the sum of the digits is not divisible by 9.

- 56874 is not divisible by 10 since the digit in its ones place is not 0.

Therefore, 56874 is divisible by 2, 3 and 6.

Example 2: Check if the following numbers are divisible by 2, 3, 5, 6, 9 and 10.

a. 5403 b. 98710

c. 10053 d. 354891

Solution:

a. 5403

- 5403 is not divisible by 2 since the digit in ones place is odd.
- 5 + 4 + 0 + 3 = 12

  5403 is divisible by 3 since the sum of the digits is divisible by 3.
- 5403 is not divisible by 5 since the digit in its ones place is not 5 or 0.
- 5403 is not divisibly by 6 since it is only divisible by 3 and not by 2.
- 5 + 4 + 0 + 3 = 12

  5403 is not divisible by 9 since the sum of the digits is not divisible by 9.
- 5403 is not divisible by 10 since the digit in its ones place is not 0.

b. 98710

- 98710 is divisible by 2 since the digit in ones place is even.
- 9 + 8 + 7 + 1 + 0 = 25

  98710 is not divisible by 3 since the sum of the digits is not divisible by 3.
- 98710 is divisible by 5 since the digit in its ones place is 0.
- 98710 is not divisibly by 6 since it is only divisible by 2 and not by 3.
- 9 + 8 + 7 + 1 + 0 = 25

  98710 is not divisible by 9 since the sum of the digits is not divisible by 9.
- 98710 divisible by 10 since the digit in its ones place is 0.

c. 10053

- 10053 is not divisible by 2 since the digit in ones place is odd.
- $1 + 0 + 0 + 5 + 3 = 9$

  10053 is divisible by 3 since the sum of the digits is divisible by 3.
- 10053 is not divisible by 5 since the digit in its ones place is not 5 or 10.
- 10053 is not divisibly by 6 since it is only divisible by 3 and not by 2.
- $1 + 0 + 0 + 5 + 3 = 9$

  10053 is divisible by 9 since the sum of the digits is divisible by 9.
- 10053 is not divisible by 10 since the digit in its ones place is not 0.

d. 356580

- 356580 is divisible by 2 since the digit in ones place is even.
- $3 + 5 + 6 + 5 + 8 + 0 = 27$

  356580 is divisible by 3 since the sum of the digits is divisible by 3.
- 356580 is divisible by 5 since the digit in its ones place is 0.
- 356580 is divisibly by 6 since it is divisible by 3 and by 2.
- $3 + 5 + 6 + 5 + 8 + 0 = 27$

  356580 is divisible by 9 since the sum of the digits is divisible by 9.
- 356580 divisible by 10 since the digit in its ones place is 0.

PRIME AND COMPOSITE NUMBERS

A number that has only two factors (1 and itself) is called a **prime number.** For example, 2 and 3.

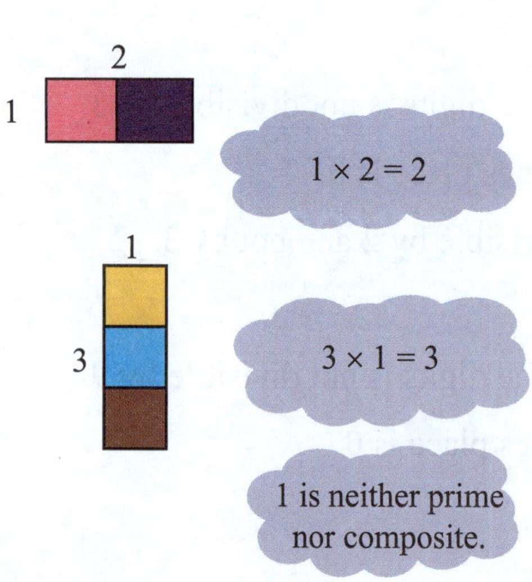

A number that has more than 2 factors is called a **composite number.** For example, 4 and 6.

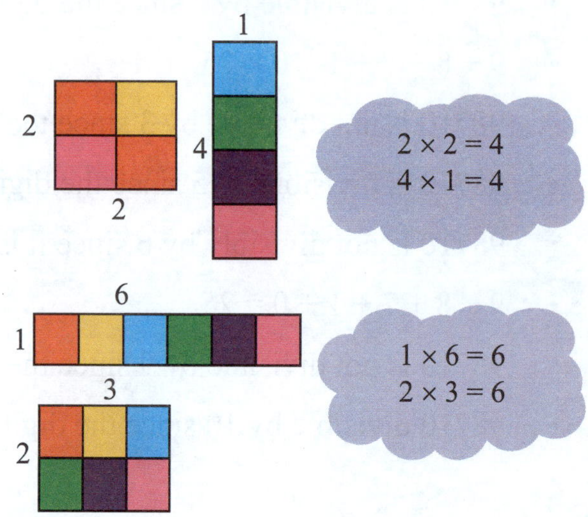

Method for Finding Prime Numbers

A Greek mathematician, **Eratosthenes**, gave a method of finding prime numbers from 1 to 100 without finding the factors.

Follow the steps given below to understand the method.

1	2	3	4	5	6	7	8	9	10
11	12	13	14	15	16	17	18	19	20
21	22	23	24	25	26	27	28	29	30
31	32	33	34	35	36	37	38	39	40
41	42	43	44	45	46	47	48	49	50
51	52	53	54	55	56	57	58	59	60
61	62	63	64	65	66	67	68	69	70
71	72	73	74	75	76	77	78	79	80
81	82	83	84	85	86	87	88	89	90
91	92	93	94	95	96	97	98	99	100

Step 1: Write down the numbers from 1 to 100.

Step 2: Cross out 1 as it is neither a prime nor a composite number.

Step 3: Circle 2 as it is a prime number.

Step 4: Shade all the multiples of 2 in green.

Step 5: Now, consider the next number after 2, that is, 3. Circle 3 and shade all the other multiples of 3 in pink.

Step 6: Similarly, consider number 5. Circle number 5 and shade all the other multiples of 5 in blue.

Step 7: Continue this process till all the numbers are either shaded or circled.

There are 25 prime numbers between 1 and 100.

Step 8: List all the numbers that are circled. The circled numbers do not have factors other than 1. They are all prime numbers.

Example 3: How many prime numbers are there between 20 and 40?

Solution: There are 4 prime numbers between 20 and 40.
They are 23, 29, 31 and 37.

Example 4: Check whether the following numbers are prime numbers.

a. 36 b. 49 c. 53 d. 97

Solution: List the factors of each number.

a. 36 has 1, 2, 3, 4, 6, 9, 12, 18 and 36 as its factors, thus it is a composite number.

b. 49 has 1, 7 and 49 as its factors, thus it is a composite number.

c. 53 has 1 and 53 as its factors, thus it is a prime number.

d. 97 has 1 and 97 as its factors, thus it is a prime number.

Twin Primes

If the difference between two prime numbers is 2, then they are said to be **twin primes**. For example, 17 and 19.

Find out other twin primes and colour the boxes as done for 17 and 19.

1	2	3	4	5	6	7	8	9	10
11	12	13	14	15	16	17	18	19	20
21	22	23	24	25	26	27	28	29	30
31	32	33	34	35	36	37	38	39	40
41	42	43	44	45	46	47	48	49	50
51	52	53	54	55	56	57	58	59	60
61	62	63	64	65	66	67	68	69	70
71	72	73	74	75	76	77	78	79	80
81	82	83	84	85	86	87	88	89	90
91	92	93	94	95	96	97	98	99	100

Co-primes

If the common factor of two given numbers is 1, then such numbers are called **co-prime numbers.**

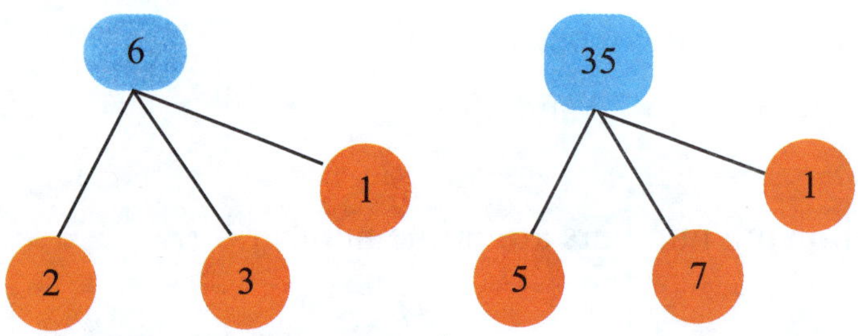

Co-prime numbers need not be prime numbers.

The only factor common of 6 and 35 is 1. Thus, 6 and 35 are co-prime numbers.

Example 5: Which of the following pair of prime numbers are twin primes?

a. 29 and 31 b. 49 and 51 c. 61 and 71 d. 7 and 11

Solution: The difference between the twin prime numbers is 2.

a. 29 and 31: Difference between 29 and 31 is 2, thus these are twin primes.

b. 49 and 51: 49 and 51 are composite numbers, thus these are not twin primes.

c. 61 and 71: Difference between 61 and 71 is 10, thus these are not twin primes.

d. 7 and 11: Difference between 7 and 11 is 4, thus these are not twin primes.

Example 6: Are 8 and 65 co-prime numbers?

Solution: List the factors of 8 and 65.

Factors of 8 are 1, 2, 4 and 8.

Factors of 65 are 1, 5, 13 and 65.

Since, 8 and 65 do not have any common factor other than 1, they are co-prime numbers.

Example 7: Are 11 and 18 co-prime numbers?

Solution: List the factors of 11 and 18.

Factors of 11 are 1 and 11.

Factors of 18 are 1, 2, 3, 6, 9 and 18.

Since, 11 and 18 do not have any common factor other than 1, they are co-prime numbers.

Exercise 4.1

1. Fill in the following table with "Yes, if divisible by the given numbers or 'No' if not divisible by given number."

Number	2	5	10	3	6	9
26352						
36000						
11011						
3996						
23484						

2. State whether the following statements are true (T) or false (F).

a. The numbers that are divisible by 6 are divisible by 2 and 3.

b. All composite numbers are even numbers.

c. The numbers divisible by 3 are divisible by 9.

d. Co-prime factors have 1 as their common factor.

e. The number 6787 is divisible by 5.

3. Fill in the blanks.

a. ________ is a factor of all even numbers.

b. ________ is the smallest odd prime number.

c. 1 is neither a ________ nor a ________ number.

d. ________ numbers have more than 2 factors.

e. Prime numbers whose difference is 2 are known as ________.

4. **Circle the prime numbers and cross the composite numbers in the box given below.**

5	15	14	17	28	27	71	41	46	81
99	60	29	49	51	63	93	86	37	10
3	1	13	22	39	45	20	67	91	43
31	47	77	50	69	30	87	56	76	23
32	11	38	42	46	98	19	26	30	12
90	21	37	61	4	33	18	92	95	25
59	88	5	24	35	20	44	66	16	58
73	18	79	7	52	55	75	14	28	40
93	34	40	64	80	70	37	9	53	36
62	23	57	2	89	25	78	44	85	72

PRIME FACTORISATION

A number that divides the given number completely without leaving any remainder is called a **factor**. If the factor is a prime number, then it is called a **prime factor**.

Listing the factors of a given number is **factorisation**. The method of expressing the number as a product of prime numbers is called **prime factorisation**.

Prime factorisation can be done by two different methods.

Division method	Factor tree method
In the division method, the given number is divided by prime numbers starting from the smallest until the new dividend is 1.	In this method, factorisation is represented pictorially that looks like an inverted tree with branches spreading out. The given number is factorised until the factors are prime numbers.

Example 8: Find the prime factorisation of 36.

Solution: Factors of 36 are 1, 2, 3, 4, 6, 9, 12, 18 and 36.

By division method

Step 1

Divide 36 by 2.
Write 18 under 36

2	36
	18

Step 2

Divide 18 by 2.
Write 9 under 18

2	36
2	18
	9

Step 3

Divide 9 by 3.
Write 3 under 3

2	36
2	18
3	9
	3

Step 4

Divide 3 by 3.
Write 1 under 3

2	36
2	18
3	9
3	3
	1

Therefore, the prime factorisation of 36 = $2 \times 2 \times 3 \times 3$.

By factor tree method

Step 1

Represent 36 as product of any 2 numbers

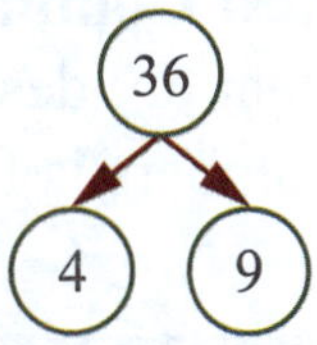

Step 2

Factorise 4 since it is a composite number.

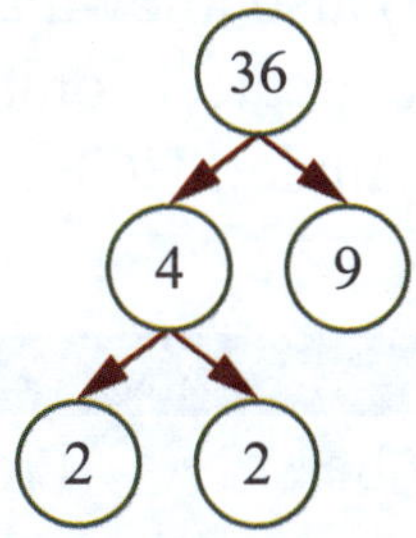

Step 3

Factorise 9 since it is a composite number.

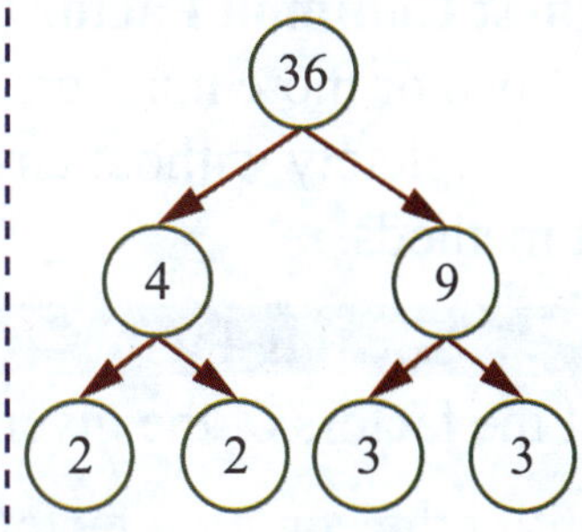

Therefore, the prime factorisation of 36 = 2 × 2 × 3 × 3.

Example 9: Find the prime factorisation of 45.

Solution:

3	45
3	15
5	5
	1

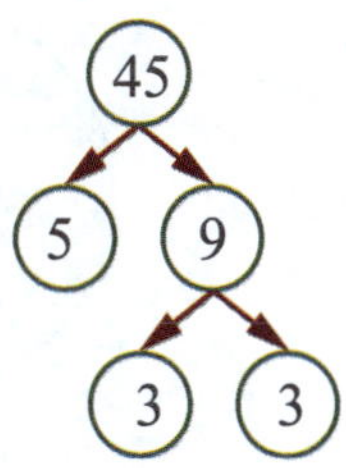

Therefore, the prime factorisation of 45 = 5 × 3 × 3.

Exercise 4.2

1. Prime factorise the following numbers using the division method.

a. 20 b. 36 c. 75 d. 600 e. 147

2. Prime factorise the following numbers using the factor tree method.

a. 40 b. 72 c. 50 d. 81 e. 48

3. Complete the prime factorisations of the following numbers.

a.

2	56
2	
2	
	1

b.

	27
3	
	1

c.

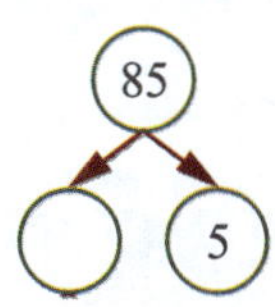

d.

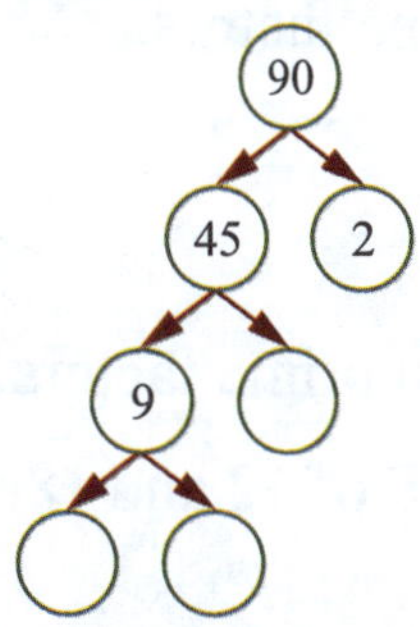

e.

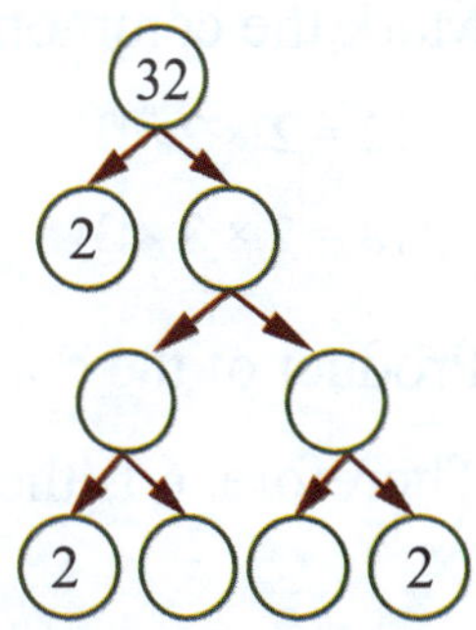

HIGHEST COMMON FACTOR (HCF)

Numbers that divide the given numbers completely without leaving any remainders are called factors. Factors that are common to a given pair of numbers are common factors.

The **Highest Common Factor** (HCF) also known as the **Greatest Common Divisor** (GCD) of two or more numbers is the greatest common factor that divides the given numbers completely without any remainder. HCF of any two numbers is found using different methods.

Listing factors	Prime factorisation method
• List the factors of the given numbers	• Prime factorise the given numbers
• Identify the common factor	• Identify the common prime factors
• HCF will be the highest among the common factors	• HCF will be the product of common prime factors

Example 10: Find the HCF of 15 and 30 by listing the factors.

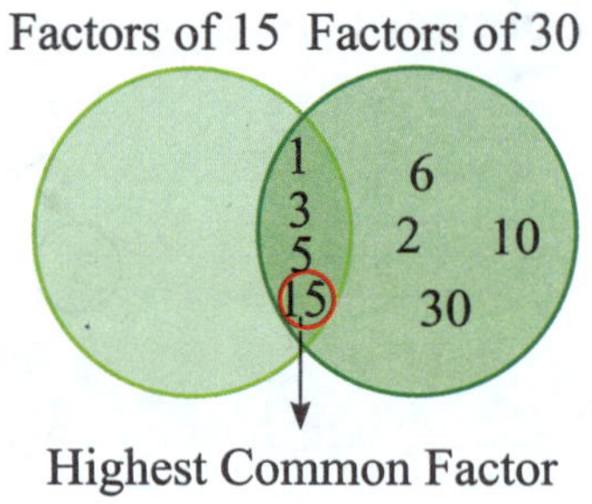

Solution:

The factors of 15 are 1, 3, 5 and 15.

The factors of 30 are 1, 2, 3, 5, 6, 10, 15 and 30.

Mark the common factors.

Factors of 15	1, 3, 5, 15
Factors of 30	1, 2, 3, 5, 6, 10, 15, 30

15 is the highest among the common factors.

Therefore, 15 is the HCF of 15 and 30.

Example 11: Find the HCF of 12 and 18 by prime factorisation method.

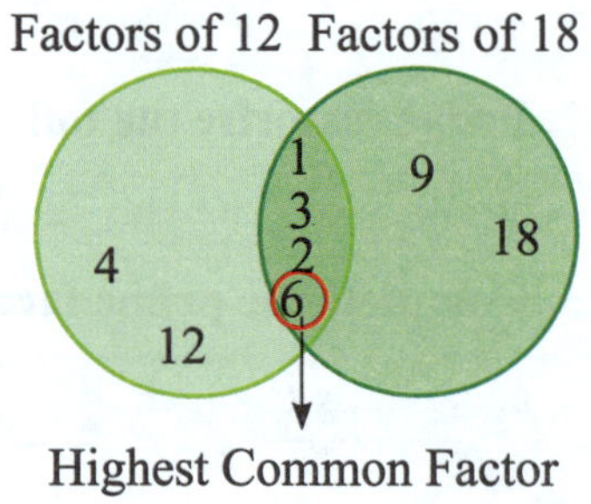

Solution:

Prime factorisation of 12 = $2 \times 2 \times 3$

Prime factorisation of 18 = $2 \times 3 \times 3$

Mark the common prime factors.

$12 = 2 \times 2 \times 3$

$18 = 2 \times 3 \times 3$

Product of the common prime factors is $2 \times 3 = 6$.

Therefore, 6 is the HCF of 12 and 18.

HCF of more than Two Numbers

Example 12: Find the HCF of 8, 12 and 36.

Solution: Prime factorise 8, 12 and 36.
Mark the common prime factors.

$8 = 2 \times 2 \times 2$

$12 = 2 \times 2 \times 3$

$36 = 2 \times 2 \times 3 \times 3$

HCF = Product of the common prime factors = $2 \times 2 = 4$.

Therefore, the HCF of 8, 12 and 36 is 4.

Example 13: Find the HCF of 45, 48 and 63.

Solution: Prime factorise 45, 48 and 63. Mark the common prime factors.

There is only one common prime factor which is 3.

Therefore, the HCF of 45, 48 and 63 is 3.

$45 = 3 \times 3 \times 5$

$48 = 2 \times 2 \times 2 \times 2 \times 3$

$63 = 3 \times 3 \times 7$

Exercise 4.3

1. Find the HCF of the following numbers by listing factors.

a. 42 and 56 b. 18 and 45 c. 36 and 54 d. 120 and 45 e. 108 and 130

2. Find the HCF of the following numbers using prime factorisation method.

a. 42, 56 and 28 b. 32, 60 and 80 c. 30, 45 and 95 d. 9, 15 and 33 e. 18, 45 and 36

LEAST COMMON MULTIPLE (LCM)

A multiple is a product of any two numbers. The multiples that are common to a given pair of numbers are called common multiples.

The **lowest common multiple** (LCM) is the smallest common multiple of two or more numbers. LCM of any two numbers is found using different methods.

Listing common multiples	Prime factorisation	Division method
• List the multiples of the given numbers • Identify the common multiple • LCM will be the smallest common multiple	• Prime factorise the given numbers • LCM will be the product of prime factors	• Divide all numbers by a common prime number • Write their quotients under the respective numbers • Continue the division till we are left with co-prime numbers • LCM will be the product of all divisors and co-prime numbers

Example 14: Find out the LCM of 12 and 18.

Solution:

Multiples of 12: 12, 24, **36**, 48, 60, **72**, 84, 96, **108**, 120, 132, **144**

Multiples of 18: 18, **36**, 54, **72**, 90, **108**, 126, **144**

Common multiples of 12 and 18 are 36, 72, 108 and 144.

Therefore, the LCM of 12 and 18 is 36.

Multiples of 12 Multiples of 18

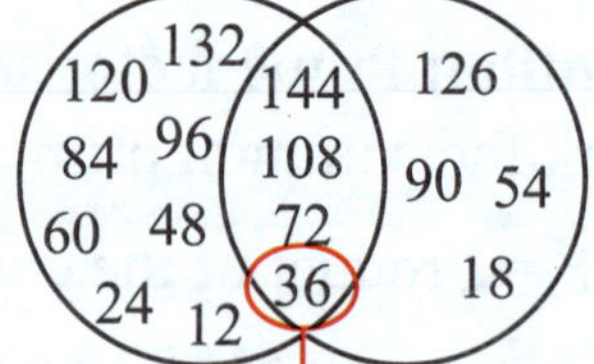

LCM of 12 and 18

Example 15: Find the LCM of 80 and 99.

Solution: Prime factorise 80 and 99.

2	80
2	40
2	20
2	10
5	5
	1

3	99
3	33
11	11
	1

Prime factorisation of 80 = 2 × 2 × 2 × 2 × 5

Prime factorisation of 99 = 3 × 3 × 11

Since there are no common factors between 80 and 99, LCM is the product of all the prime factors.

LCM = 2 × 2 × 2 × 2 × 3 × 3 × 5 × 11 = 7920.

Therefore, the LCM of 80 and 99 is 7920.

Prime factorisation of

80 99

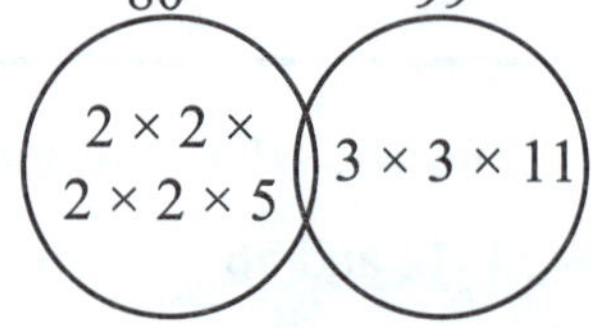

Example 16: Find the LCM of 45 and 60 by division method.

Solution:

Divide 45 and 60 by a common prime number and write their quotients under the respective numbers.

Continue the division till we are left with co-prime numbers.

Multiply all the divisors and the numbers in the last row.

LCM = 2 × 2 × 3 × 3 × 5 = 180

Therefore, the LCM of 45 and 60 is 180.

LCM of 45 and 60

2	45	60
2	45	30
3	45	15
3	15	5
5	5	5
	1	1

LCM of Three or More Numbers

Example 17: Find the LCM of 10, 15 and 20 using all the three methods.

Solution:

- **By listing common multiples**

  Multiples of 10 = 10, 20, 30, 40, 50, 60, 70, 80, 90, 100, 110, 120, 130, 140

  Multiples of 15 = 15, 30, 45, 60, 75, 90, 105, 120, 135, 150

  Multiples of 20 = 20, 40, 60, 80, 100, 120, 140, 160, 180

  Common multiples are 60 and 120.

  The LCM of 10, 15 and 20 is 60.

- **By prime factorisation**

  Prime factorisation of 10 = 2 × 5

  Prime factorisation of 15 = 3 × 5

  Prime factorisation of 20 = 2 × 2 × 5

  2 occurs twice in 20, 5 occurs once and 3 occurs once.

  The LCM of 10, 15 and 20 = 2 × 2 × 5 × 3 = 60.

- **By division method**

  Divide 10, 15 and 20 by a common prime number and write their quotients under the respective numbers.

  Continue the division till we are left with co-prime numbers.

  Multiply all the divisors and the numbers in the last row.

  The LCM of 10, 15 and 20 = 2 × 2 × 3 × 5 = 60

LCM of 10, 15 and 20

2	10	15	20
2	5	15	10
3	5	15	5
5	5	5	5
	1	1	1

Exercise 4.4

1. Find the LCM of the following numbers using the prime factorisation method.

a. 18 and 24 b. 16 and 18 c. 48 and 56 d. 25, 75 and 50 e. 10, 15 and 20

2. Find the LCM of the following by the division method.

a. 20, 25 b. 40, 60 c. 30, 15, 75 d. 85, 51 e. 26, 39, 52

RELATIONSHIP BETWEEN HCF AND LCM

Let us find the LCM and HCF of any two pair of numbers.

HCF and LCM of 6 and 21

Multiples of 6: 6, 12, 18, 24, 30, 36, **42**, 48

Multiples of 21: 21, **42**, 63, 84

LCM of 6 and 21 is 42.

Prime factors of 6 are: 2 × **3**

Prime factors of 21 are: **3** × 7

HCF of 6 and 21 is 3.

HCF and LCM of 9 and 12

Multiples of 9: 9, 18, 27, **36**, 45, 54

Multiples of 12: 12, 24, **36**, 48, 60

LCM of 9 and 12 is 36.

Prime factors of 9 are: 3 × **3**

Prime factors of 12 are: **3** × 2 × 2

HCF of 9 and 12 is 3.

How are the products of the given numbers and their HCF and LCM related to each other?

Product of the given number, $6 \times 21 = 126$

Product of HCF and LCM, $42 \times 3 = 126$

Product of the given number, $9 \times 12 = 108$

Product of HCF and LCM, $36 \times 3 = 108$

From the above examples, we can conclude that,

Product of two numbers = HCF × LCM

Example 18: Is the product of 12 and 18 equal to their product of HCF and LCM if their HCF is 6 and LCM is 36?

Solution: HCF of 12 and 18 = 6 and LCM of 12 and 18 = 36

- Product of HCF and LCM = $6 \times 36 = 216$
- Product of the numbers = $12 \times 18 = 216$

Therefore, the product of 12 and 18 is equal to product of 6 and 36.

Example 19: Find the HCF of 20 and 25 if the LCM is 100.

Solution: Product of two numbers = HCF × LCM

LCM of 20 and 25 = 100 and Product of 20 and 25 = 500

HCF = Product of two numbers ÷ LCM = $500 \div 100 = 5$

Therefore, HCF of 20 and 25 is 5.

Activity

a

Aim: Deduce the relation between HCF and LCM.

Material Required: Two colours of unit cubes that can be inter-locked.

Procedure:

1. Divide the students into small groups.
2. Ask them to represent a pair of numbers by taking those number of unit cubes.
3. Ask the students to group the cubes of both the colours separately such that each group has the same number of cubes without leaving any cube.
4. Allow students to find all possible combination of equal grouping of both numbers without any remainders.
5. Inform students that the possible combinations of equal groups of numbers are the common factors and the highest among them is the HCF.

Example: 18 and 24

- Represent 18 using red cubes and 24 using yellow cubes.
- Regroup 18 red cubes and 24 yellow cubes evenly.

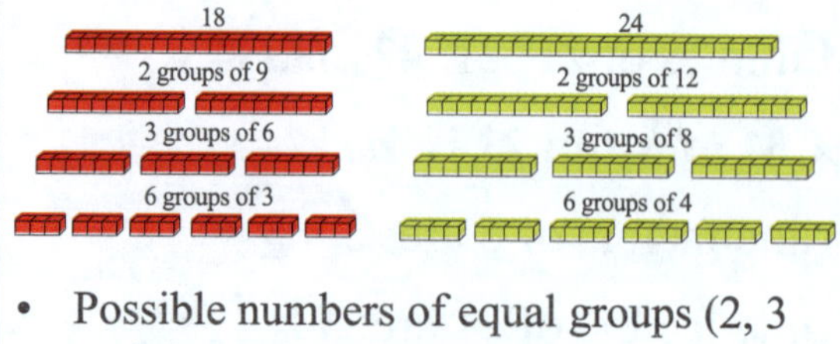

- Possible numbers of equal groups (2, 3 and 6) are the common factors.
- 6 is the HCF since it is the highest among the common factors.

6. Now, ask each group of students to represent a pair of numbers by placing red and yellow coloured unit cubes one beside the other.
7. Allow students to repeat placing the same number of red cubes and yellow cubes one beside the other until the lengths of both are the same.
8. Inform students that the number of cubes that are repeatedly added are the factors of the respective numbers.
9. Now, allow students to count the number of red and yellow cubes they have used. This number is the first common multiple or LCM of the given number.

> Example: 18 and 24
>
> - Represent 18 using red cubes and 24 using yellow cubes.
> - Add 18 more red cubes and 24 more yellow cubes and arrange them one beside the other. Repeat the process to find the multiples of each number.
>
> 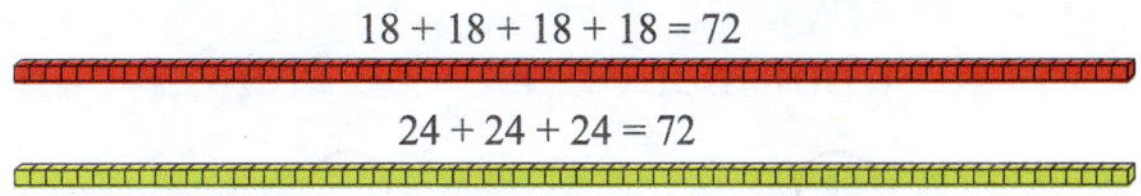
>
>
> Multiples of 18 are 18, 36, 54, 72
>
> Multiples of 24 are 24, 48, 72
>
> 72 is the first common multiple and it is the LCM of 18 and 24.

10. Now, ask students to find the product of the given numbers and the product of LCM and HCF of the given numbers.
    - Product of 18 and 24 is 432.
    - Product of 72 and 6 is 432.
11. Ask students to find the relationship of the products of the given numbers and their HCF and LCM.

Conclusion: Students deduce the relationship between HCF and LCM.

Exercise 4.5

Answer the following questions.

1. If the LCM of two numbers 4 and 5 is 20, what is their HCF?
2. Find the LCM of the numbers 27 and 18 if their HCF is 9.
3. Find the HCF of 78 and 21 if their LCM is 546.
4. If the HCF and LCM of two numbers is 6 and 90 and one of the numbers is 18, find the other.
5. Find the HCF and LCM of 66 and 44. Verify the relation between their product and the product of HCF and LCM.

APPLICATION OF HCF AND LCM

Example 20: Shubham has 12 red pens and 15 blue pens. He wants to put these into pen stands in equal number, but with each pen stand having only one colour of pen. What is the greatest number of pens he can have in one pen stand?

Solution:

Number of red pens = 12 Number of blue pens = 15

The greatest number of pens he can have in one pen stand

$12 = 2 \times 2 \times 3$ $15 = 3 \times 5$ HCF = 3

So, the greatest number he can have in each pen stand is 3 pens.

Example 21: Ashang and Akanksha have their taekwondo class today. Ashang goes to the taekwondo class every 9 days and Akanksha goes to the taekwondo class every 12 days. When will both have their taekwondo classes on the same day again at the earliest?

Solution:

To find when both will have their taekwondo classes again on the same day, we have to find the LCM of 9 and 12.

2	12, 9
2	6, 9
3	3, 9
3	1, 3
	1, 1

$LCM = 2 \times 2 \times 3 \times 3 = 36$

Both children will have their taekwondo classes on the same day again on 36th day.

Exercise 4.6

Solve the following.

1. Karim has 24 storybooks and 30 colouring books. He wants to divide the books in equal stacks, but he wants each stack to have only storybooks or only colouring books. What is the greatest number he can have in each stack?
2. The traffic lights at two different crossroads change after every 48 seconds and 72 seconds. If they change simultaneously at 7 a.m., at what time will the traffic lights change simultaneously again?
3. Nazia, Prashansha and James jog around a circular park. They complete the round in 36 seconds, 42 seconds and 48 seconds, respectively. After how many seconds will they be together at the starting point?

Concept Map

Number	Divisibility rule
2	The digit in the ones place of the number should end with 0, 2, 4, 6, or 8
3	The sum of the digits of the number should be divisible by 3
5	The digit in the ones place of the number should end with 0 or 5
6	The number is divisible by both 2 and 3
9	The sum of the digits of the number should be divisible by 9
10	The digit in the ones place of the number should end with 0

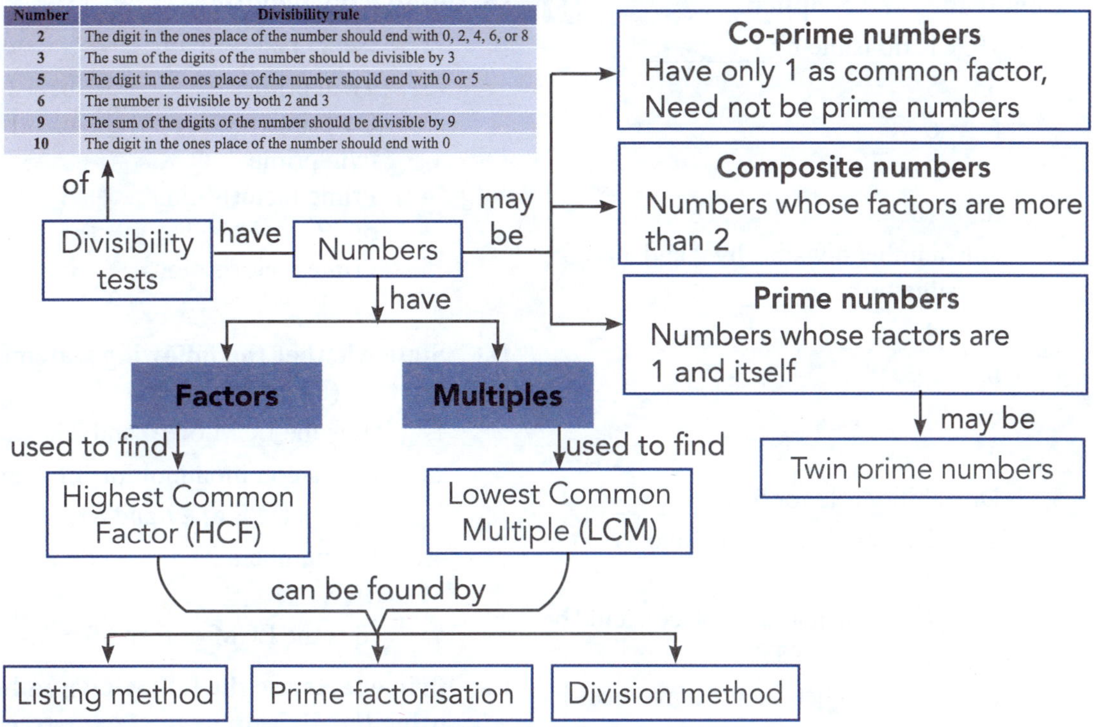

Projects

A. Representation of HCF and LCM

Represent the HCF and LCM of any three random numbers using Venn diagrams on a chart as shown here. Make these representations for 10 sets of numbers.

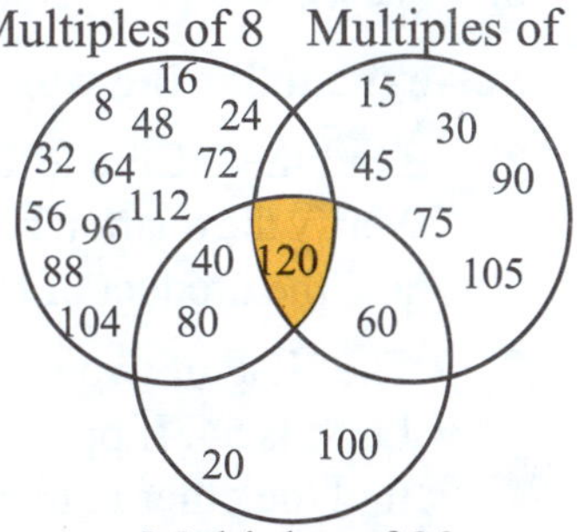

LCM of 8, 15, and 20 is 120.

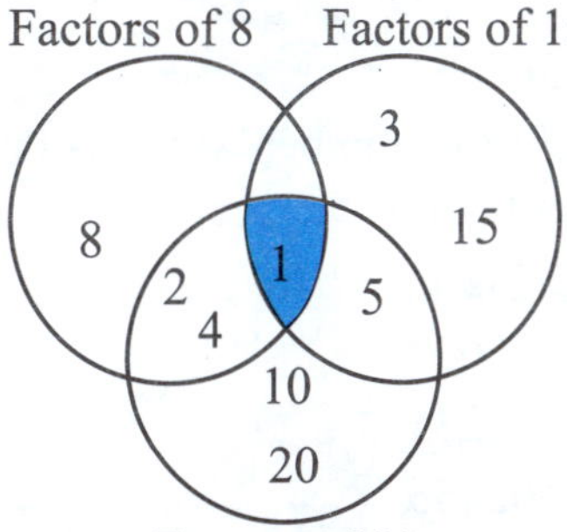

HCF of 8, 15, and 20 is 1.

B. Physical Education

Physical Education aims to develop students' physical competence and ability to perform in a wide range of activities associated with an active and healthy lifestyle.

Group performances in physical education means to carry out activities in groups. To divide the number of students into different groups, HCF and LCM may be used. Find out the name of any five group performances that would need arranging into groups. Make a presentation on how HCF and LCM can be used in these performances to plan groups.

Revision Exercise

A. Choose the correct option.

1. 1092 is divisible by ________.
   a. 5
   b. 6
   c. 9
   d. 10
2. Any number divisible by 2 and 3 is also divisible by ________.
   a. 4
   b. 2
   c. 5
   d. 6
3. Divisibility rule for 5 is ________.
   a. The number should have 5 or 0 in its ones place
   b. The digit in its ones place should be an even number
   c. The number should have 0 in its ones place
   d. The sum of the digits of the number is divisible by 5
4. The number divisible by both 2 and 10 is:
   a. 175480
   b. 174584
   c. 8011745
   d. 56767
5. Identify the number which is divisible by 3 but not by 9.
   a. 234562
   b. 19563
   c. 901235
   d. 102456

B. Fill in the blanks.

1. HCF of 18, 6 and 9 is ________.
2. LCM of 5 and 7 is ________.
3. LCM of 18, 45 and 90 is ________.
4. The product of 2 numbers is 48. If the HCF is 2 then the LCM is ________.
5. The product of HCF and LCM of 2 numbers is 150. If one of the numbers is 10 then the other number is ________.

C. Match the following.

1.	Prime factor of 32	a.	3×29
2.	Twin primes	b.	2
3.	Co-prime but not twin prime	c.	11, 13
4.	Prime factorisation of 87	d.	7×13
5.	Prime factorisation of 91	e.	24, 11

D. State whether the following statements are true (T) or false (F).

1. 50 is the LCM of 10 and 25.
2. 18 is a common multiple of 4 and 6.
3. 3 is the HCF of 27 and 81.
4. The numbers 24 and 35 do not have an HCF.
5. 18 is the LCM of 6 and 9.

E. Prime factorise the following numbers using the division or the factor-tree method.

1. 38
2. 84
3. 76
4. 155
5. 120

F. Solve the following word problems.

1. Find the HCF and LCM of 24 and 12. Verify the relation between their product and the product of HCF and LCM.
2. The HCF of two numbers is 3 and their LCM is 54. If one of the numbers is 27, find the other number.
3. The LCM of 63 and 28 is 252. Find their HCF.
4. The LCM of 2 numbers is 1088 and HCF is 2. If one of the numbers is 34, find the other.
5. The HCF and LCM of 2 numbers is 5 and 75. If one of the numbers is 15, find the other.

G. Application-based questions.

1. 60 oranges and 48 apples have to be packed in baskets such that each basket has the same fruit in same numbers. Find the maximum number of fruits that can be packed in each basket.
2. In a class, students can be arranged in groups of 2, 3 and 5. What could be the minimum number of students in the class?
3. Ravi cleans his house every 6th day and his sister cleans it every 4th day. How many times will they clean together in the month of April?
4. The dimensions of a box are 30 cm, 18 cm and 48 cm. What is the maximum length of tape that can be used to measure the dimensions of the box?
5. A train station has two tracks that start together daily at 7 am. Trains on track A leave the track every 10 minutes and trains on track B leave every 15 minutes. How many times do trains on tracks A and B leave together between 7 am and 11 am?

Space for rough work

Did You Master?

A. The greatest number that divides two numbers completely is known as _______.

1. composite number
2. HCF
3. LCM
4. prime number

B. What is the HCF of 12 and 18?

1. 2
2. 3
3. 6
4. 4

C. Using the divisibility rule, find which of the following numbers is divisible by 6.

1. 10973
2. 42389
3. 12558
4. 81237

D. What is the LCM of 51 and 85?

1. 255
2. 120
3. 67
4. 35

E. Which of the following is not a factor of 20, 30 and 60?

1. 2
2. 10
3. 5
4. 7

F. Which of the following is NOT a multiple of 3, 5 and 11?

1. 165
2. 330
3. 300
4. 495

G. The number 101 is an _________.

1. even prime number
2. odd prime number
3. even composite number
4. odd composite number

H. Which of the following is the prime factorisation of 100?

1. $2 \times 2 \times 5$
2. $2 \times 2 \times 10$
3. $2 \times 2 \times 5$
4. $2 \times 2 \times 5 \times 5$

I. The product of 32 and 96 is equal to the product of their HCF and LCM. If the LCM is 96, then what would be the HCF?

1. 64
2. 96
3. 6
4. 32

J. What would be the HCF of 14 and 21, if the LCM is 42?

1. 14
2. 21
3. 7
4. 28

How many questions did you answer correctly? Score yourself.

easy ☐ average ☐ advanced ☐ remembering ☐ understanding ☐ applying ☐ analysing ☐ evaluating ☐ creating ☐

communication ☐ representation ☐ devising strategies ☐ mathematisation ☐ reasoning and argument ☐ using symbols ☐ using mathematical tools ☐ creativity ☐

5 Fractions

Curricular Goals

- Understand numbers and sets of numbers (Whole numbers, Fractions) and carry out the four basic operations (CG-1)

Competencies

- Represent and compare commonly used fractions in daily life (such as $\frac{1}{2}, \frac{1}{4}$) as parts of unit wholes, as locations on number lines and as divisions of whole numbers (C-1.2)

Why This Topic?

We use fractions in many situations in our daily lives.

Birthday party planning

Total Budget: ₹50,000

Budget allocation for various events:

Event	Food	Games	Return gifts	Decoration
Fraction of allocation	$\frac{1}{2}$	$\frac{1}{5}$	$\frac{2}{5}$	$\frac{2}{5}$

Architect scale

When using the architect's scale, accurate measurements require knowledge of fractions.

Can you think of two examples from your daily life where comparison and operations such as addition, subtraction, multiplication and division of fractions are used?

Are You Ready?

A. Identify the fraction represented by the shaded portion.

1. $\frac{1}{6}$ 2. $\frac{1}{3}$

3. $\frac{2}{4}$ 4. $\frac{1}{4}$

B. Which of the following represents a proper fraction?

1. $\frac{3}{6}$ 2. $\frac{9}{3}$

3. $\frac{48}{47}$ 4. $\frac{15}{6}$

C. Which of the following are equivalent fractions?

i. 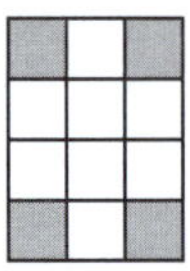

ii. 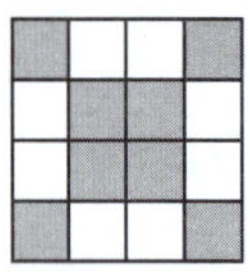

iii. 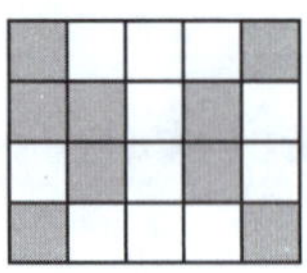

iv. 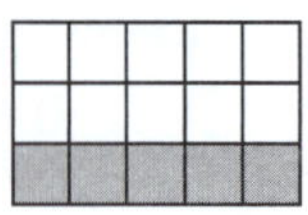

1. i and ii 2. ii and iii

3. i and iii 4. i and iv

D. Add the given fractions.

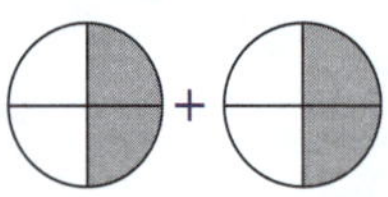

1.  2. 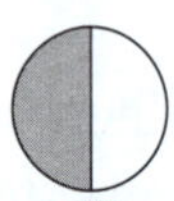

3. 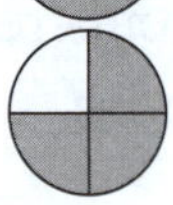 4. 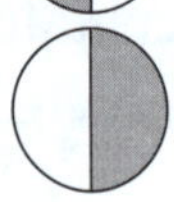

E. Compare: $\frac{3}{6}+\frac{2}{6}$ ☐ $\frac{1}{6}+\frac{1}{6}$

1. > 2. <

3. = 4. Cannot be solved

F. $\frac{3}{4}-\frac{1}{2}=$ ☐

1. $\frac{2}{2}$ 2. $\frac{1}{8}$

3. $\frac{1}{4}$ 4. $\frac{1}{2}$

G. A bundle consists of 1 m thread. If $\frac{1}{8}$ m of thread is used, how much is left?

1. $\frac{9}{8}$ m 2. $\frac{1}{4}$ m

3. $\frac{3}{4}$ m 4. $\frac{7}{8}$ m

H. An apple, an orange and a guava weigh $\frac{2}{6}$ kg, $\frac{1}{6}$ kg and $\frac{3}{6}$ kg, respectively. Which fruit is the heaviest?

1. Orange
2. Apple
3. Gauva
4. All are equal in weight

I. While preparing a juice, Riya used $\frac{3}{5}$ litres of water and $\frac{1}{5}$ litres of fruit syrup. If it is filled in a 1 litre jar, how much portion of the jar will be left empty?

1. $\frac{3}{5}$ litres 2. $\frac{1}{5}$ litres

3. $\frac{2}{5}$ litres 4. $\frac{4}{5}$ litres

J. $\frac{2}{49}+\frac{1}{7}=$ ☐

1. $\frac{9}{49}$ 2. $\frac{3}{49}$

3. $\frac{3}{56}$ 4. $\frac{3}{7}$

How many questions did you answer correctly? Score yourself.

easy ☐ average ☐ advanced ☐ remembering ☐ understanding ☐ applying ☐ analysing ☐ evaluating ☐ creating ☐

communication ☐ representation ☐ devising strategies ☐ mathematisation ☐ reasoning and argument ☐ using symbols ☐ using mathematical tools ☐ creativity ☐

FRACTIONS

Let us recall what we learnt about fractions in the previous grade.

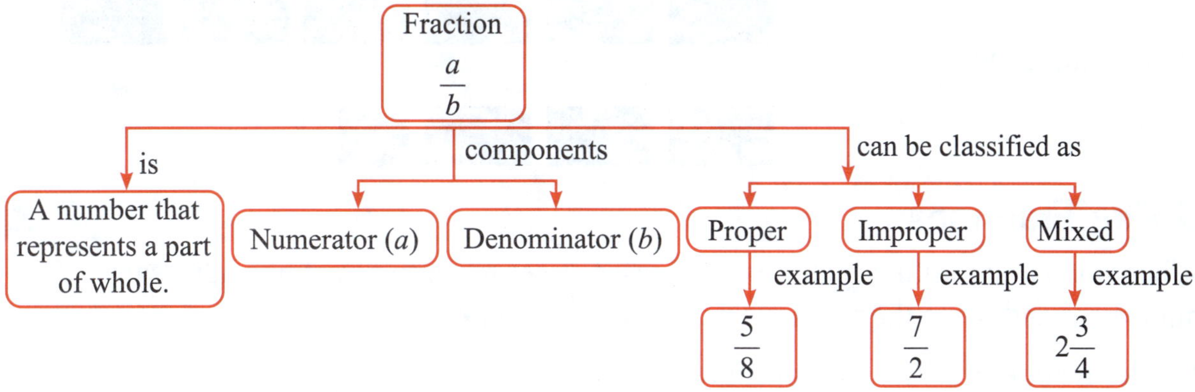

COMPARISON OF FRACTIONS

All types of fractions can be compared using some techniques. Let us learn them.

Like Fractions

Rohanpreet eats $\frac{5}{8}$ parts and Ayuub eats $\frac{3}{8}$ parts of a watermelon. Who ate more?

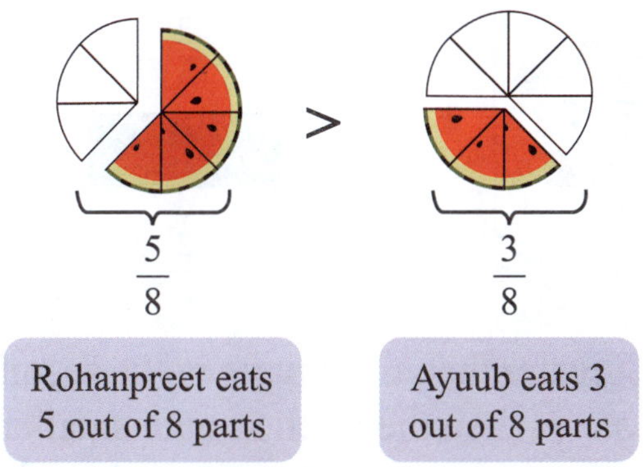

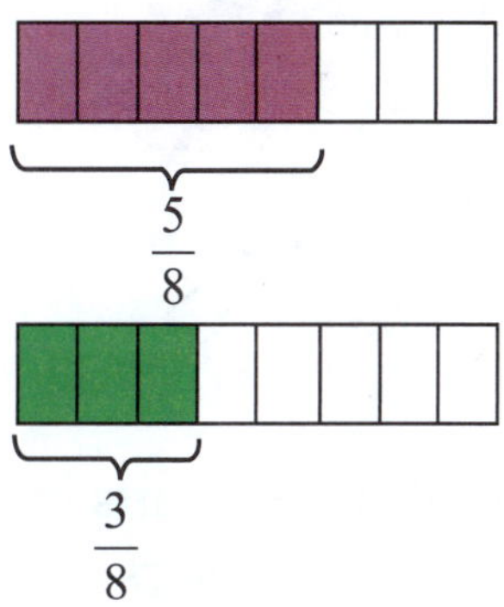

Note that if the denominators of the fractions are same, then the fraction with greater numerator is the greater one. Since, $\frac{5}{8}$ has greater numerator than $\frac{3}{8}$, we get $\frac{5}{8} > \frac{3}{8}$. Therefore, Rohanpreet ate more watermelon than Ayuub.

For like fractions, the fraction with the greater numerator is the greater fraction.

Example 1: Compare $\frac{3}{5}$ and $\frac{4}{5}$.

Solution: Since $\frac{4}{5}$ has greater numerator than $\frac{3}{5}$, we get $\frac{3}{5} < \frac{4}{5}$.

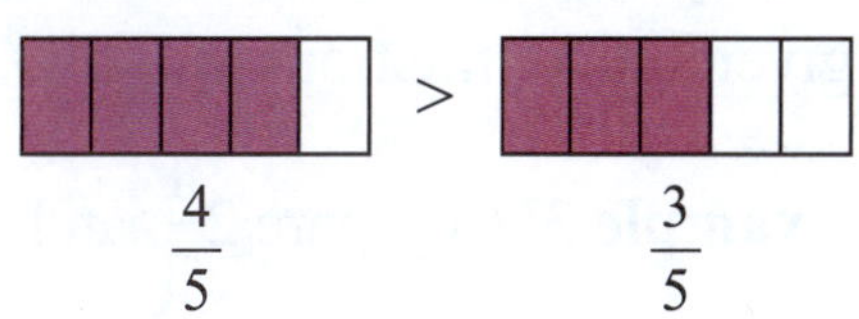

Example 2: Compare $\frac{18}{3}$ and $\frac{11}{3}$.

Solution: Since $\frac{18}{3}$ has greater numerator than $\frac{11}{3}$, we get $\frac{18}{3} > \frac{11}{3}$.

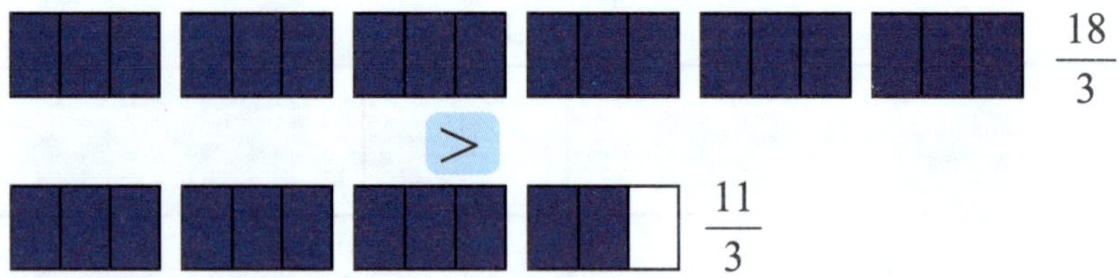

Unlike Fractions

When comparing unlike fractions, two cases arise: when the fractions have same numerator and when the fractions have different numerators.

Unlike fractions with same numerator

Niharika made 2 rotis and gave 1 to her brother. She cut the rotis into pieces, as shown in the following pictures. When 2 pieces of both the rotis are compared, they seemed to be of different sizes. Can you tell why?

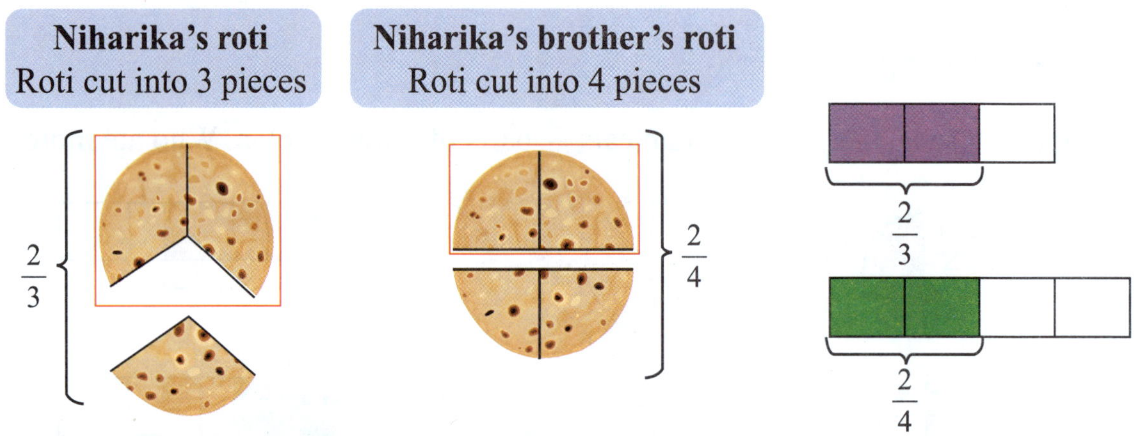

We can see that the 2 parts in the first roti are greater than the 2 parts in the second roti. So, if the numerators of the fractions are same, then the fraction with smaller denominator is greater. Since $\frac{2}{3}$ has smaller denominator than $\frac{2}{4}$, we get $\frac{2}{3} > \frac{2}{4}$.

For unlike fractions with the same numerators, the fraction with smaller denominator is greater.

Unlike fractions with different numerators

Unlike fractions can be compared using two methods.

1. Finding the LCM: Here, we find the LCM of the denominators and convert the given unlike fractions into like fractions. Then, we compare the fractions.

Example 3: Compare $2\frac{1}{3}$ and $1\frac{1}{4}$.

Solution: Converting the mixed fractions into improper fractions, we get $\frac{7}{3}$ and $\frac{5}{4}$.

LCM of 3 and 4 is 12. So, converting $\frac{7}{3}$ and $\frac{5}{4}$ into like fractions,

we get $\frac{7}{3} = \frac{7}{3} \times \frac{4}{4} = \frac{28}{12}$ and $\frac{5}{4} = \frac{5}{4} \times \frac{3}{3} = \frac{15}{12}$.

Since 28 > 15, we get $\frac{28}{12} > \frac{15}{12}$, that is, $\frac{7}{3} > \frac{5}{4}$.

2. Cross-multiplication method: We can compare two unlike fractions by cross-multiplying the numerator of one fraction with the denominator of the other fraction and vice-versa and then comparing the products.

If $\frac{a}{b}$ and $\frac{c}{d}$ are any two fractions, then their cross products are $a \times d$ and $c \times b$.

Example 4: Compare $\frac{4}{5}$ and $\frac{3}{8}$ by cross multiplication method.

Solution: The cross products are $4 \times 8 = 32$ and $5 \times 3 = 15$. Since, 32 > 15, we get $\frac{4}{5} > \frac{3}{8}$.

Mixed Fractions

Mixed fractions can be compared by two methods, that are shown in the following examples.

Example 5: Compare $1\frac{1}{3}$ and $1\frac{2}{3}$.

Solution: Compare the whole number parts first and then the fractional parts.

Since the whole numbers are same, we move to the fractional parts. As the denominators are same and 1 < 2, we get $1\frac{1}{3} < 1\frac{2}{3}$.

Example 6: Compare $3\frac{4}{5}$ and $2\frac{1}{5}$.

Solution: Convert the given fractions into improper fractions and then compare.

$$\text{We have, } 3\frac{4}{5} = \frac{19}{5} \quad \text{and} \quad 2\frac{1}{5} = \frac{11}{5}$$

Since the denominators are same and 19 > 11, we get $\frac{19}{5} > \frac{11}{5}$, that is, $3\frac{4}{5} > 2\frac{1}{5}$.

ORDERING FRACTIONS

We can arrange the given fractions in ascending or descending order by comparing the fractions. Following are the steps involved.

Step 1: Find the LCM of the denominators.

Step 2: Convert all the fractions into like fractions using the LCM.

Step 3: Compare the fractions obtained and arrange them in ascending or descending order.

Example 7: Arrange the fractions $\frac{5}{6}, \frac{3}{4}, \frac{2}{3}$ and $\frac{11}{12}$ in ascending order.

Solution: We find the LCM of the denominators of all the fractions and then convert them into like fractions.

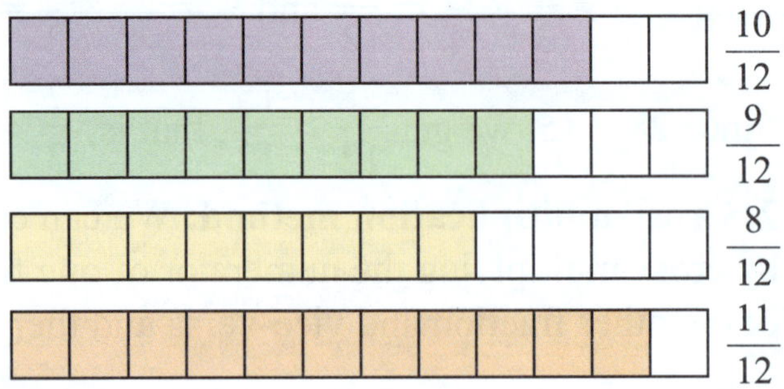

LCM of 3, 4, 6 and 12 is 12.

$\frac{5}{6} = \frac{5}{6} \times \frac{2}{2} = \frac{10}{12}$ $\frac{3}{4} = \frac{3}{4} \times \frac{3}{3} = \frac{9}{12}$

$\frac{2}{3} = \frac{2}{3} \times \frac{4}{4} = \frac{8}{12}$ $\frac{11}{12} = \frac{11}{12} \times \frac{1}{1} = \frac{11}{12}$

On comparing the numerators, we get $8 < 9 < 10 < 11$

$\Rightarrow \frac{8}{12} < \frac{9}{12} < \frac{10}{12} < \frac{11}{12}$ or $\frac{2}{3} < \frac{3}{4} < \frac{5}{6} < \frac{11}{12}$.

Example 8: Arrange the fractions $\frac{3}{10}, \frac{8}{3}, \frac{4}{5}$ and $\frac{7}{6}$ in descending order.

Solution: LCM of 10, 3, 5 and 6 is 30.

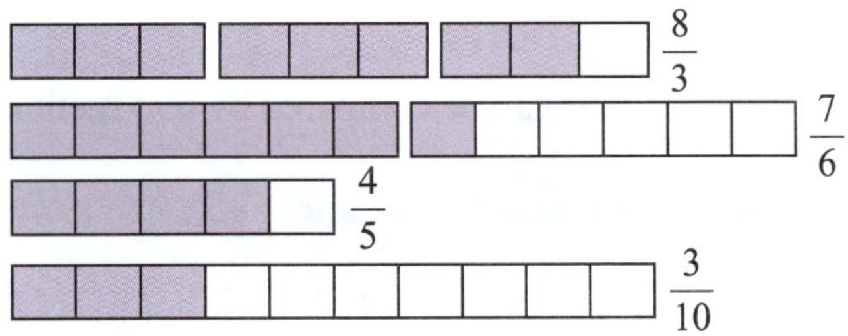

$\frac{3}{10} = \frac{3}{10} \times \frac{3}{3} = \frac{9}{30}$ $\frac{8}{3} = \frac{8}{3} \times \frac{10}{10} = \frac{80}{30}$

$\frac{4}{5} = \frac{4}{5} \times \frac{6}{6} = \frac{24}{30}$ $\frac{7}{6} = \frac{7}{6} \times \frac{5}{5} = \frac{35}{30}$

On comparing the numerators, we get $80 > 35 > 24 > 9$

$\Rightarrow \frac{80}{30} > \frac{35}{30} > \frac{24}{30} > \frac{9}{30}$ or $\frac{8}{3} > \frac{7}{6} > \frac{4}{5} > \frac{3}{10}$

Exercise 5.1

1. Compare the following like fractions.

a. $\frac{3}{8}$ ☐ $\frac{5}{8}$ b. $\frac{14}{9}$ ☐ $\frac{11}{9}$ c. $\frac{7}{14}$ ☐ $\frac{1}{2}$ d. $\frac{15}{11}$ ☐ $\frac{21}{11}$ e. $\frac{4}{7}$ ☐ $\frac{6}{7}$

2. Compare the following unlike fractions.

a. $\frac{2}{7}$ ☐ $\frac{3}{5}$ b. $\frac{10}{3}$ ☐ $\frac{7}{7}$ c. $\frac{3}{4}$ ☐ $\frac{4}{9}$ d. $\frac{13}{10}$ ☐ $\frac{13}{6}$ e. $\frac{3}{2}$ ☐ $\frac{12}{8}$

3. Arrange the following fractions in ascending order.

a. $\frac{2}{3}, \frac{4}{5}, \frac{1}{2}, \frac{3}{8}$ b. $\frac{3}{4}, \frac{5}{6}, \frac{5}{2}, \frac{5}{8}$ c. $\frac{3}{4}, \frac{2}{3}, \frac{1}{3}, \frac{1}{2}$ d. $\frac{16}{25}, \frac{4}{5}, \frac{9}{10}, \frac{13}{15}$ e. $\frac{11}{21}, \frac{5}{6}, \frac{5}{2}, \frac{9}{14}$

4. **Arrange the following fractions in descending order.**

a. $\frac{5}{12}, \frac{7}{8}, \frac{3}{4}, \frac{1}{2}$ b. $\frac{2}{5}, \frac{1}{4}, \frac{2}{3}, \frac{1}{10}$ c. $\frac{3}{2}, \frac{5}{2}, \frac{2}{5}, \frac{5}{3}$ d. $\frac{4}{7}, \frac{2}{5}, \frac{1}{2}, \frac{3}{8}$ e. $\frac{1}{6}, \frac{4}{9}, \frac{5}{12}, \frac{1}{3}$

ADDITION OF FRACTIONS

Just like comparison, all types of fractions can be added and subtracted.

Like Fractions

Arun eats $\frac{13}{18}$ parts of his protein bar and Sunil eats $\frac{7}{18}$ parts of his protein bar. What is the amount of chocolate eaten by both Arun and Sunil?

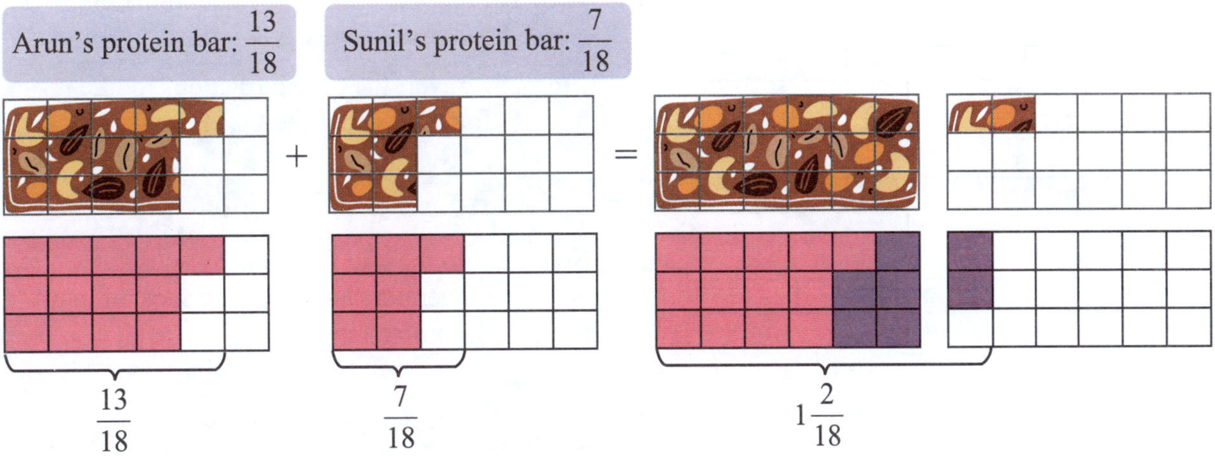

Since the denominators are same, add the numerators and retain the common denominator.

$$\frac{13}{18} + \frac{7}{18} = \frac{13+7}{18} = \frac{20}{18}$$

Express the answer in the simplest form. If it is an improper fraction, express it as a mixed fraction. So, $\frac{20}{18} = \frac{10}{9} = 1\frac{1}{9}$.

Hence, the amount of protein bar eaten by both Arun and Sunil is $1\frac{1}{9}$.

Example 9: Add $\frac{3}{5}$ and $\frac{6}{5}$.

Solution: $\frac{3}{5} + \frac{6}{5} = \frac{3+6}{5} = \frac{9}{5} = 1\frac{4}{5}$

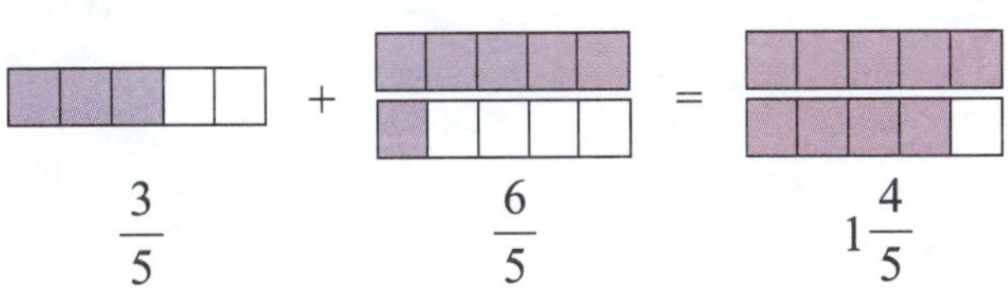

Unlike Fractions

Ritesh is a fashion designer. He used $\frac{1}{2}$ m of fabric A and $\frac{3}{4}$ m of fabric B in designing a cloth. What is the total length of the fabric used by Ritesh?

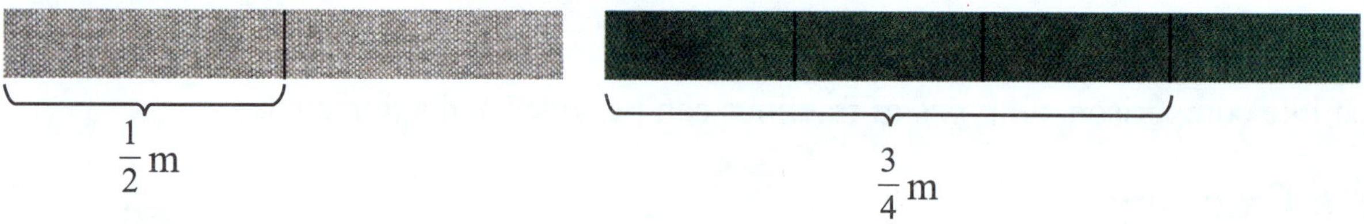

Total fabric used by Ritesh = $\frac{1}{2}$ m + $\frac{3}{4}$ m

Let us divide the two fabrics into equal number of parts and then add.

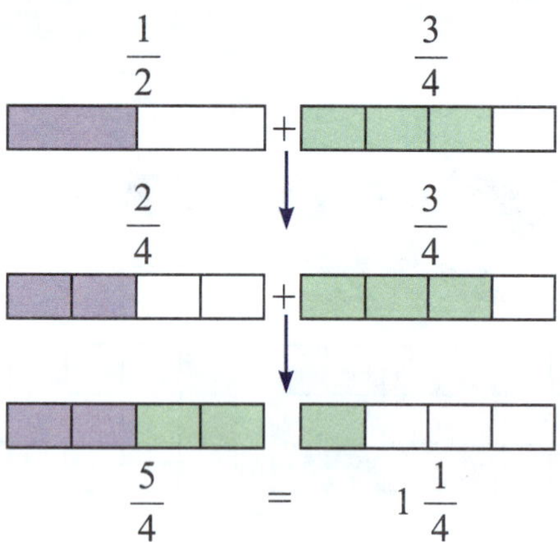

So, $\frac{1}{2} + \frac{3}{4} = \frac{5}{4} = 1\frac{1}{4}$

Step 1: Find the LCM of the denominators. LCM of 2 and 4 is 4.

Step 2: Convert the unlike fractions to like fractions using the LCM.

$$\frac{1}{2} = \frac{1}{2} \times \frac{2}{2} = \frac{2}{4} \qquad \frac{3}{4} \times \frac{1}{1} = \frac{3}{4}$$

Step 3: Add the like fractions by adding the numerators and retaining the common denominator.

$$\frac{1}{2} + \frac{3}{4} = \frac{2}{4} + \frac{3}{4} = \frac{2+3}{4} = \frac{5}{4}$$

Step 4: Express the answer in simplest form.

$$\frac{5}{4} = 1\frac{1}{4}$$

Therefore, Ritesh has used $\frac{5}{4}$ m or $1\frac{1}{4}$ m of fabric to make the cloth.

Example 10: Add $\frac{1}{2}$ and $\frac{2}{3}$.

Solution: LCM of 2 and 3 is 6.

$$\frac{1}{2} = \frac{1}{2} \times \frac{3}{3} = \frac{3}{6} \qquad \frac{2}{3} = \frac{2}{3} \times \frac{2}{2} = \frac{4}{6}$$

So, $\frac{1}{2} + \frac{2}{3} = \frac{3}{6} + \frac{4}{6}$

$= \frac{3+4}{6} = \frac{7}{6} = 1\frac{1}{6}$.

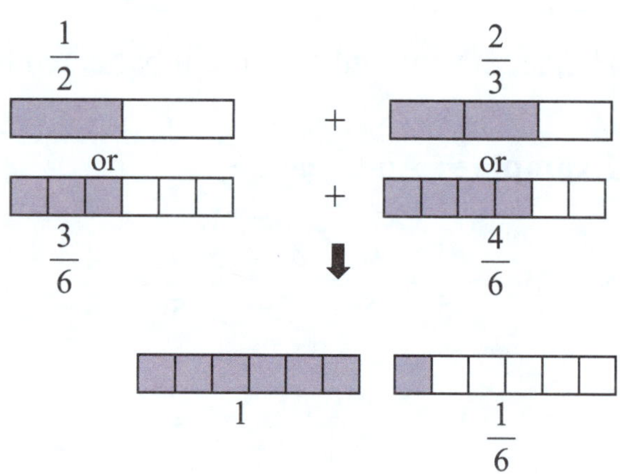

Example 11: Add $\frac{4}{15}, \frac{2}{5}$ and $\frac{1}{3}$.

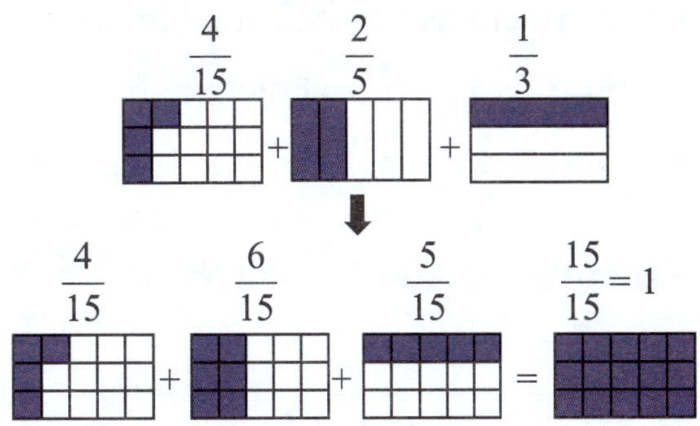

Solution: LCM of 15, 5 and 3 is 15.

$$\frac{4}{15} = \frac{4}{15} \times \frac{1}{1} = \frac{4}{15} \qquad \frac{2}{5} = \frac{2}{5} \times \frac{3}{3} = \frac{6}{15}$$

$$\frac{1}{3} = \frac{1}{3} \times \frac{5}{5} = \frac{5}{15}$$

So, $\frac{4}{15} + \frac{2}{5} + \frac{1}{3} = \frac{4}{15} + \frac{6}{15} + \frac{5}{15} = \frac{4+6+5}{15} = \frac{15}{15} = 1$

Mixed Fractions

Roy drinks $1\frac{1}{2}$ litres of water in the first half of the day and $2\frac{1}{4}$ litres in the second half of the day. How many litres of water does Roy drink in all?

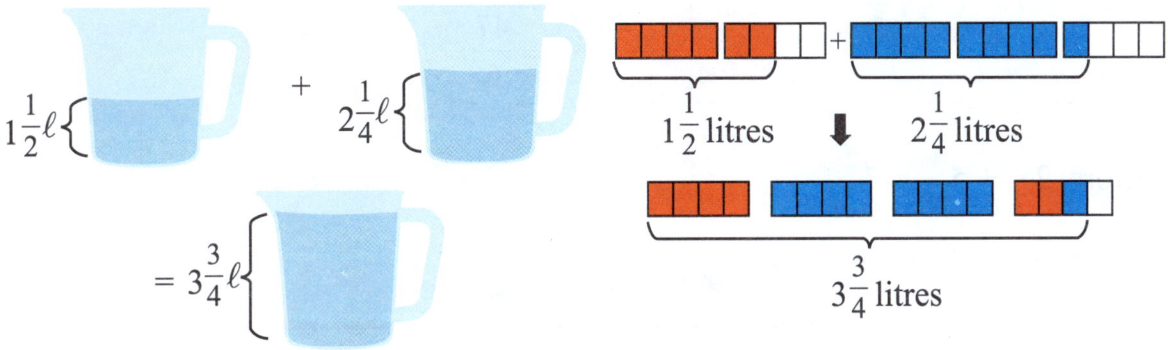

Step 1: Convert the mixed fractions into improper fractions.

$$1\frac{1}{2} + 2\frac{1}{4} = \frac{3}{2} + \frac{9}{4}$$

Step 2: Find the LCM of the denominators. LCM of 2 and 4 is 4.

Step 3: Convert the unlike fractions into like fractions with LCM as their denominator.

$$\frac{3}{2} = \frac{3}{2} \times \frac{2}{2} = \frac{6}{4} \qquad \frac{9}{4} \times \frac{1}{1} = \frac{9}{4}$$

Step 4: Add the like fractions by adding the numerators and retaining the common denominator. $\frac{3}{2} + \frac{9}{4} = \frac{6}{4} + \frac{9}{4} = \frac{6+9}{4} = \frac{15}{4}$

Step 5: Express the answer in simplest form. $\frac{15}{4} = 3\frac{3}{4}$

Therefore, Roy drinks $3\frac{3}{4}$ litres of water in a day.

Mixed fractions can be added by using any of the following methods.

Method 1: Add the whole number part and the fractional part separately.

Method 2: Convert the mixed fractions into improper fractions and then add them.

Example 12: Add $2\frac{1}{3}$ and $5\frac{1}{2}$.

Solution:

Method 1	Method 2
$2\frac{1}{3}+5\frac{1}{2}=\left(2+\frac{1}{3}\right)+\left(5+\frac{1}{2}\right)$ $=(2+5)+\left(\frac{1}{3}+\frac{1}{2}\right)$ $=7+\left(\frac{1}{3}+\frac{1}{2}\right)$ $=7+\frac{5}{6}=7\frac{5}{6}$	$2\frac{1}{3}+5\frac{1}{2}=\frac{7}{3}+\frac{11}{2}$ LCM of 3 and 2 is 6. $\frac{7}{3}=\frac{7}{3}\times\frac{2}{2}=\frac{14}{6}$ $\quad\frac{11}{2}=\frac{11}{2}\times\frac{3}{3}=\frac{33}{6}$ $2\frac{1}{3}+5\frac{1}{2}=\frac{7}{3}+\frac{11}{2}=\frac{14}{6}+\frac{33}{6}$ $=\frac{14+33}{6}=\frac{47}{6}=7\frac{5}{6}$

Therefore, $2\frac{1}{3}+5\frac{1}{2}=7\frac{5}{6}$.

Exercise 5.2

1. Add the following like fractions.

a. $\frac{2}{7}+\frac{6}{7}$ b. $\frac{7}{13}+\frac{5}{13}$ c. $\frac{16}{27}+\frac{22}{27}$ d. $\frac{8}{10}+\frac{7}{10}$ e. $\frac{8}{3}+\frac{5}{3}$

f. $\frac{15}{11}+\frac{9}{11}$ g. $\frac{34}{23}+\frac{21}{23}$ h. $\frac{14}{40}+\frac{30}{40}$ i. $\frac{15}{31}+\frac{8}{31}$ j. $\frac{19}{55}+\frac{13}{55}$

2. Add the following unlike fractions.

a. $\frac{5}{18}+\frac{4}{9}$ b. $\frac{7}{8}+\frac{3}{10}$ c. $\frac{4}{7}+\frac{2}{5}$ d. $\frac{5}{8}+\frac{3}{16}+\frac{1}{10}$ e. $\frac{9}{4}+\frac{7}{6}$

f. $\frac{12}{7}+\frac{8}{3}$ g. $\frac{13}{6}+\frac{11}{9}$ h. $\frac{3}{2}+\frac{7}{6}+\frac{11}{4}$ i. $\frac{6}{5}+\frac{13}{6}$ j. $\frac{9}{15}+\frac{3}{10}$

3. Add the following mixed fractions.

a. $1\frac{5}{6}+3\frac{1}{2}$ b. $5\frac{7}{10}+2\frac{3}{4}$ c. $4\frac{2}{3}+1\frac{1}{6}$ d. $2\frac{3}{5}+1\frac{1}{3}$ e. $5\frac{1}{7}+2\frac{4}{5}$

f. $1\frac{3}{4}+6\frac{2}{7}$ g. $4\frac{1}{3}+3\frac{2}{7}$ h. $7\frac{1}{4}+5\frac{1}{6}$ i. $2\frac{1}{9}+1\frac{5}{7}$ j. $3\frac{4}{5}+6\frac{1}{8}$

SUBTRACTION OF FRACTIONS

Subtraction of like fractions, unlike fractions and mixed fractions follows the same rules as their addition.

Like Fractions

Alia had $\frac{5}{6}$ parts of watermelon with her. She gave $\frac{1}{6}$ parts to her sister. How much watermelon is left with Alia now?

$\frac{5}{6}-\frac{1}{6}$ $\qquad$ $\frac{4}{6}$

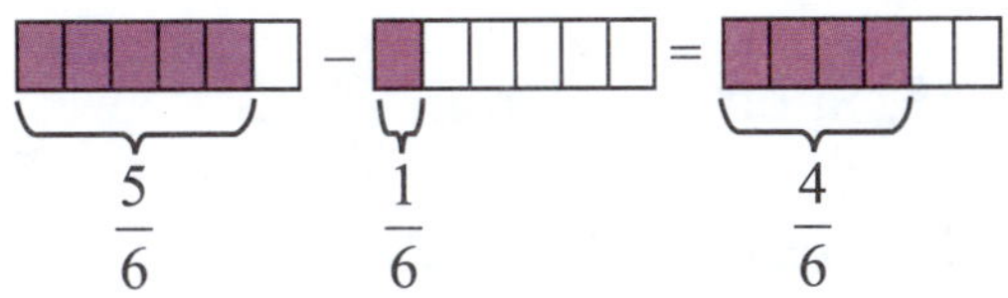

Since the denominators are the same, subtract the numerators and retain the common denominator.

So, $\frac{5}{6}-\frac{1}{6}=\frac{5-1}{6}=\frac{4}{6}=\frac{2}{3}$, that is, the amount of watermelon left with Alia is $\frac{2}{3}$.

Example 13: Subtract $\frac{5}{8}$ from $\frac{9}{8}$.

Solution: $\frac{9}{8}-\frac{5}{8}=\frac{9-5}{8}=\frac{4}{8}=\frac{1}{2}$

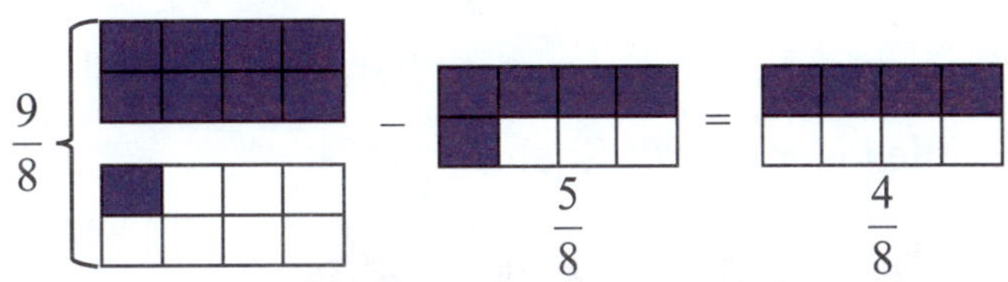

Unlike Fractions

A tailor had $\frac{7}{8}$ m of cloth material. He used $\frac{3}{4}$ m of cloth for stitching a handbag. What is the length of cloth left with the tailor?

Length of cloth left with tailor = $\frac{7}{8}$ m − $\frac{3}{4}$ m

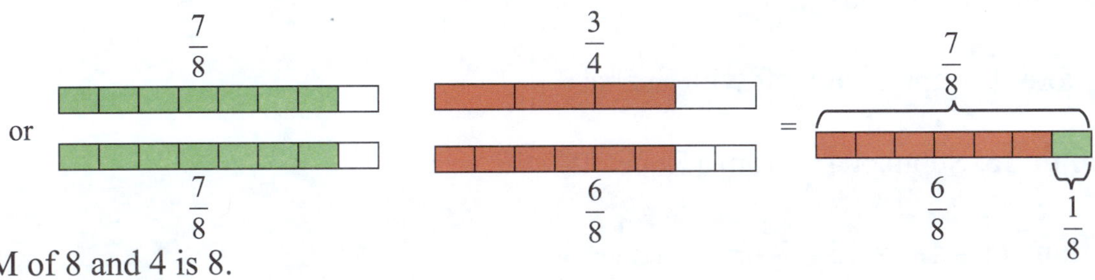

LCM of 8 and 4 is 8.

$\frac{7}{8}=\frac{7}{8}\times\frac{1}{1}=\frac{7}{8}$ $\qquad$ $\frac{3}{4}\times\frac{2}{2}=\frac{6}{8}$ $\qquad\Rightarrow\qquad$ $\frac{7}{8}-\frac{3}{4}=\frac{7}{8}-\frac{6}{8}=\frac{7-6}{8}=\frac{1}{8}$

Therefore, the length of cloth left with the tailor is $\frac{1}{8}$ m.

Example 14: Subtract $\frac{5}{9}$ from 10.

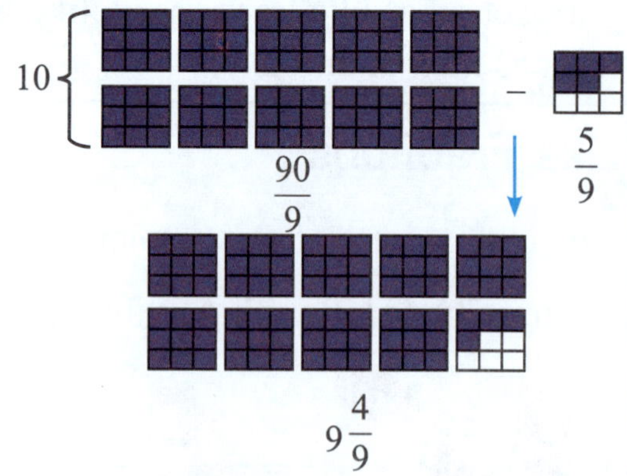

Solution: $10 - \frac{5}{9} = \frac{10}{1} - \frac{5}{9}$

LCM of 1 and 9 is 9.

$\frac{10}{1} = \frac{10}{1} \times \frac{9}{9} = \frac{90}{9}$ $\qquad$ $\frac{5}{9} = \frac{5}{9} \times \frac{1}{1} = \frac{5}{9}$

$10 - \frac{5}{9} = \frac{90}{9} - \frac{5}{9} = \frac{90-5}{9} = \frac{85}{9} = 9\frac{4}{9}$

Example 15: Subtract $\frac{3}{7}$ from $\frac{5}{3}$.

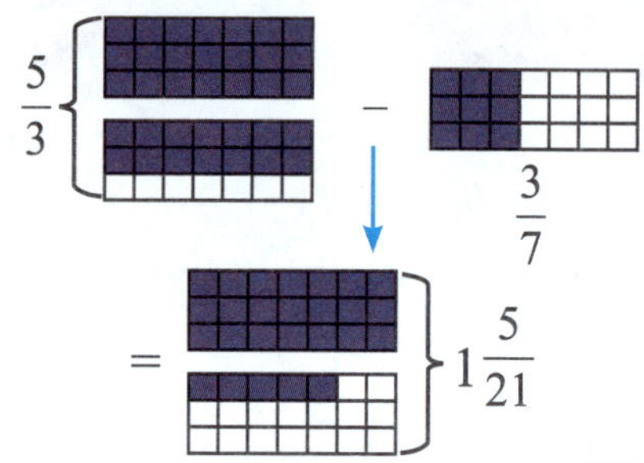

Solution: LCM of 3 and 7 is 21.

$\frac{5}{3} = \frac{5}{3} \times \frac{7}{7} = \frac{35}{21}$ $\qquad$ $\frac{3}{7} = \frac{3}{7} \times \frac{3}{3} = \frac{9}{21}$

$\frac{5}{3} - \frac{3}{7} = \frac{35}{21} - \frac{9}{21} = \frac{35-9}{21} = \frac{26}{21} = 1\frac{5}{21}$

Mixed Fractions

Sneha had $2\frac{3}{4}$ apples with her. She gives $1\frac{1}{4}$ apples to her sister. What fraction of apples is left with Sneha?

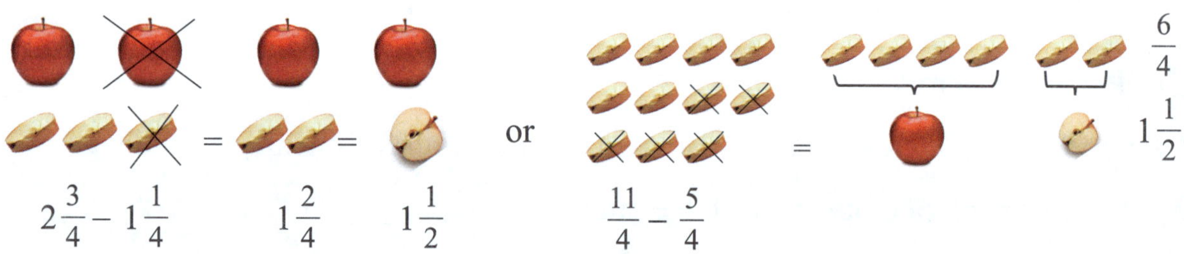

Apples left with Sneha $= 2\frac{3}{4} - 1\frac{1}{4} = \frac{11}{4} - \frac{5}{4} = \frac{11-5}{4} = \frac{6}{4} = \frac{3}{2} = 1\frac{1}{2}$

Therefore, $1\frac{1}{2}$ apples are left with Sneha.

Example 16: Subtract $4\frac{2}{3}$ from 15.

Solution: $15 - 4\frac{2}{3} = 15 - \frac{14}{3} = \frac{15}{1} - \frac{14}{3}$

LCM of 1 and 3 is 3.

$$15-\frac{14}{3}=\frac{15\times3}{1\times3}-\frac{14\times1}{3\times1}=\frac{45}{3}-\frac{14}{3}=\frac{45-14}{3}=\frac{31}{3}=10\frac{1}{3}$$

Example 17: Subtract $4\frac{3}{5}$ from $12\frac{2}{5}$.

Solution: $12\frac{2}{5}-4\frac{3}{5}=\frac{62}{5}-\frac{23}{5}=\frac{62-23}{5}=\frac{39}{5}=7\frac{4}{5}$

Exercise 5.3

1. Subtract the following like fractions.

a. $\frac{7}{8}-\frac{3}{8}$ b. $\frac{9}{11}-\frac{5}{11}$ c. $\frac{12}{19}-\frac{9}{19}$ d. $\frac{24}{26}-\frac{11}{26}$ e. $\frac{12}{7}-\frac{4}{7}$

f. $\frac{22}{15}-\frac{13}{15}$ g. $\frac{47}{30}-\frac{28}{30}$ h. $\frac{36}{19}-\frac{15}{19}$ i. $\frac{51}{22}-\frac{13}{22}$ j. $\frac{9}{10}-\frac{3}{10}$

2. Subtract the following unlike fractions.

a. $9-\frac{2}{3}$ b. $\frac{12}{5}-\frac{7}{10}$ c. $\frac{11}{12}-\frac{13}{18}$ d. $\frac{21}{4}-\frac{18}{5}$ e. $11-\frac{8}{5}$

f. $\frac{22}{15}-\frac{17}{12}$ g. $\frac{20}{13}-\frac{3}{5}$ h. $16-\frac{7}{4}$ i. $\frac{16}{25}-\frac{2}{5}$ j. $\frac{8}{20}-\frac{1}{4}$

3. Subtract the following mixed fractions.

a. $3\frac{1}{2}-1\frac{1}{4}$ b. $15-7\frac{2}{3}$ c. $5\frac{3}{10}-2\frac{7}{15}$ d. $22-10\frac{1}{5}$ e. $7\frac{3}{7}-4\frac{2}{3}$

f. $10\frac{3}{4}-9\frac{4}{5}$ g. $20-10\frac{7}{9}$ h. $14\frac{1}{6}-9\frac{1}{9}$ i. $7\frac{1}{15}-2\frac{2}{15}$ j. $5\frac{1}{2}-1\frac{3}{10}$

MULTIPLICATION OF A FRACTION

A fraction can be multiplied either by a whole number or a fraction. In case of a whole number, the method of repeated addition of fractions is used. In case of a fraction, we multiply the numerators and the denominators separately.

Example 18: Find $\frac{3}{7}$ of 5.

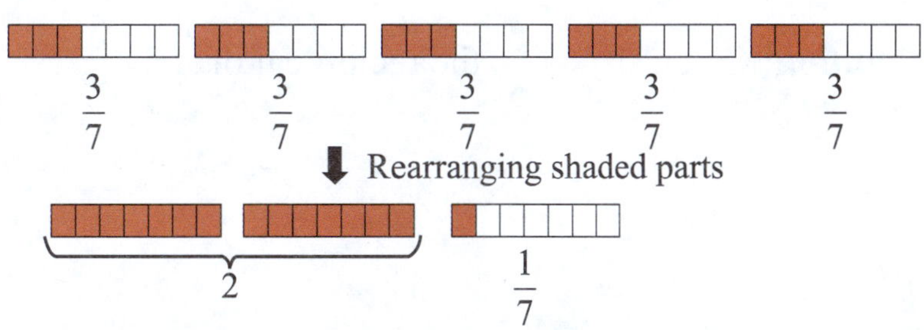

Solution:

$\frac{3}{7}\times5=\frac{3\times5}{7}=\frac{15}{7}=2\frac{1}{7}$

Example 19: Find the value of $\frac{3}{7} \times \frac{5}{8}$.

Solution: Multiply the numerators and denominators separately, that is, $\frac{3}{7} \times \frac{5}{8} = \frac{3 \times 5}{7 \times 8}$ $= \frac{15}{56}$.

Exercise 5.4

1. Solve the following.

a. $\frac{5}{6} \times 12$ b. $\frac{2}{3} \times 24$ c. $\frac{5}{12} \times 48$ d. $1\frac{2}{7} \times 8$ e. $1\frac{5}{8} \times 11$

2. Multiply the following fractions and reduce the answers to the simplest form.

a. $\frac{1}{3} \times \frac{2}{10}$ b. $\frac{2}{5} \times \frac{4}{9}$ c. $\frac{3}{8} \times \frac{4}{5}$ d. $\frac{1}{4} \times \frac{16}{21}$ e. $\frac{7}{22} \times \frac{11}{14}$

f. $\frac{5}{16} \times \frac{1}{15}$ g. $\frac{14}{15} \times 6\frac{3}{7}$ h. $\frac{2}{3} \times \frac{3}{5}$ i. $\frac{3}{11} \times \frac{5}{6}$ j. $\frac{1}{6} \times \frac{5}{10}$

RECIPROCAL

Reciprocal of any number is a number which when multiplied with the original number gives 1 as the answer.

- The reciprocal of a whole number a ($\neq 0$) is $\frac{1}{a}$.
- The reciprocal of 1 is 1 itself and the reciprocal of 0 does not exist as $\frac{1}{0}$ is not defined.
- The reciprocal of a fraction $\frac{a}{b}$ is $\frac{b}{a}$.

Observe that the reciprocal of a proper fraction is an improper fraction and vice versa. For example, reciprocal of $\frac{5}{8}$ is $\frac{8}{5}$ and reciprocal of $\frac{7}{6}$ is $\frac{6}{7}$.

Example 20: Find the reciprocal of $1\frac{3}{5}$.

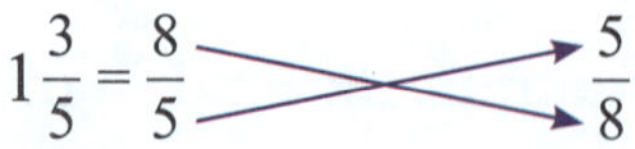

Solution: Given, $1\frac{3}{5} = \frac{8}{5}$, the reciprocal of $\frac{8}{5}$ is $\frac{5}{8}$.

DIVISION OF A WHOLE NUMBER BY A FRACTION

Lokesh wants to give $\frac{1}{2}$ of an apple to each of his friends. He has 2 apples. With how many friends can he share the apples?

Observe that 1 whole is divided into 2 equal parts. Similarly, 2 wholes can be divided into 4 equal parts. This means $2 \div \frac{1}{2} = 4$.

So, Lokesh can share 2 apples with 4 friends by giving $\frac{1}{2}$ apple to each of his friends.

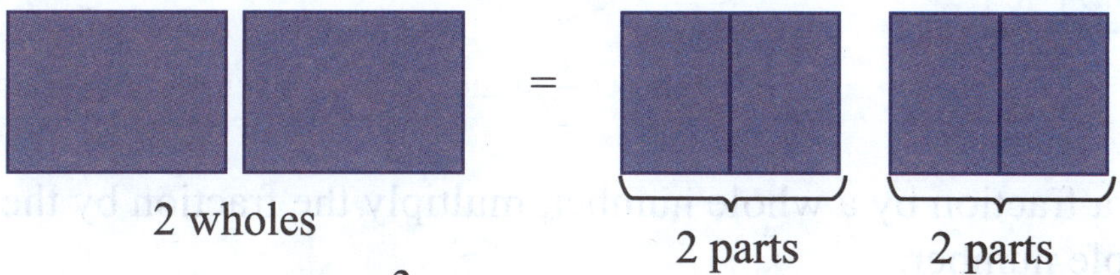

$2 \div \frac{1}{2} = 4$

Example 21: What is $3 \div \frac{3}{4}$?

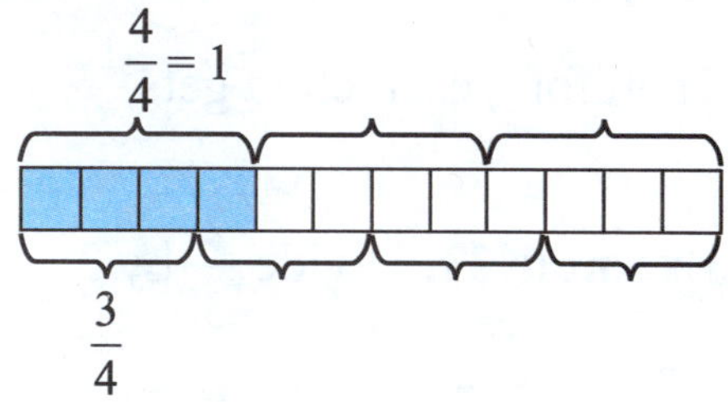

Solution: This question can be understood as how many parts of $\frac{3}{4}$ are there in 3 wholes.

Since, reciprocal of $\frac{3}{4}$ is $\frac{4}{3}$, we get $3 \times \frac{4}{3} = 4$.

Example 22: How much is $6 \div \frac{3}{6}$?

Solution: $6 \div \frac{1}{2} = 6 \times \frac{2}{1} = 12$

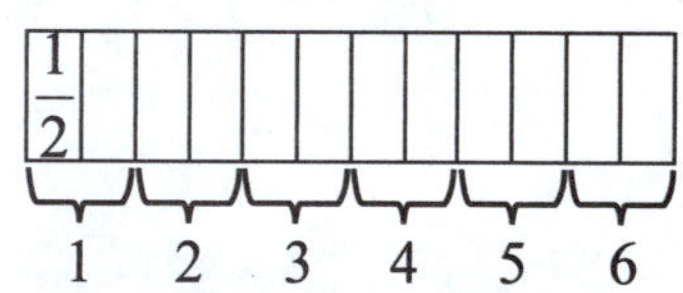

To divide a whole number by any fraction, multiply the whole number by the reciprocal of that fraction. Keep the answer in the simplest form.

DIVISION OF A FRACTION BY A FRACTION

Ganesh is a farmer. He has harvested watermelons in his field. If he wants to distribute equal pieces of half a watermelon among 4 of his grandchildren, how much does each child get?

To find this, we have to divide $\frac{1}{2}$ by 4.

$\frac{1}{8}$

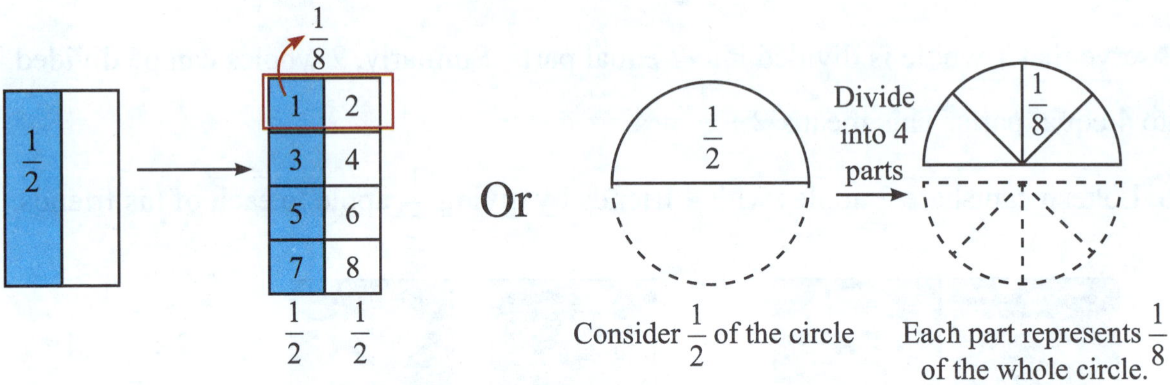

In general, to divide a fraction by a whole number, multiply the fraction by the reciprocal of the whole number.

Therefore, each child gets $\frac{1}{2} \div 4 = \frac{1}{2} \times \frac{1}{4} = \frac{1}{8}$ of the watermelon.

Example 23: Divide $\frac{2}{3}$ by 3.

Solution: $\frac{2}{3} \div 3 = \frac{2}{3} \times \frac{1}{3} = \frac{2}{9}$

Example 24: Divide $\frac{4}{5}$ by 4.

Solution: $\frac{4}{5} \div 4 = \frac{4}{5} \times \frac{1}{4} = \frac{1}{5}$

Exercise 5.5

1. Solve the following.

a. $20 \div \frac{4}{5}$ b. $\frac{7}{15} \div 2$ c. $45 \div \frac{5}{9}$ d. $\frac{4}{5} \div 6$ e. $\frac{2}{3} \div 9$

f. $\frac{5}{8} \div 15$ g. $56 \div \frac{7}{9}$ h. $\frac{5}{18} \div 10$ i. $54 \div \frac{2}{3}$ j. $\frac{6}{7} \div 8$

2. Divide the following.

a. $\frac{4}{9} \div \frac{13}{27}$ b. $\frac{1}{6} \div \frac{7}{15}$ c. $\frac{11}{20} \div \frac{33}{35}$ d. $\frac{2}{5} \div \frac{10}{3}$ e. $\frac{9}{11} \div \frac{8}{5}$

f. $\frac{13}{16} \div \frac{39}{22}$ g. $\frac{22}{3} \div \frac{5}{6}$ h. $\frac{38}{7} \div \frac{16}{21}$ i. $\frac{65}{19} \div \frac{50}{57}$ j. $\frac{7}{4} \div \frac{11}{10}$

WORD PROBLEMS

Till now, we have studied various operations on fractions. Let us solve some problems based on them.

Example 25: Arjun wrote a unit test in Mathematics and Science. He answered $\frac{3}{4}$ questions correctly in Mathematics and $\frac{2}{3}$ questions correctly in Science. In which subject will he score more?

Solution: Let us compare the fractions $\frac{3}{4}$ and $\frac{2}{3}$.

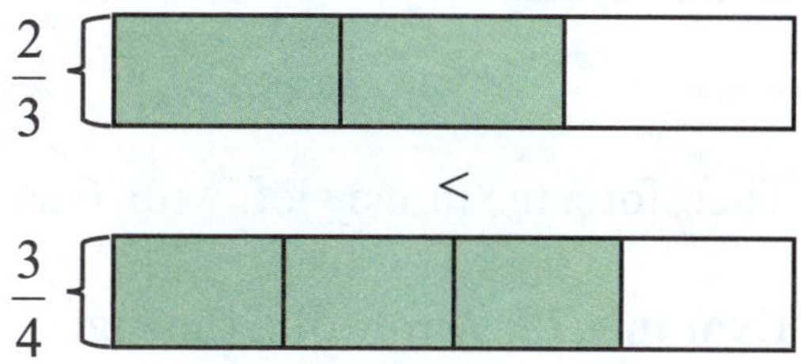

LCM of 4 and 3 is 12.

$$\frac{3}{4}=\frac{3\times3}{4\times3}=\frac{9}{12} \qquad \frac{2}{3}=\frac{2\times4}{3\times4}=\frac{8}{12}$$

Since $\frac{9}{12}>\frac{8}{12}$, we can say that Arjun will score more marks in Mathematics.

Example 26: Chitra participated in two marathons successively in two weekends. In the first marathon, she ran $7\frac{1}{2}$ km and in the second marathon, she ran $6\frac{2}{3}$ km. What is the total distance covered by her in the two marathons?

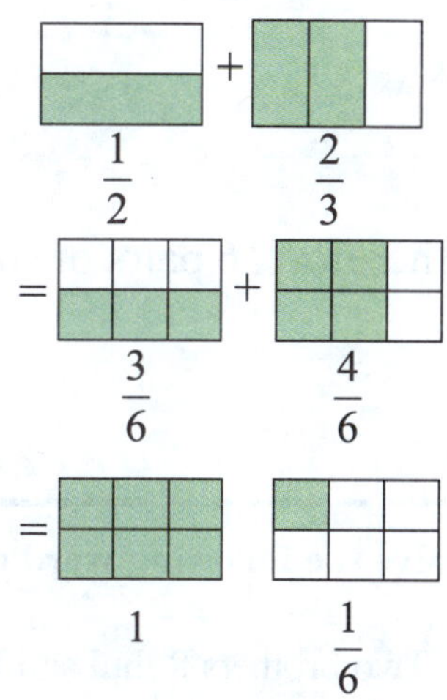

Solution: Total distance covered $= 7\frac{1}{2}+6\frac{2}{3}$

$$= (7+6)+\left(\frac{1}{2}+\frac{2}{3}\right)$$

$$= 13+\left(\frac{1}{2}+\frac{2}{3}\right)$$

Now, $\frac{1}{2}+\frac{2}{3}=\frac{1\times3}{2\times3}+\frac{2\times2}{3\times2}=\frac{3}{6}+\frac{4}{6}=\frac{7}{6}=1\frac{1}{6}$.

So, $13+\left(\frac{1}{2}+\frac{2}{3}\right)=13+1\frac{1}{6}=14\frac{1}{6}$.

Therefore, the total distance covered by Chitra in the two marathons is $14\frac{1}{6}$ km.

Example 27: Tina's father gave her ₹1000 as pocket money to spend during her summer vacations. She spent $\frac{1}{4}$ of the money to buy a dress and $\frac{2}{5}$ of the money to buy a schoolbag. How much money is left with her?

Solution: Fraction of money spent on both items $=\frac{1}{4}+\frac{2}{5}$

LCM of 4 and 5 is 20.

$$\frac{1}{4}+\frac{2}{5}=\frac{1\times5}{4\times5}+\frac{2\times4}{5\times4}=\frac{5}{20}+\frac{8}{20}=\frac{5+8}{20}=\frac{13}{20}$$

Fraction of money remaining $= 1-\frac{13}{20}=\frac{20-13}{20}$

$= \frac{7}{20}$

Remaining money $= \frac{7}{20}\times ₹1000$

$= ₹350$

Therefore, the money left with Tina is ₹350.

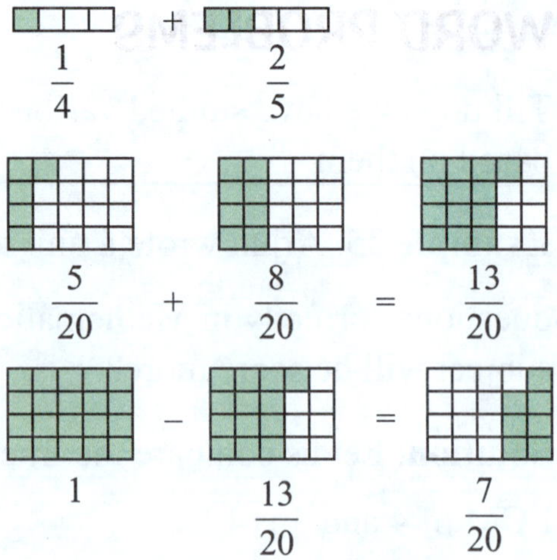

Example 28: A row of a shoe rack is 4 feet long. One pair of shoes occupies $\frac{2}{3}$ feet space. How many pairs of shoes can fit in one row of the shoe rack?

Solution: Number of pairs of shoes that can fit in one row of the shoe rack

$$= 4\div\frac{2}{3}=4\times\frac{3}{2}=6$$

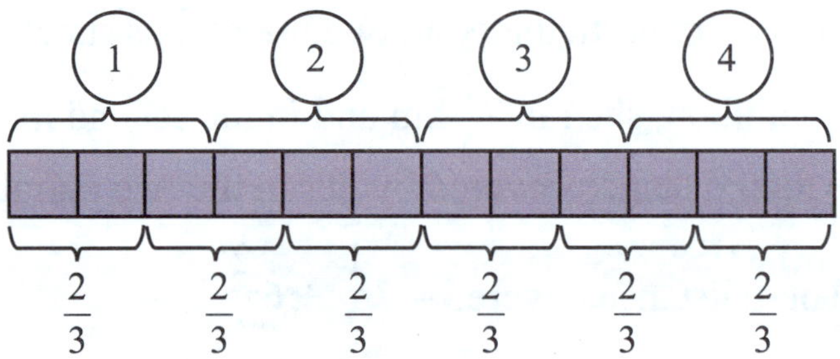

Therefore, 6 pairs of shoes can be placed in one row of the shoe rack.

Exercise 5.6

Solve the following word problems.

1. Two brothers Rahul and Vinay reached home in $\frac{5}{6}$ of an hour and $\frac{4}{9}$ of an hour respectively. Who took less time to reach home?
2. Anil walked $5\frac{1}{5}$ km on Saturday and $2\frac{4}{5}$ km on Sunday. How many kilometers did he walk altogether?
3. Mary purchased $\frac{3}{7}$ kg of sugar. She used $\frac{1}{3}$ kg of it to bake cookies. How much sugar is left with her?
4. There are 32 pencils with you. You gave $\frac{1}{4}$ of it to your friend. How many pencils did you give?
5. A rope is 24 m long. How many pieces of length $\frac{3}{12}$ m can be cut from it?

Concept Map

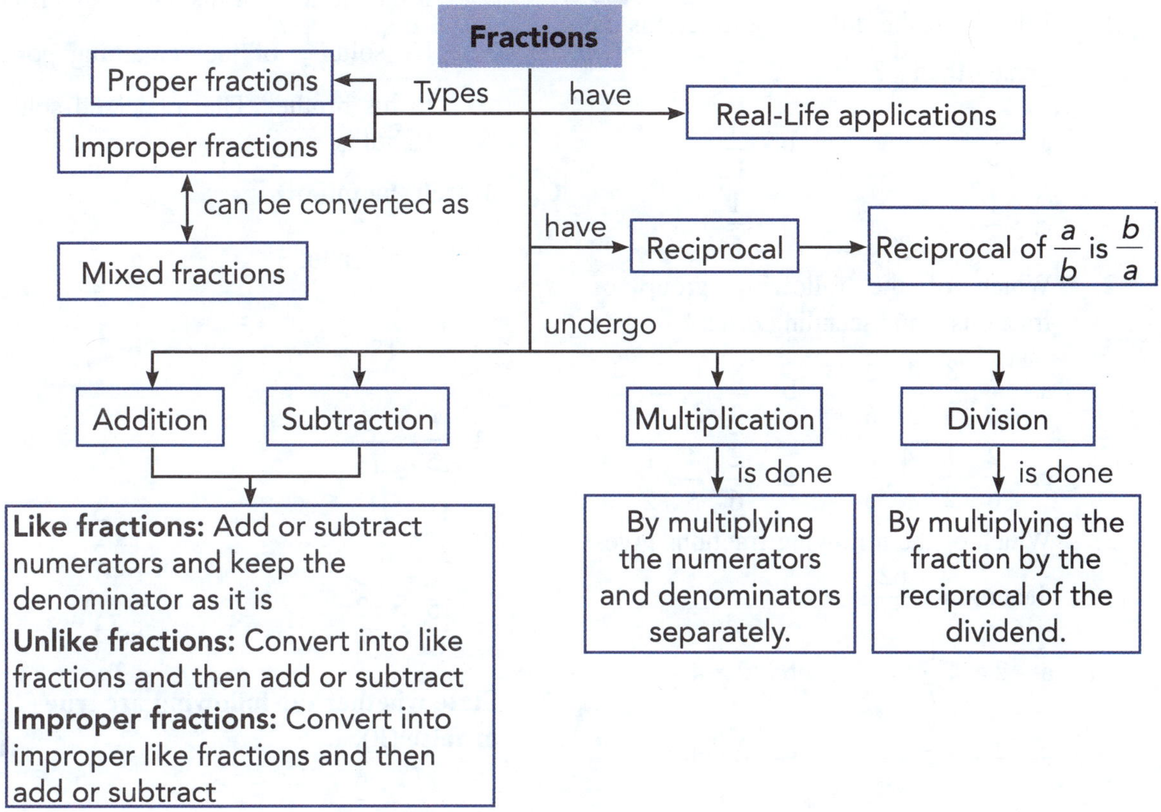

Project

Maths in Event Management

A school is planning a trip for the students. The total budget allocated for the trip is ₹50,000. The following table shows the fractions of budget allocated for each event.

Event	Food	Games	Travel	Stay
Fraction Allocated	$\frac{1}{2}$	$\frac{1}{5}$	$\frac{2}{5}$	$\frac{2}{5}$

Answer the following questions based on the data given in the table.

1. For which event is the most budget allocated? ________
2. For which event is the least budget allocated? ________
3. What is the difference between the allocation of budget for food and for travel?
4. ₹_______ is allocated for travel.
5. ₹_______ is allocated for food.

Revision Exercise

A. Choose the correct option.

1. Which of the following fractions is greater than $\frac{1}{5}$?

   a. $\frac{1}{9}$ b. $\frac{1}{12}$

   c. $\frac{1}{2}$ d. $\frac{1}{6}$

2. Which of the following group of fractions is in ascending order?

   a. $\frac{1}{2}, \frac{8}{3}, \frac{4}{5}, \frac{2}{6}$ b. $\frac{8}{3}, \frac{1}{2}, \frac{2}{6}, \frac{4}{5}$

   c. $\frac{2}{6}, \frac{1}{2}, \frac{4}{5}, \frac{8}{3}$ d. $\frac{2}{6}, \frac{4}{5}, \frac{1}{2}, \frac{8}{3}$

3. Which of the following fractions gives the product $\frac{62}{7}$?

   a. $2 \times 4\frac{1}{7}$ b. $2 \times 4\frac{3}{7}$

   c. $2 \times 4\frac{5}{7}$ d. $2 \times 4\frac{7}{7}$

4. What is the sum of $\frac{9}{8}$ and $\frac{7}{6}$?

   a. $2\frac{7}{24}$ b. $1\frac{2}{14}$

   c. $\frac{1}{3}$ d. $1\frac{5}{8}$

5. What is the reciprocal of $3\frac{1}{2}$?

   a. $\frac{1}{2}$ b. $\frac{7}{6}$

   c. 2 d. $\frac{2}{7}$

B. Fill in the blanks.

1. $\frac{2}{7}$ ____ $\frac{1}{3}$ (Use symbol >/</=)
2. $\frac{3}{5} - \frac{1}{4} =$ ____
3. The quotient obtained when $\frac{3}{4}$ is divided by 2 is ____.
4. $\frac{1}{3}$ of an hour = ____ minutes
5. Rahul sold $\frac{1}{2}$ of his land to his friend. He sold $\frac{1}{2}$ of the remaining portion to his brother. The total land sold by Rahul is ____.

C. Match the following.

1. Reciprocal of 3	a. $\frac{1}{20}$
2. $\frac{1}{6} \times 18$	b. 2
3. $\frac{4}{15} \times \frac{3}{16}$	c. 3
4. $\frac{1}{3} \div \frac{1}{6}$	d. $\frac{5}{2}$
5. $\frac{15}{9} \div \frac{12}{18}$	e. $\frac{1}{3}$

D. State whether the following are true (T) or false (F).

1. $\frac{7}{7} - \frac{6}{6} = \frac{1}{1}$
2. Reciprocal of 1 is 1.
3. To divide a fraction by a whole number, multiply the reciprocal of the fraction by the whole number.
4. The product of $\frac{7}{10}$ and $\frac{4}{5}$ is $\frac{11}{15}$.
5. On dividing $\frac{2}{3}$ by 10, we get $\frac{1}{15}$.

E. Application-based questions.

1. Tarun drank $\frac{3}{8}$ of orange juice and Varun drank $\frac{4}{5}$ of apple juice from cartons kept on the table. Find the difference in the quantity of juice they drank.
2. Nithin bought $2\frac{1}{7}$ litres of milk on 1st day and $\frac{1}{3}$ litres more on the 2nd day. How many litres of milk did he buy in all?

3. Anup has 54 cookies. He shared $\frac{2}{3}$ of them with his friend. How many cookies did Anup share?

4. A statue is 100 feet tall. Find the number of cloth pieces required to cover the statue if one piece can cover $\frac{10}{3}$ feet.

5. Sahil has ₹2000 with him. He spent $\frac{1}{8}$ of it for buying a shirt and $\frac{3}{5}$ of it for buying shoes. How much money is remaining with him?

6. A train arrives at a station with 350 passengers on board. $\frac{4}{7}$ of the passengers get off the train but only $\frac{1}{4}$ of them boarded the train again. How many passengers are on the train when it leaves the station?

7. The cost of a fairytale book is ₹$63\frac{3}{4}$ and that of a historical fiction is ₹$17\frac{1}{2}$ more than the fairytale book. What is the cost of the historical fiction book?

8. A flask contains $1\frac{1}{2}$ litres of tea. It is poured equally into 9 similar cups. What is the volume of tea in each cup?

9. Amruta read $\frac{1}{6}$ of a book on Saturday and $\frac{7}{9}$ of the book on Sunday. If the book has 450 pages, how many pages is Amrutha yet to read?

10. An object weighs $\frac{1}{6}$ of its mass on the Moon. If a person weighs $58\frac{1}{2}$ kg on the Earth, how much would he weigh on the moon?

Space for rough work

Did You Master?

A. $\frac{2}{8} \times 2 =$ ________

1. $\frac{2}{16}$ 2. $\frac{1}{2}$
3. $\frac{1}{4}$ 4. $\frac{3}{4}$

B. Subtract $\frac{1}{4}$ from $\frac{4}{8}$.

1. $\frac{1}{4}$ 2. $\frac{3}{8}$
3. $\frac{2}{4}$ 4. $\frac{3}{4}$

C. What is the reciprocal of 0?

1. 1 2. –1
3. 0 4. does not exist

D. Dividing a number by $\frac{a}{b}$ is same as ______.

1. adding $\frac{a}{b}$ to it
2. multiplying it with $\frac{a}{b}$
3. multiplying it with $\frac{b}{a}$
4. subtracting $\frac{b}{a}$ from it

E. In a coffee shop, one-fifth of the customers prefer cold coffee. What fraction of the customers prefer hot coffee?

1. $\frac{1}{2}$
2. $\frac{3}{5}$
3. $\frac{2}{5}$
4. $\frac{4}{5}$

F. $\frac{3}{2} \div 4 =$ ________

1. $\frac{3}{8}$ 2. 6
3. $\frac{3}{4}$ 4. 1

G. Three athletes A, B and C spend $\frac{1}{6}$ of an hour, $\frac{1}{8}$ of an hour and $\frac{4}{9}$ of an hour daily on warm up exercises. Who takes the maximum time?

1. A
2. B
3. C
4. All take equal time

H. In a box, there are 24 packets of rice bags. If each bag weighs $\frac{3}{4}$ kg, what is the total weight of the box?

1. 28 kg 2. 32 kg
3. 18 kg 4. 24 kg

I. $\frac{6}{9} \times \frac{1}{3} =$ ________

1. $\frac{2}{9}$ 2. 2
3. $\frac{1}{2}$ 4. $\frac{1}{3}$

J. The length of a rope is $2\frac{1}{2}$ m. Another rope of length $\frac{3}{4}$ m is tied to one end of the first rope. What is the total length of the rope?

1. $3\frac{1}{6}$ m 2. $3\frac{1}{4}$ m
3. $\frac{4}{13}$ m 4. $4\frac{4}{5}$ m

How many questions did you answer correctly? Score yourself.

easy	average	advanced	remembering	understanding	applying	analysing	evaluating	creating

communication	representation	devising strategies	mathematisation	reasoning and argument	using symbols	using mathematical tools	creativity

6 Decimals

Curricular Goals

- Understand numbers and sets of numbers (whole numbers, fractions and carry out the basic operations (CG-1)

Competencies

- Represent and compare commonly used decimals in daily life such as $\frac{1}{10}, \frac{1}{100}$, etc. as parts of unit wholes, as locations on number lines, and as divisions of decimal numbers (C-1.2)

Why This Topic?

Consider the following real-world situations where decimals are used.

Who weighs more?

Tanvi and Manvi are twin babies and they weigh 2.85 kg and 2.6 kg, respectively.
To find who weighs more, we will require the knowledge of comparing decimal numbers.

Total fabric required

Clothing material	Girls	Boys
Shirt	1.5 m	1.5 m
Trouser/Skirt	1.75 m	1.55 m

To find the total fabric required for 45 boys and 25 girls, we must know how to multiply and add decimal numbers.

Can you think of two more examples from your daily life where decimal numbers are used?

Are You Ready?

A. Which digit is in the tenth place in 23.91?

1. 2
2. 3
3. 9
4. 1

B. Which decimal number is represented in the given picture?

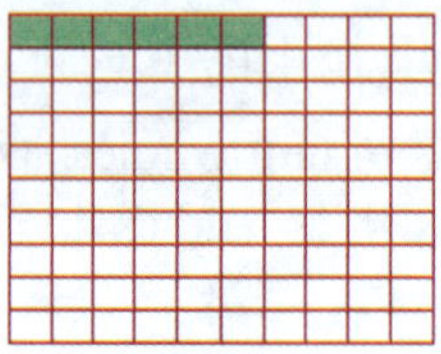

1. 0.6
2. 0.8
3. 6
4. 0.06

C. What is decimal part of the given number 132.245?

1. 13 2. 245
3. 24 4. 132

D. $\frac{7}{1000}$ can be written as ______.

1. 7 2. 0.007
3. 0.07 4. 0.7

E. Which of the following is a pair of like decimals?

1. 3.8, 3.98 2. 456.5, 45.05
3. 0.78, 0.56 4. 34.890, 34.78

F. In which of the following number lines the number 4.231 is represented?

1. 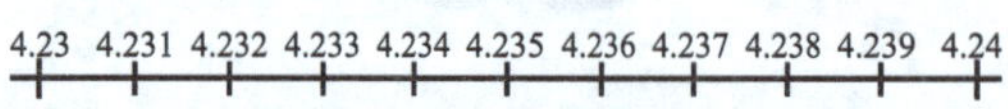

2. 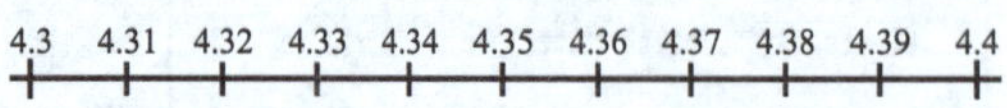

3. 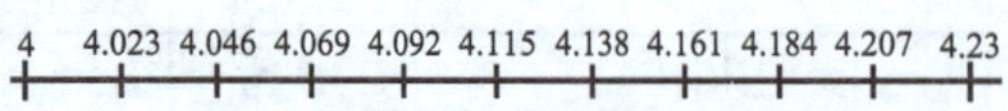

4. 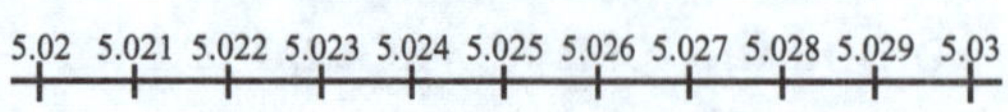

G. What is the fractional form of 6.72?

1. $6\frac{18}{25}$ 2. $\frac{18}{25}$
3. $5\frac{8}{5}$ 4. $\frac{8}{5}$

H. What is the decimal form of $\frac{9}{5}$?

1. 0.8
2. 2.8
3. 1.8
4. 0.008

I. The heights of Rekha, Sahana and Roger are 145.45 cm, 145.4 cm and 145.045 cm, respectively. Who is the tallest person?

1. Sahana
2. Roger
3. Both Roger and Sahana
4. Rekha

J. Arun cuts a ribbon into different pieces of 78.3 cm, 37.8 cm, 378.09 cm and 0.387 cm. Write these lengths in ascending order.

1. 378.09 cm, 78.3 cm, 37.8 cm, 0.387 cm
2. 0.387 cm, 37.8 cm,78.3 cm, 378.09 cm
3. 78.3 cm, 37.8 cm, 378.09 cm, 0.387 cm
4. 0.387 cm , 78.3 cm, 37.8 cm, 378.09 cm

How many questions did you answer correctly? Score yourself.

easy, average, advanced, remembering, understanding, applying, analysing, evaluating, creating

communication, representation, devising strategies, mathematisation, reasoning and argument, using symbols, using mathematical tools, creativity

LIKE AND UNLIKE DECIMALS

Recall that a decimal number consists of a whole number and a fractional part, separated by a dot called decimal point.

Decimals with the same number of decimal places are called **like decimals,** whereas decimals with different number of decimal places are called **unlike decimals**.

Examples:

1. 0.5, 13.1, 54.6, 123.7 and 95.2 are like decimals with one decimal place.
2. 4.54, 23.86, 6.06 and 1.40 are like decimals with two decimal places.
3. 1.5 and 1.25 are unlike decimals since they have different number of decimal places.
4. 7.5, 9.94 and 15.705 are unlike decimals since they have different number of decimal places.

> Recall that adding any number of zeros on the right of the fractional part of a number does not change its value. This way we can change unlike decimals into like decimals by adding the required number of zeros.

Example 1: State whether the following group of decimals are like or unlike.

a. 19.6, 9.68, 11.081, 109.02 b. 6.21, 3.44, 4.61, 8.42

Solution:

a. 19.6, 9.68, 11.081, 109.02: These are unlike decimals as they have different number of decimal places.

b. 6.21, 3.44, 4.61, 8.42: These are like decimals as they have same number of decimal places.

Example 2: Convert 0.3333, 127.01 and 69.4 into like decimals.

Solution: Unlike decimals are converted into like decimals by adding the required number of 0s at the end of the fractional part.

Since 0.3333 has 4 decimal places, we add 0 after the decimal parts in 127.01 and 69.4. Therefore, the like decimals are 0.3333, 127.0100 and 69.4000.

CONVERTING FRACTIONS INTO DECIMALS AND VICE-VERSA

Janaki walks a distance of $\frac{1}{2}$ km everyday from her home to school. Here, the distance is given in fraction. To convert fractions into decimals, the numerator and the denominator of the fraction should be multiplied by the same number so that the denominator becomes a multiple of 10.

So, we multiply by $\frac{1}{2}$ by $\frac{5}{5}$ to obtain $\frac{5}{10}$. Then, the decimal form becomes 0.5.

$\frac{5}{10}$ or 0.5

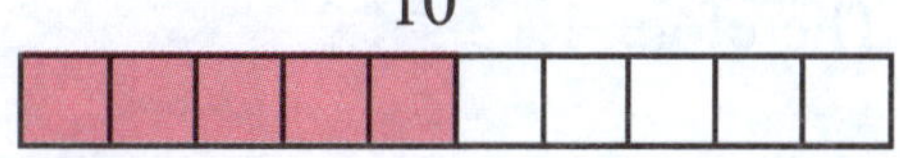

Example 3: Convert $\frac{3}{4}$ into its decimal form.

$\frac{3}{4}$ or $\frac{75}{100}$ or 0.75

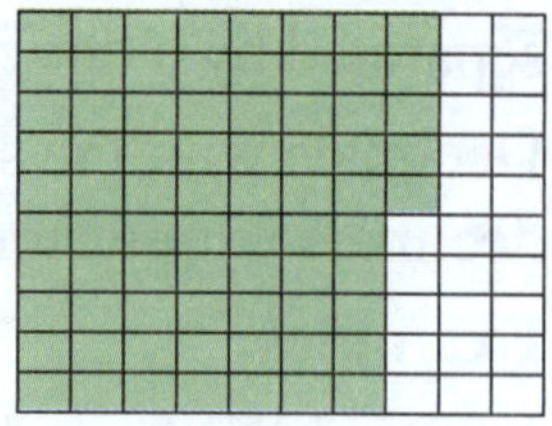

Solution: $\frac{3}{4} = \frac{3\times25}{4\times25} = \frac{75}{100} = 0.75$

To convert a decimal number into a fraction, write the decimal number in the expanded form, according to the place value system, and add the resultant unlike fractions.

Example 4: Convert 1.4 into a fraction and write the answer in the simplest form.

Solution: We write 1.4 in expanded form and then simplify.

$1.4 = 1 + \frac{4}{10} = \frac{14}{10} = \frac{7}{5} = 1\frac{2}{5}$

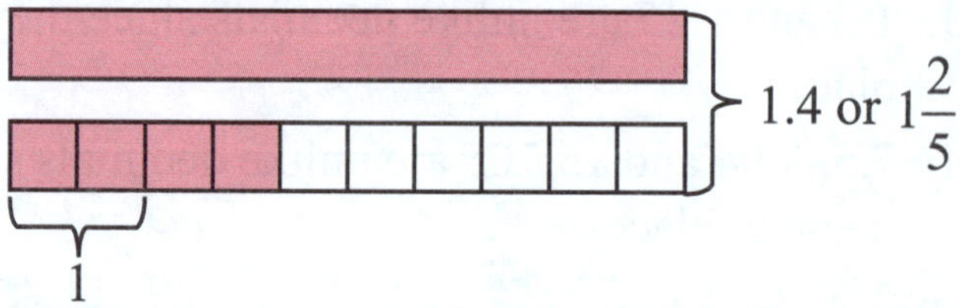

COMPARISON OF DECIMALS

Consider two jars of capacity 1.2 litres and 1.12 litres. Which jar's capacity is more?

Let us first recall the place value chart of decimal numbers.

Whole number part				Decimal number part		
Thousands	Hundreds	Tens	Ones	Tenths	Hundredths	Thousandths
1000	100	10	1	$\frac{1}{10} = 0.1$	$\frac{1}{100} = 0.01$	$\frac{1}{1000} = 0.001$

The steps followed to compare decimal numbers are listed below.

Step 1: Compare the whole number parts of the numbers. The greater whole number part will be greater of the two decimal numbers.

Step 2: If the whole number parts are equal, then compare the digits in the tenths place, hundredths place and thousandths place one after the other. Remember to convert unlike decimals into like decimals before comparing the decimal numbers.

Example 5: Which is greater: 1.12 or 1.2?

Solution: 1.12 and 1.2 are unlike decimals. So, we convert them into like decimals and represent them in the place value chart.

Whole number	Tenths	Hundredths
1	. 1	2
1	. 2	0

Therefore, 1.12 < 1.2.

Example 6: Arrange the numbers 3.64, 3.54, 3.05, 3.259 and 3.32 in ascending order.

Solution: We convert the given decimals into like decimals and represent them in the place value chart to compare.

Whole number		Tenths	Hundredths	Thousandths
3	.	6	4	0
3	.	5	4	0
3	.	0	5	0
3	.	2	5	9
3	.	3	2	0

As $3.050 < 3.259 < 3.320 < 3.540 < 3.640$

Ascending order: 3.050, 3.259, 3.320, 3.540 and 3.640

Exercise 6.1

1. Write whether the following decimal numbers are like or unlike.

a. 3.56, 16.95, 780.54
b. 1.1, 42.43, 435.768
c. 0.81, 1.18, 23.45
d. 12.76, 16.7, 9.865
e. 123.5, 1567.8, 23.34

2. Convert the following fractions into decimals.

a. $\frac{2}{5}$
b. $\frac{4}{3}$
c. $\frac{7}{50}$
d. $\frac{17}{20}$
e. $\frac{12}{25}$

3. Convert the following decimals into fractions.

a. 0.5
b. 1.9
c. 1.15
d. 1.344
e. 5.76

4. Compare the given decimals and put the appropriate symbols (< or >).

a. 3.6 ☐ 3.9
b. 6.81 ☐ 6.44
c. 18.5 ☐ 18.42
d. 17.27 ☐ 17.35
e. 34.86 ☐ 28.12

5. Arrange the following decimal numbers in ascending order.

a. 4.62, 462, 0.462, 4.26, 0.4, 46.2, 42
b. 35.7, 3.57, 3.75, 53.7, 357, 0.537, 0.5
c. 13.75, 1.375, 15.73, 5.75, 137.5, 51.37
d. 0.02, 0.2, 1, 1.2, 0.211, 0.088, 0.75
e. 1.986, 19.01, 18.45, 1.009, 11.209, 23.6, 29.4

6. Arrange the following decimal numbers in descending order.

a. 0.032, 0.32, 0.102, 0.302, 0.233
b. 4.09, 4.90, 14.009, 14.99
c. 1.001, 0.11, 0.111, 11.01, 111.1
d. 3.90, 3.09, 3.009, 13.8, 1.38
e. 0.12, 0.002, 1.02, 1.2, 0.02

ADDITION OF DECIMALS

There are two pieces of strings of length 2.5 m and 3.12 m. Can you find the total length of these pieces?

Following are the steps to add any given decimals numbers.

1. Write the given decimal numbers in columns according to their place values.
2. Add each digit starting from the right.
3. Place the decimal point in the sum exactly below the decimal points in the given numbers.

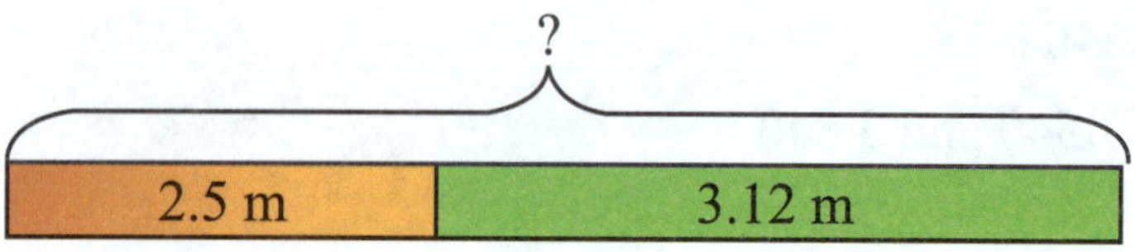

	T	O		Ots	Ohs
		2	.	5	0
+		3	.	1	2
		5	.	6	2

Therefore, the sum of the lengths of the strings is 2.5 m + 3.12 m = 5.62 m.

Example 7: Add 7.25 and 3.74.

Solution:

	T	O		Ots	Ohs
		7	.	2	5
+		3	.	7	4
	1	0	.	9	9

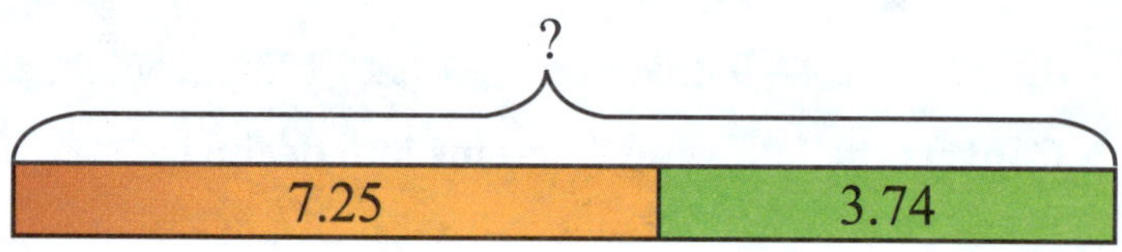

Therefore, 7.25 + 3.74 = 10.99

Example 8: Find the sum of 72.53 and 26.14.

Solution:

	T	O		Ots	Ohs
	7	2	.	5	3
+	2	6	.	1	4
	9	8	.	6	7

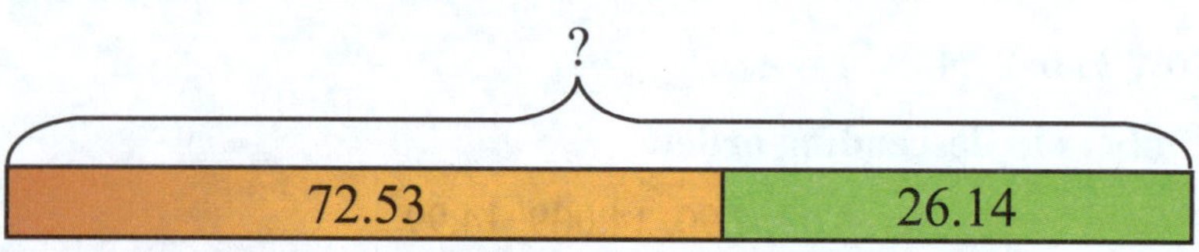

Therefore, the sum of 72.53 and 26.14 is 98.67.

SUBTRACTION OF DECIMALS

Two decimal numbers can be subtracted using the same method as addition.

Example 9: Subtract 53.26 from 86.40.

Solution:

	T	O		Ots	Ohs
	8	6	.	3 ~~4~~	10 ~~0~~
−	5	3	.	2	6
	3	3	.	1	4

Therefore, 86.4 – 53.26 = 33.14.

Example 10: What is the difference between 94.25 and 43.62?

Solution:

	T	O		Ots	Ohs
	9	3 ~~4~~	.	12 ~~2~~	5
−	4	3	.	6	2
	5	0	.	6	3

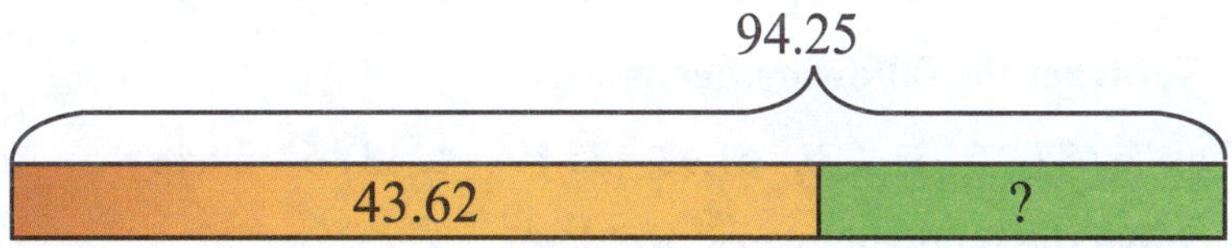

Therefore, the difference between 94.25 and 43.62 is 50.63.

WORD PROBLEMS

We come across many instances of adding and subtracting decimal numbers in our daily life.

Example 11: If the annual rainfall of a district in Karnataka was 12.3 inches in 2012, 13.2 inches in 2011 and 11.5 inches in 2010, what was the total rainfall in the 3 years?

Solution: Annual rainfall in 2012 = 12.3 inches

Annual rainfall in 2011 = 13.2 inches

Annual rainfall in 2010 = 11.5 inches

Total rainfall in 3 years = 12.3 inches + 13.2 inches + 11.5 inches

	T	O		Ots
	1	1 2	.	3
	1	3	.	2
+	1	1	.	5
	3	7	.	0

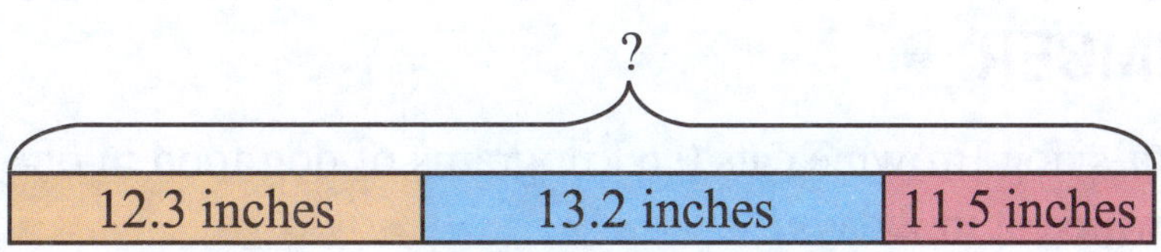

Therefore, the total rainfall in the 3 years was 37 inches.

Example 12: Harish's salary is ₹576.65 per day and Raveesh's salary is ₹248.50 per day. What is the difference between Harish's and Raveesh's per day salary?

Solution: Harish's per day salary = ₹576.65

Raveesh's per day salary = ₹248.50

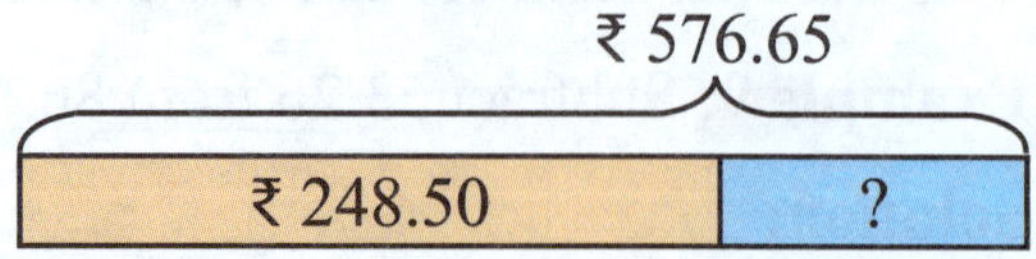

Difference between per day salary
= ₹576.65 – ₹ 248.50

	H	T	O		Ots	Ohs
	5	$\overset{6}{\cancel{7}}$	$\overset{16}{\cancel{6}}$	.	6	5
–	2	4	8	.	5	0
	3	2	8	.	1	5

Therefore, the difference between Harish's and Raveesh's per day salary is ₹328.15.

Exercise 6.2

ia

1. Add the following decimals.

a. 97.71 + 1.3 b. 40.3 + 44.6 c. 28.93 + 43.12 d. 15.55 + 68.7 e. 77.5 +71.6

2. Subtract the following decimals.

a. 62.87 – 54.31 b. 61.92 – 25.19 c. 31.5 – 29.48 d. 99.61 – 30.3 e. 59.26 – 27.66

3. Solve the following word problems.

a. If you drive 15.4 km, 24.2 km, 10.4 km and 7.5 km for four consecutive days, how many kilometres did you drive in all in these 4 days?

b. A weatherman was measuring the amount of rain in two cities received over a week. City A received 10.97 inches and City B received 8.4 inches. How much rain did both the cities receive in total?

c. In the 1st year, Saima grew by 4.83 cm and by 9.5 cm in the 2nd year. How much more did she grow in the 2 years altogether?

d. The total mass of cherry and lime jelly bought for a birthday party was 5.4 kg. If cherry jelly weighs 4.20 kg, find the weight of the lime jelly.

e. Tom and Jack were running a relay race. The race was 33.03 kilometres in total. If Tom ran 16.93 kilometres, how far did Jack run?

MULTIPLICATION OF A DECIMAL NUMBER BY A WHOLE NUMBER

Anita's dog Brownie eats 0.6 kilograms of dog food in one day. How much food does Brownie eat in 2 days?

The answer will be (0.6 + 0.6 or 0.6 × 2) kilograms of dog food. When a decimal number is multiplied by a whole number, multiply the numbers by ignoring the decimal point. Count the number of digits to the right of the decimal point in the decimal number and put the decimal point in the product by counting the same number of digits from the right.

So, (0.6 × 2 = 1.2) kilograms which is the amount of dog food Brownie eats in 2 days.

Example 13: Multiply 12.51 by 6.

Solution: Multiply 1251 by 6. We get 7506 as the product. Now place the decimal point in the product after two digits from the right.

$$\begin{array}{r} 1\ 2\ 5\ 1 \\ \times \quad\quad\ 6 \\ \hline 7\ 5\ 0\ 6 \\ \hline \end{array}$$

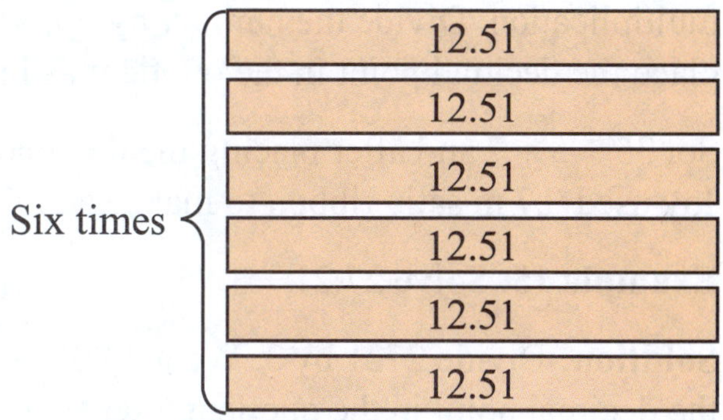

Therefore, 12.51 × 6 is 75.06.

When a decimal number is multiplied by 10, 100 or 1000, the digits in the product are the same as in the decimal number. The decimal point in the product simply shifts to the right by as many number of places as there are zeros after one.

Example 14: Multiply 1.42 by 10, 100 and 1000.

Solution: 1.42 × 10 = 14.2 1.42 × 100 = 142 or 142.0

1.42 × 1000 = 1420 or 1420.0

Exercise 6.3

1. Multiply the following with 10, 100 and 1000 and complete the table.

		10	100	1000
a.	6.63			
b.	0.457			
c.	9.91			
d.	3.456			
e.	456.7			

2. Multiply the following decimal numbers by the given whole numbers.

a. 32.1 × 8 b. 72.9 × 9 c. 441.8 × 4

d. 32.4 × 12 e. 764.3 × 163

DIVISION OF A DECIMAL NUMBER BY A WHOLE NUMBER

Joy had 3.5 m satin ribbon. He made 5 flowers out of it. Find the length of satin ribbon that was used to make each flower if he used the same length for all the 5 flowers.

The answer can be obtained by dividing 3.5 by 5. To divide a decimal number by a whole number, we follow the same procedure as multiplication. Divide the number by ignoring the decimal symbol and place the decimal point in the quotient as in the decimal number.

$$\begin{array}{r|rr} & & 7 \\ \hline 5 & 3 & 5 \\ - & 3 & 5 \\ \hline & & 0 \\ \hline \end{array}$$

So, 35 ÷ 5 = 7 and after placing the decimal point, we get 0.7 as the answer. Therefore, Joy used 0.7 m satin ribbon to make each flower.

Example 15: Solve 27.21 ÷ 3.

Solution: Divide 2721 by 3. We get 907 as the quotient. Now place the decimal point in the quotient after two digits from the right.

$$\begin{array}{r|rrrr} & & 9 & 0 & 7 \\ \hline 3 & 2 & 7 & 2 & 1 \\ - & 2 & 7 & & \\ \hline & & 0 & 2 & 1 \\ - & & & 2 & 1 \\ \hline & & & 0 & 0 \\ \hline \end{array}$$

Therefore, 27.21 ÷ 3 = 9.07.

When we divide a decimal number by 10, 100 or 1000, simply shift the decimal point to the left by as many number of places as there are zeros after one.

Example 16: Divide 87.6 by 10, 100 and 1000.

Solution: 87.6 ÷ 10 = 8.76 87.6 ÷ 100 = 0.876

87.6 ÷ 1000 = 0.0876

Exercise 6.4

1. Divide the following.

a. 0.9 ÷ 3 b. 2.4 ÷ 8 c. 25.935 ÷ 15

d. 36.24 ÷ 12 e. 0.2717 ÷ 132

2. Divide the following by 10, 100 and 1000 and complete the table.

	÷	10	100	1000
a.	34.5			
b.	456.60			
c.	34.9			
d.	11.289			
e.	0.08			

Concept Map

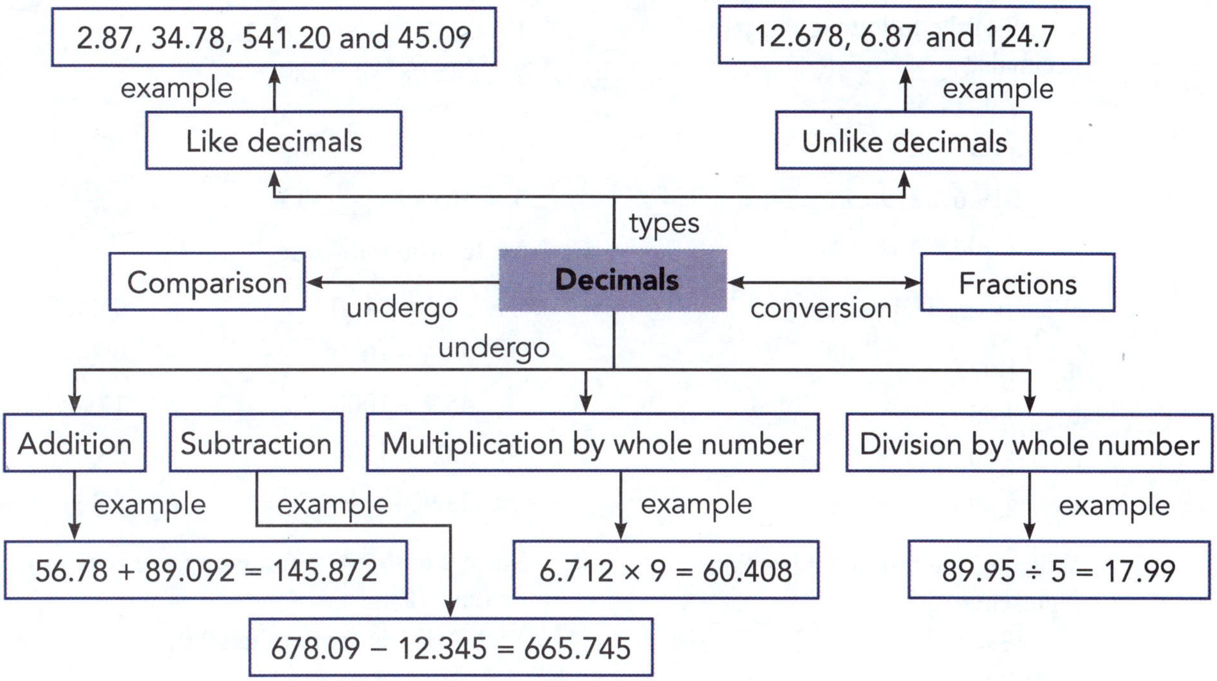

Project

Use of decimals in sports!

The concept of decimal numbers is used in sports, like swimming, to represent the time taken by each swimmer in the event. The following table shows the results of a 50 m freestyle swimming competition held in 2022 Commonwealth Games.

Medal	Timings in seconds for 50 m freestyle swimming			
	Men		Women	
Gold	Ben Pround (England)	21.36	Emma McKeon (Australia)	23.99
Silver	Lewis Burras (England)	21.88	Meg Harris (Australia)	24.32
Bronze	Josh Liendo (Canada)	22.02	Shayna Jack (Australia)	34.36

Compare the timings of men and women in all the three medal categories.

Revision Exercise

A. Choose the correct option.

1. Which of the following is a pair of like decimals?
   a. 2.3, 14.56
   b. 1.34. 134.01
   c. 219.67, 2196.7
   d. 2.908, 24.78
2. What is the decimal form of $\frac{13}{8}$?
   a. 1.625
   b. 3.45
   c. 1.29
   d. 2.678
3. Which of the following fractions represents 1.25?
   a. $\frac{3}{4}$
   b. $\frac{5}{7}$
   c. $\frac{5}{4}$
   d. $\frac{3}{8}$
4. Which of the following is a pair of unlike decimals?
   a. 4.92, 4.789
   b. 2.13, 3.89
   c. 4.23, 5.78
   d. 8.2, 872.9
5. Which is the greatest among 6.89, 0.87, 16.09 and 16.006?
   a. 016.006
   b. 6.89
   c. 16.09
   d. 0.87

B. Fill in the blanks. Use symbols < or >.

1. 567.23 _____ 67.12
2. 45.98 _____ 89.7
3. 1.001 _____ 1.01
4. 2.34 _____ 2.67
5. 13.89 _____ 13.7

C. Match the following.

1. 12.34 × 100	a. 0.0459
2. 23.6 ÷ 10	b. 9030
3. 45.9 ÷ 1000	c. 1234
4. 9.03 × 1000	d. 239.01
5. 23.901 × 10	e. 2.36

D. State whether the following are true (T) or false (F).

1. 9.001 is greater than 9.01.
2. $\frac{15}{100}$ is same as 0.15.
3. The sum of 45.87 and 134.005 is 179.875.
4. 123.09 + 1.78 = 15.08.
5. The difference between 45.89 and 23.98 is 21.91.

E. Answer the following questions.

1. Add the following decimals.
   a. 3345.9 + 3.98
   b. 45.901 + 67891.093
   c. 6789.09 + 123.456
   d. 4091.178 + 5.789
   e. 3.890 + 79.295
2. Subtract the following decimals.
   a. 89.7 – 34.44
   b. 35.16 – 31.158
   c. 50.455 – 1.22
   d. 37.221 – 21.851
   e. 26.809 – 5.232

3. Multiply the following decimals.
   a. 3.6 × 6
   b. 128.12 × 9
   c. 2.3 × 7
   d. 4.56 × 3
   e. 1.232 × 4
4. Divide the following decimals with the given whole numbers.
   a. 23.5 ÷ 100
   b. 12.90 ÷ 3
   c. 127.89 ÷ 18
   d. 80.08 ÷ 1000
   e. 190.869 ÷ 21

F. Application-based questions.

1. Mridul has ₹230.65 and Jaya has ₹125.35. How much money do they have altogether?
2. Nisha runs daily as part of an exercise plan. She ran 8.3 km on Sunday, 5.1 km on Monday, 5.75 km on Tuesday, 5.6 km on Wednesday, 4.25 km on Thursday, 4 km on Friday and 6 km on Saturday. How many kilometres did she run during the week?
3. Bhavya bought 14.50 kg of carrots and 14.25 kg of tomatoes. Which vegetable did he buy more and how much more?
4. Jasmeet walked for 9.58 kilometres for 2 days of the fair. On the first day, he walked for 4.68 kilometres. How much did he walk on the second day?
5. Raghav has ₹25 to spend at an Internet cafe. He spends ₹15.83 on playing games. How much money is left with him?

Space for rough work

Did You Master?

A. Which of the following is a pair of like decimals?

1. 4.67, 4.7
2. 12.56, 920.23
3. 1.098, 10.98
4. 40.987, 12.98

B. Which of the following is greater than 521.67?

1. 52.216
2. 521.89
3. 67.98
4. 345.67

C. Which of the following is true?

1. 7890.9 ÷ 10 = 78.909
2. 345.89 ÷ 7 = 48.902
3. 234.6 ÷ 4 = 58.65
4. 346.98 ÷ 100 = 34.698

D. What is the fractional form of 4.567?

1. $4\frac{56}{100}$
2. $5\frac{567}{100}$
3. $5\frac{56}{100}$
4. $4\frac{567}{1000}$

E. $\frac{14}{25}$ can be written as _______.

1. 5.6
2. 0.76
3. 0.56
4. 7.6

F. What is the sum of 17.89 and 45.562?

1. 56.98
2. 65.45
3. 63.54
4. 63.452

G. Find the difference between 345.89 and 34.782.

1. 311.108
2. 334.788
3. 380.672
4. 345.908

H. What is the product of 45.891 and 23?

1. 1234.87
2. 2349.812
3. 1055.493
4. 1278.492

I. Shalini's house is 4.678 km away from school, whereas Rani's house is 3.57 km away. Who lives nearer to the school and by how many kilometres?

1. Shalini, 1.108 km
2. Rani, 1.108 km
3. Shalini, 8.248 km
4. Rani, 8.248 km

J. Naveen's father gave him ₹56.78, and his mother gave him ₹456.79 to buy a school bag for his birthday.
What is the total amount he has?

1. ₹567.98
2. ₹609.89
3. ₹456.12
4. ₹513.57

How many questions did you answer correctly? Score yourself.

easy ☐ average ☐ advanced ☐ remembering ☐ understanding ☐ applying ☐ analysing ☐ evaluating ☐ creating ☐

communication ☐ representation ☐ devising strategies ☐ mathematisation ☐ reasoning and argument ☐ using symbols ☐ using mathematical tools ☐ creativity ☐

7 Percentage

Curricular Goals

- Understand numbers and sets of numbers (whole numbers and fractions) (CG-1)

Competencies

- Represent and compare commonly used fractions in daily life as percentage (C-1.2)
- Understand and visualise arithmetic operations and the relationships among them, knows addition and multiplication and apply the four basic operations on whole numbers to solve daily life problems (C-1.3)

Why This Topic?

Consider the following examples to relate percentage to everyday life.

Festival discount offers

Many of the shops display sale signs during festival seasons with percentages written on them. Most products have this discount. Instead of displaying each item's discount, shops display a percentage instead.

Fruits packed in a basket

A percentage is useful when packing large quantities of fruits in baskets to estimate the number of fruits of a specific type in a basket. There is a lot of effort and time involved in writing the individual numbers.

Can you think of two more examples where you see percentage being used in daily life?

Are You Ready?

A. What is the fraction representation of the shaded portion?

1. $\frac{4}{3}$ 2. $\frac{1}{3}$

3. $\frac{1}{4}$ 4. $\frac{4}{1}$

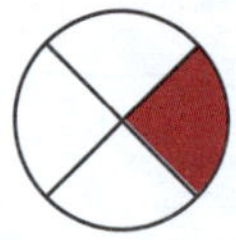

B. What is the decimal representation of the shaded portion?

1. 4.04
2. 0.4
3. 4.4
4. 0.04

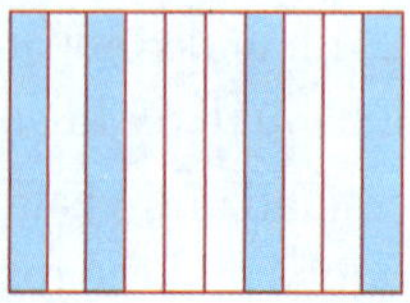

C. What is the decimal representation of the unshaded portion?

1. 0.18
2. 18.018
3. 8.08
4. 0.82

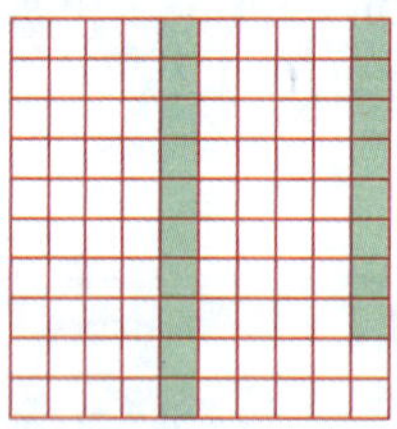

D. Which of the following represents a fraction having 3 in the denominator?

1. 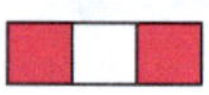 2. 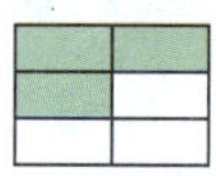

3. 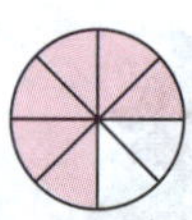 4. 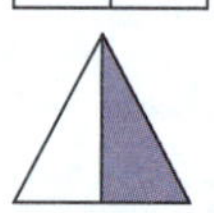

E. What is the decimal form of $\frac{3}{8}$?

1. 0.3 2. 1.375

3. 1.35 4. 0.375

F. What is the fraction form of 2.76?

1. $\frac{19}{25}$ 2. $3\frac{9}{16}$

3. $1\frac{21}{17}$ 4. $2\frac{19}{25}$

G. Renuka walks $\frac{4}{5}$ km on Monday and $\frac{2}{5}$ km on Tuesday. What is the total distance covered by Renuka in 2 days?

1. $\frac{2}{10}$ km 2. $\frac{6}{5}$ km

3. $\frac{4}{5}$ km 4. $\frac{5}{9}$ km

H. Sameer bought 3.8 kg of carrots, 3.09 kg of potatoes and 3.27 kg of tomatoes. Which vegetable did he buy the most?

1. Carrots
2. Tomatoes
3. Potatoes
4. Both potatoes and tomatoes

I. Jayshree bought a book for ₹47.56. If she gives ₹100 note to the shopkeeper, how much amount does she get back?

1. ₹34.89 2. ₹53.9

3. ₹64.07 4. ₹52.44

J. In a long jump competition, Sanjay jumped $2\frac{2}{5}$ m and Shankar jumped $3\frac{7}{9}$ m. Who jumped longer and by how many metres?

1. Sanjay; by $1\frac{7}{9}$ m
2. Shankar; by $1\frac{17}{45}$ m
3. Sanjay; $1\frac{7}{9}$ m
4. Shankar; by $\frac{17}{45}$ m

How many questions did you answer correctly? Score yourself.

easy ☐ average ☐ advanced ☐ remembering ☐ understanding ☐ applying ☐ analysing ☐ evaluating ☐ creating ☐

communication ☐ representation ☐ devising strategies ☐ mathematisation ☐ reasoning and argument ☐ using symbols ☐ using mathematical tools ☐ creativity ☐

PERCENTAGE

The distribution of water and land on the earth is shown in the figure. It shows some numerical value along with a symbol.

71% water and 29% land

How do we read it? What does it mean?

The symbol % is called **percentage**. Percent is derived from the Latin word *per centum* meaning **per hundred** that means hundredths.

Therefore, 71% is read as seventy-one percent, meaning $\frac{71}{100}$ and 29% is read as twenty-nine percent, meaning $\frac{29}{100}$.

Converting Fractions into Percentage and Vice-Versa

Suhani read $\frac{1}{4}$ of a book on a holiday. Find the percentage of the book she read.

$$\frac{1}{4}=\frac{1\times25}{4\times25}=\frac{25}{100}=25\%$$

or

$$\frac{1}{4}=\frac{1}{4}\times100=\frac{1}{\cancel{4}_1}\times\cancel{100}^{25}=25\%$$

Therefore, Suhani read 25% of the book on her holiday.

Fractions are converted into percentage by multiplying by 100. Write the answer using "%" symbol.

Example 1: Convert $\frac{3}{5}$ into percentage.

Solution: Multiply $\frac{3}{5}$ by 100.

$$\frac{3}{5}=\frac{3}{5}\times100=\frac{3}{\cancel{5}_1}\times\cancel{100}^{20}=60$$

Add % symbol after 60 to get $\frac{3}{5}=60\%$.

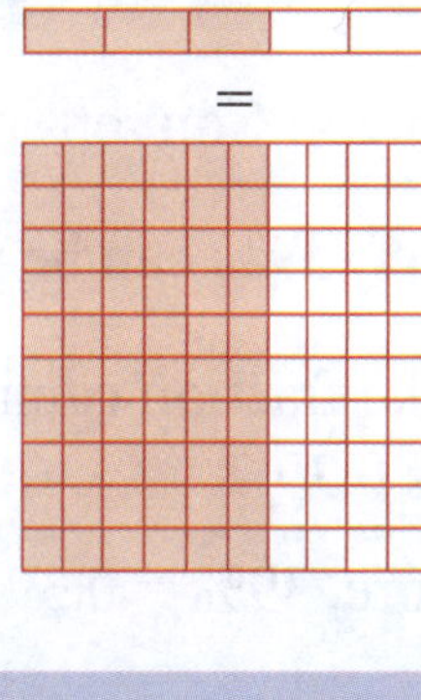

Percentages are converted into fraction by dividing by 100. Retain the answer in its simplest form.

Example 2: Convert 45% into fraction.

Solution: 45% can be written as $\frac{45}{100}$.

On simplifying the fraction, we get $\frac{45}{100} = \frac{9}{20}$.

Therefore, 45% = $\frac{9}{20}$.

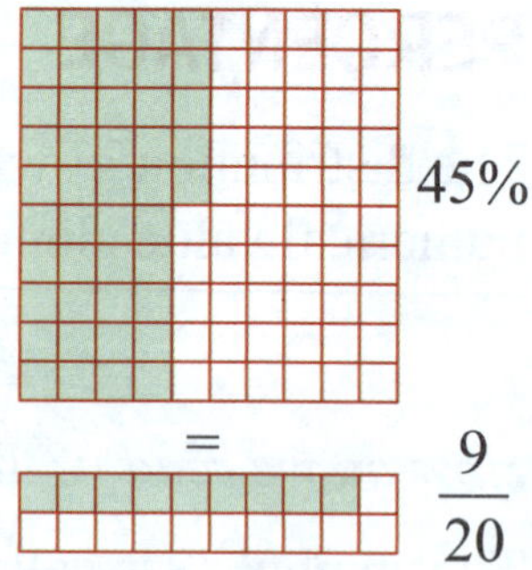

Converting Decimals into Percentage and Vice-Versa

Pooja is carrying a pumpkin weighing 0.9 kg. How can we represent the weight of pumpkin in percentage?

0.9 × 100 = 90 = 90%

Decimal numbers are converted into percentage by multiplying by 100. Write the answer using "%" symbol.

Therefore, 0.9 kg is 90% of a kg.

Example 3: Convert 0.65 into percentage.

Solution: Multiply 0.65 by 100.

0.65 × 100 = 65

Add the % symbol after 65 to get 0.65 = 65%.

0.65 or 65%

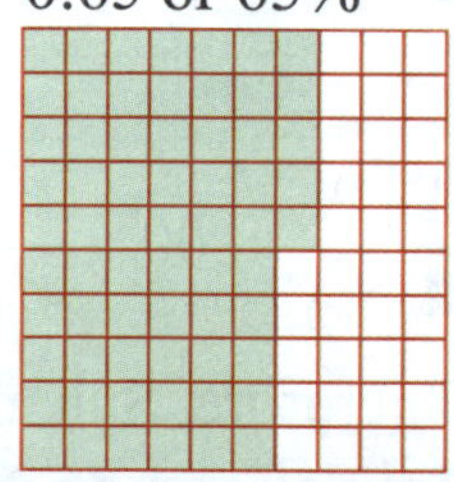

Percentages are converted into decimal numbers by dividing by 100. Retain the answer in its simplest form.

Example 4: Convert 39% into decimal number.

Solution: 39% can be written as $\frac{39}{100}$.

Since the fraction cannot be simplified further, we get the decimal form as 0.39.

Therefore, 39% = 0.39

39% = 0.39

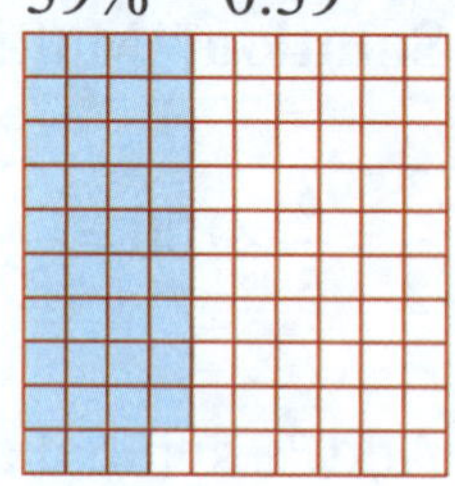

Exercise 7.1

1. Convert the following fractions into percentages.

a. $\frac{1}{5}$ b. $\frac{3}{10}$ c. $\frac{6}{8}$ d. $\frac{12}{24}$ e. $\frac{9}{20}$

2. Convert the following percentages into fractions.

a. 4% b. 75% c. 11% d. 48% e. 38%

3. Convert the following decimals into percentages.

a. 0.6 b. 0. 27 c. 0.45 d. 1.25 e. 3.48

4. Convert the following percentages into decimals.

a. 4% b. 112% c. 16% d. 24% e. 103%

PERCENTAGE OF A NUMBER

a

A decorator used 200 balloons while decorating the background of a stage. If 40% of them are red, then find the number of red balloons used.

Divide 40% by 100 to get $\frac{40}{100}$.

Now, multiply $\frac{40}{100}$ by 200 and simplify.

To find the percentage of a given number, divide the given % by 100 and multiply the given number.

$$\frac{40}{\cancel{100}} \times \cancel{200}^{2} = 80$$

Therefore, 80 red balloons are used in decorating the background of the stage.

Example 5: Find 85% of 40.

Solution: Divide 85% by 100 and multiply by 40.

$$\frac{\cancel{85}^{17}}{\cancel{100}_{5}} \times \cancel{40}^{2} = 34$$

85% of 40 = 34

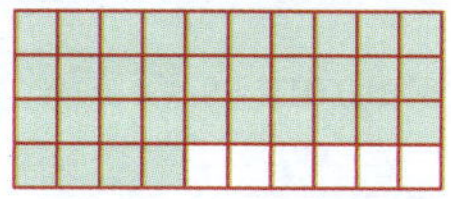

Therefore, 85% of 40 is 34.

Mental Maths

Find the following.

a. 50% of 20 b. 50% of 100 c. 100% of 50 d. 48% of 50

Goods and Services Tax (GST) is an indirect tax imposed by the Government of India on various goods and services provided to us in India.

Example 6: Daniel bought a pair of shoes worth ₹2200. If 5% GST is added on this price, find the total cost of a pair of shoes.

Solution: GST at 5% on ₹2200 = $22\cancel{00} \times \frac{5}{1\cancel{00}}$ = ₹110.

Therefore, the total cost of a pair of shoes is ₹2200 + ₹110 = ₹2310.

Exercise 7.2

1. Find the value of each of the following:

a. 12% of 35 b. 78% of 600 c. 64% of 75 d. 35% of 80 e. 98% of 50

2. Solve the following word problems.

a. There are 240 animals in a national park out of which 30% are mammals. How many mammals are there in the national park?

b. 320 employees work for Mr. Y. If 40% workers are men, how many employees are women?

c. Out of a collection of 80 books, 20% are comic books. How many comic books are there in the collection?

d. There are 60 fruits in a basket. If 60% are apples and the rest are oranges, find the number of apples and oranges.

e. A swimming club had 720 members last year. This year, the membership increased by 5%. Find the number of members this year.

f. Vismaya bought a comic that cost ₹50. In addition, she had to pay 10% sales tax. How much did she pay for the comic?

g. The usual price of a vase was ₹190. At a sale, it was sold at a discount of 30%. What was the sale price?

h. Ishaan shot 15 arrows. 40% of the arrows hit the target. How many arrows did not hit the target?

i. A library has a reading club. 30% of the members of the club are boys, 40% are girls and the rest are adults. If there are 280 members, how many of them are adults?

j. The bill of a dinner party in a restaurant is ₹1778, including a GST of 7%. What was the amount of GST?

Concept Map

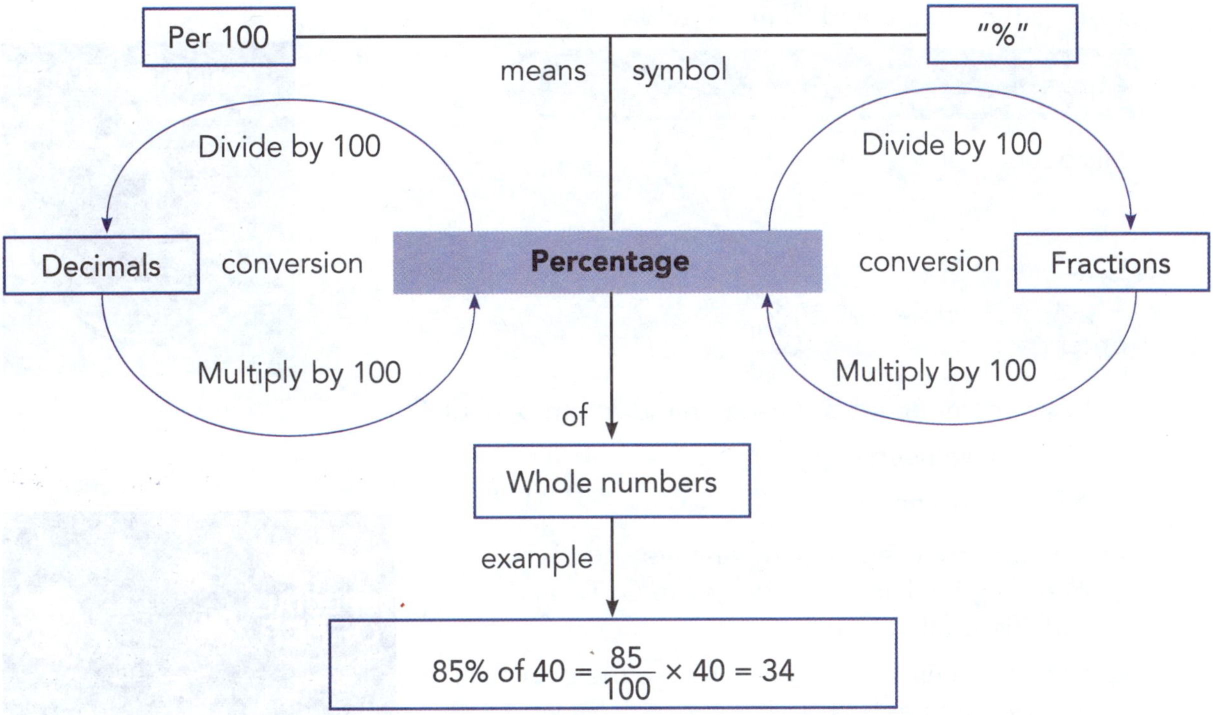

Projects

A. My Meal Plate for a Week

Every meal plate must have 4 sections: 30% grains, 30% vegetables, 20% fruits and 20% protein, along with some dairy product.

- Carbohydrates are obtained from grains, such as rice, wheat, brown rice, ragi, jawar, etc.
- Fruits and vegetables give us dietary fibres, vitamins and minerals.
- Proteins help our bones become strong and healthy, which we get from nuts, pulses, poultry, seafood, etc.
- Dairy products are milk, butter, curd, lassi or buttermilk, etc.

Based on this, prepare a chart showing your meal plate plan for a week.

B. Composition of Air

Air in our atmosphere is made up of different components. The percentage of each component is given in the picture.

Observe the picture and fill in the table.

Components	Present (in %)
Nitrogen	
Oxygen	
Argon, carbon dioxide and other gases	

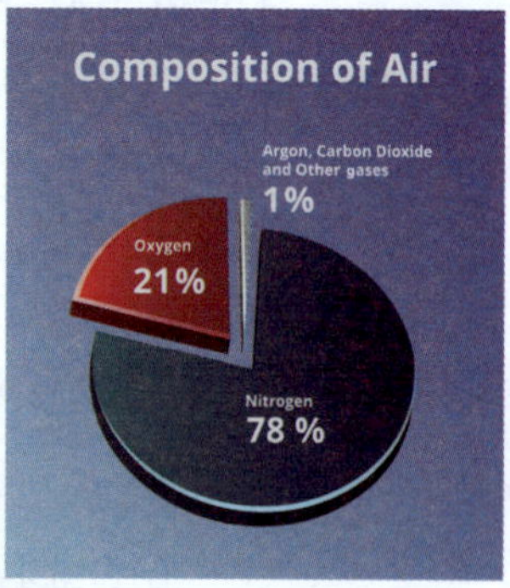

1. Which component is present in maximum quantity?
2. Why do we need oxygen?

C. Maths in shopping

Percentages are used in many real-life situations. For example, bank interest, taxes like GST, service tax, and discounts/offers.

Here are some exciting offers. Choose the best deal for your requirements and give a reason for your choice.

Buy 3 with 25% off on the total price!

Buy 1 and get the 2nd and 3rd for 35% of the original price!

Buy 1 and get the 2nd for 20% off and 3rd for 60% off !

Buy 2 and get the 3rd for 75% off !

1. What is the best deal if you want to buy three of the same items?
2. When shopping with your elders, check for discounts and use your Maths skills to find the best price. List two or three similar discounts you find.

Revision Exercise

A. Choose the correct option.

1. The decimal form of 65% is ______.
   a. 0.65 b. 0.065
   c. 6.5 d. 0.06
2. The percentage form of $\frac{20}{25}$ is ______.
   a. 75% b. 60%
   c. 80% d. 120%
3. What is the fractional form of 70%.
   a. $\frac{7}{10}$ b $\frac{15}{20}$
   c. $\frac{1}{10}$ d. $\frac{7}{100}$
4. The percentage form of 18.5 is ______.
   a. 185% b. 1.85%
   c. 1850% d. 18500%
5. 30% of 90 is ______.
   a. 26 b. 27
   c. 28 d. 29

B. Fill in the blanks.

1. The fractional form of 12% is _______.
2. _______ is the percentage form of 0.8.
3. The decimal form of 9% is _________.
4. The percentage form of $\frac{4}{5}$ is _______.
5. 25% of 640 is __________.

C. Match the following.

1. 36%	a. 140%
2. 1.4	b. 0.65
3. 32% of 1100	c. 50%
4. $\frac{7}{14}$	d. 352
5. 65%	e. $\frac{9}{25}$

D. State whether the following are true (T) or false (F).

1. The percentage form of 2.3 is 230%.
2. The percentage form of $\frac{1}{4}$ is 50%.
3. The fractional form of 70% is $\frac{3}{4}$.
4. The decimal form of 37% is 0.37.
5. 13% of 456 is 59.28.

E. Solve the following.

1. 50% of 800
2. 55% of 140
3. 25% of 80
4. 84% of 900
5. 8% of 5402

F. Application-based questions.

1. In a scrapbook, there are 40 pictures. If 40% of these pictures are of dried leaves and the rest are pictures of flowers, how many pictures of flowers are there?
2. Out of 140 fishes in an aquarium, 84 are big fishes. Find the percentage of big fishes.
3. In a stadium, there are 80 children. 36 of them are undergoing cricket coaching. What percentage of children is undergoing cricket coaching?
4. Shri earns ₹60,800 a month. If she saves 25% of her income every month, how much will she save in a year?
5. Arun goes to a shop to buy a shirt. The price of the shirt, including GST of 15%, is ₹2345. What is the amount of GST?

Did You Master?

A. What does "%" represent?
1. per 10
2. per 50
3. per 1000
4. per 100

B. 0.05 is expressed as _______
1. 50%
2. 500%
3. 5%
4. 55%

C. $\frac{42}{30}$ is equal to _______
1. 42%
2. 140%
3. 30%
4. 160%

D. What is the decimal form of 83%?
1. 8.3
2. 0.083
3. 0.0083
4. 0.83

E. 22% of 350 = _______
1. 77
2. 68
3. 93
4. 86

F. Which of the following is greater?
1. 25% of 600
2. 50% of 500
3. 50% of 600
4. 75% of 200

G. Read the following statements and choose the correct alternative.
i. 87% of 500 is 435.
ii. 87% of 400 is 348.
1. Both i. and ii. are correct.
2. Both i. and ii. are wrong.
3. Only i. is correct.
4. Only ii. is correct.

H. In a school, there are 136 students out of which 25% are girls. How many girls are there in the school?
1. 45
2. 34
3. 24
4. 43

I. 45% of 500 mℓ of milk was used for making a milkshake. What is the amount of milk unused?
1. 150 mℓ
2. 240 mℓ
3. 190 mℓ
4. 275 mℓ

J. The price of a mobile phone is ₹15,600, excluding 28% GST. What is the amount of GST charged?
1. ₹908
2. ₹4368
3. ₹5678
4. ₹450

How many questions did you answer correctly? Score yourself.

easy ☐ average ☐ advanced ☐ remembering ☐ understanding ☐ applying ☐ analysing ☐ evaluating ☐ creating ☐

communication ☐ representation ☐ devising strategies ☐ mathematisation ☐ reasoning and argument ☐ using symbols ☐ using mathematical tools ☐ creativity ☐

8 Measurement

Curricular Goals

- Understand measurable attributes of objects and the units, systems and the processes of such measurement related to length, mass and capacity using standard units (CG-3)

Competencies

- Carry out simple unit conversions, such as from centimetres into metres, within a system of measurement (C-3.3)
- Evaluate the conservation of attributes like length and solve daily-life problems related to them (C-3.7)

Why This Topic?

Measurement is required in every aspect of our life. We use different measurement tools every day, without which we cannot live our normal daily lives.

To find the distance between 1st and 3rd tree

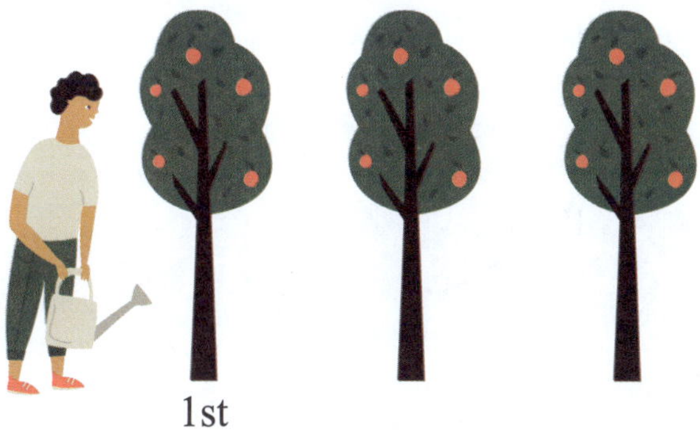

To measure the amount of cough syrup taken for required number of days

Can you think of other examples where we use measurements in day-to-day activities?

Are You Ready?

A. 1675 cm = _______ m _______ cm
1. 1 m 675 cm
2. 16 m 75 cm
3. 167 m 5 cm
4. 1675 m 50 cm

B. Express 5 kg 400 g in grams.
1. 5040 g
2. 5440 g
3. 5004 g
4. 5400 g

C. 65 litres = _______
1. 6000500 *mℓ*
2. 65000 *mℓ*
3. 6500 *mℓ*
4. 60500 *mℓ*

D. Which unit of measurement is commonly used to calculate the distance between two cities?
1. Litre
2. Metre
3. Kilogram
4. Kilometre

E. 4700 metres + 3 km = _______
1. 7.7 km
2. 770 km
3. 47.03 km
4. 473 km

F. 1234 mℓ + 1 *l* 767 *mℓ* = _______ ℓ _______ *mℓ*
1. 3 *l* 1 *mℓ*
2. 2 *l* 999 *mℓ*
3. 3 *l* 1001 *mℓ*
4. 3 *l* 4 *mℓ*

G. 165 kg + 1467 g = _______ kg _______ g
1. 1664670 g
2. 165 kg 467 g
3. 166 kg 467 g
4. 16 kg 6467 g

H. Kritika had a roll of rope which was 56 m long. She gave 750 cm of the rope to Milind. How much rope is left with Kritika?
1. 4850 cm
2. 4825 cm
3. 4800 cm
4. 4775 cm

I. In Ananya's stamp collection, the horse stamp is 7 cm long. The fish stamp is 5 cm longer than the horse stamp. What is the total length of both the stamps?
1. 12 cm
2. 12 m
3. 19 m
4. 19 cm

How many questions did you answer correctly? Score yourself.

easy ☐ average ☐ advanced ☐ remembering ☐ understanding ☐ applying ☐ analysing ☐ evaluating ☐ creating ☐

communication ☐ representation ☐ devising strategies ☐ mathematisation ☐ reasoning and argument ☐ using symbols ☐ using mathematical tools ☐ creativity ☐

MEASUREMENT OF LENGTH, MASS AND CAPACITY

a

We have learnt about measurement in previous classes. Let us learn more about the units used to measure them.

Measure	Common units
Length	mm, cm, m, km
Weight (mass)	mg, g, kg
Capacity	mℓ, ℓ

Relation Between Different Units

There are other units of metric measures to measure smaller lengths, masses and capacities. Larger units are used to measure larger lengths, masses and capacities. There is a definite relationship among the various units of metric measures.

Look at the place value table given below.

Thousands	Hundreds	Tens	Ones	Tenths	hundredths	thousandths
Kilometre (km)	hectometre (hm)	decametre (dam)	metre (m)	decimetre (dm)	centimetre (cm)	millimetre (mm)
1000	100	10	1	$\frac{1}{10}$	$\frac{1}{100}$	$\frac{1}{1000}$
Kilogram (kg)	hectogram (hg)	decagram (dag)	gram (g)	decigram (dg)	centigram (cg)	milligram (mg)
1000	100	10	1	$\frac{1}{10}$	$\frac{1}{100}$	$\frac{1}{1000}$
Kilolitre (kℓ)	hectolitre (hℓ)	decalitre (daℓ)	litre (ℓ)	decilitre (dℓ)	centilitre (cℓ)	millilitre (mℓ)
1000	100	10	1	$\frac{1}{10}$	$\frac{1}{100}$	$\frac{1}{1000}$

This chart will help you convert bigger units into smaller units and smaller units into bigger units.

- To change from bigger units to smaller units, **multiply**.
- To change from smaller units to bigger units, **divide**.

We use **decimals** to express measurements of length, mass and capacity in higher units.

For example, Shreya's father travels a distance of 6 km 700 m from his office to home.

6 km 700 m is same as 6700 m (6 × 1000 m + 700 m).

Using decimals, 6 km 700 m can be written as 6.700 km.

6 km 700 m = 6.700 km

CONVERSION OF UNITS OF MEASUREMENT

Example 1: The length of the cloth required to stitch the school uniform is 3.75 metres. How much cloth is required in centimetres?

Solution:

Length of the cloth required = 3.75 m

We know that the conversion factor for 1 m = 100 cm

Length of the cloth = 3.75 m × 100 cm = 375 cm

Therefore, the length of cloth required to stitch the uniform is 375 cm.

Example 2: Convert 313 km 56 m into kilometres.

Solution: we know that 1000 m = 1 km

$$313 \text{ km } 56 \text{ m} = 313 + \frac{56}{1000} = 313.056 \text{ km}$$

Example 3: Convert 832 mg into grams.

Solution: We know that 1000 mg = 1 g.

$$832 \text{ mg} = \frac{832}{1000} \text{ g} = 0.832 \text{ g}$$

Example 4: A school bag weighs 5.25 kilograms. How much does it weigh in grams?

Solution: Weight of the school bag = 5.25 kg

We know that 1 kilogram = 1000 grams

Therefore, weight of the school bag in grams

= 5.25 kg × 1000 g = 5250 g

Therefore, the weight of the school bag is 5250 grams.

Example 5: The capacity of a small water tank is 68565 mℓ. What is the capacity in litres?

Solution: Capacity of the tank = 68,565 mℓ

We know that 1000 *mℓ* = 1 litre

Capacity (in litres) = 68565 *mℓ* ÷ 1000 mℓ

= 68.565 litres

Hence, the capacity of the tank is 68.565 litres.

Exercise 8.1

1. Convert the following measurements.

a. 0.285 ℓ = _____ mℓ   b. 2.75 ℓ = _____ mℓ   c. 0.085 km = _____ m

d. 0.706 kg = _____ g   e. 1.54 m = _____ cm   f. 3.825 kg = _____ g

2. Find the equivalent measures.

a. 20.08 km = _____ km _____ m   b. 16.5 ℓ = _____ ℓ _____ mℓ

c. 2.08 kg = _____ kg _____ g   d. 40.006 ℓ = _____ ℓ _____ mℓ

e. 56.075 km = _____ km _____ m   f. 64.10 cm = _____ cm _____ mm

3. Find the equivalent measures. Express each answer as a decimal.

a. 670 mℓ = _____ ℓ   b. 105 m = _____ km   c. 69 g = _____ kg

d. 2870 g = _____ kg   e. 3500 mℓ = _____ ℓ   f. 4060 m = _____ km

4. Complete the table.

Measurement	In bigger unit	In smaller unit
5 m 40 cm	5.40 m	540 cm
		427 cm
	16.05 m	
5 kg 350 g		
	7.35 kg	
		2595 g
1 ℓ 770 mℓ		
		2725 mℓ
	7.45ℓ	

OPERATION ON MEASUREMENTS

We can perform different operations (+, –, ×, ÷) on the same units. To do this, first convert them into the same units before performing any operation on them.

Addition and Subtraction of Length, Mass and Capacity

Example 6: Add: 54 m and 25 m 7 cm.

Solution: 54 m + 25 m 7 cm = ?

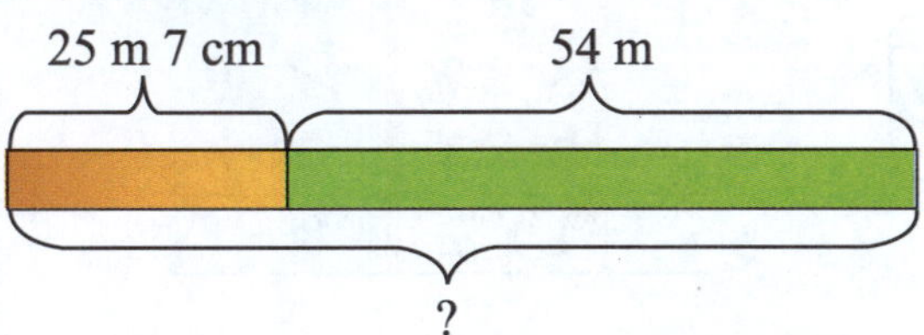

	m	cm
	54	0
+	25	7
	79	7

Therefore, the sum of 54 m and 25 m 7 cm is equal to 79 m 7 cm.

Example 7: Add: 3 kg 425 g + 35 kg 5 g + 192 kg + 23 kg 55 g (Express your answer in kg.)

Solution: The given weight measures can be shown as:

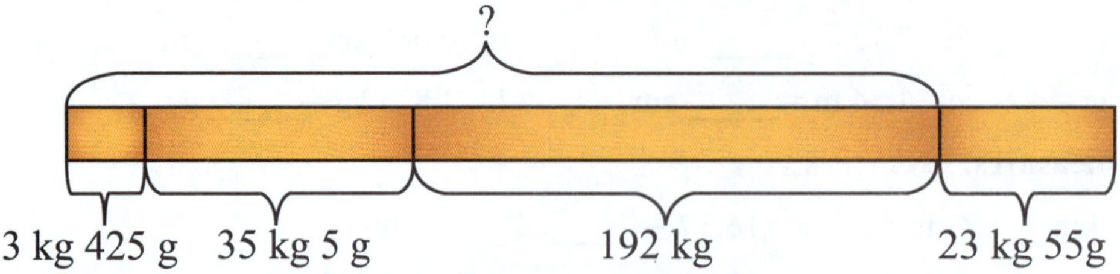

Convert all the measurements into the same units.

3 kg 425 g = 3.425 kg

35 kg 5 g = 35.005 kg

192 kg = 192.000 kg

23 kg 55g = 23.055 g

3 kg 425 g + 35 kg 5 g + 192 kg + 23 kg 55g = 253.485 kg

	Kg
	3.425
	35.005
	192.000
+	23.055
	253.485

Therefore, the sum of 3 kg 425 g + 35 kg 5 g + 192 kg + 23 kg 55g is 253.485 kg.

Example 8: Find the sum: 9 *ℓ* 650 *mℓ* and 15 *ℓ* 375 *mℓ*

Solution: Consider the two containers with given measurements.

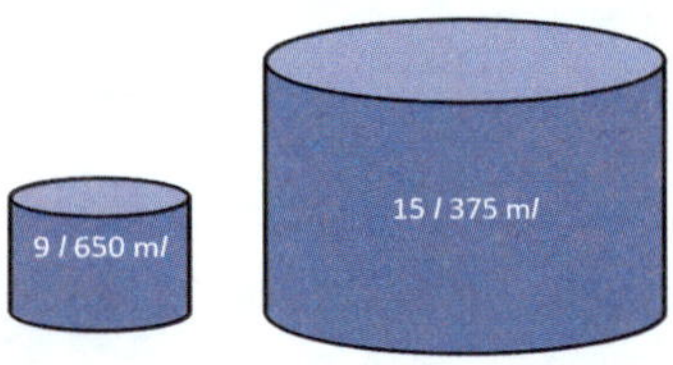

	l	*ml*
	[1][1]9	[1]650
+	15	375
	25	025

9 *ℓ* 650 *mℓ* + 15 *ℓ* 375 *mℓ*

= 9000 *mℓ* + 650 *mℓ* + 15,000 *mℓ* + 375 *mℓ*

= 9650 *mℓ* + 15,375 *mℓ*

= 25,025 *mℓ* = 25 *ℓ* 25 *mℓ*

Therefore, 9 *ℓ* 650 *mℓ* + 15 *ℓ* 375 *mℓ* is 25 *ℓ* 25 *mℓ*.

Example 9: Find the difference: 37 m 59 cm and 24 m 78 cm.

Solution: 37 m 59 cm – 24 m 78 cm = ?

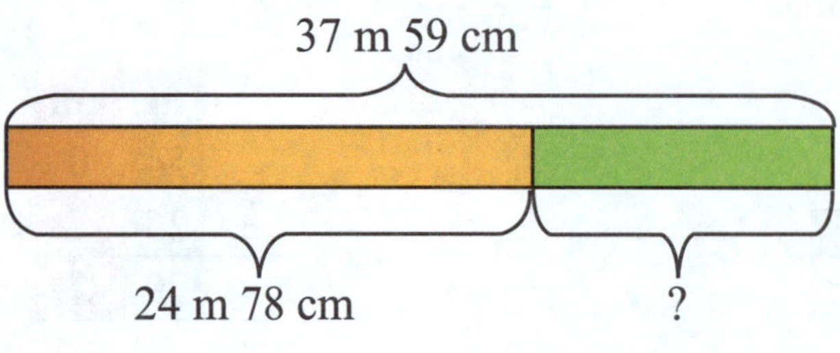

	m			**cm**	
	3	[6]~~7~~	.	[15]~~5~~	9
–	2	4	.	7	8
	1	2	.	8	1

Therefore, 37 m 59 cm – 24 m 78 cm = 12 m 81 cm.

Example 10: Find the difference: 70 kg 90 g and 50 kg 760 g

Solution: 70 kg 90 g – 50 kg 760 g = ?

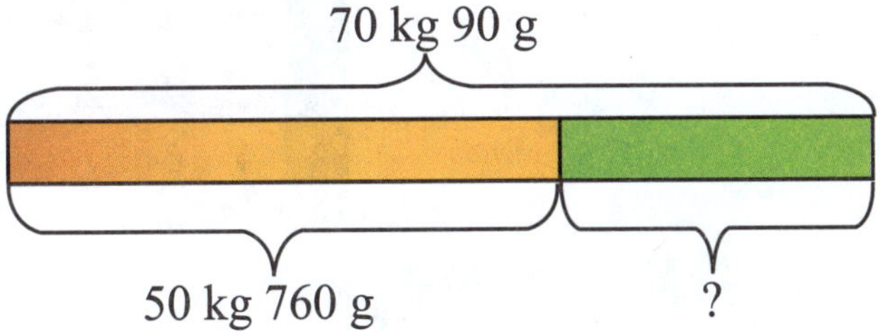

	kg		.	g		
	6 ~~7~~	9 ~~10~~ ~~0~~	.	10 ~~0~~	9	0
–	5	0	.	7	6	0
	1	9	.	3	3	0

Therefore, 70 kg 90 g – 50 kg 760 g is 19 kg 330 g.

Example 11: Find the difference: 4 ℓ 920 *m*ℓ and 450 *m*ℓ.

Solution: 4 ℓ 920 *m*ℓ – 450 *m*ℓ = ?

	ℓ	.	*m*ℓ		
	4	.	8 ~~9~~	12 ~~2~~	0
–	0	.	4	5	0
	4	.	4	7	0

Therefore, 4 ℓ 920 *m*ℓ – 450 *m*ℓ = 4 ℓ 470 *m*ℓ.

Multiplication of Length, Mass and Capacity

Example 12: Multiply 26 m 14 cm by 18.

Solution: 26 m 14 cm × 18 = ?

26 m × 100 cm + 14 cm

= 2600 cm + 14 cm

= 2614 cm

	2	6	1	4
		×	1	8
2	0	9	1	2
2	6	1	4	0
4	7	0	5	2

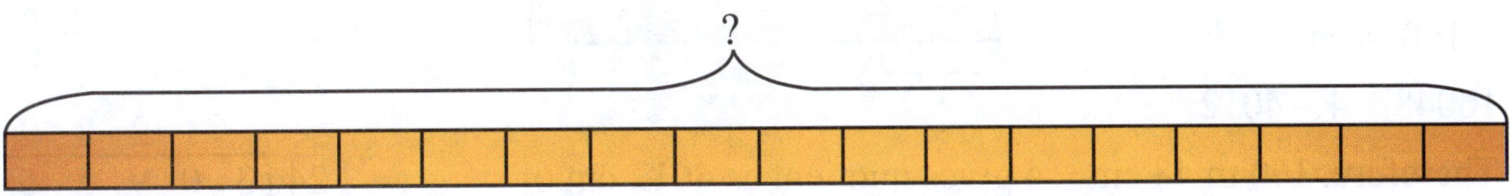

Multiplying 2614 cm by 18, we get 47052 cm.

Adding the decimal point (.) after two numbers from the right, we get 470.52.

Therefore, 26 m 14 cm × 18 is 470 m 52 cm or 470.52 m.

Example 13: Multiply 122 kg 250 g by 12.

Solution: 122 kg 250 g × 12

= (122 × 1000 g + 250 g) × 12

= (1,22,000 g + 250 g) × 12

= 1,22,250 g × 12

= 14,67,000 g

	1	2	2	2	5
			×	1	2
	2	4	4	5	0
1	2	2	2	5	0
1	4	6	7	0	0

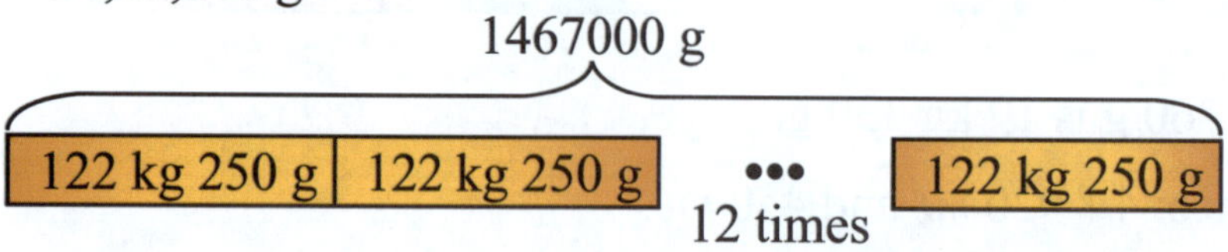

Adding three decimal points, we get 1467.000 kg or 1467 kg.

Therefore, 122 kg 250 g × 12 = 1467 kg.

Example 14: Multiply 7512 mℓ by 64.

Solution: 7512 × 64 = ?

		7	5	1	2
			×	6	4
	3	0	0	4	8
4	5	0	7	2	0
4	8	0	7	6	8

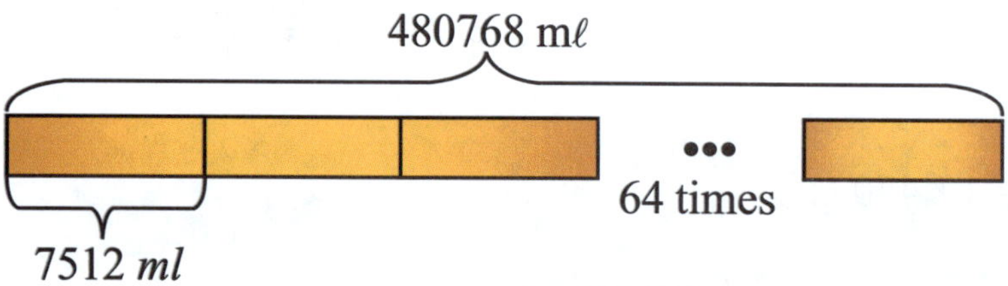

Therefore, 7512 *mℓ* × 64 = 4,80,768 *mℓ*.

Division of Length, Mass and Capacity

Example 15: Divide 160 m 48 cm by 4.

Solution: 160 m 48 cm ÷ 4

= (160 × 100) cm + 48 cm

= 16000 cm + 48 cm

= 16048 cm

16048 ÷ 4 = 4012

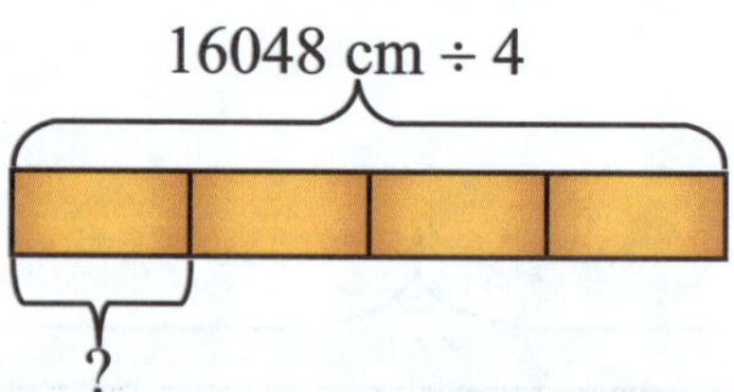


```
      4 0 1 2
4 | 1 6 0 4 8
  − 1 6
      0 0
    − 0
      0 4
      − 4
        0 8
        − 8
          0
```

Therefore, 160 m 48 cm ÷ 4 gives quotient as 4012 cm or 40.12 m.

Example 16: Divide 30 kg 936 g by 24.

Solution: 30 kg 936 g ÷ 24 = ?

(30 × 1000) kg + 936 g

= 30000 g + 936 g = 30936 g

```
         1 2 8 9
24 | 3 0 9 3 6
   − 2 4
       6 9
     − 4 8
       2 1 3
     − 1 9 2
         2 1 6
       − 2 1 6
             0
```

Now, 30936 g ÷ 24 = 1289 g

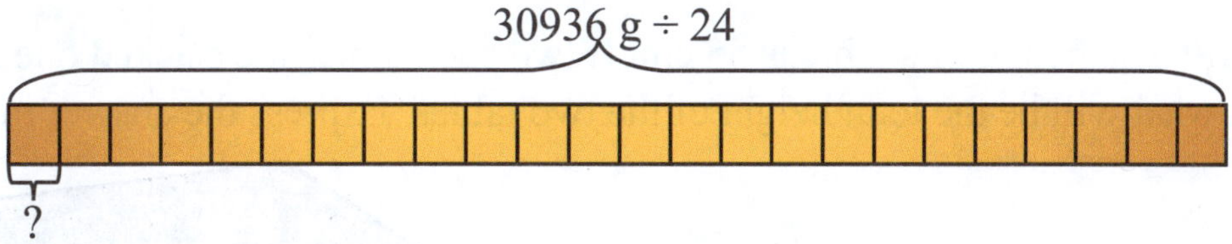

Therefore, 30936 g ÷ 24 gives quotient as 1289 g or 1 kg 289 g.

Example 17: Divide 14 *ℓ* 500 *mℓ* by 5.

Solution: 14 *ℓ* 500 *mℓ* ÷ 5 = ?

= 14 × 1000 *mℓ* + 500 *mℓ*

= 14000 *mℓ* + 500 *mℓ*

= 14500 *mℓ*

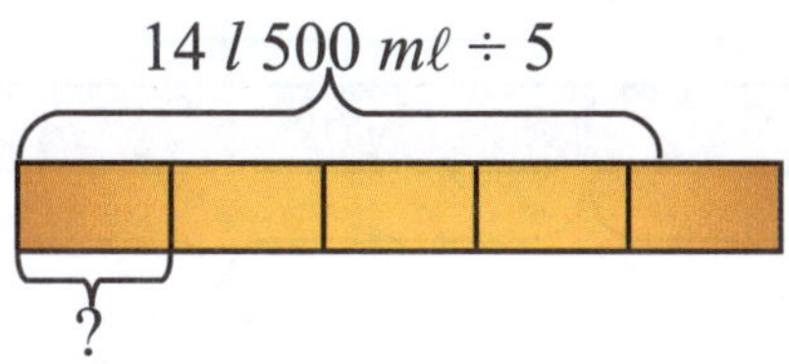


```
      2 9 0 0
5 ) 1 4 5 0 0
  − 1 0
      4 5
    − 4 5
        0 0
      −   0
          0 0
        −   0
            0
```

Now, 14500 *mℓ* ÷ 5 = ?

Therefore, 14 *ℓ* 500 *mℓ* ÷ 5 gives quotient as 2900 *mℓ* or 2 *ℓ* 900 *mℓ*.

Exercise 8.2

1. Add the following.

a. 456 m + 1674 cm
b. 876 cm + 12 m 77 cm
c. 254 *l* + 5676 *ml*
d. 12.768 *l* + 364 *ml*
e. 1234 g + 43 kg 21 g
f. 214 km 624 m + 73 km 82 m

2. Subtract the following.

a. 6 m – 3m 24 cm
b. 86.46 m − 6.35 m
c. 40000 g – 26 kg 750 g
d. 87667 *ml* – 52447 *ml*
e. 14 kg – 878 g
f. 825 kg –216 kg 750 g

3. Multiply the following.

a. 230 m 73 cm × 33
b. 25 kg 25 g × 5
c. 745 cm × 256
d. 123 *l* 25 *ml* × 14
e. 12678 *ml* × 12
f. 97.354 *l* × 17

4. Divide the following.

a. 625 m 75 cm ÷ 25
b. 5416 kg 416 g ÷ 16
c. 20 *l* 90 *ml* ÷ 3
d. 45.450 *l* ÷ 15
e. 8652 cm ÷ 12
f. 98 *l* ÷ 16

WORD PROBLEMS

Example 18: The height of a table is 55 cm. If two such tables are stacked one above the other, then what will be the total height of the two tables. Express the answer in metres.

Solution:

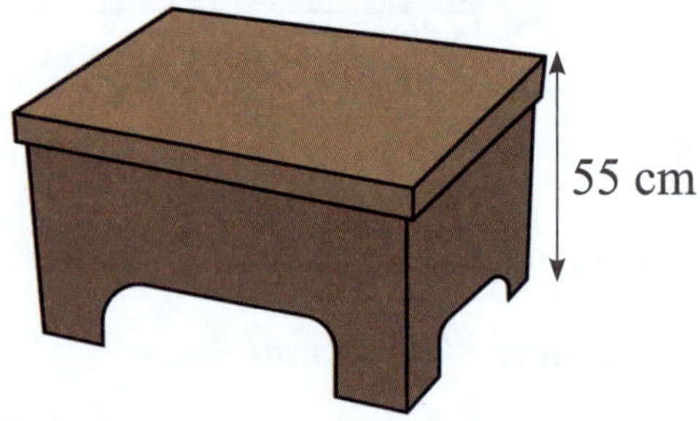

Height of one table = 55 cm

Height of two tables = 55 cm + 55 cm

= 110 cm

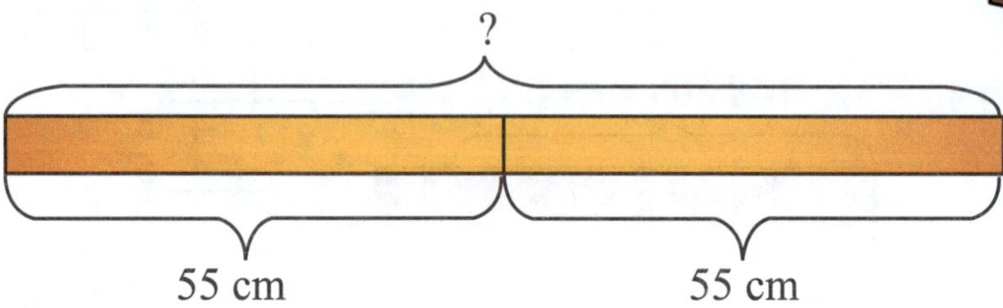

Therefore, the height of the two tables is 1.10 m.

Example 19: The mass of a bag of oranges is 1600 g. The mass of a bag of lemons is 850 g. What is the total mass of the bag of oranges and lemons. Express your answers in kilograms.

Solution:

1600 g

850 g

	[1]1	6	0	0
+		8	5	0
	2	4	5	0

Bag of oranges = 1600 g

Bag of lemons = 850 g

Total mass = 1600 g + 850 g

= 2450 g

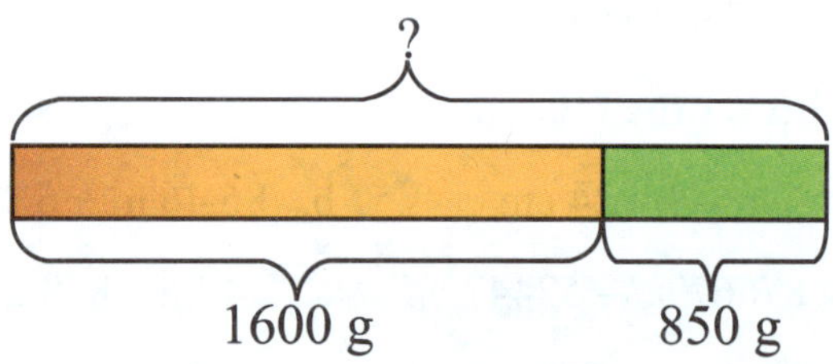

Therefore, the total mass of the bag of oranges and lemons is 2450 g or 2.45 kg.

Example 20: There are two cylinders filled with different amounts of water. Calculate the total water in the two cylinders.

Solution:

Water in the first cylinder = 250 *ml*

Water in the second cylinder = 350 *ml*

Total water = 250 *ml* + 350 *ml*

= 600 *ml* or 0.6 *l*

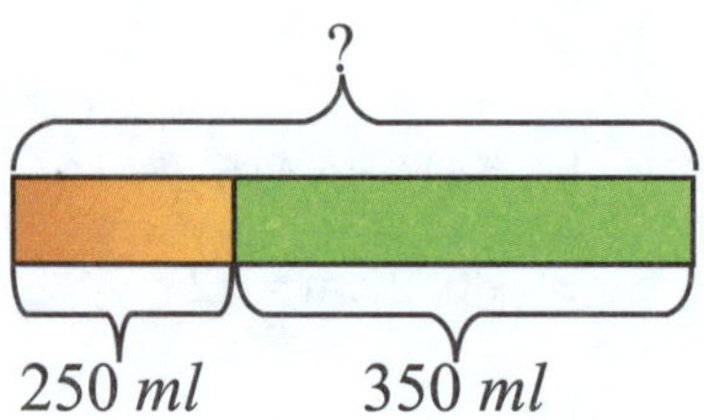

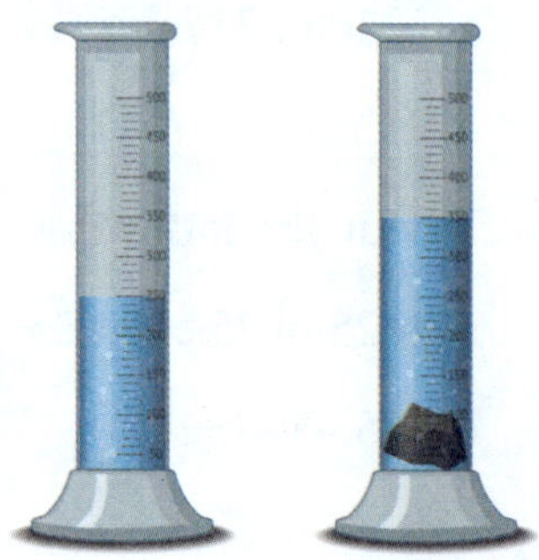

Therefore, the total quantity of water in the two cylinders is 600 *ml* or 0.6 *l*.

	[1]2	5	0
+	3	5	0
	6	0	0

Example 21: The length of Pole A is 438.8 m and the length of Pole B is 367.5 m. By how many metres is Pole B shorter than Pole A?

Solution: Length of Pole A = 438.8 m

Length of Pole B = 367.5 m

Now, 438.8 – 367.5

(since B is shorter than A)

Therefore, Pole B is shorter by 71.3 m as compared to Pole A.

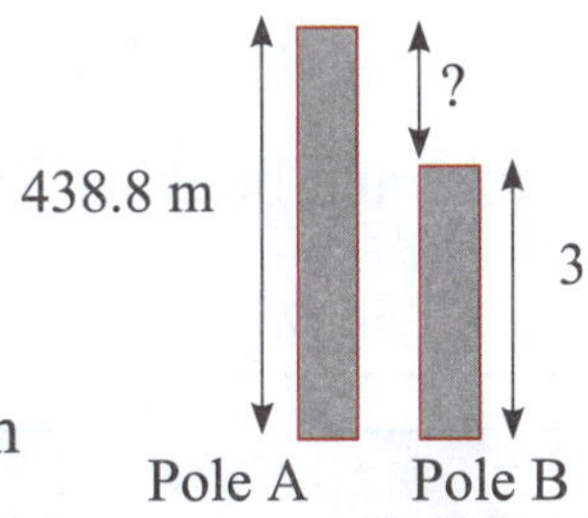

	$\overset{3}{\cancel{4}}$	$\overset{13}{\cancel{3}}$	8	.	8
–	3	6	7	.	5
	0	7	1	.	3

Example 22: A storage jar can hold 1000 grams of sugar, and 287 grams of sugar is already in it. How many grams of sugar should you add to fill the container?

Solution: Capacity of the jar = 1000 g

Sugar already in the jar = 287 grams

Sugar that can be added

= 1000 g – 287 g

= 713 g

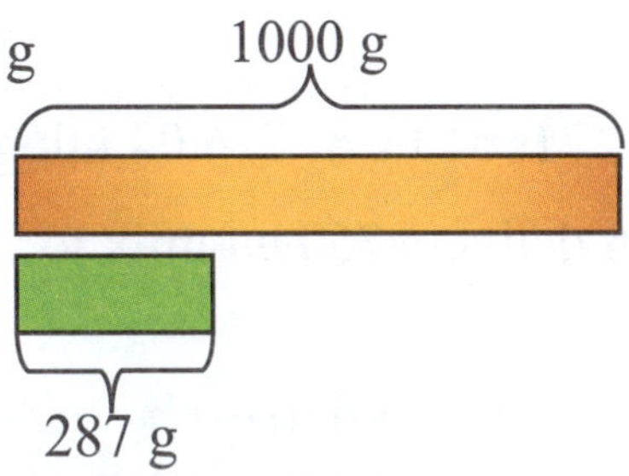

	$\overset{0}{\cancel{1}}$	$\overset{9}{\cancel{10}}$	$\overset{9}{\cancel{10}}$	$\overset{10}{\cancel{0}}$
–	0	2	8	7
	0	7	1	3

Therefore, 713 grams of sugar must be added to fill the container.

Example 23: Mridula needed water for her home, and she ordered a water tanker of 6000 litres capacity. Her overhead water storage tank has a capacity of 4725 litres. How much water is remaining in the water tanker?

Solution: Water in the tanker = 6000 ℓ

Capacity of the overhead tank = 4725 ℓ

Remaining water

= 6000 ℓ – 4725 ℓ = 1275 ℓ

Therefore, the water remaining in the water tanker is 1275 ℓ.

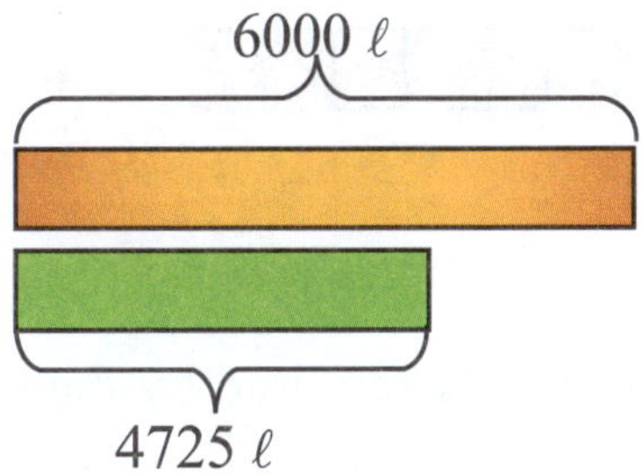

	$\overset{5}{\cancel{6}}$	$\overset{9}{\cancel{10}}$	$\overset{9}{\cancel{10}}$	$\overset{10}{\cancel{0}}$
–	4	7	2	5
	1	2	7	5

Example 24: A chair made of plastic weighs 2.45 kilograms. How much will 67 such chairs weigh in total?

Solution: Weight of one chair = 2.45 kg

Weight of 67 such chairs = 2.45 kg × 67 = 164.15 kg

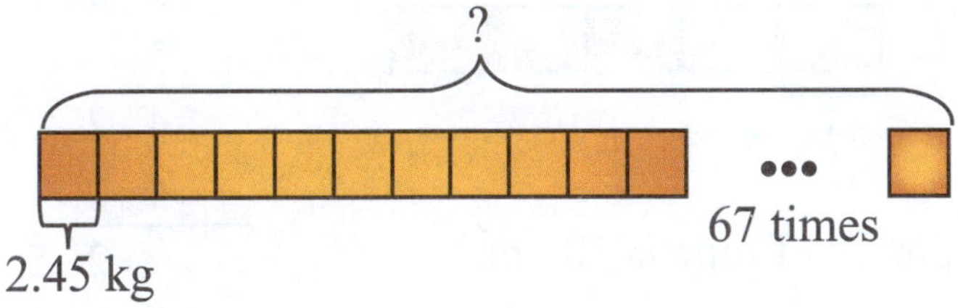

		2	4	5
		×	6	7
	1	7	1	5
1	4	7	0	0
1	6	4	1	5

Therefore, the total weight of 67 chairs is 164.15 kg.

Example 25: The weight of a pencil box and a book put together is 780 g.

There are 918 such pencil boxes and books. What is the total weight?

Solution: Weight of one pencil box and one book together = 780 g

Weight of 918 sets of pencil boxes and books = 780 g × 918 = 716040 g

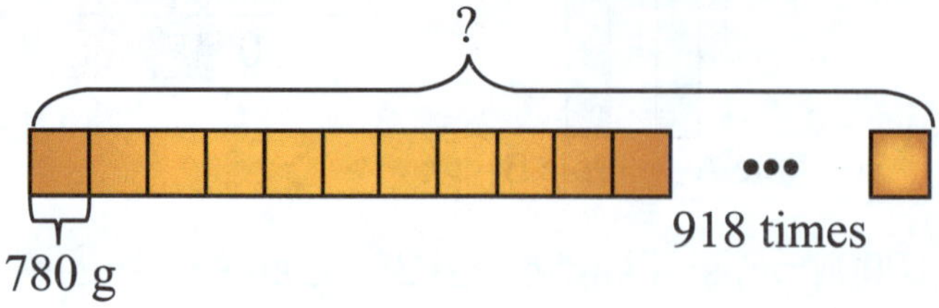

			7	8	0
		×	9	1	8
		6	2	4	0
		7	8	0	0
7	0	2	0	0	0
7	1	6	0	4	0

Therefore, total weight is 716040 g or 716.04 kilograms.

Example 26: A milkman delivers 750 *ml* milk to 76 houses every day. How much milk does he need every day?

Solution: Quantity of milk delivered to each house = 750 *ml*

Number of houses = 76

Milk required for 76 houses = 750 *ml* × 76 = 57,000 *ml* or 57 *l*

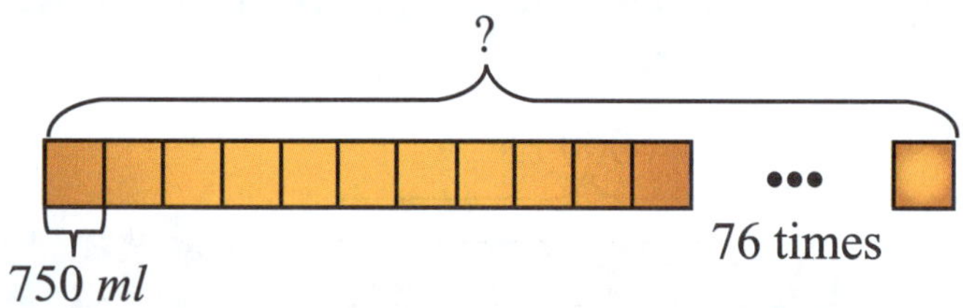

		7	5	0
		×	7	6
	4	5	0	0
5	2	5	0	0
5	7	0	0	0

Therefore, the amount of milk required by the milkman is 57000 m*l* or 57 litres.

Example 27: A rope of length 925 m is cut into five equal pieces. What is the length of each piece of rope?

Solution: Length of the rope = 925 m

Number of equal pieces = 5

Length of each piece of rope

= 925 m ÷ 5

= 185 m

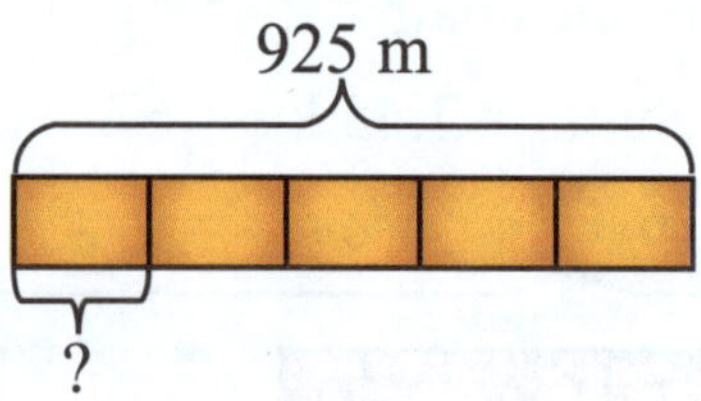

$$
\begin{array}{r}
185 \\
5\overline{)925} \\
-5 \\
\hline
42 \\
-40 \\
\hline
25 \\
-25 \\
\hline
0
\end{array}
$$

Therefore, the length of each of the five pieces of rope is 185 m.

Example 28: A total of 3256 litres of petrol is to be distributed equally among the eight battle tanks. How many litres of petrol will each battle tank get?

Solution: Petrol available = 3256 ℓ

Number of battle tanks = 8

Petrol for each battle tank = 3256 ℓ ÷ 8 = 407 ℓ

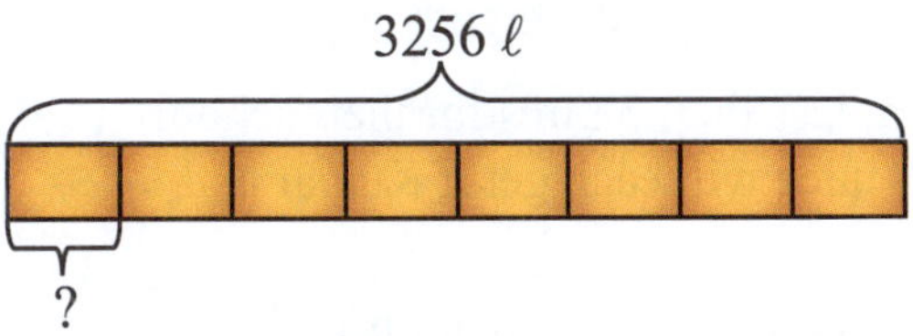


```
      4 0 7
  8 )3 2 5 6
   - 3 2
       0 5
     -   0
         5 6
       - 5 6
           0
```

Therefore, each battle tank will get 407 litres of petrol.

Mental Maths

1. If a pen is 12 cm in length and another pen is 8 cm in length, what is their total length in centimetres?
2. A pumpkin weighs 4 kilograms and a watermelon weighs 2.250 kilograms. What is the total weight in kilograms and grams?
3. A rope is 8 metres long. If you cut off 2.5 metres from the rope, how much rope is left?

ESTIMATING MEASURES

In real life, measures are usually estimated. To estimate measures, we must know the real measures of objects in our surroundings.

To estimate any measure, compare with a known measure.

Look at the following examples.

The thickness of a pencil lead: about 1 mm

The length of an ant: about 1 cm

The weight of a feather: about 1 mg

The weight of a cake: about 1 kg

Exercise 8.3

1. Solve the following word problems.

a. Navneeta bought 7 m 30 cm white ribbon, 3 m 45 cm red ribbon and 24 m 87 cm green ribbon. Find the total length of the ribbons together.

b. Kriti weighs 67.43 kg and Lalit weighs 87.545 kg. What is their total weight?

c. Kumar and Shravya made mango juice which was 23 ml less than 7 litres for their school friends. There are 32 students in their class. How much juice will each get if Kumar and Shravya give each of them equal quantity of juice.

d. The total weight of a box of cereal is 746 g. What is the weight of the cereal inside if the weight of the packaging is 39 g?

e. A boy is filling a bucket with water using a mug. The boy carries 900 mℓ of water each time. The bucket gets filled on the 81st mug. How much water is in the bucket?

2. Choose the most appropriate option for the descriptions shown below.

		i	ii	iii
a.	 The length of a book	25 m	25 cm	25 km
b.	 The length of a pair of spectacles	10 cm	10 m	100 cm
c.	 The weight of a bunch of keys	100 kg	100 g	1 kg
d.	 The capacity of a water bottle	1000 litres	100 *ml*	1000 *ml*
e.	 The weight of a motorcycle	100 kg	100 g	1 kg

Concept Map

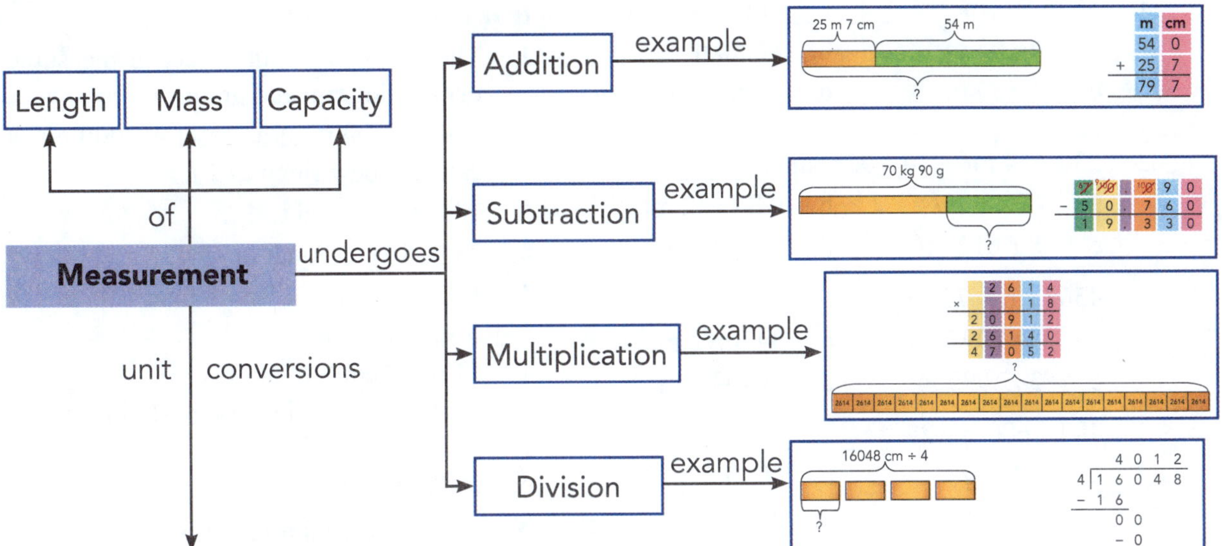

Length	Weight	Capacity
1 km = 1000 m	1 kg = 1000 g	1 ℓ = 1000 mℓ
1 m = 100 cm	1 g = 1000 mg	

Project

Desks in Line!

Observe the furniture in your classroom. Are all the student desks the same kind and of the same measure?

- Measure the length of each desk
- Measure the width of each desk

Now, if you placed all the desks (same kind and of the same measure) in a single line along the width, what will be the length of the line of desks?

Similarly, if you placed all the desks (same kind and of the same measure) in a single line along the length, what will be the length of the line of desks?

How many desks will fit in the corridor of your school: along the width or along the length?

Revision Exercise

A. Choose the correct option.

1. 86 m 50 cm = __________ m
   a. 86.05 m b. 86.50 m
   c. 50.85 m d. 86 m
2. 23 ℓ 654 mℓ – 14 ℓ 958 mℓ = _______
   a. 80 ℓ 6 mℓ b. 0.8 ℓ 612 mℓ
   c. 8 ℓ 612 mℓ d. 8 ℓ 696 mℓ
3. 4567 cm × 76 = ________
   a. 34.7092 m b. 3470.92 m
   c. 347.092 m d. 34709.2 m
4. 48 kg 600 g ÷ 24 = _______
   a. 2005 g b. 2010 g
   c. 2025 g d. 2050 g
5. 14 cm + 24.56 m + 12 cm = _______
   a. 50.56 m b. 5056 cm
   c. 248.2 m d. 24.82 m

B. Fill in the blanks.

1. The sum of 4.5 kg and 3.2 kg is _____ kg.
2. If a box weighs 1.4 kg and another box weighs 700 g, their total weight in kilogram is _______ kg.
3. A 20-year-old weighs 84 kg. The total weight if 16 people with the same weight as the 20-year-old will be _____ kg.
4. If Kadam walks 2.6 km every day, he would have walked ____ km in a week.
5. If 158000 mℓ of drinking water is distributed equally among 632 people, each person will get _____ *l* of water.

C. Match the following. (Estimate the measures)

1.	Length of a log	a.	75 kg
2.	Capacity of an earthen pot	b.	10 *ml*
3.	Weight of a grown-up man	c.	50 g
4.	Weight of a computer mouse	d.	10 m
5.	Capacity of a syringe	e.	10 *l*

D. State whether the following are true (T) or false (F).

1. The capacity of an object is measured using kilogram and gram.
2. If the capacity of a vessel is 2000 *mℓ*, it can also be written as 2 *l*.
3. 100 cm is equal to 1 *l*.
4. 75.025 kg is equal to 75,025 g.
5. 150 cm is bigger length than 1.05 m.

E. Solve the following.

1. 72 m 87 cm + 68 m 99 cm
2. 4 kg 376 g + 18 kg 234 g + 11 kg 954 g
3. 326370 cm ÷ 258
4. 1578 kg × 74

F. Application-based questions.

1. A coffee shop gets 16 kg 250 g of coffee beans every month. How many kilos of coffee beans are required by them in a year?
2. Roads in a city are being asphalted. The total length of the road is 13650 m and the government is asphalting 8250 m road in the first phase. What is the remaining length of the road being left for asphalting?
3. The prime minister is visiting your city. The police are building a wall with wooden legs for security. The mass of each log is 12 kg 290 g. What is the total weight of the log if they are using 1765 logs.
4. There are 67 students and there is 916225 ml of water. How much water will each student get?
5. If 45 post graduate students are being given laptops each weighing 4.12 kg. What is the total mass of all the laptops?
6. There are 10 bags full of coins. Each bag contains 1000 coins. But there is one bag that has forged coins. Each real coin weighs 1g and each forged coin weighs 1.1 g. How will you find the bag of forged coins? You are allowed to weigh only once.

Did You Master?

A. 13 m 74 cm + 1234 cm = ______
1. 2608 m
2. 26 m 8 cm
3. 2 m 608 cm
4. 260 m 8 cm

B. 40750 *mℓ* – 15 ℓ = ______
1. 25750 *mℓ*
2. 257.50 *mℓ*
3. 2.5750 *mℓ*
4. 25.750 *mℓ*

C. 190 g × 49 = ______
1. 9.310 g
2. 9.310 kg
3. 9310 kg
4. 93.10 kg

D. 22865 cm ÷ 17 = ______
1. 1315 cm
2. 1325 cm
3. 1335 cm
4. 1345 cm

E. There are 2816 students and each student will be given 50 g of sweet after the Independence Day celebration. How much sweet is required in total?
1. 140800 kg
2. 140008 kg
3. 140.8 kg
4. 14.08 kg

F. What is the height of a stack of 23 books if each book in the stack is 7.5 cm in height?
1. 169.5 cm 2. 127.5 cm
3. 171.5 cm 4. 172.5 cm

G. 16 kg bags of rice were given to each of 145 families. What is the total amount of rice that was given altogether?
1. 2300 kg
2. 2310 kg
3. 2320 kg
4. 2330 kg

H. 15 bags of sugar of the same weight were delivered to a grocery shop and the total weight is 1136 kg 250 g. How much does each bag weigh?
1. 75 kg
2. 75.750 kg
3. 757.50 kg
4. 75.50 kg

I. A 15 ℓ oil can was purchased at the start of the month by a family. By the end of the month there was 2 ℓ 346 mℓ oil left in the can. How much oil did the family use in that month?
1. 12654 ℓ
2. 126.45 ℓ
3. 12654 *mℓ*
4. 12.654 *mℓ*

J. What would be the estimated weight of the feather?
1. 500 g
2. 50 g
3. 5 g
4. 5 kg

How many questions did you answer correctly? Score yourself.

easy ☐ average ☐ advanced ☐ remembering ☐ understanding ☐ applying ☐ analysing ☐ evaluating ☐ creating ☐

communication ☐ representation ☐ devising strategies ☐ mathematisation ☐ reasoning and argument ☐ using symbols ☐ using mathematical tools ☐ creativity ☐

9 Time and Temperature

Curricular Goals

- Understand measurable attributes of objects and the units, systems and processes of measurement of time (CG-3)

Competencies

- Uses an appropriate unit and tool for the attribute being measured (C-3.2)
- Carry out simple unit conversions within a system of measurement (C-3.3)

Why This Topic?

Both time and temperature are important aspects of our lives. Their knowledge is useful for most of our everyday tasks, such as planning schedules and travel, meeting deadlines at school or at office, calculating time duration, etc.

School timetable

Tracking timetable helps in managing time; whether it is getting to school on time or arranging the bag according to the class schedule, study time, TV time, and sleep, etc.

Temperature of a human body

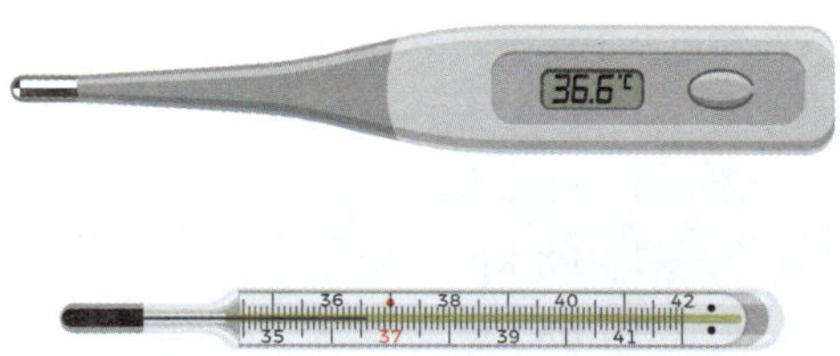

How do you know when you have a fever?
What is the instrument used to measure the temperature of your body?

Can you think of two more examples from your daily life where the concepts of time and temperature are used?

Are You Ready?

A. A digital watch is showing the time as 1845. What time is it in a 12-hour system?

1. 5:45 a.m.
2. 5:45 p.m.
3. 6:45 a.m.
4. 6:45 p.m.

B. What is 10:22 p.m. in a 24-hour system?

1. 2122
2. 2222
3. 2322
4. 2022

C. 7 hours 30 min = ______ min

1. 420   2. 430
3. 440   4. 450

D. ______ quarter hours = 45 minutes

1. 4   2. 3
3. 2   4. 1

E. 333 minutes = ______ hours ______ minutes

1. 5 hours 33 minutes
2. 5 hours 30 minutes
3. 6 hours 33 minutes
4. 6 hours 30 minutes

F. 6 minutes and 58 seconds + 6 seconds = ______

1. 6 minutes 4 seconds
2. 7 minutes
3. 7 minutes 4 seconds
4. 7 minutes 12 seconds

G. How much time has elapsed?

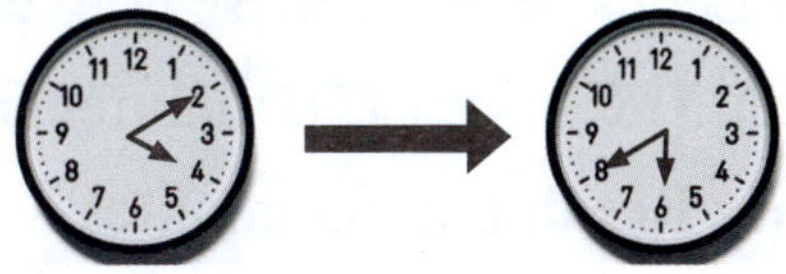

Start time   End time

1. 2 hours 10 minutes
2. 2 hours 20 minutes
3. 2 hours 30 minutes
4. 2 hours 40 minutes

H. Science exhibition at a school started at 10:15 a.m. and ended at 3:20 p.m. How long was the exhibition for?

1. 5 hours 15 minutes
2. 5 hours 10 minutes
3. 5 hours 5 minutes
4. 5 hours

I. Karan had Diwali holidays from 25th October to 29th October. How many days were his Diwali holidays?

1. 5 days
2. 6 days
3. 7 days
4. 4 days

J. Jessy started working on her home assignments at 6:15 p.m. and completed them at 9:00 p.m. How much time did she take to complete her assignments?

1. 1 hour 45 minutes
2. 2 hours 15 minutes
3. 2 hours 30 minutes
4. 2 hours 45 minutes

How many questions did you answer correctly? Score yourself.

easy ☐ average ☐ advanced ☐ remembering ☐ understanding ☐ applying ☐ analysing ☐ evaluating ☐ creating ☐

communication ☐ representation ☐ devising strategies ☐ mathematisation ☐ reasoning and argument ☐ using symbols ☐ using mathematical tools ☐ creativity ☐

CONVERSION OF UNITS OF TIME

Conversion of different units of time helps in comparing and expressing time duration clearly. Let us see how these conversions are done.

Example 1: Convert 150 minutes into hours.

Solution: Recall that 60 minutes = 1 hour.

So, divide 150 by 60 to get 2 as the quotient and 30 as the remainder.

Since, 30 minutes = half hour.

Therefore, 150 minutes = 2.5 hours or two and a half hours or two hours thirty minutes.

Example 2: Convert 3840 hours into days.

Solution: Recall that 24 hours = 1 day.

So, divide 3840 by 24 to get 160 as the quotient and no remainder.

Therefore, 3840 hours is equal to 160 days.

Example 3: Convert 6 days into hours.

Solution: Since, 1 day = 24 hours, 6 days = 6 × 24 hours = 144 hours.

Therefore, 6 days is 144 hours.

Example 4: Convert 6 days into minutes.

Solution: 1 day = 24 hours × 60 minutes = 1440 minutes

So, 6 days = 6 × 1440 minutes = 8640 minutes.

Therefore, 6 days is 8640 minutes.

ADDITION AND SUBTRACTION OF TIME

Time can be added and subtracted just like any other number with a few rules applied. Let us understand these rules with the help of a few examples.

Example 5: Harshita is flying from Bengaluru to Delhi via Mumbai. Her first flight from Bengaluru to Mumbai is for 1 hour 20 minutes and her second flight from Mumbai to Delhi is for 2 hours 35 minutes. How long will it take her to reach Delhi?

Solution: First flight from Bengaluru to Mumbai = 1 h 20 min

Second flight from Mumbai to Delhi = 2 h 35 min

Total time taken = 1 h 20 min + 2 h 35 min = 3 h 55 min

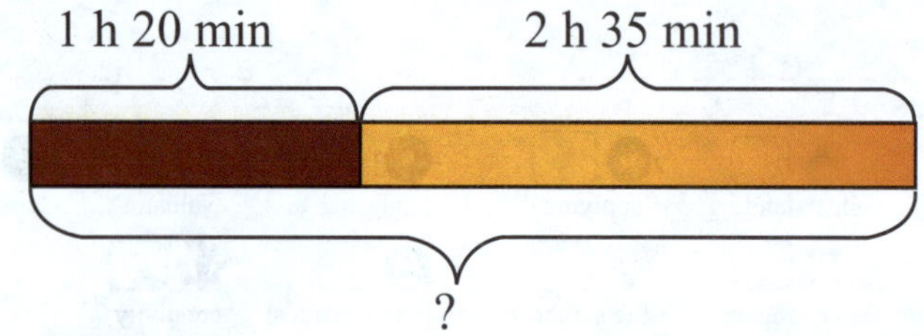

	h	min
	1	20
+	2	35
	3	55

Therefore, it will take 3 hours 55 mins for Harshita to reach Delhi via Mumbai.

Example 6: Shreeja and Shailesh took 1 h 30 min to cook food and 45 min to clean the kitchen. What is the total time taken to complete both the activities?

Solution:

Time taken for cooking = 1 h 30 min

Time taken for cleaning = 45 min

Total time taken = 1 h 30 min + 45 min

= 1 h 75 min

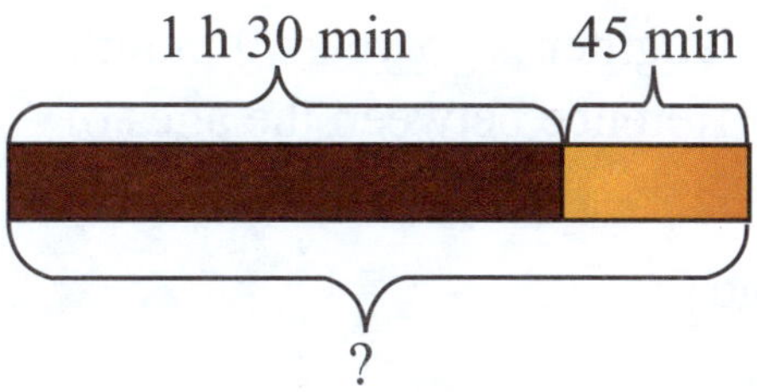

	h	min
	1	30
+		45
	2	75

75 min → 60 min, 15 min

60 min = 1 hour

+ 1 hour

Now, 75 min = 60 min + 15 min = 1 h 15 min.

Therefore, 1 h 75 min = 1 h + 1 h 15 min = 2 h 15 min.

So, Shreeja and Shailesh took 2 h 15 min to complete both the activities.

Example 7: Saavan and Seema decided to paint both the sides of their compound wall. Saavan took 4 hours 50 minutes to complete painting on one side. Seema took 3 hours 20 minutes to paint the other side. How much less time did Seema take to paint?

Solution: Time taken by Saavan = 4 h 50 min

Time taken by Seema = 3 h 20 min

Difference in time = 4 h 50 min – 3 h 20 min = 1 h 30 min

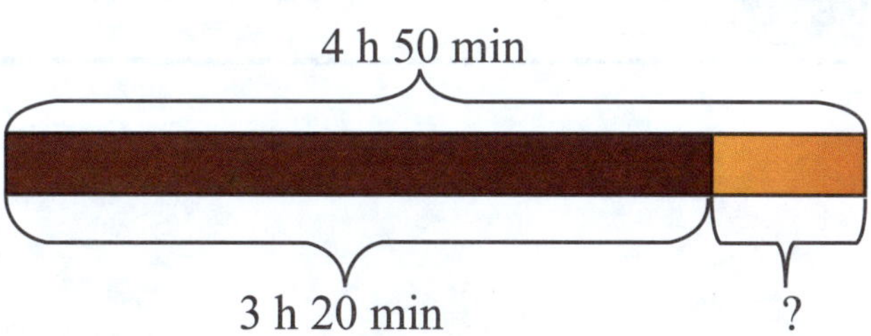

	h	min
	4	50
–	3	20
	1	30

Therefore, Seema took 1 hour 30 minutes lesser than Saavan to paint one side of the compound wall.

Example 8: Sudhir and Sumit ran a city marathon on World Environment Day. Sudhir clocked a time of 5 hours 30 minutes and Sumit clocked a time of 4 hours 45 minutes. What is the difference in their time?

Solution: Sudhir's time = 5 hours 30 minutes

Sumit's time = 4 hours 45 minutes

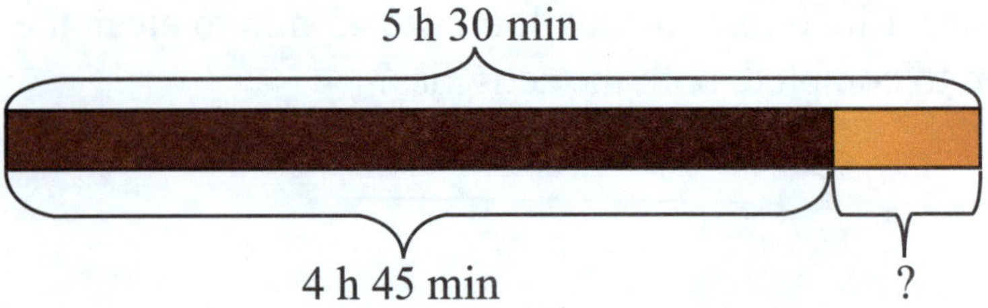

	h	min
	~~5~~ 4	30 + 60 = 90 ~~30~~
–	4	45
	0	45

Difference in time = 4 hours 90 minutes – 4 hour 45 minutes = 45 minutes

Therefore, the difference in their time is 45 minutes.

Example 9: Mr. and Mrs. Prakash have two kids. Their daughter is 15 years 9 months old and their son is 12 years 7 months old. What is the difference between the ages of the two kids?

Solution: Difference in age = Daughter's age – Son's age

= 15 years 9 months – 12 years 7 months = 3 years 2 months

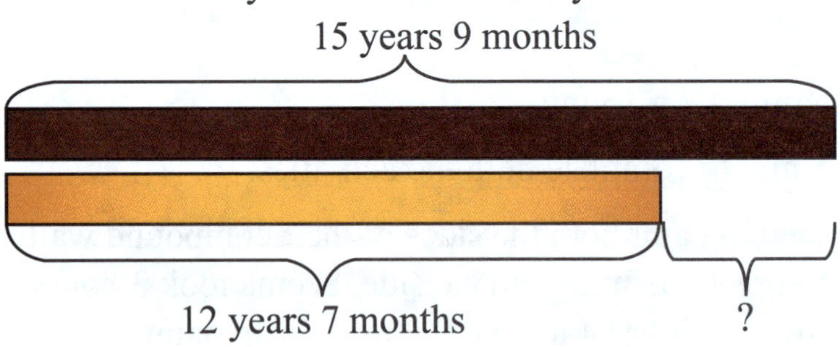

	Years	Months
	15	9
–	12	7
	3	2

Therefore, the difference between their ages is 3 years 2 months.

Exercise 9.1

1. Answer the following.

a. How many minutes is 7.5 hours?

b. How many hours is 3.5 days?

c. How many minutes is 8 days?

d. Madhumati stayed at a hotel for 3 days. How many hours did she stay for?

e. If a movie is 3 hours 15 minutes, how many minutes is the movie for?

2. Solve the following word problems.

a. Mr. Singh's family went to a beach on Sunday. After spending 4 hours 45 minutes on the beach, they visited a park nearby. If they spent 1 hour 45 minutes there, how many hours did they spend outside their home on Sunday?

b. Christine was the winner of the reading competition. If the runner-up took 2 minutes 24 seconds to read the passage and Christine beat her by 20 seconds, how much time did Christine take?

c. The school arranged for the screening of a children's movie. The movie was for 2 h 15 mins followed by lunch which was for 1 h 10 min. What was the total time spent for the movie and the lunch?

d. Kirti was supposed to come home by 8 p.m., but he came at 2345. How late was he?

e. Mihir built a brick wall in 7 hours 12 minutes whereas Kalyan built the same wall in 6 hours 50 minutes. How much less time did Kalyan take?

TIME DURATION OR TIME ELAPSED

a

Karan, Kirti and their sister Neha went shopping with their parents for the coming festival. They left home at 10:15 a.m. and drove to the biggest mall in the city. They reached the mall at 11:00 a.m. They went into a clothing store and bought clothes for all. When they finished shopping, it was 12:25 p.m. They window shopped at the mall for some time and then went to the top floor for juice and cold drinks. They spent half an hour there. When they left the mall, it was 1:45 p.m. As they were hungry, they drove to a restaurant for lunch. From the restaurant, they left for the footwear shop and reached there at 3:10 p.m. The parents bought footwear for all three children and headed home. They reached home at 5:15 p.m.

Example 10: How much time did they spend from the time they left home and finished shopping for clothes?

Solution: Time spent to reach the mall = 45 minutes (From 10:15 a.m. to 11:00 a.m.)

Time spent in shopping for clothes = 1 hour 25 minutes

(From 11:00 a.m. to 12:25 p.m.)

Total time spent = 45 min + 1 h 25 min

(45 min + 25 min

= 70 min = 60 min + 10 min = 1 h 10 minutes

= 1 h + 1 h 10 min = 2 h 10 min

They spent 2 hours 10 minutes.

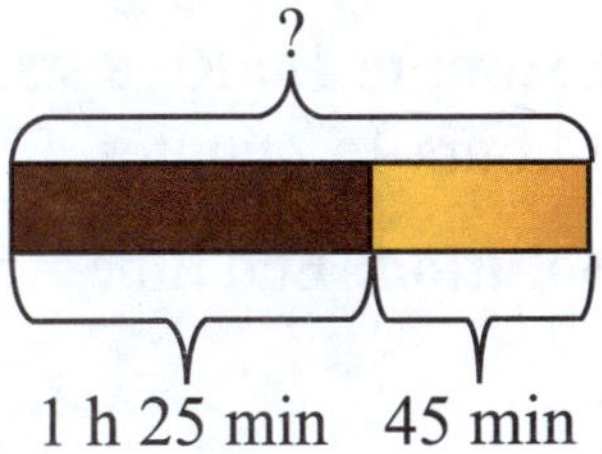

Example 11: After how many hours of leaving the mall did they reach the footwear shop?

Solution: Time when they left the mall = 1:45 p.m.

Time when they reached the footwear shop = 3:10 p.m.

Time interval between 1:45 p.m. and 3:10 p.m. = 3:10 p.m. − 1: 45 p.m.

(Since the number of minutes is not enough in 3:10, borrow from the hour.

Borrowing an hour (60 minutes) from 3 we get 2 hours 70 minutes.

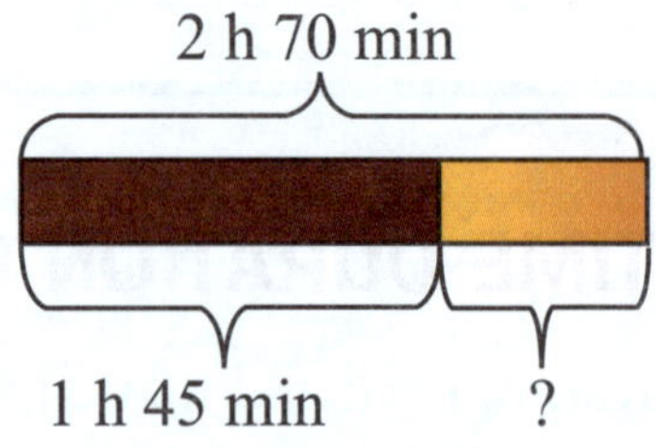

2 h 70 min − 1 h 45 min = (2 h − 1 h) + (70 min − 45 min)

= 1 h 25 min

So, the time taken between leaving the mall and reaching the footwear shop is 1 h 25 min.

Finding the Start Time and the End Time

Example 12: Asif is drawing pictures for Rajan's story book. He took 4 hours 10 minutes to draw the pictures. If he finished drawing at 2:40 p.m., at what time did he start?

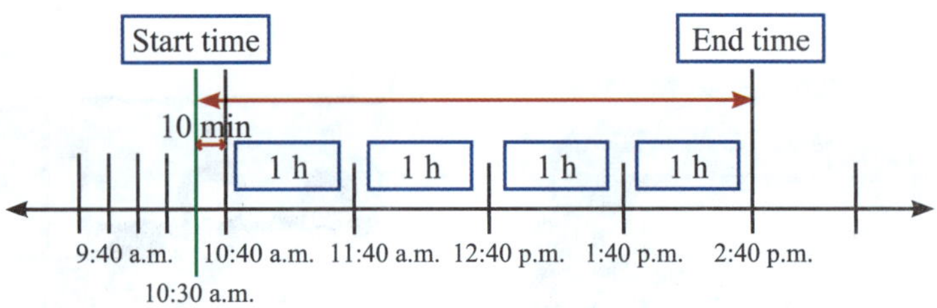

Solution: We are given the time duration and the end time. To find the start time, count backwards from the end time.

Start time = End time – Time duration

= 2:40 p.m. – 4 hours 10 minutes

Break up the time period to make it easier to subtract.

2:40 p.m. – 4 hours = 10:40 a.m.

10 hours 40 minutes – 10 minutes = 10 hours 30 minutes

Therefore, Asif started drawing the pictures at 10:30 a.m.

Example 13: Riya started her homework at 7:20 p.m. and completed it in 2 hours 15 minutes. Find the time at which she completed her homework?

Solution: End time = Start time + Time duration

= 7:20 p.m. + 2 hours 15 minutes

Break up the time period to make it easier to add.

7:20 p.m. + 2 hours = 9:20 p.m.

9 hours 20 minutes + 15 minutes = 9 hours 35 minutes

Therefore, Riya completed her homework at 9:35 p.m.

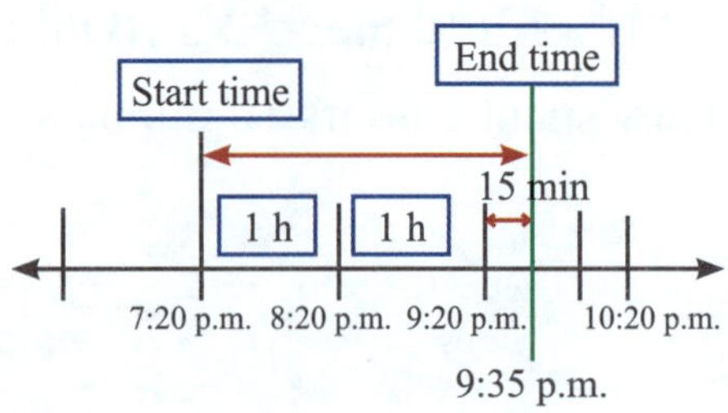

Finding the Number of Days

Example 14: The Tokyo Olympics started on 23 July 2021 and ended on 8 August 2021. How many days did the Olympics go on for?

Solution: Start date = 23 July 2021 and we know that the month of July has 31 days.

End date = 8 August 2021

Break up the number of days to make it easier to count

JULY & AUGUST 2021

1	2	3	4	5	6	7	8	9	10	
11	12	13	14	15	16	17	18	19	20	
21	22	~~23~~	~~24~~	~~25~~	~~26~~	~~27~~	~~28~~	~~29~~	~~30~~	~~31~~
~~1~~	~~2~~	~~3~~	~~4~~	~~5~~	~~6~~	~~7~~	~~8~~	9	10	
11	12	13	14	15	16	17	18	19	20	
21	22	23	24	25	26	27	28	29	30	31

23rd July to 31st July = 9 days

1st August to 8th August = 8 days

Total number of days = 9 days in July + 8 days in August = 17 days

Therefore, the Tokyo Olympics went on for 17 days.

Example 15: The Rio de Janeiro 2016 Olympics ended on 21st August. If they lasted for 17 days, on which date did they begin?

Solution: Start date = End date – Number of days

= 21st August – 17 days

Break up the number of days to make it easier to subtract.

AUGUST 2016

1	2	3	4	~~5~~	~~6~~	~~7~~	~~8~~	~~9~~	~~10~~	
~~11~~	~~12~~	~~13~~	~~14~~	~~15~~	~~16~~	~~17~~	~~18~~	~~19~~	~~20~~	
~~21~~	22	23	24	25	26	27	28	29	30	31

21st August to 12th August = 10 days

11th August to 5th August = 7 days

Therefore, the Rio de Janeiro 2016 Olympics started on 5th August 2016.

Exercise 9.2

Solve the following word problems.

1. A car wash service started work at 8:20 a.m. and continued for 4 hours 10 minutes before taking a lunch break. At what time did the lunch break start?
2. The gardener came to a clients place to trim the grass and completed the task in 50 minutes. If the gardener completed the work at 2:05 p.m., at what time did the gardener start trimming the grass?
3. The Class 10 annual exams start on 3rd May and go on for 17 days with breaks in between. On what date will the exam end?
4. A baker takes 3 hours 20 minutes to bake one batch of biscuits. If he started at 7 a.m., at what time did he finish baking one batch of biscuits.
5. How many days are there between March 6 and May 20?

TEMPERATURE

Temperature is a measure of the amount of heat present in a body, in the environment or in an object. It tells the hotness or the coldness of an object or a substance in either degree Celsius or degree Fahrenheit.

Thermometer

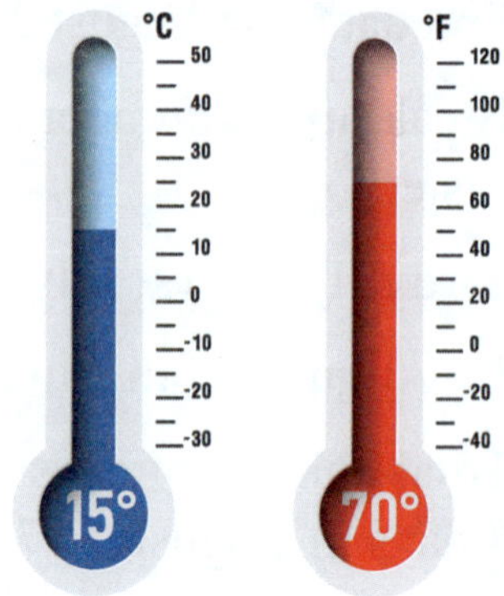

Thermometer is an instrument used to measure how cold or hot something is. It usually consists of a long narrow tube that contains a liquid, such as mercury or alcohol. This liquid inside the thermometer expands and rises when the temperature increases and when the temperature decreases, this liquid contracts and moves down the tube.

Units of Temperature

The Celsius scale is also known as the centigrade scale. Here, 0°C represents the freezing point of water and 100°C represents the boiling point of water.

On the Fahrenheit scale, 32°F represents the freezing point of water and 212°F represents the boiling point of water. The Fahrenheit scale is commonly used in the United States of America.

How to use a thermometer?

Step 1: Check if the thermometer has a Celsius scale or a Fahrenheit scale.

Step 2: Place the thermometer inside the object or the substance whose temperature needs to be measured.

Step 3: Wait for the thermometer reading to stabilise. This may take a few seconds.

Step 4: Read the temperature from the scale on the thermometer.

The normal temperature of our body is 37°C or 98.6 °F.

Conversion of temperature from degree Celsius to degree Fahrenheit

The formula used for this conversion is $°F = \left(\frac{9}{5} \times °C\right) + 32$.

Example 16: Convert 15°C into °F.

Solution: $°F = \left(\frac{9}{5} \times °C\right) + 32$

$= \left(\frac{9}{5} \times 15\right) + 32$

$= 27 + 32 = 59$

Therefore, 15°C is equal to 59°F.

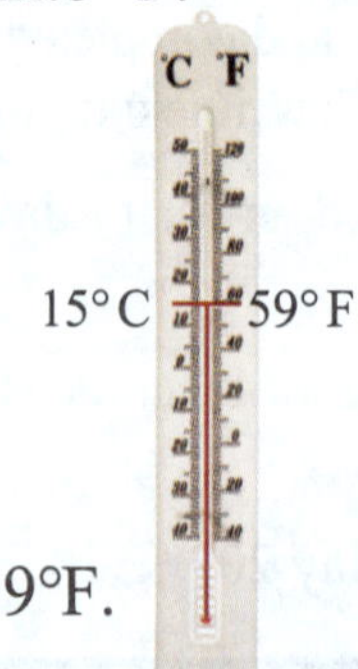

Example 17: Convert 55°C into °F

Solution: $°F = \left(\frac{9}{5} \times °C\right) + 32$

$= \left(\frac{9}{5} \times 55\right) + 32$

$= 99 + 32 = 131$

Therefore, 55°C is equal to 131°F.

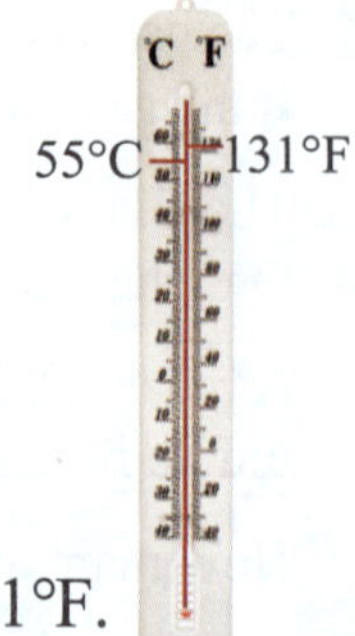

Conversion of temperature from degree Fahrenheit to degree Celsius

The formula used for this conversion is $°C = \frac{5}{9} \times (°F - 32)$.

Example 18: Convert 50°F into °C.

Solution: $°C = \frac{5}{9} \times (°F - 32)$

$= \frac{5}{9} \times (50 - 32)$

$= \frac{5}{9} \times 18 = 10$

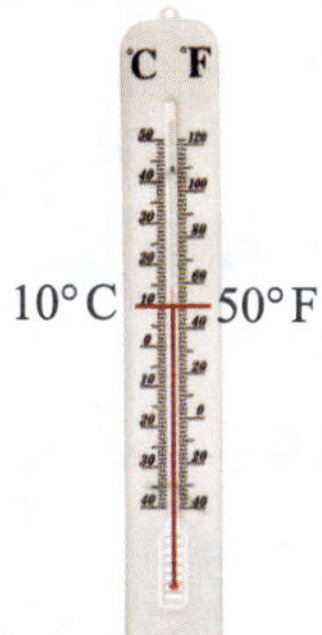

Therefore, 50°F is equal to 10°C.

Example 19: Convert 113°F into °C.

Solution: $°C = \frac{5}{9} \times (°F - 32)$

$= \frac{5}{9} \times (113 - 32)$

$= \frac{5}{9} \times 81 = 45$

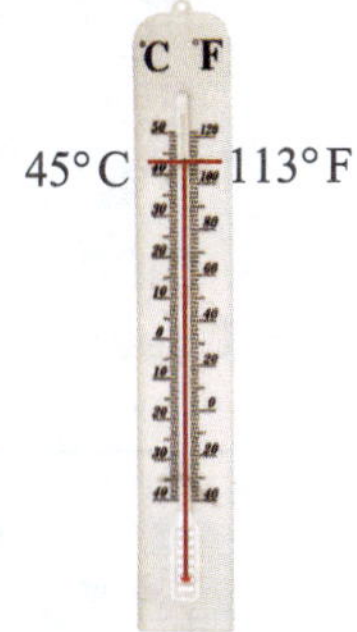

Therefore, 113°F is equal to 45°C.

Exercise 9.3

1. Write the temperature indicated on each thermometer.

a.

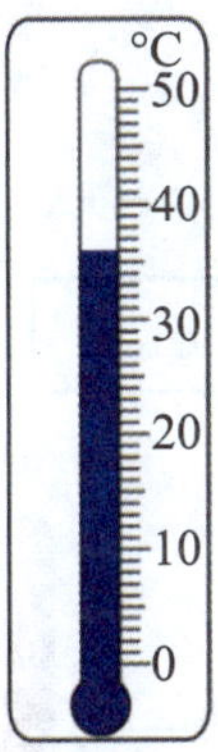

b.

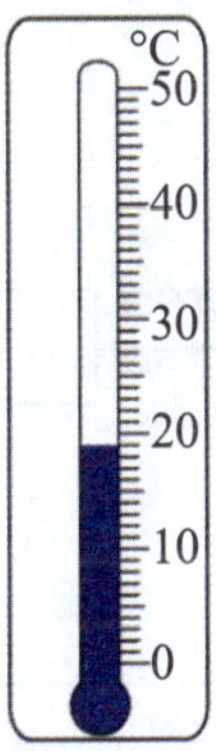

c.

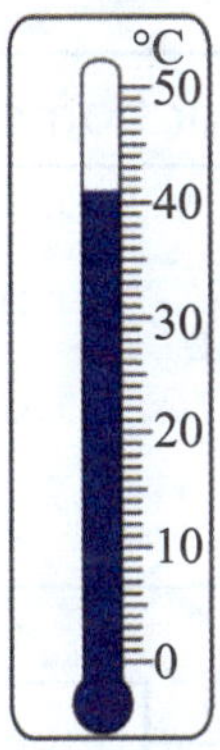

d.

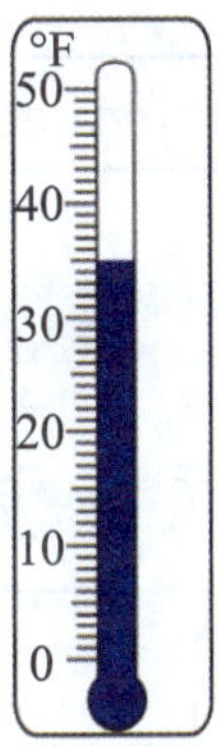

e.

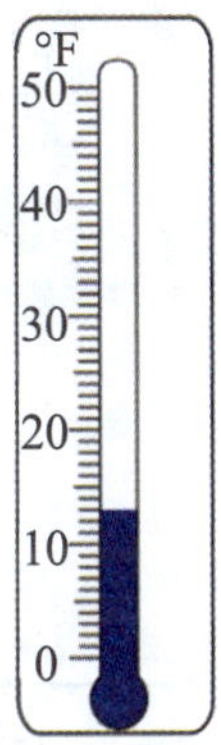

2. Convert the following temperatures into degree Fahrenheit.

a. 65°C b. 5°C c. 200°C d. 35°C e. 75°C

3. Convert the following temperatures into degree Celsius.

a. 68°F b. 104°F c. 446°F d. 77°F e. 176°F

Concept Map

1 hour → 60 minutes
1 day → 24 hours
1 week → 7 days
1 month → 4/5 weeks → 28/29/30/31 days
1 year → 12 months → 365/366 days

Time measured in → Different units

Different units undergo → Conversions

Conversions are → (the conversions above)

Time leads to → Start time; End time; Duration

Temperature is → Degree of coldness or hotness

Temperature measured using → Thermometer

Temperature measured in → Degree Celsius (°C); Degree Fahrenheit (°F)

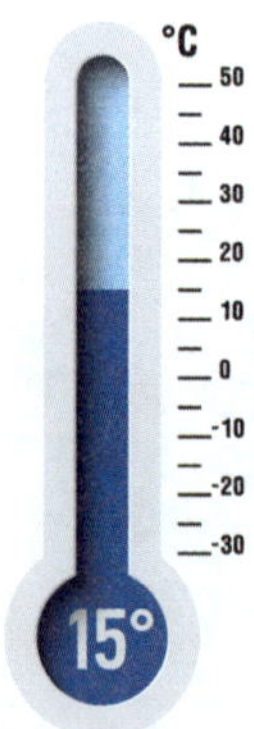

Degree Celsius (°C) and Degree Fahrenheit (°F): conversion formulae

$$°C = \frac{5}{9} \times (°F - 32)$$

$$°F = \left(\frac{9}{5} \times °C\right) + 32$$

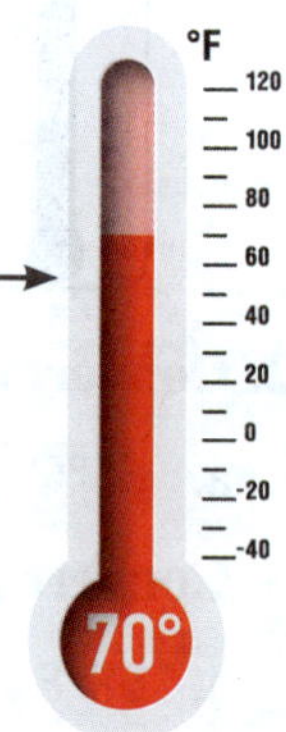

Project

Weather Report

Prepare a temperature data sheet for 1 week of the city/town of your choice. Cut out the weather reports of the last 1 week from the newspaper or find the weather report on the Internet. Record the information in the following table and answer the questions that follow.

Day	Date	Maximum Temperature (in °C)	Minimum Temperature (in °C)	Minimum Temperature (in °F)	Maximum Temperature (in °F)
1					
2					
3					
4					
5					
6					
7					

1. Do all the 7 days have the same maximum and minimum temperatures?
2. What may be the factors that affect the observed maximum and minimum temperatures?
3. Which day has the hottest temperature?
4. Which day has the coldest temperature?

Revision Exercise

A. Choose the correct option.
Listed below are some of the deadliest volcanoes that have erupted over the years. Answer the questions based on the information given in the table.

Name of Volcano	Year of Eruption
Mount Etna, Italy	1669
Krakatoa, Indonesia	1883
Mount Pele, Martinique, Caribbean Island	1902
Mount St. Helens, USA	1980
Nevada de Ruiz Volcano, Columbia	1985
Mount Merapi, Indonesia	2010

1. After how many years of Mount Etna's eruption did Krakatoa eruption take place?
   a. 244 years
   b. 214 years
   c. 212 years
   d. 215 years
2. How many years before Mount St. Helens eruption did Mount Pele eruption take place?
   a. 75 years
   b. 76 years
   c. 77 years
   d. 78 years
3. What is the difference in the number of years of Nevada de Ruiz Volcano eruption and Mount Merapi eruption?
   a. 25 months
   b. 25 years
   c. 25 days
   d. 25 centuries
4. How many years before Mount Merapi eruption did Mount St. Helens eruption take place?
   a. 33 years b. 32 years
   c. 30 years d. 35 years
5. If Mount Merapi had erupted in 2000 and Mount St. Helens in 1960, what would be the difference in the number of years between both eruptions?
   a. 30
   b. 60
   c. 60
   d. 40

B. Fill in the blanks.

1. 18°C = ____°F
2. 176°F = ____°C
3. 40°C = ____°F
4. 95°F = ____°C
5. 37°C = ____°F

C. Match the following.

1. 5:20 a.m. to 7.30 a.m.	a. 51 min
2. 11:15 a.m. to 3:45 p.m.	b. 3 h 20 min
3. 7:56 p.m. to 8.47 p.m.	c. 7 h 5 min
4. 8:30 p.m. to 11:50 p.m.	d. 2 h 10 min
5. 2:15 p.m. to 9:20 p.m.	e. 4 h 30 min

D. State whether the following statements are true (T) or false (F).

1. 72 hours make 3 days.
2. 32°F is the boiling point of water.
3. 60°C is equal to 145°F.
4. 203°F is equal to 95°C.
5. We can find the end time if we know the start time and the duration.

E. Find the following times.

1. 2 hours 15 minutes after 1:20 a.m.
2. 4 hours 20 minutes after 6:40 p.m.
3. 7 hours 40 minutes before 11:10 a.m.
4. 3 hours 10 minutes before 4:20 a.m.
5. 2 hours 50 minutes after 10:50 p.m.

F. Application-based questions.

1. Mr. Advani took a train to visit his daughter. He got on the train at 12:30 p.m. and got off at his daughter's town 6 hours and 45 minutes later. What time was it when he got off the train?
2. If Karan spent 12 hours and Kavya spent 16 hours in the workshop, How many minutes did they spend altogether in the workshop?
3. Ms. Malini conducted a science laboratory session for 4 hours 15 minutes on day 1 and 2 hours 50 minutes on day 2. What is the difference in the time on the 2nd day?
4. Sheetal wanted to bake a cake. She preheated the oven at 450°F. She then increased the temperature by 5°F for 10 minutes of baking. At what temperature, in Celsius, did she bake the cake?
5. Karan wanted to go out to play but it was very hot outside. He checked the temperature and it showed 95°F. What is the temperature in °C?

Space for rough work

Did You Master?

A. 1 h 36 min + 4 h 44 min = _____

1. 6 h 50 min
2. 6 h 10 min
3. 6 h 15 min
4. 6 h 20 min

B. 4 h 17 min – 2 h 59 min = _____

1. 1 h 16 min
2. 1 h 17 min
3. 1 h 18 min
4. 1 h 19 min

C. 2135 min = _____ h _____ min

1. 35 h 30 min
2. 35 h 35 min
3. 35 h 40 min
4. 35 h 45 min

D. What is the elapsed time if the start time is 5:55 a.m. and the end time is 7:15 a.m.?

1. 1 h 20 min
2. 1 h 25 min
3. 1 h 15 min
4. 1 h 30 min

E. What is 554°F in degree Celsius?

1. 190°C
2. 289°C
3. 290°C
4. 390°C

F. The Farmer's Market started at 7:30 a.m. and went on for 5 hours 40 minutes. At what time did it end?

1. 1:10 p.m.
2. 1:05 p.m.
3. 1:00 p.m.
4. 12:55 p.m.

G. At the annual summer camp, students are supposed to spend 2 hours 15 minutes practicing gymnastics, 2 hours 55 minutes studying and 45 minutes in prayer every day. How much time do the students spend altogether on these activities in one day?

1. 5 h 40 min
2. 5 h 45 min
3. 5 h 50 min
4. 5 h 55 min

H. The temperature in Bengaluru is said to be pleasant throughout the year with average temperature at 77°F. What is this temperature in degree Celsius?

1. 24°C
2. 25°C
3. 26°C
4. 27°C

I. The temperature in Hyderabad is 39°C. What is this temperature in degree Fahrenheit?

1. 101.2°F
2. 102.2°F
3. 103.2°F
4. 104.2°F

J. The temperature in Mumbai was 89.6°F. Convert it to degree Celsius.

1. 33°C
2. 31.5°C
3. 32.5°C
4. 32°C

How many questions did you answer correctly? Score yourself.

easy ☐ average ☐ advanced ☐ remembering ☐ understanding ☐ applying ☐ analysing ☐ evaluating ☐ creating ☐

communication ☐ representation ☐ devising strategies ☐ mathematisation ☐ reasoning and argument ☐ using symbols ☐ using mathematical tools ☐ creativity ☐

10 Average and Unitary Method

Curricular Goals

- Develop problem-solving skills with procedural fluency, to solve daily life problems, and as a step towards developing computational thinking (CG-4)

Competencies

- Solve daily life problems involving one or more operations on whole numbers (C-4.1)
- Select appropriate methods for computing with whole numbers such as mental computation or paper and pencil calculation, in accordance with the context (C-4.3)

Why This Topic?

In real life, we come across the concept of finding the average of a number or solving problems using unitary method in many situations.

Finding weight of one pumpkin

Weight of 5 pumpkins = 12 kg
Average weight of each pumpkin can be found by dividing total weight by number of pumpkins.

Finding cost of three balloons

Cost of 15 balloons = ₹120
The cost of 3 balloons can be found using unitary method.

Can you think of one example each of average and of unitary method being applied in your daily life?

Are You Ready?

A. What is the sum of 234 and 568?

1. 782 2. 873
3. 802 4. 762

B. What is the difference between 2134 and 6572?

1. 4438 2. 3467
3. 4129 4. 8706

C. What is the product of 45 and 23?

1. 2315 2. 1782
3. 4562 4. 1035

D. There are some children at the fair and some balloons in a bunch. Which operation will you use to find the number of balloons that each child can have?

1. Multiplication
2. Addition
3. Division
4. Subtraction

E. The seating capacity of a bus is 54 people. How many people can travel in 9 such buses?

1. 486 2. 345
3. 673 4. 398

F. Rahul had 78 cookies. He gave 18 cookies to Sahana and 7 cookies to Vandana. How many cookies are left with him?

1. 71 2. 60
3. 103 4. 53

G. In basket A, there are 347 apples and in basket B, there are 671 apples. What is the total number of apples in A and B?

1. 1204
2. 1018
3. 1362
4. 2713

H. The cost of 5 cars is ₹32,50,250, each having the same price. What is the cost of one car?

1. ₹3,45,000
2. ₹6,50,005
3. ₹26,781
4. ₹6,50,050

I. A vendor earns ₹17,184 in 6 months by selling toys. If the cost of 1 toy is ₹48, find the number of toys he sold in 6 months.

1. 538
2. 583
3. 358
4. 385

J. A chair and a table cost ₹456 and ₹1278, respectively. What will be the cost of 12 chairs and 24 tables?

1. ₹19,834
2. ₹5671
3. ₹36,144
4. ₹4528

How many questions did you answer correctly? Score yourself.

easy | average | advanced | remembering | understanding | applying | analysing | evaluating | creating

communication | representation | devising strategies | mathematisation | reasoning and argument | using symbols | using mathematical tools | creativity

AVERAGE

There are 25 students in a section of Class 5. Some of them are 9 years old, some are 10 years old and some others are 11 years old. When we need to find the general age of a student in this section, we take the average of the ages of all 25 students.

Average is the value that is evenly distributed among a given number of quantities. Average is also called **arithmetic mean** or **mean**.

$$\text{Average} = \frac{\text{Sum of quantities}}{\text{Number of quantities}}$$

Example 1: Find the average of 5 and 7.

Solution: $\text{Average} = \frac{\text{Sum of quantities}}{\text{Number of quantities}} = \frac{5+7}{2} = \frac{12}{2} = 6$

Therefore, the average of 5 and 7 is 6.

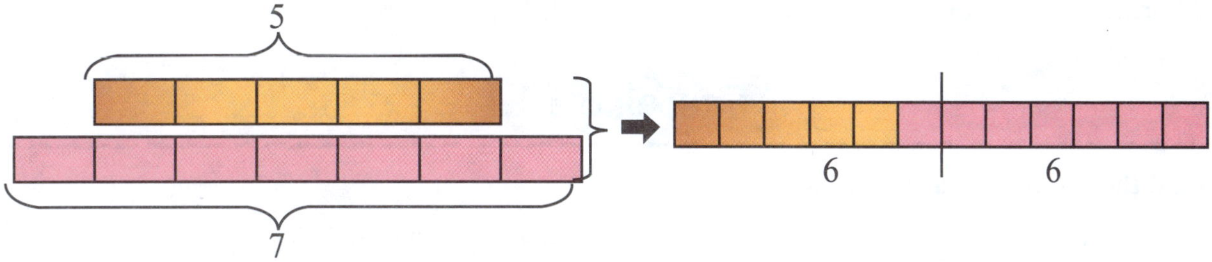

Example 2: Find the average of 12 kg, 11 kg and 13,000 g.

Solution: Note that 13,000 g = 13 kg.

$$\text{Average} = \frac{\text{Sum of quantities}}{\text{Number of quantities}} = \frac{12+11+13}{3} = \frac{36}{3}$$
$$= 12$$

Before calculating an average, make sure that all the measurements are in the same unit.

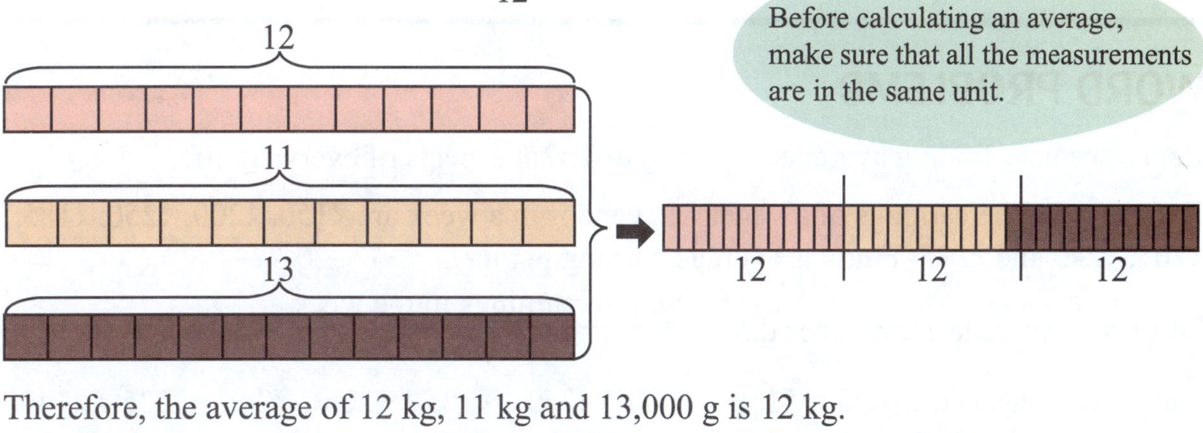

Therefore, the average of 12 kg, 11 kg and 13,000 g is 12 kg.

Average of Fractions and Decimals

Finding average of fractions and decimals is same as finding the average of whole numbers.

Example 3: Find the average of $\frac{1}{2}$, $\frac{1}{3}$ and $\frac{1}{6}$.

Find the sum of the fractions before finding the average.

Solution: Average = $\frac{\text{Sum of quantities}}{\text{Number of quantities}}$

Sum of quantities = $\frac{1}{2}+\frac{1}{3}+\frac{1}{6}=\frac{3+2+1}{6}=\frac{6}{6}=1$

So, average = $\frac{\frac{1}{2}+\frac{1}{3}+\frac{1}{6}}{3}=\frac{1}{3}$.

Therefore, the average of $\frac{1}{2}$, $\frac{1}{3}$ and $\frac{1}{6}$ is $\frac{1}{3}$.

Example 4: Find the average of 4.3 m, 5.1 m, 4.7 m and 5.5 m.

Solution: Average = $\frac{\text{Sum of quantities}}{\text{Number of quantities}}=\frac{4.3+5.1+4.7+5.5}{4}=\frac{19.6}{4}=4.9$

Therefore, the average of 4.3 m, 5.1 m, 4.7 m and 5.5 m is 4.9 m.

Exercise 10.1

Find the average of the following.

1. 3, 5 and 7
2. 10 g, 20 g, 30 g, 40 g, and 50 g
3. 2, 4, 6, 8, 10 and 12
4. 12 cm, 7 cm, 9 cm and 12 cm
5. 2.62 m, 2.08 m, 3.9 m and 0.96 m
6. $\frac{1}{4}$, $\frac{2}{4}$ and $\frac{1}{4}$
7. 3 cm, 2.5 cm, 1.5 cm and 5 cm
8. 2.4, 3.1, 1.2 and 1.33
9. $\frac{1}{5}$, $\frac{1}{15}$ and $\frac{1}{10}$
10. 1.4 kg, 2.3 kg, 3.5 kg, and 4.8 kg

WORD PROBLEMS

Let us see how finding average is used in different aspects of everyday life.

Example 5: The earnings of a vegetable vendor in a week are ₹150, ₹200, ₹250, ₹185, ₹205, ₹245 and ₹235. Find his average earning per day.

Solution: Average earning per day = $\frac{\text{Sum of earnings in the week}}{7}$

Sum of earnings in the week = ₹150 + ₹200 + ₹250 + ₹185 + ₹205 + ₹245 + ₹235 = ₹1470

So, average earning per day = $\frac{1470}{7}$ = ₹210

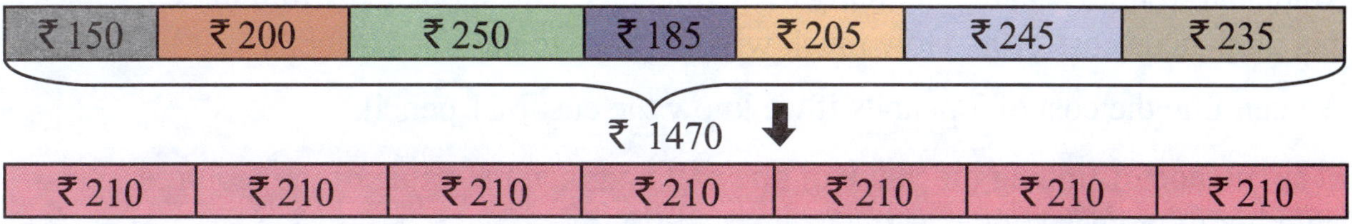

Therefore, the average earning of the vegetable vender is ₹210 per day.

Example 6: Sneha weighs 25 kg. Rajeev weighs 11 kg more than Sneha and Ritika weighs 5 kg less than Sneha. Find the average weight of these three friends.

Solution: Weight of Sneha = 25 kg

Weight of Rajeev = 25 kg + 11 kg = 36 kg

Weight of Ritika = 25 kg – 5 kg = 20 kg

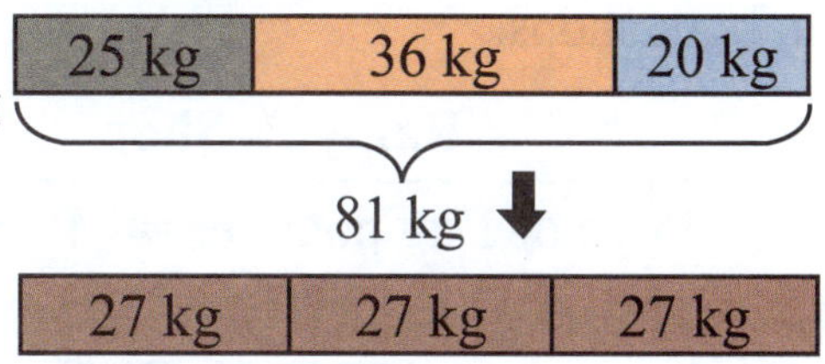

Average weight = $\frac{\text{Sum of weights}}{3} = \frac{81}{3}\text{kg} = 27\text{ kg}$

Therefore, the average weight of Sneha, Rajeev and Ritika is 27 kg.

Example 7: The average weight of Kashvi and Vinati is 27 kg. If Kashvi's weight is 24 kg, how much does Vinati weigh?

Solution: Vinati's weight = Total weight – Kashvi's weight

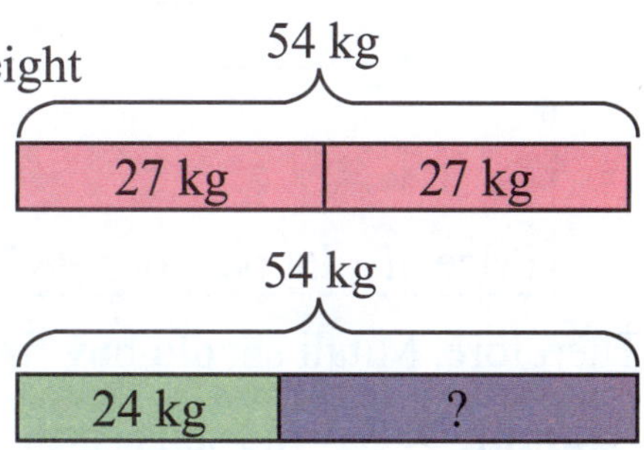

Note that the total weight can be calculated by multiplying the average weight with 2 (number of quantities).

So, total weight = 27 × 2 = 54 kg.

Therefore, Vinati's weight = 54 kg – 24 kg = 30 kg.

Exercise 10.2

Solve the following word problems.

1. The maximum temperatures in a city for a week are 35.4°C, 30.2°C, 33.3°C, 38.3°C, 32.5°C, 37°C and 31.3°C. What is the average temperature of the week?
2. The lengths of three threads are 1.5 m, 5 m and 35.5 m. Find the average length, in m, of the threads.
3. The average height of A, B and C is 140 cm. A's height is 148 cm and B's height is 132 cm. Find the height of C.
4. What is the average of the first 6 odd numbers?
5. Jena completes $\frac{1}{6}$ of a work and Kavitha completes $\frac{3}{4}$ of the same work in a day. Find the average work done by Jena and Kavitha in a day.

UNITARY METHOD

Aradhana went to a stationary shop to buy pencils. The shopkeeper told her that 20 pencils cost ₹100. How much will she have to pay for 7 pencils?

We can find the cost of 7 pencils if we know the cost of 1 pencil.

> The method of finding the value of one unit and then the value of the required number of units is known as the **unitary method**.

Example 8: Ramya sells 6 kg potatoes for ₹45 and Gayatri sells 10 kg potatoes for ₹72.50. From whom should Mitali buy from so that she profits?

Solution: To find which deal is profitable, we compare the price of 1 kg potatoes in both shops.

Ramya's Shop	Gayatri's Shop
Price of 1 kg potatoes = ₹45 ÷ 6	Price of 1 kg potatoes = ₹72.50 ÷ 10
$\begin{array}{r} 7.50 \\ 6\,\overline{)\,45.00} \\ -42 \\ \hline 30 \\ -30 \\ \hline 0 \end{array}$	$\begin{array}{r} 7.25 \\ 10\,\overline{)\,72.50} \\ -70 \\ \hline 25 \\ -20 \\ \hline 50 \\ -50 \\ \hline 0 \end{array}$
Price of 1 kg potatoes = ₹7.50	Price of 1 kg potatoes = ₹7.25

Therefore, Mitali should buy from Gayatri's shop as ₹7.25 < ₹7.50.

Example 9: Sayyad sells earthen lamps in packs of 5 and as single pieces also. If the cost of 5 lamps is ₹125, how much should Anuj pay for 7 such lamps?

Solution: To find the cost of 7 lamps, we first need to find the cost of 1 lamp.

Since the cost of 5 lamps is ₹125, the cost of 1 lamp will be ₹125 ÷ 5 = ₹25.

So, cost of 7 lamps = ₹25 × 7 = ₹175.

Therefore, Anuj should pay ₹175 for 7 lamps.

Exercise 10.3

Solve the following word problems.

1. There is a sale at Sahana's furniture shop. The price list of different items is given below.

Items	Quantity	Price (₹)
Chairs	7	28,000
Tea table	3	12,000
Dining table	8	32,000
TV unit	5	15,000
Bean bags	4	8000
Garden chairs	9	7200

How much should I pay if I buy the following items?

Items	Quantity	Price (₹)
Tea table	2	
Dining table	1	
Bean bags	3	
Garden chairs	12	
Total		

2. Deenu sells 7 bamboo curtains for ₹17,192 and Ranjana sells 4 bamboo curtains for ₹9300. Which is a better deal?
3. Shop A sells onions in 5 kg bags at ₹45.50 and 9 kg bags at ₹76.50. Buying which bag is profitable?
4. Twenty-three children equally planted 506 trees in one day on Earth Day. How many trees would have been planted if there were 15 students?
5. On the scale of a map, 6 cm represents 18 km. Find the actual distance between two points if the distance between them on the map is 12 cm.

Concept Map

Average

is: The value that is evenly distributed among a given number of quantities

is calculated using:

$$\text{Average of quantities} = \frac{\text{Sum of the quantities}}{\text{Number of quantities}}$$

example:

Weight of 3 friends is 25 kg, 36 kg and 20 kg.

Average weight of 3 friends $= \frac{81}{3} = 27$ kg

Unitary Method

is: Method of finding the value of one unit and then the value of the required number of units

is calculated using:

Value of required number of units

$$= \frac{\text{Value of total number of units}}{\text{Total number of units}} \times \text{No. of required units}$$

example:

Cost of 5 lamps is ₹125.

Cost of 7 lamps $= \frac{125}{5} \times 7 =$ ₹175

Projects

A. Average Temperature

Tabulate the temperature of your city over a period of 7 days at different times. Find the average temperature of the week and write a report on the same.

B. Microsoft Excel or Google Spreadsheets

A spreadsheet is a computer program that is used to record, calculate and compare numerical data. Following is an example showing how average can be determined using Microsoft Excel or Google Spreadsheets.

1. Enter some numbers in a column and select any empty cell.
2. In the **Home** tab, click the arrow next to **Σ** (**AutoSum**), click on **Average** and press Enter.

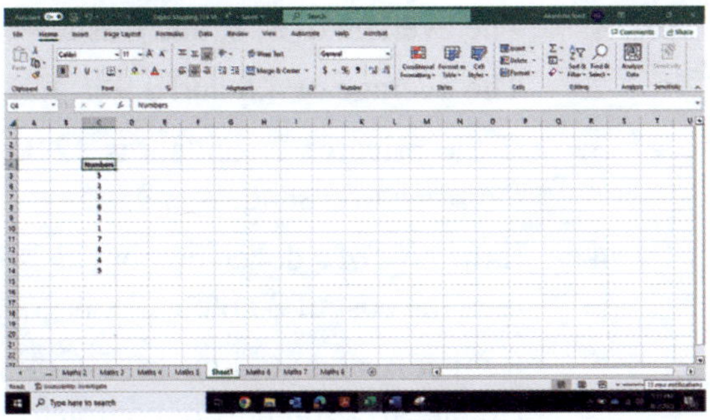

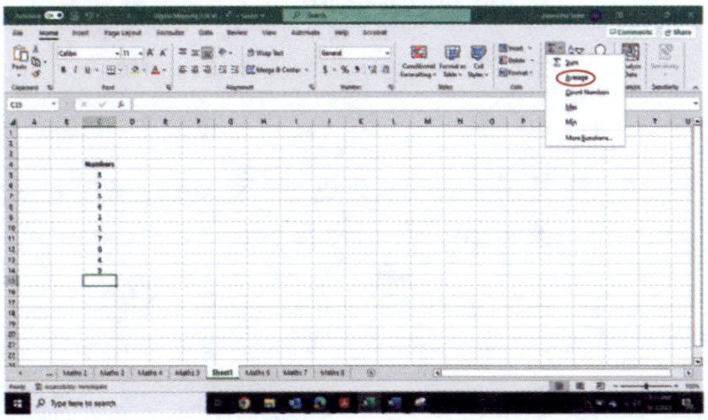

3. Select the numbers for which you want to find the average and press Enter. The average appears in the selected cell.

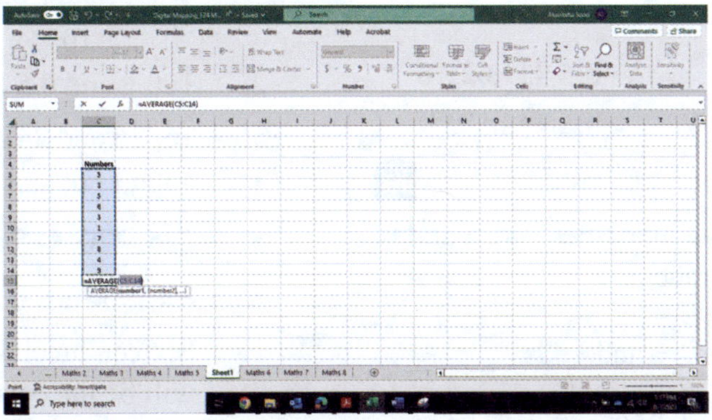

Now, enter five sets of data in the spreadsheet and calculate their individual averages. Take printouts of the screen and show it to your class teacher for evaluation.

Revision Exercise

A. Choose the correct option.

1. What is the average of 13 cm and 9 cm?
   a. 12 cm b. 11 cm
   c. 10 cm d. 22 cm
2. If Razia weighs 61 kg and Rashmi weighs 57 kg, what is their average weight?
   a. 148 kg b. 56 kg
   c. 67 kg d. 59 kg
3. What is the average of 3.5, 4.7 and 3.8?
   a. 6 b. 12
   c. 5 d. 4
4. If 48 kg rice costs ₹2688, what is the cost of 7 kg rice?
   a. ₹445 b. ₹56
   c. ₹278 d. ₹392
5. Sujay earns ₹5580 for his 12 days of work. If he worked for 25 days in a month, then how much did he earn in that month?
   a. ₹10,725 b. ₹11,625
   c. ₹12,075 d. ₹12,575

B. Fill in the blanks.

1. If there are two quantities, say a and b, then their average is ________.
2. The average of $\frac{6}{7}$ and $\frac{3}{7}$ is _______.
3. The average of 250 mℓ and 1.5 ℓ is _______.
4. If the price of 3 pairs of slippers is ₹297, then the price of 7 such pairs is ________.
5. Renuka types 360 words in half an hour. She can type _______ words in 20 minutes.

C. Match the following. (by finding average)

1. $\frac{1}{2}$ and $\frac{1}{5}$	a. 6.7
2. 7 and 13	b. 13
3. 10, 13 and 16	c. 11
4. 4 and 18	d. $\frac{7}{20}$
5. 5.8 and 7.6	e. 10

D. State whether the following are true (T) or false (F).

1. The average of 8, 6, and 4 is 5.
2. The average of 4.5 and 3.9 is 4.2.
3. If the price of 2 sandals is ₹210, then the price of 3 sandals is ₹305.
4. If the cost of a dozen notebooks is ₹384, then the cost of 2 notebooks is ₹64.
5. Ranjan walks 6 km in 50 minutes. He takes 12 minutes to complete 1 km.

E. Find the average of the following.

1. $\frac{2}{5}$ and $\frac{3}{10}$
2. 100 g and 0.5 kg
3. 16, 26 and 24
4. 32, 34, 36 and 38
5. ₹25, ₹20, ₹15 and ₹40

F. Application-based questions.

1. Sixteen lunch boxes cost ₹592. What will be the cost of 7 lunch boxes?
2. If the cost of 27 m of cloth is ₹1512, what is the cost of 1 m?
3. Rani takes 26 minutes to make 13 paper flowers. How much time will she take to complete 32 paper flowers?
4. A man earns ₹868 in 2 weeks. How much will he earn in 12 weeks?
5. Nikhil can paint 5 signboards in 2 hours. How many of them can he paint in 6 hours?

Did You Master?

A. The value that is evenly distributed among a given number of quantities is called _____.

1. Unitary method
2. Average
3. Division method
4. Arithmetic

B. What is the average of $\frac{2}{3}$, $\frac{4}{3}$ and $\frac{5}{3}$?

1. $\frac{11}{3}$ 2. $\frac{6}{3}$
3. $\frac{11}{9}$ 4. $\frac{12}{9}$

C. What is the average of 2.3, 0.4 and 0.3?

1. 3 2. 0.5
3. 0.75 4. 1

D. The runs scored by a batsman in five matches are 45, 38, 75, 52 and 40. What is his average run score?

1. 46 2. 50
3. 38 4. 55

E. The temperature of a city for 5 days is 32°C, 40°C, 28°C, 27°C and 23°C. What is the average temperature?

1. 28°C 2. 30°C
3. 32°C 4. 25°C

F. If 5 pencils cost ₹15 and 2 erasers cost ₹5, what is the total cost of 1 pencil and 1 eraser?

1. ₹20 2. ₹6.25
3. ₹3 4. ₹5.5

G. Which of the following is a better buy?

1. ₹164.50 for 7 bowls
2. ₹307.5 for 15 bowls
3. ₹94 for 4 bowls
4. ₹270 for 12 bowls

H. Given below are the times Sandy studied for in a week. How long did Sandy study for on an average?

Day	Mon	Tue	Wed	Thu	Fri	Sat	Sun
Minutes	45	50	60	55	30	35	40

1. 30 minutes
2. 40 minutes
3. 50 minutes
4. 45 minutes

I. If 64 jackfruits weighed 192 kg, what is the weight of 18 jackfruits?

1. 54 kg
2. 78 kg
3. 39 kg
4. 46 kg

J. In a sale, 4 pairs of shoes cost ₹1000 and 4 pairs of socks cost ₹160. Which of the following is correct?

1. 1 pair of shoes costs ₹500 and pair of socks costs ₹80.
2. 1 pair of shoes costs ₹250 and 1 pair of socks costs ₹80.
3. 1 pair of shoes costs ₹250 and 1 pair of socks costs ₹40.
4. 2 pairs of shoes cost ₹250 and 2 pairs of socks cost ₹8.

How many questions did you answer correctly? Score yourself.

easy ☐ average ☐ advanced ☐ remembering ☐ understanding ☐ applying ☐ analysing ☐ evaluating ☐ creating ☐

communication ☐ representation ☐ devising strategies ☐ mathematisation ☐ reasoning and argument ☐ using symbols ☐ using mathematical tools ☐ creativity ☐

11 Profit and Loss

Curricular Goals

- Develop problem-solving skills with procedural fluency, to solve mathematical puzzles as well as daily life problems, and as a step towards developing computational thinking (CG-4)

Competencies

- Solve daily life problems involving one or more operations on whole numbers (C-4.1)
- Select appropriate methods and tools for computing with whole numbers such as mental computation, estimation, or paper and pencil calculation, in accordance with the context (C-4.3)

Why This Topic?

In real life, we come across many situations of buying and selling things. Sometimes, we pay more than expected for an item and sometimes we pay less. Let us understand more the concept of profit and loss.

Birthday shopping

Rhea's parents bought a pair of dress marked at ₹1400.

Its actual price was ₹800.

Did they pay more or less for the pair of dress?

Money spent on baking a cake

The baker spent ₹750 on baking a cake. He charged ₹75 for delivery.

The customer paid ₹100 less because the cake had been damaged.

Whose loss is this?

Can you think of two more examples where we spend more or less money than the actual price?

Are You Ready?

A. If ₹5 = 500 paise, then, ₹9 = ___

1. 900 paise
2. 90 paise
3. 500 paise
4. 1000 paise

B. Which of the following fruits is expensive?

₹110 ₹70 ₹47

1. All are of same price
2. Grapes
3. Papaya
4. Cherries

C. The price of a T-shirt is ₹847, and the price of a formal shirt is ₹874. Which is cheaper?

1. Formal shirt
2. Both are of same cost
3. T-shirt
4. Cannot be compared

D. Who among the following has more money?

1. 2. 3. 4.

₹4120 ₹4012 ₹4102 ₹4201

E. Manu's father gave ₹200 to Manu and ₹310 to his sister to buy notebooks and no money to Sita. Who has more money?

1. Manu
2. Manu's sister
3. Sita
4. All have same amount

F. Neha buys grocery worth ₹418 and paid ₹500 to the shopkeeper. How much money will she get back in return?

1. ₹28
2. ₹84
3. ₹82
4. ₹86

G. Amar bought a second-hand car from his friend for ₹2,26,974. After a few months, he sold the same car for ₹2,58,675. How much more money did he get?

1. ₹31,701
2. ₹13,701
3. ₹13,107
4. ₹13,017

H. Which is a better deal: 2 dozen bananas at ₹120 or 10 bananas at ₹60?

1. 2 dozen bananas at ₹120
2. 10 bananas at ₹60
3. Both are good deals
4. Cannot say

I. The price of a sofa is ₹4250. How much money is needed to buy 3 such sofas?

1. ₹12,250
2. ₹12,570
3. ₹12,750
4. ₹12,075

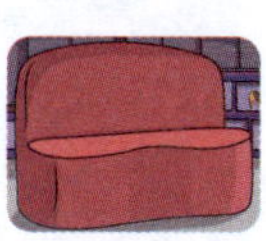

How many questions did you answer correctly? Score yourself.

easy ☐ average ☐ advanced ☐ remembering ☐ understanding ☐ applying ☐ analysing ☐ evaluating ☐ creating ☐

communication ☐ representation ☐ devising strategies ☐ mathematisation ☐ reasoning and argument ☐ using symbols ☐ using mathematical tools ☐ creativity ☐

COST PRICE AND SELLING PRICE

Kumar sells designer pottery in his shop. He spends money to buy things such as clay, colour, moulds, etc. that are required for making pottery. The cost of making something is called its **cost price (C.P.)**.

He sells his pottery for a price that is more than the cost of making it. The price at which something is sold is called its **selling price (S.P.)**.

Cost Price = ₹275

Selling Price = ₹299

Cost Price = ₹435

Selling Price = ₹480

Cost Price = ₹573

Selling Price = ₹610

Cost Price = ₹580

Selling Price = ₹625

The potter was making these items and then selling them. The price at which the item was bought is its cost price. The price at which he sells the item is its selling price.

The difference what the potter gets on selling the pot is called **profit** (that he gains).

The cost price (C.P.) of pot 1 is ₹275 and its selling price (S.P) is ₹299.

$$\begin{array}{rr} \text{Selling price (S.P.)} = & 2\ 9\ 9 \\ \text{Cost price (C.P.)} = & -\ 2\ 7\ 5 \\ \hline & 2\ 4 \end{array} \rightarrow \text{Profit}$$

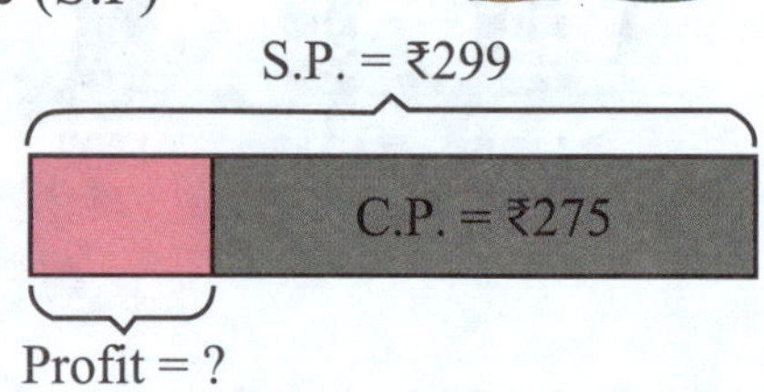

Kumar earns ₹24 on this pot.

Here the selling price (S.P.) is more than the cost price (C.P.).

So the difference is the **profit**. The profit is also referred as **gain**.

The lid of Pot 3 fell down and broke. Kumar had to sell it without the lid.

So, he reduced its cost and sold it for ₹550 instead of selling it for ₹610.

$$\begin{array}{rr} \text{Cost price (C.P.)} = & 5\ 7\ 3 \\ \text{Selling price (S.P.)} = & -\ 5\ 5\ 0 \\ \hline = & 2\ 3 \end{array} \rightarrow \text{Loss}$$

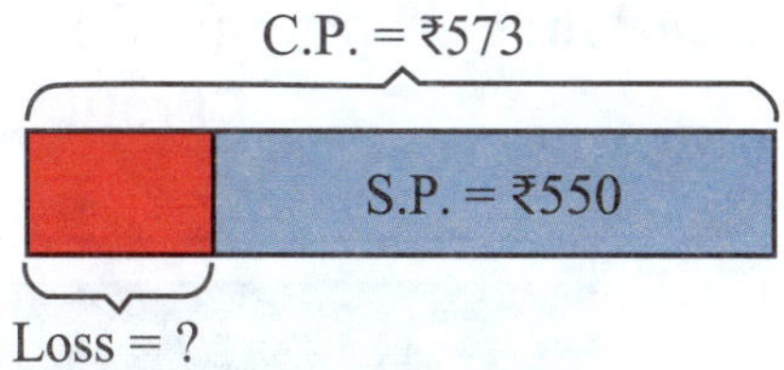

Kumar lost ₹23 on this pot. Here, the cost price (C.P.) is more than the selling price (S.P.), so the difference is the **loss**.

- If S.P. > C.P., then Profit = S.P. – C.P.
- If C.P. > S.P., then Loss = C.P. – S.P.
- If S.P. = C.P., then there is neither profit nor loss.

FINDING COST PRICE AND SELLING PRICE

Example 1: Bindu sells handmade jewellery. If she had sold one set of jewellery for ₹447 at a loss of ₹52, what was the cost price of the jewellery?

Solution: Selling price (S.P.) = ₹447

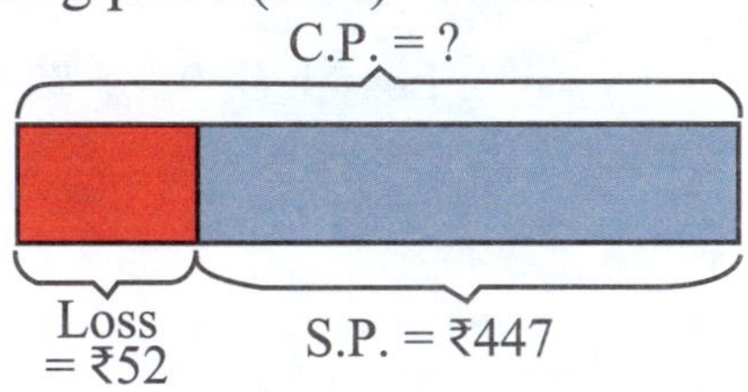

If Loss then, C.P. = S.P. + Loss

If Profit then, C.P. = S.P. – Profit

Cost price (C.P.) = Selling price (S.P.) + Loss
= ₹447 + ₹52 = ₹499

Therefore, the cost price of the jewellery was ₹499.

Example 2: Raju sold a study table for ₹2035 and made a profit of ₹350. What was its cost price?

Solution: Selling price (S.P.) = ₹2035 and Profit = ₹350

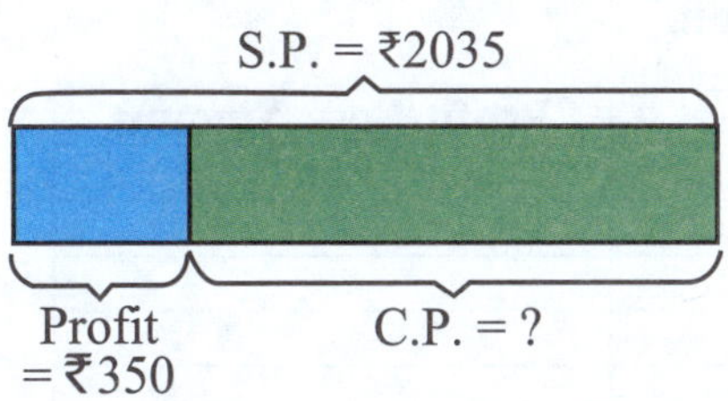

Cost price (C.P.) = Selling price (S.P.) – Profit = ₹2035 – ₹350 = ₹1685

Therefore, the cost price of the study table was ₹1685.

Example 3: Altaf bought a wooden cabinet of the Mughal period for ₹31,560 and sold it for a profit of ₹2250. What was the selling price of the wooden cabinet?

Solution: Cost price (C.P.) = ₹31,560

Profit = ₹2250

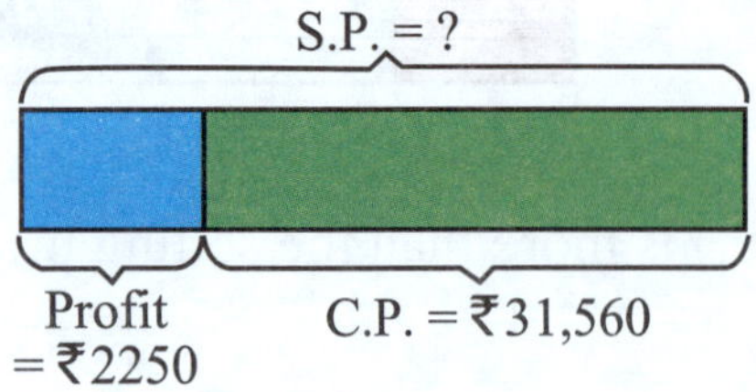

Selling price (S.P.) = Cost price + Profit

S. P. = ₹31,560 + ₹2250 = ₹33,810

Therefore, the selling price of the wooden cabinet is ₹33,810.

Example 4: Casper bought a bicycle for ₹19,260, and after some years sold it at a loss of ₹4260. What was the selling price of the bicycle?

Solution: Cost price (C.P.) = ₹19,260

Loss = ₹4260

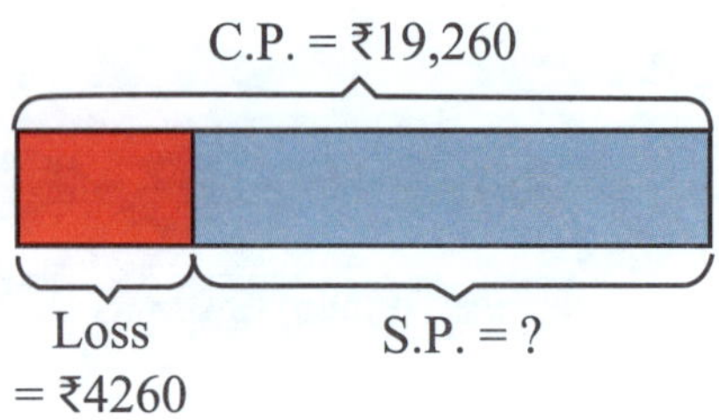

If Profit then, S.P. = C.P. + Profit

If Loss then, S.P. = C.P. – Loss

Selling price (S.P.) = Cost price (C.P.) – Loss

= ₹19,260 – ₹4260 = ₹15,000

Therefore, Casper sold the bicycle for ₹15,000.

Exercise 11.1

1. Complete the following table. One has been done for you.

a.

S. No.	C.P.	S.P.	Profit/Loss	Profit/Loss Amount
1.	₹5630	₹5580	S.P. < C.P. then Loss	₹50
2.	₹10,475	₹10,754		
3.	₹22,958	₹22,589		
4.	₹3650	₹3565		
5.	₹12,261	₹13,126		

b.

S. No.	S.P.	Profit	Loss	C.P.
1.	₹1542	--	₹200	S.P. + Loss = ₹1542 + ₹200 = ₹1742
2.	₹55,761	₹1700	--	
3.	₹4500	₹344	--	
4.	₹13,763	--	₹525	
5.	₹15,025	₹268	--	

c.

S. No.	C.P.	Profit	Loss	S.P.
1.	₹8642	₹200	--	C.P. + Profit = ₹8642 + ₹200 = ₹8842
2.	₹4,050	--	₹300	
3.	₹1033	₹215	--	
4.	₹12,377	--	₹650	
5.	₹17,456	₹345	--	

2. Find the profit or loss of an item that was bought for ₹536 and sold for ₹563.
3. Ritika sold a Christmas tree for ₹4675 and made a profit of ₹500. What was the cost price of the Christmas tree?
4. If some fruits were bought for ₹320 and sold at a profit of ₹78, then what was the selling price of the fruits?
5. A glass painting was bought for ₹2270 and sold at a loss of ₹350. What was the selling price of the painting?

Concept Map

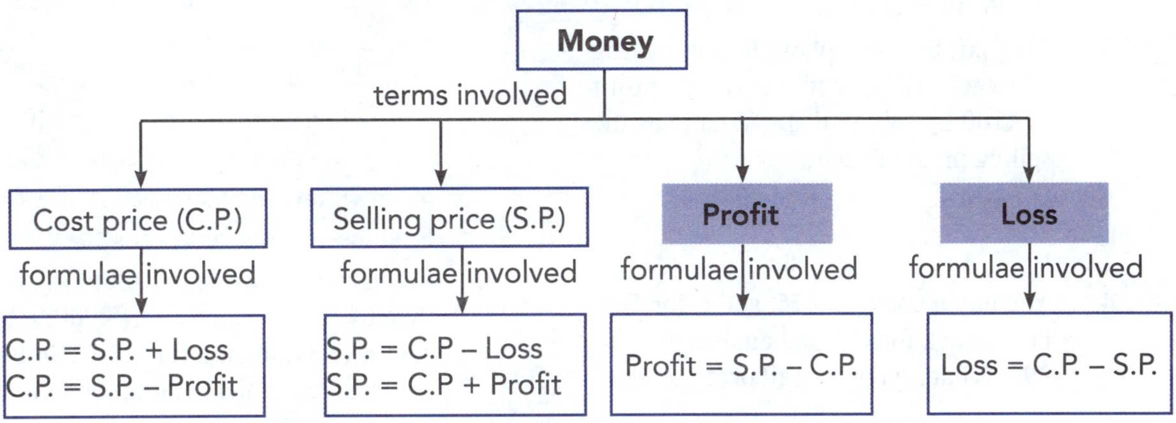

Project

Survey at school

Visit your school office and find out the following:

1. The actual cost of furniture and the amount paid by the school
2. The actual cost of stationery items and the amount paid by the school

Now, find out if the school saved money or spent more.

Revision Exercise

A. Choose the correct option.

1. Suri buys a calculator for ₹700 and sells it at a loss of ₹42. What is the selling price of the calculator?

   a. ₹568 b. ₹856

   c. ₹658 d. ₹758

2. A shopkeeper purchased an article for ₹10,000 and spent ₹1000 on transportation. He sold the article for ₹8800. Find the amount of loss or profit incurred by the shopkeeper.

   a. Loss = ₹2200

   b. Profit = ₹2200

   c. Loss = ₹1100

   d. Profit = ₹1100

3. Mr Dixit bought 4 photo frames paying ₹27 each. He earned an overall profit of ₹100 by selling them. What was the selling price of each?

   a. ₹31.75 b. ₹25

   c. ₹73 d. ₹52

4. You buy a book for ₹75, sell it for ₹85, buy it back for ₹90 and again sell it for ₹90. What is your overall profit or loss?

   a. Loss of ₹10

   b. Profit of ₹10

   c. Profit of ₹15

   d. Neither profit nor loss

5. The cost of a toy is ₹400. Nagu sold it at a profit of ₹80. Find the selling price of the toy.

   a. S.P. = ₹240

   b. S. P. = ₹420

   c. S. P. = ₹480

   d. S. P. = ₹400

B. Fill in the blanks.

1. When the cost price is more than the selling price, then it is a ______.
2. When the selling price is more than the cost price, then it is a ______.
3. If there is a profit, then selling price = ________.
4. If there is a loss, then cost price = _________.
5. If a bicycle worth ₹2000 was sold for ₹3000, then it is a _________.

C. Application based questions.

1. Prakash, a vegetable vendor, bought 25 kg beans, 20 kg carrots and 15 kg onions from the market paying ₹1150. He sold them at the following prices.
   - 15 kg beans were sold at ₹30 and the remaining was sold at ₹25.
   - 12 kg carrots were sold at ₹40 and the remaining were sold at ₹30.
   - Onions were sold at ₹15 per kg.

   Find his actual profit or loss.
2. Rahul sold a bicycle to Rohit for ₹8750 thereby making a profit of ₹900. Rohit sold it to Karan at a loss of ₹250. Find the cost at which Karan bought the bicycle.
3. A trader mixes three varieties of groundnuts costing ₹50, ₹40 and ₹60 per kg measuring 10 kg, 12 kg and 8 kg respectively. He sold the entire quantity at ₹55 per kg. Find the profit or loss made by the trader.

Did You Master?

A. Which of these, best explains the terms, profit, and loss?
   1. Gaining and profit
   2. Losing and loss
   3. No loss, no gain
   4. Gaining and losing

B. What is the definition of selling price?
   1. The price at which something is sold.
   2. The gain after selling something.
   3. The price at which something is bought.
   4. The amount of loss.

C. If SP = ₹120 and CP = ₹150, then find the loss.
   1. ₹40
   2. ₹35
   3. ₹30
   4. ₹25

₹120

D. If CP = ₹444 and SP = ₹600 then find the profit.
   1. ₹146 2. ₹156
   3. ₹136 4. ₹126

E. Ramya sold a sofa set for ₹20,354 and incurred a loss of ₹745. Find the cost price.
   1. ₹21,099 2. ₹19,609
   3. ₹20,609 4. ₹19,099

F. What is the amount of profit or loss, if the selling price is ₹5670 and the cost price is ₹5000?
   1. Profit of ₹760
   2. Loss of ₹760
   3. Loss of ₹670
   4. Profit of ₹670

G. What would be the cost price, if the selling price is ₹9843 and the loss is ₹67?
   1. ₹9890 2. ₹9990
   3. ₹9190 4. ₹9910

H. Rachel sold 1 kg apple for ₹865. If she made a profit of ₹33, what was the price at which she bought the apples?
   1. ₹823 2. ₹657
   3. ₹832 4. ₹856

I. If the cost price of an object is ₹400 and there is a loss of ₹10, what would be the selling price?
   1. ₹390 2. ₹930
   3. ₹903 4. ₹309

J. A baker sold a cake for ₹290 and made a profit of ₹29. What is the cost price of the cake?

   1. ₹216 2. ₹126
   3. ₹261 4. ₹262

How many questions did you answer correctly? Score yourself.

easy ☐ average ☐ advanced ☐ remembering ☐ understanding ☐ applying ☐ analysing ☐ evaluating ☐ creating ☐

communication ☐ representation ☐ devising strategies ☐ mathematisation ☐ reasoning and argument ☐ using symbols ☐ using mathematical tools ☐ creativity ☐

12 Geometry

Curricular Goals

- Analyse the characteristics and properties of two- and three-dimensional geometric shapes (CG-2)

Competencies

- Identify, compare, and analyse attributes of two- and three-dimensional shapes and develop vocabulary to describe their attributes/properties (C-2.1)

Why This Topic?

In mathematics, geometry is the study of shapes and figures. It is used in many different fields, from building houses and bridges to planning for space exploration.

Sun rays

Have you ever watched the beautiful sunrays falling on you during sunrise or sunset?

What do you mean by a ray?

Shapes and angles in construction

Can you identify angles and polygons in the picture of this bungalow?

Can you think of naming two other objects/places where you find lines, angles and polygons from your everyday experience?

Are You Ready?

A. Name the following figure.

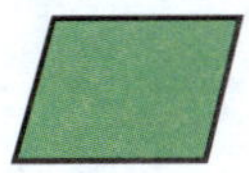

1. Square
2. Rectangle
3. Quadrilateral
4. Triangle

B. Which of the following figures shows the reflected image?

1. 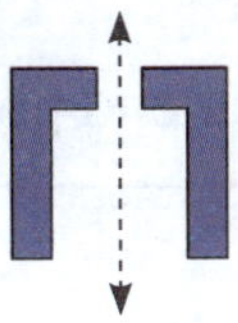
2. 
3. 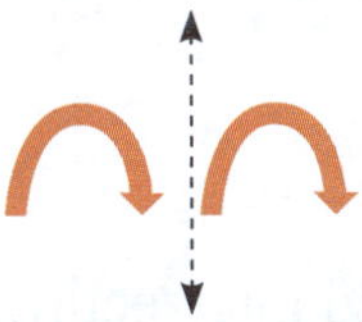
4. 

C. Which of the following is not a mirror image?

1. 
2. 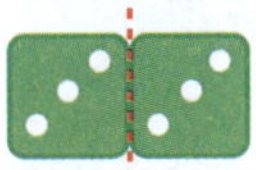
3. 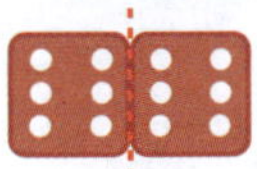
4. 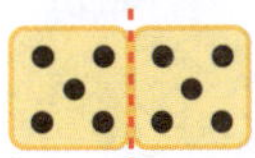

D. What is the measure of the line segment shown below?

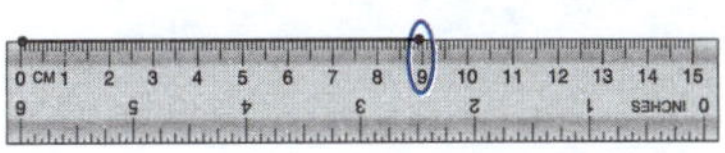

1. 8 cm
2. 6 cm
3. 10 cm
4. 9 cm

E. Which of the following is not a simple closed curve?

1. 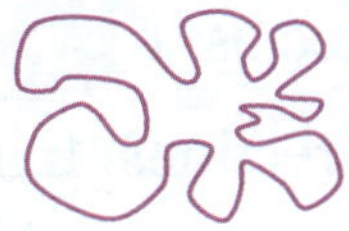
2. 
3. 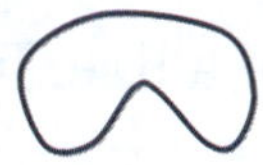
4. 

F. What is a polygon?

1. A simple closed curve
2. A closed curve which is not simple
3. A closed figure made up of line segments
4. None of the above

G. What is the radius of the circle if the diameter of the circle is 28 cm?

1. 14 cm 2. 12 cm
3. 11 cm 4. 10 cm

H. Which of the following is true about a circle?

1. It is a polygon.
2. It is round.
3. It is a quadrilateral.
4. None of the above

I. Which of the following shapes tessellates?

1. Circle 2. Trapezium
3. Hexagon 4. Oval

J. What is the diameter of a circle if the radius is 17 cm?

1. 34 cm 2. 32 cm
3. 36 cm 4. 30 cm

How many questions did you answer correctly? Score yourself.

easy ☐ average ☐ advanced ☐ remembering ☐ understanding ☐ applying ☐ analysing ☐ evaluating ☐ creating ☐

communication ☐ representation ☐ devising strategies ☐ mathematisation ☐ reasoning and argument ☐ using symbols ☐ using mathematical tools ☐ creativity ☐

BASIC CONCEPTS OF GEOMETRY

A **point** determines an exact location. It is represented by a dot (·) and denoted by a capital letter.

Point K can be represented as ·K .

A **line** extends in both directions. It has no a definite length. It has no end points.

$\overleftrightarrow{LM}$ represents a line.

A **line segment** is a part of a line. It has a definite length. It has two end points.

$\overline{AB}$ represents a line segment.

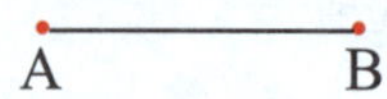

A **ray** begins at a point and extends only in one direction. It has only one end point.

$\overrightarrow{AB}$ represents a ray.

TYPES OF LINES

Intersecting Lines

If two or more lines meet at the same common point, then they are called intersecting lines.

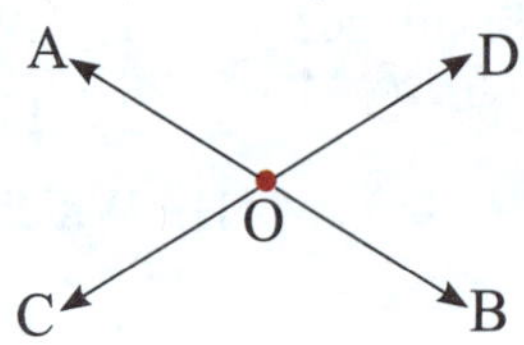

Here, line AB and line CD are intersecting at the same point O.

Perpendicular Lines

Perpendicular lines meet at the same point creating a right angle (90°). Here, line PQ and MN meet at point O creating right angles only.

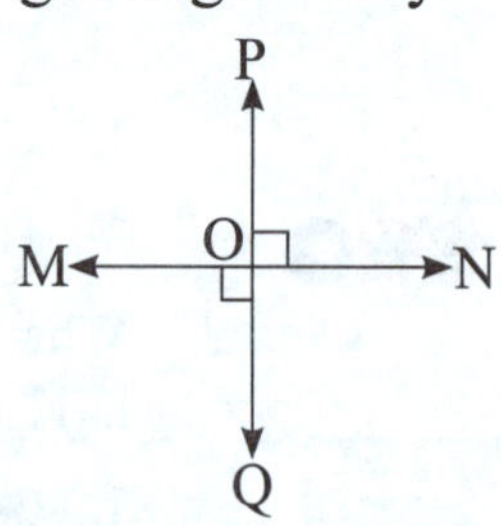

Lines PQ and MN are perpendicular to each other.

Parallel Lines

Parallel lines never meet each other at any point.

They do not intersect.

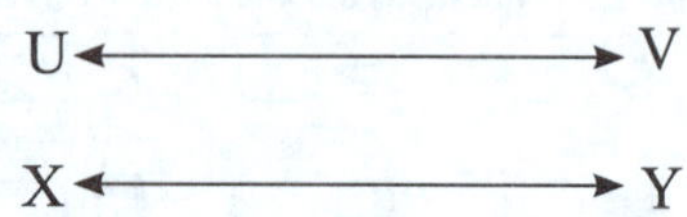

Here lines UV and XY are parallel lines since they do not meet each other even on extending them on either sides.

Exercise 12.1

1. Identify each of the following figures as line, line segment and ray.

a. 

b. 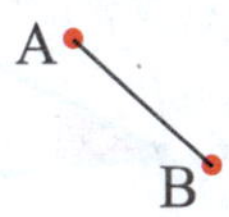

c. 

d. 

e. 

2. Name the rays and lines in the given figure.

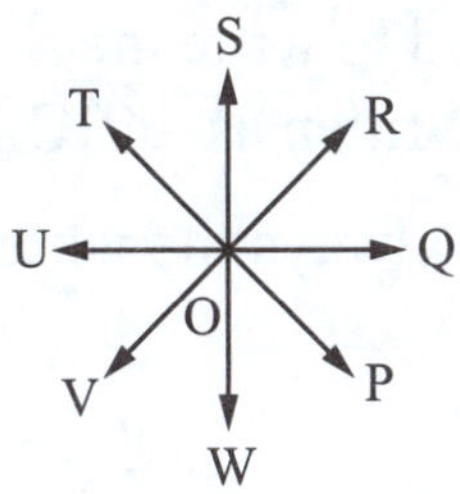

Rays	Lines

3. Identify the types of lines and name them.

a. 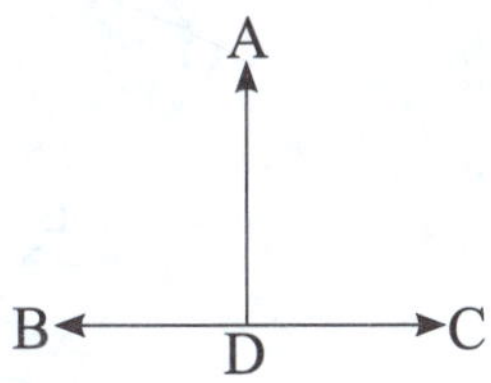

b. 

c. 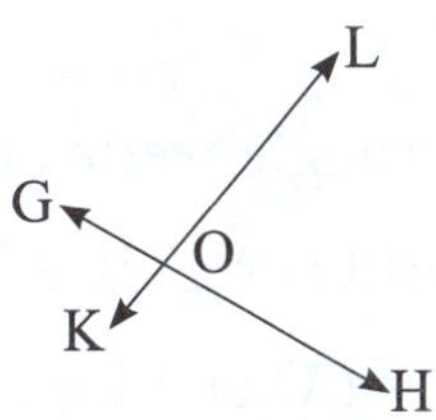

d. 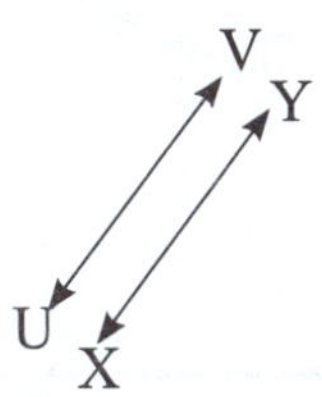

e. 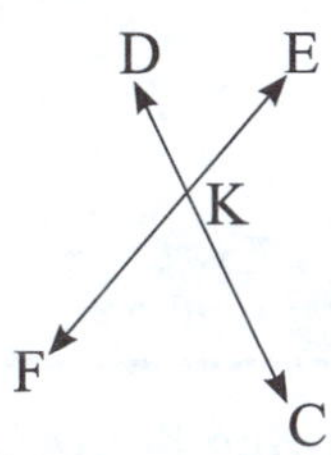

ANGLES

Two sides that meet at a corner form an **angle**.

Angles marked in some of the objects we see in our everyday life:

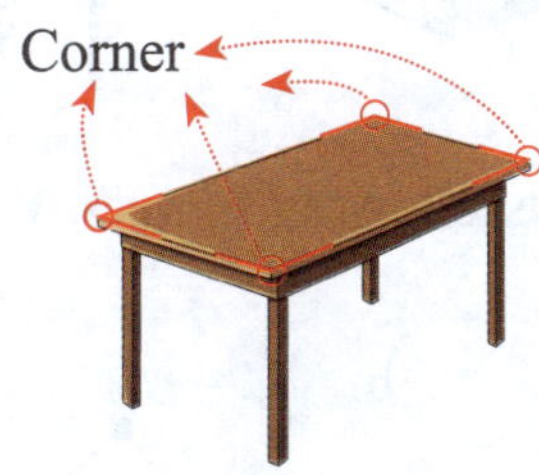

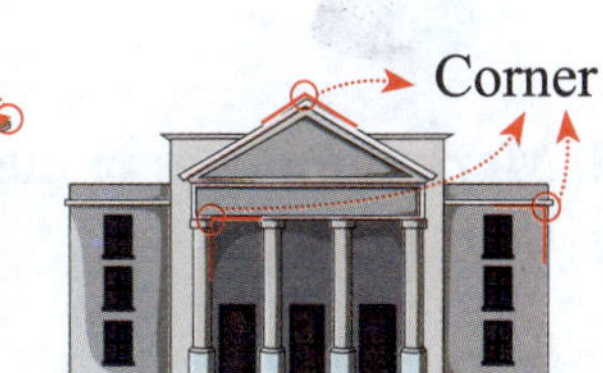

In geometry, when two rays meet at a point, they form an angle.

Parts of an Angle

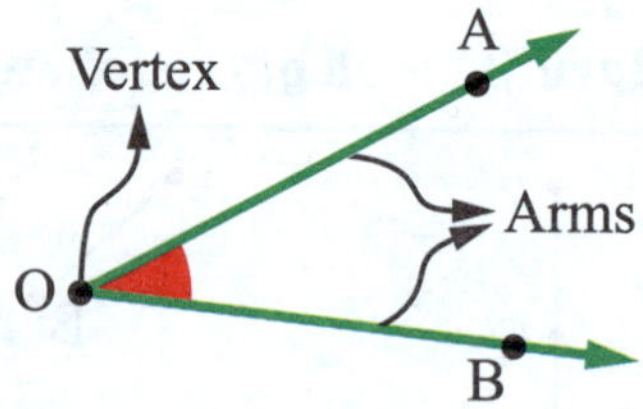

- Consider the rays **OA** and **OB**. They meet at point **O** to form an angle.
- The point where two rays meet is called the **vertex** of the angle. Here, **O** is the vertex.
- The rays that form the angles are called the arms of the angles. Here, **OA** and **OB** are the arms.
- This angle is named as **angle AOB** or **angle BOA**. ∠ symbol is used to write the word "angle". Angle AOB is written as **∠AOB** and angle BOA is written as **∠BOA**.
- The middle letter denotes the angle to which we are referring. It is always the vertex of the angle.

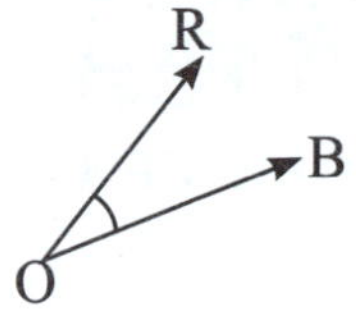

Example 1: Name the vertices and the arms of the angle shown.

Solution: Vertex = O

Arms = OR and OB

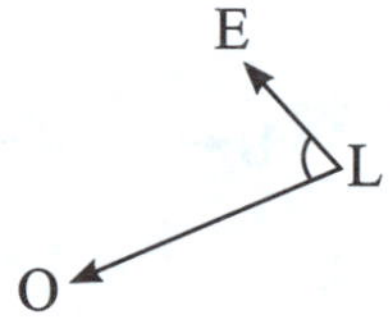

Example 2: Name the angle, vertex and arms of the angle shown.

Solution: Angle = ∠ELO or ∠OLE

Vertex = L and Arms = LO and LE

Exercise 12.2

1. Identify and mark different angles in the following figures.

a.  b.  c.  d.  e. 

2. Mark the angles in the following figures. Write the names of the angles, their vertices, and their arms.

a.

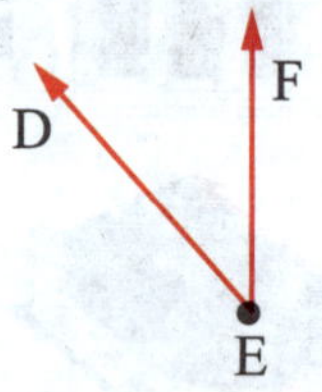

Angle:

Vertex:

Arms:

b.

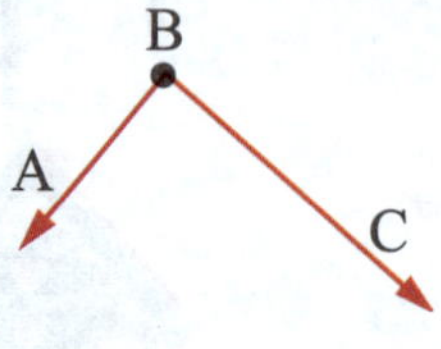

Angle:

Vertex:

Arms:

c.

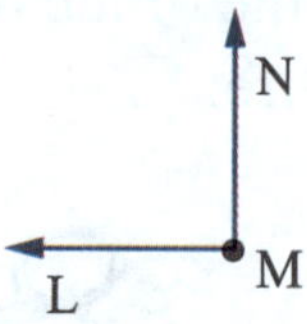

Angle:

Vertex:

Arms:

d.

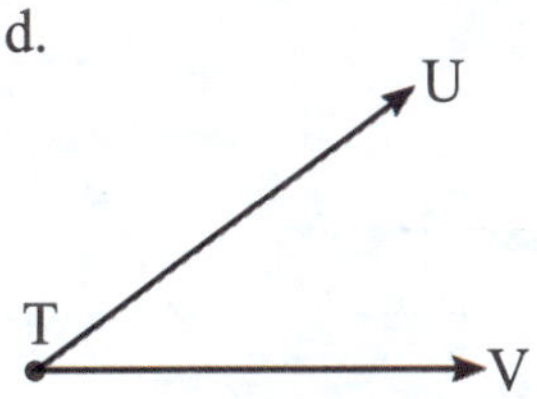

Angle:

Vertex:

Arms:

e.

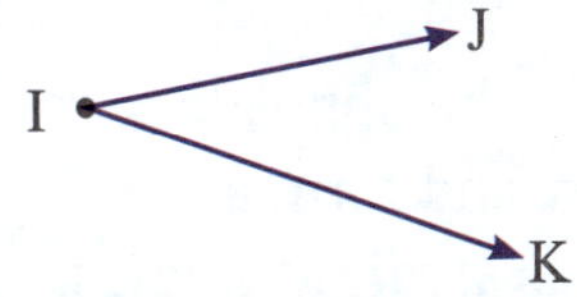

Angle:

Vertex:

Arms:

TYPES OF ANGLES

Right Angle

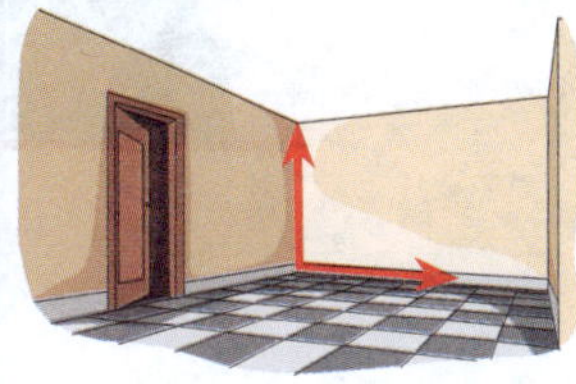

Look at the angles in the following figures.

Which shape do they remind you of?

The “L” shape. The angles that are in the L shape are known as **right angles**.

You can make a right-angle tester using a sheet of paper. Cut a circle from a sheet of paper.

Fold it into half. Again, fold it into half.

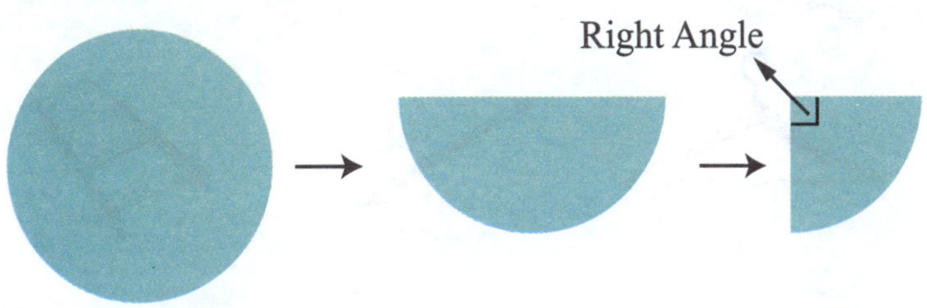

Acute and Obtuse Angles

Look at the angles in the following figures.

Use your right-angle tester and observe whether each angle is more than a right angle or less than a right angle.

Less than a right angle

Less than a right angle

The angles that are less than a right angle are called **acute angles.**

The angles that are more than a right angle are called **obtuse angles.**

More than a right angle

More than a right angle

Straight Angle

Angles whose arms lie in the opposite direction from the vertex and form a straight line are known as **straight angles**.

When two right angles are placed next to one another, we get a straight angle.

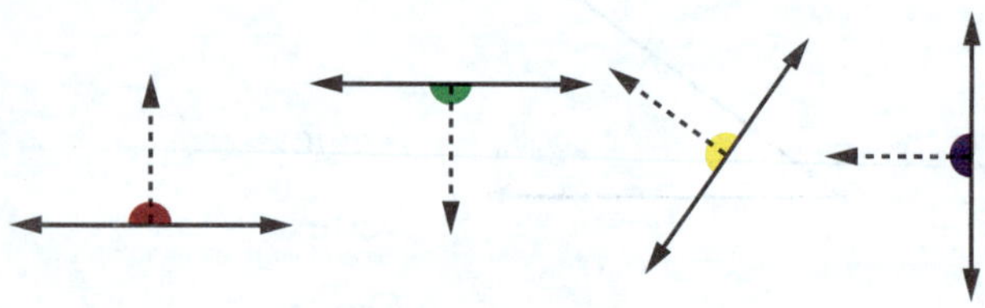

Example 3: Give a few examples for straight angles.

Solution: The following figures represent straight angles.

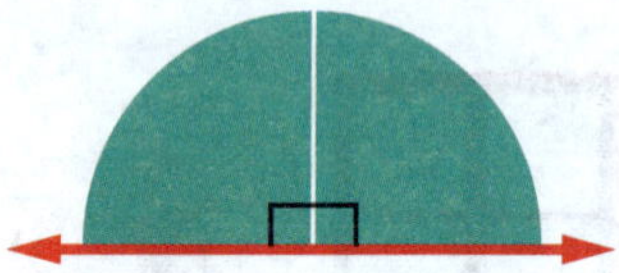

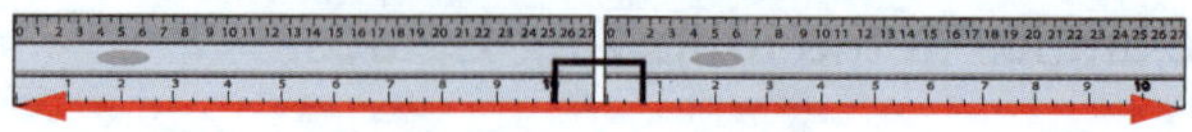

Exercise 12.3

1. Identify whether the angles marked in the following figures are acute (A), obtuse (O), right (R) or straight (S) angles.

a. 

b. 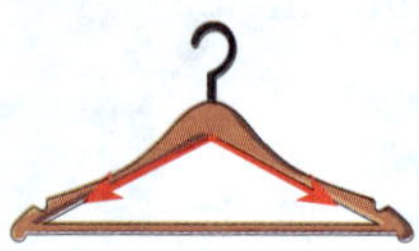

c. 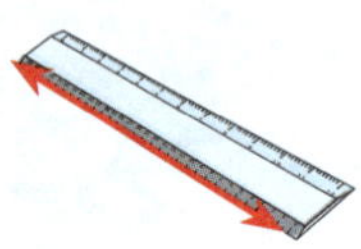

d. 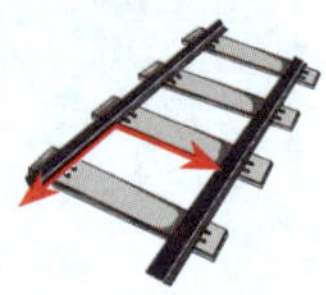

e. 

2. The following are different postures in yoga. Write the type of angle formed in each posture.

a. 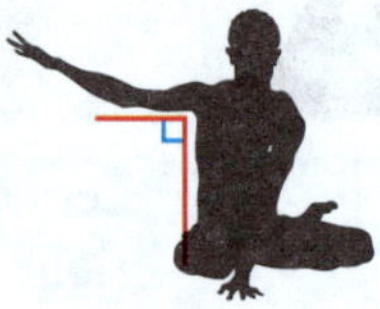

____

b. 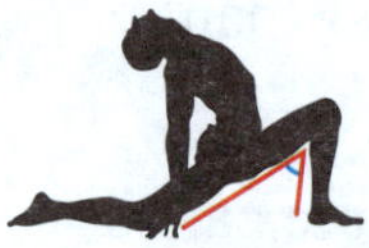

____

c. 

____

d. 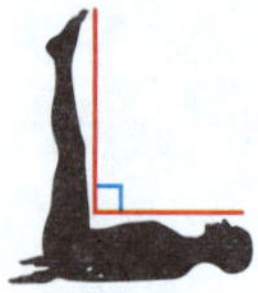

____

e. 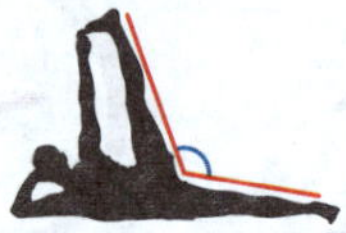

____

3. **Identify all the right angles, acute angles, obtuse angles and straight angles in the figure shown here.**

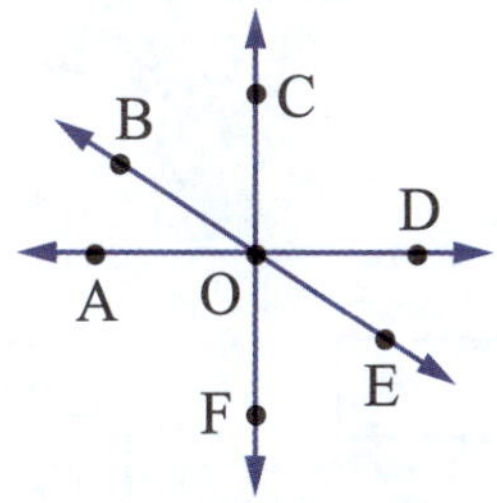

4. **Identify the types of angles and write them in the boxes with their names.**

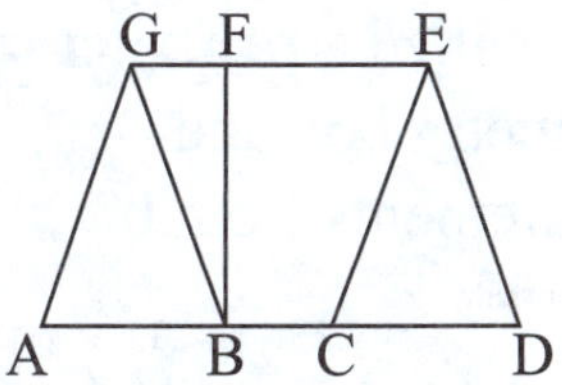

Acute Angles	**Obtuse Angles**	**Right Angles**

5. **Mark at least 15 right angles in the following football field.**

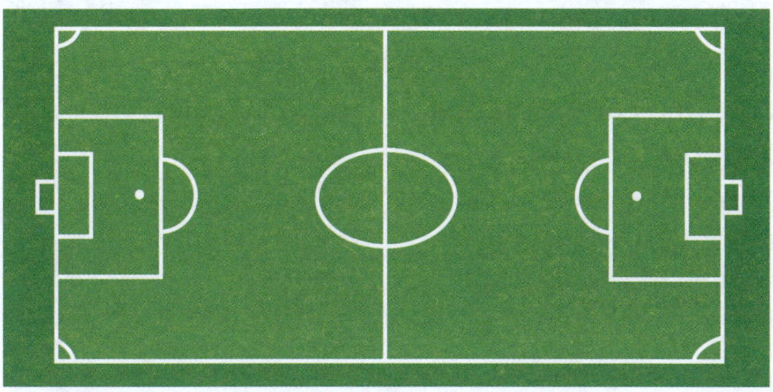

Measurement of Angles

Take two sticks and form different angles by keeping one stick constant and moving the other slowly without changing the meeting point of the two sticks. Observe that the gap between the two sticks increases. Here, the two sticks represent the arms of an angle. The gap between the two arms of any angle can be measured in **degrees.**

A **degree** is a unit of measurement of an angle. The symbol used for representing degrees is °.

Example 4: Write the measurements of the following angles.

Solution: The measurements of the following angles are:

∠QPR = 1° (one degree)

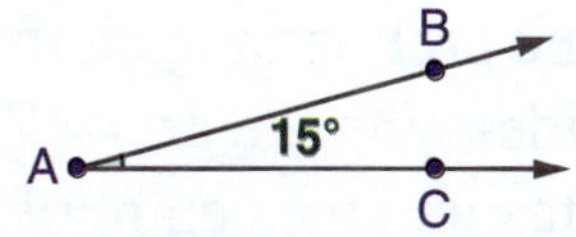

∠BAC = 15° (fifteen degrees)

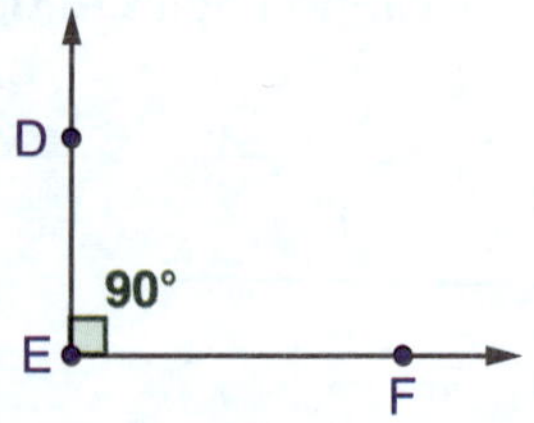

∠DEF = 90° (ninety degrees)

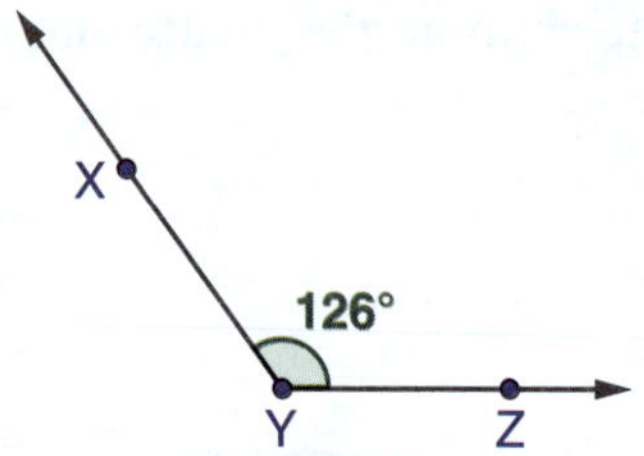

∠XYZ = 126° (one hundred twenty-six degrees)

Have you seen a D-shaped instrument in your geometry box? It is called a **protractor** and is used to measure angles. Take the protractor from your geometry box and observe it carefully. You can see that there are two rows of measurements from 0° to 180° going in opposite directions. They are called **scales.** One is the **inner scale** and the other is the **outer scale**. There are 180 divisions between 0° and 180°. Each division represents **one degree**. The bottom line is known as the **base line.**

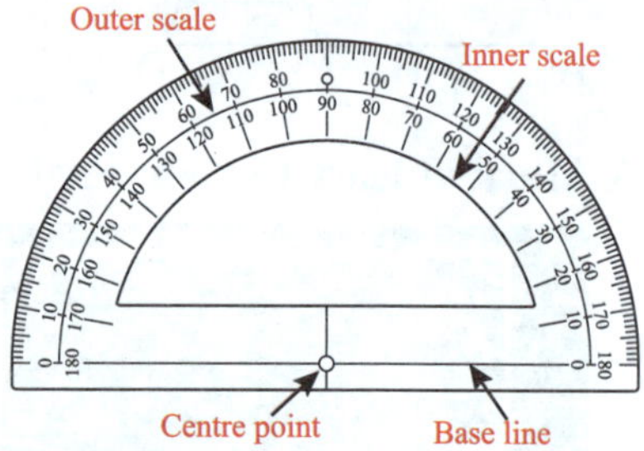

The point where the base line and the line corresponding to 90° meet is known as the **centre point.**

The protractor that is there in the geometry box is known as **half-circle protractor**. There is also a **full-circle protractor**. It also has an inner scale and an outer scale marking from **0° to 360°**.

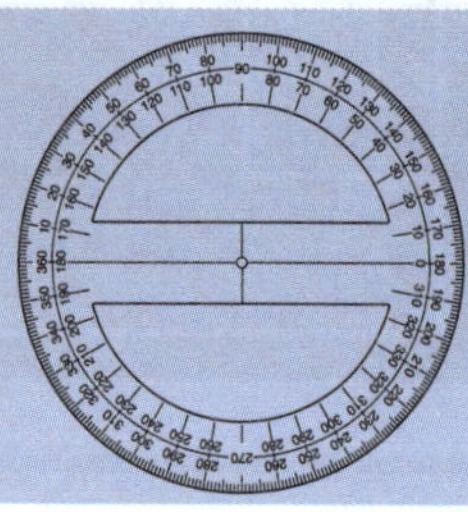

Measuring Angles Using Protractor

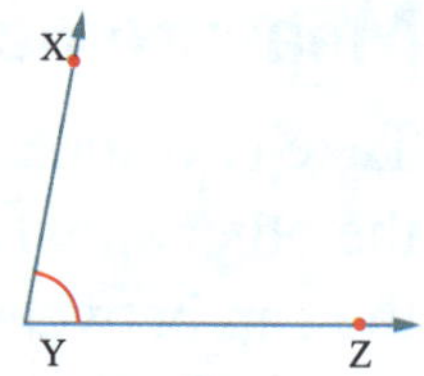

Let us measure the ∠XYZ given here using the protractor. Here, XY and YZ are the arms of the angle and Y is the vertex of the angle.

Follow the steps given below while measuring ∠XYZ.

Step 1: Place the protractor over the angle to be measured, i.e., ∠XYZ, such that the centre point of the protractor coincides with the vertex of the angle, that is, Y.

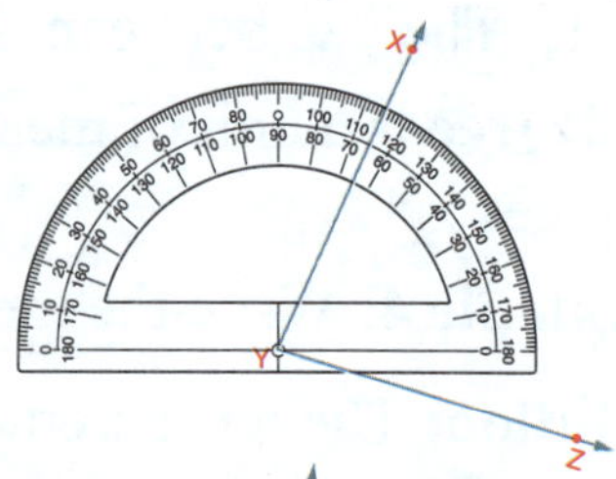

Step 2: Adjust the protractor such that the base line of the protractor coincides with the arm YZ of the protractor. Make sure that the vertex and the centre of the protractor lie on the same point.

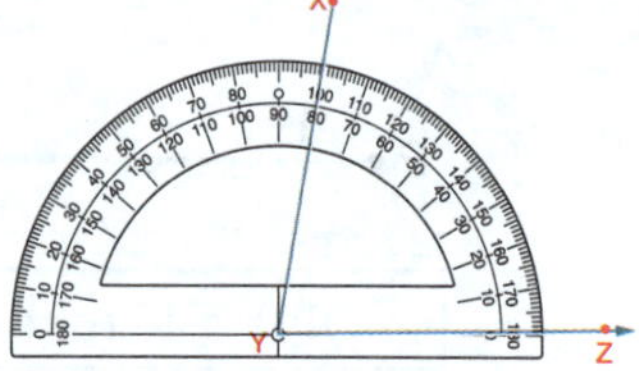

Step 3: Choose the scale (inner or outer) to be used.

Look at the scale where the baseline arm is coinciding with 0°.

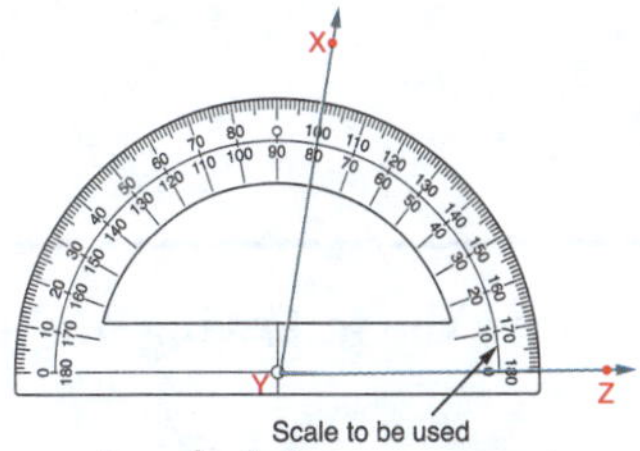

Angle Measurement

Step 4: Now, read the measure of the angle and figure out the degree by which the other arm, that is, XY is coinciding. Here, XY is coinciding with the 80° line on the inner scale.

Hence, the measure of the $\angle XYZ$ is 80°.

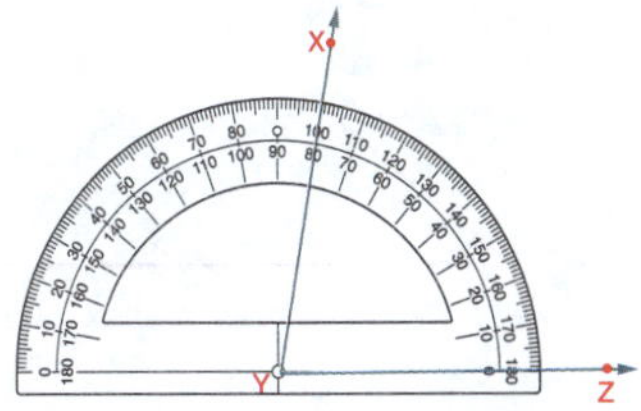

APPLICATIONS OF ANGLES IN REAL LIFE

We use angles everywhere in our everyday life right from the construction of buildings, roads, bridges, etc., to sports.

Angles in Construction

Angles in Sports

In the construction of roads, an angle called a **banking angle** is used at the turns. It is the angle at which a vehicle is inclined towards the inside of the turn.

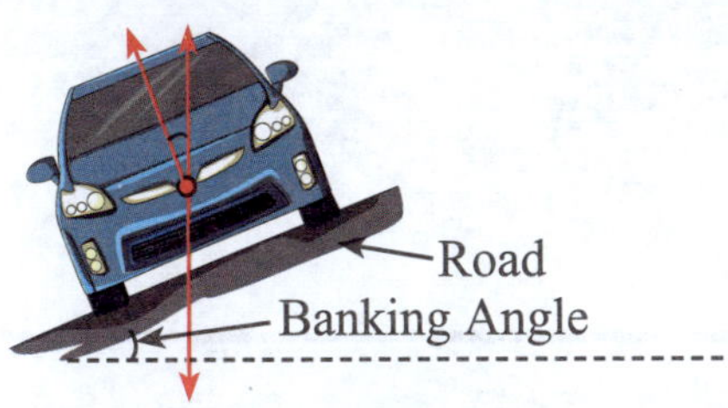

Exercise 12.4

1. Measure the following angles using a protractor and write them in the boxes provided.

a.

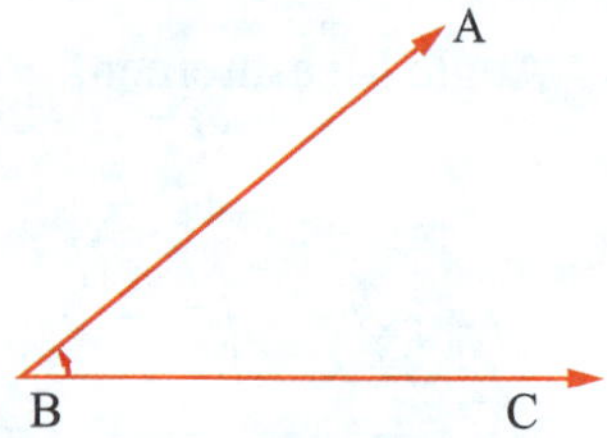

∠ABC = ____

b.

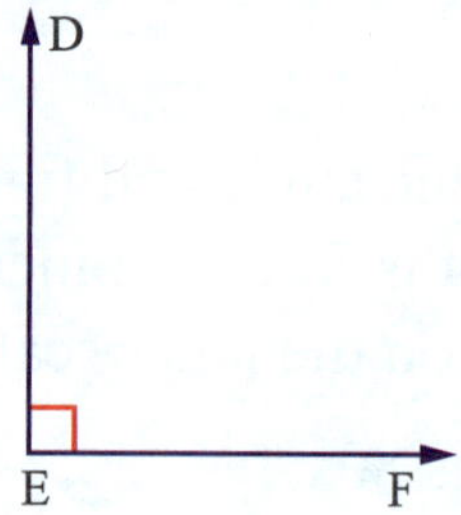

∠DEF = ____

c.

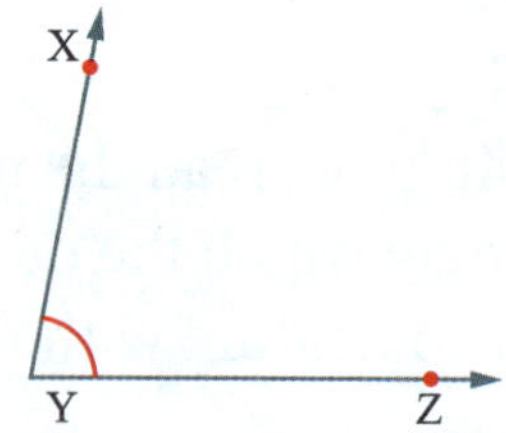

∠XYZ = ____

d.

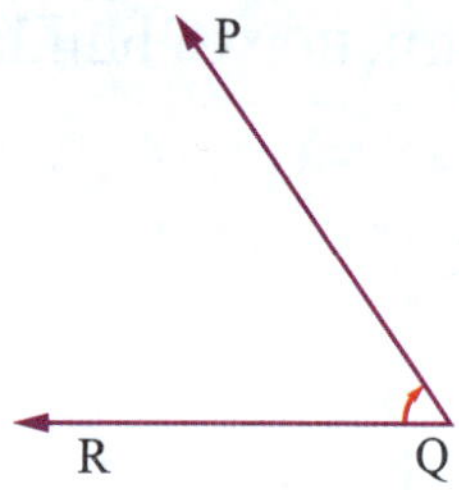

∠PQR = ____

e.

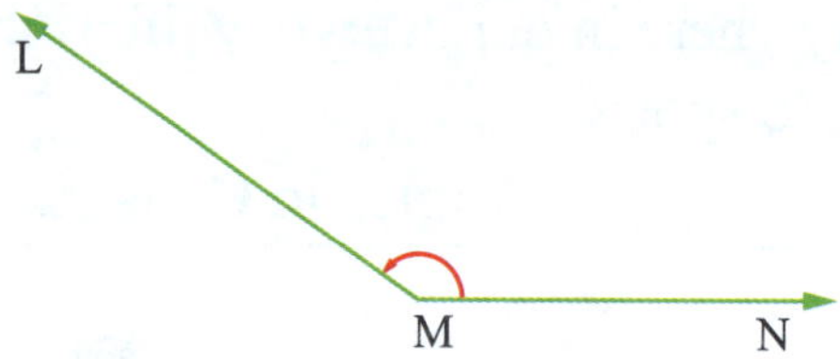

∠LMN = ____

2. Draw the following angles using a protractor.

a. ∠ABC = 25°
b. ∠RST = 55°
c. ∠XYZ = 75°
d. ∠MNO = 90°
e. ∠BCD = 105°
f. ∠PQR = 140°

3. Use a ruler and draw five angles (acute, obtuse and right angles) in the space given below. Measure them using a protractor and write their measurements.

Concept Map

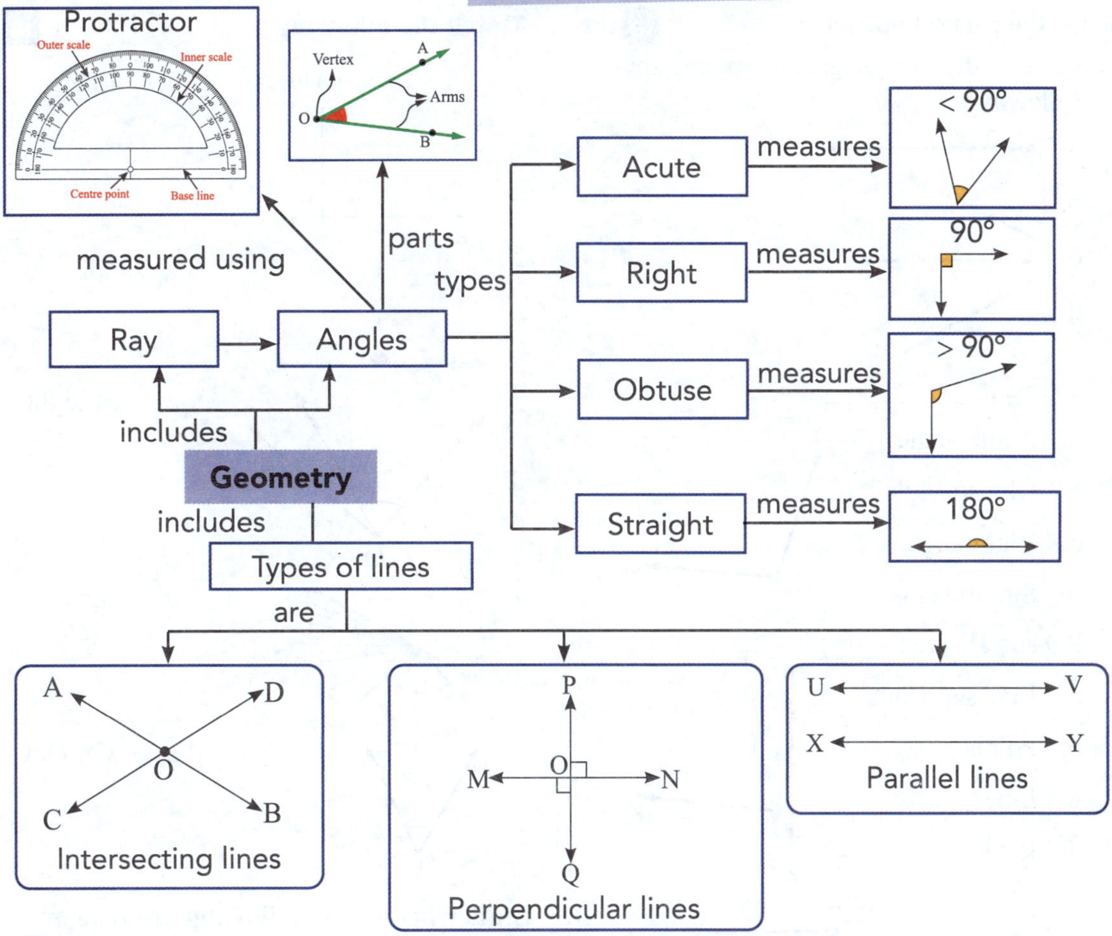

Projects

A. Angles in the house

1. Look at different parts of your house, walls, doors, windows, etc. Observe the angles and classify them as acute/right/obtuse angles. Also, guess their approximate measures.
2. Draw a floor plan of your dream house/room using different angles in the plan. List the angles used.

B. Angles in body parts

1. Collect some photos of Olympic sports events.
2. Identify the angles at which the athletes hold their body or their arms or legs. Identify the angles at which they hold the equipment they use.

Revision Exercise

A. Choose the correct option.

1. Choose the line segment among the following.

a.
b.
c.
d.

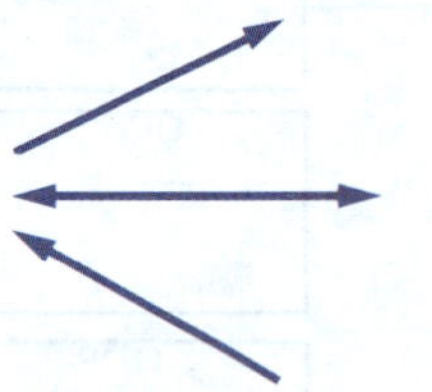

2. ∠ABC is __________ .

a. Acute angle
b. Obtuse angle
c. Right angle
d. Straight angle

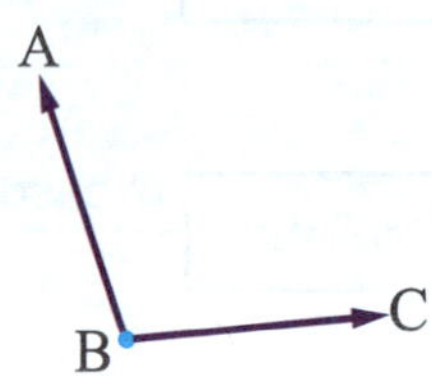

3. PQ and JK are __________ .

a. Line segments
b. Points
c. Lines
d. Rays

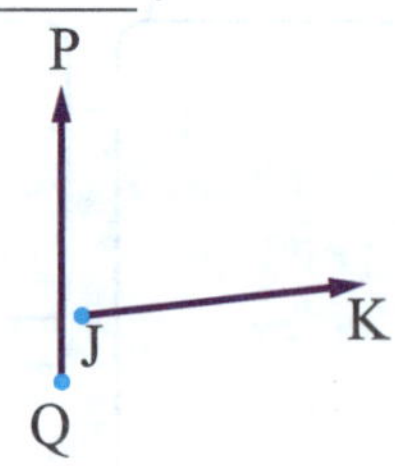

4. ∠TUV is __________ .

a. 60°
b. 80°
c. 90°
d. 30°

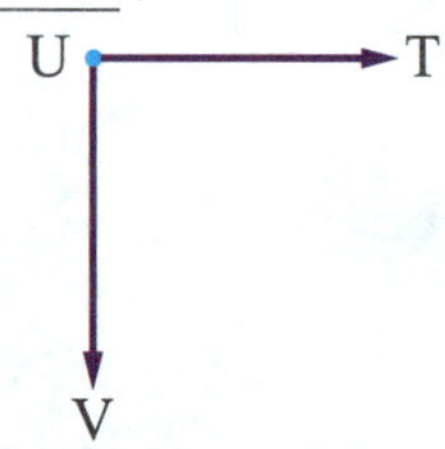

5. ∠OPN is __________ .

a. Acute angle
b. Obtuse angle
c. Right angle
d. Straight angle

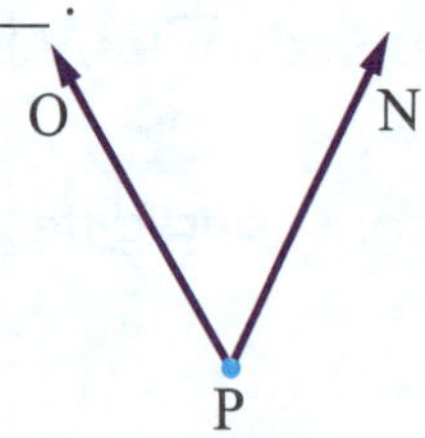

B. Fill in the blanks. (by observing the figure given below)

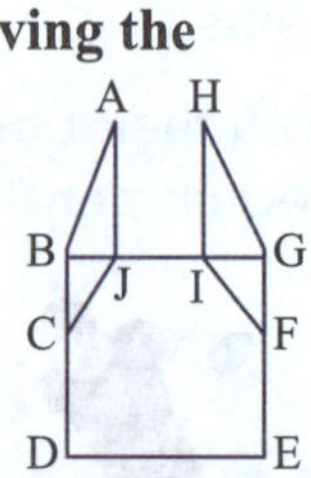

1. BDE is _____ degrees.
2. BAJ is _____ angle.
3. AJC is _____ angle.
4. BGE is _____ angle.
5. ______ is an acute angle on the line EG.

C. Match the following.

1. 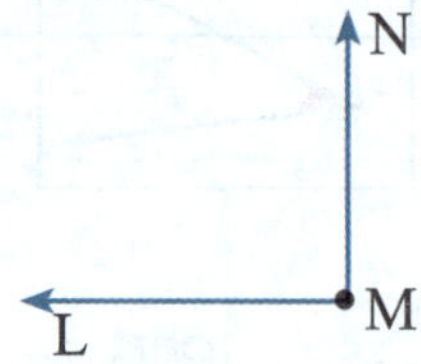

a. Lines

2. 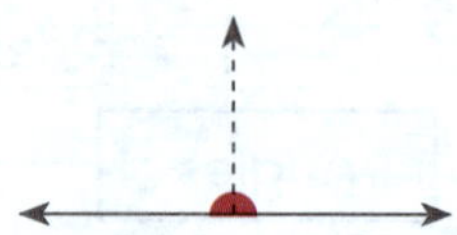

b. 90°

3. 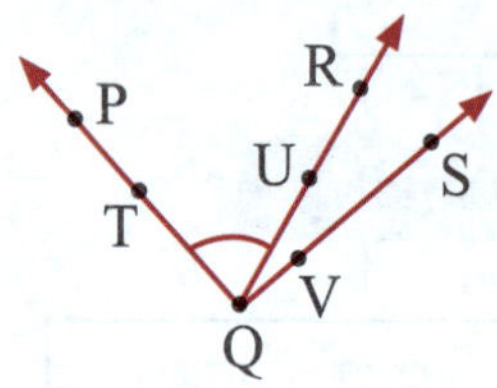

c. Straight angle

4. 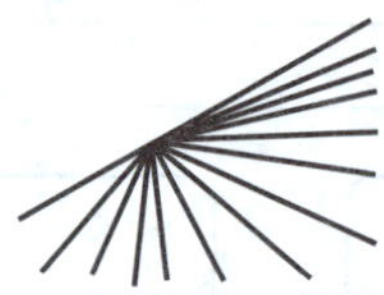

d. Acute angle

5. 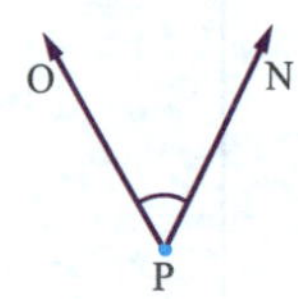

e. Vertex Q

D. State whether the following are true or false.

1. 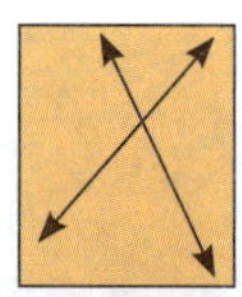 These are intersecting lines.

2. 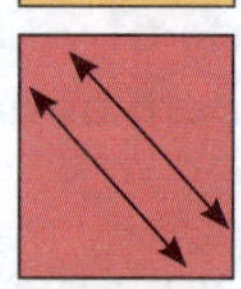 These are not parallel lines.

3. 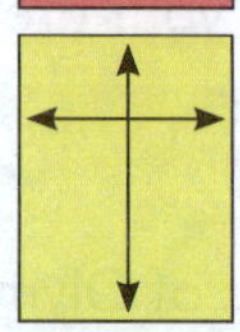 Perpendicular lines meet at the same point creating a right angle.

4. 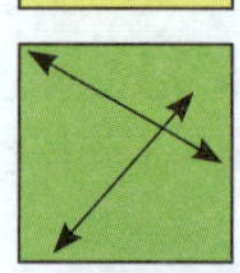 The given rays form an angle.

5. 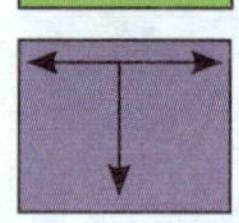 We can find only one right angle here.

E. Measure the following angles and write the type.

1. 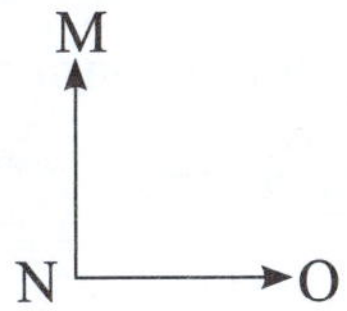

2. 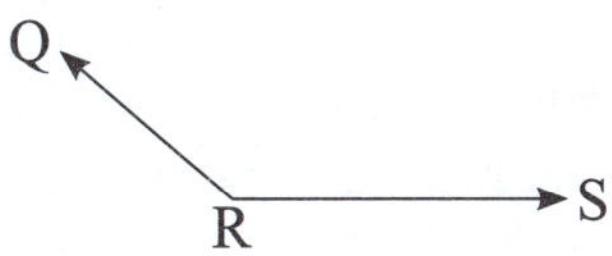

3. 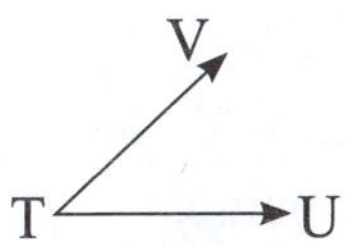

4. 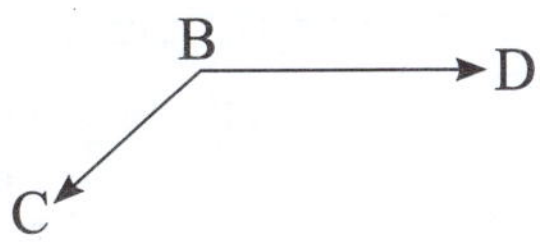

5. 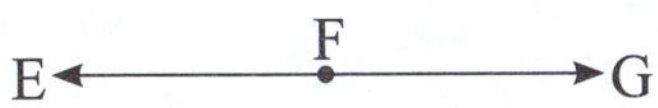

F. Application-based questions.

1. Name the type of angle formed between the tree and its shadow during different times of the day

2. Observe the position of cars parked in the parking lot, and name the type of the parking as parallel parking or perpendicular parking.

Space for rough work

Did You Master?

A. Which of the following is an example of a ray?

1. 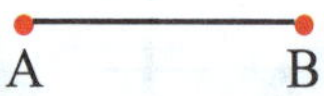

2. 

3. 

4. ΔAB

B. Name the vertex in the angle PQR of the given figure.

1. P
2. PQ
3. Q
4. QR

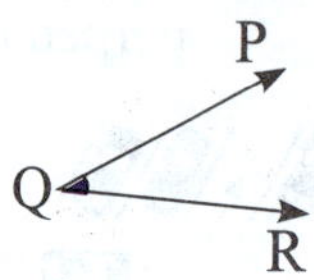

C. Name the arms of the angle MNO in the given figure.

1. NM and MO
2. NM and NO
3. MO and NO
4. MNO

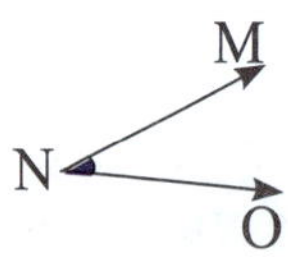

D. The marked angle in the given figure is:

1. Obtuse angle
2. Acute angle
3. Right angle
4. Straight angle

E. An acute angle is always

1. Equal to 90°
2. Equal to straight angle
3. More than 120°
4. Less than 90°

F. In the constructing of roads, which of the given angles is used in turns?

1. Right angle
2. Banking angle
3. Acute angle
4. Obtuse angle

G. The D-shaped instrument in your geometry box is called ______________.

1. Ruler
2. Perimeter
3. Compass
4. Protractor

H. An angle that measures more than 90° is ________ .

1. always a right angle
2. always a straight angle
3. always an obtuse angle
4. either an obtuse or a straight angle

I. Identify the parallel lines among the following.

1. 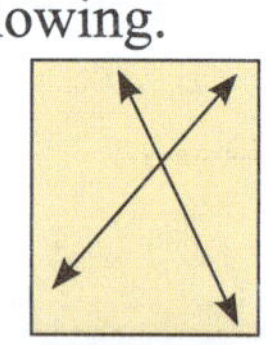
2. 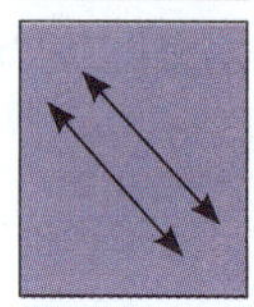
3. 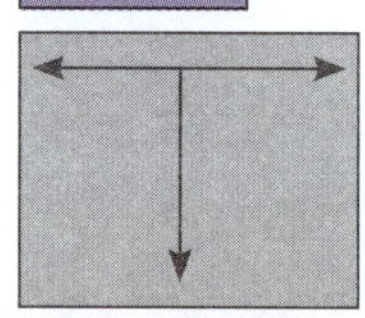
4. 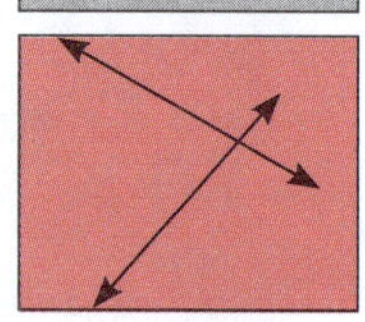

J. Which among the following is not a type of lines in geometry?

1. Intersecting lines
2. Perpendicular lines
3. Parallel lines
4. Introductory lines

How many questions did you answer correctly? Score yourself.

easy ☐ average ☐ advanced ☐ remembering ☐ understanding ☐ applying ☐ analysing ☐ evaluating ☐ creating ☐

communication ☐ representation ☐ devising strategies ☐ mathematisation ☐ reasoning and argument ☐ using symbols ☐ using mathematical tools ☐ creativity ☐

13 Perimeter, Area and Volume

Curricular Goals

- Understand measurable attributes of objects and the units, systems and processes of such measurement, including those related to distance, length, mass, weight, area, volume and time, using non-standard and standard units (CG-3)

Competencies

- Devise strategies for estimating the distance, length, time, perimeter (for regular and irregular shapes), area (for regular and irregular shapes), weight, and volume and verify the same using standard units (C-3.5)
- Deduce that shapes having equal areas can have different perimeters and shapes having equal perimeters can have different areas (C-3.6)
- Evaluate the conservation of attributes of volume, and solve daily-life problems related to them (C-3.7)

Why This Topic?

In real life, we come across many situations of finding perimeter, area and volume.

Finding the area of region and length of boundary

We can find the area of the region where plants are grown and the length of the boundary by measuring the dimensions of the farm and the farmhouse.

Finding the capacity of the boxes

We can find the capacity of each box by measuring the dimensions of each box.

Can you think of listing some more examples of finding the area, perimeter and volume from your daily life?

Are You Ready?

A. The total length of the boundary of an object is called ________.

1. area 2. vertices
3. perimeter 4. none of these

B. What is the perimeter of the shaded part in the figure, if each side of the square is 1 cm?

1. 15 cm
2. 24 cm
3. 13 cm
4. 16 cm

C. What is the perimeter of the rectangular frame?

1. 21 cm
2. 42 cm
3. 26 cm
4. 16 cm

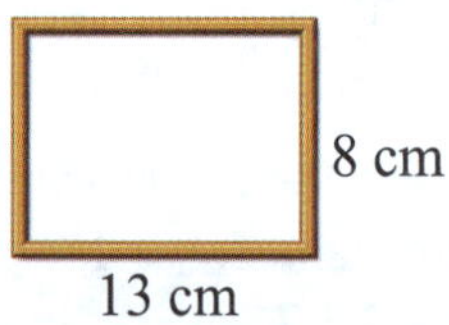

D. The perimeter of the given figure is ________.

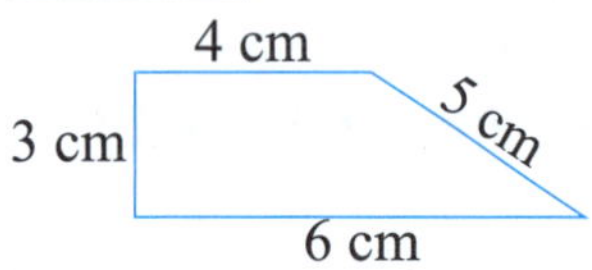

1. 17 cm 2. 23 cm
3. 18 cm 4. 12 cm

E. What is the area of the shaded portion, if the side of each square measures 1 unit?

1. 9 sq. units
2. 11 sq. units
3. 15 sq. units
4. 13 sq. units

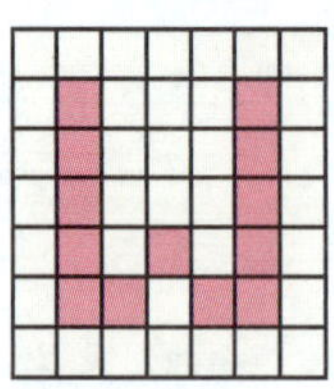

F. Find the missing length of the figure if its perimeter is 42 cm.

1. 5 cm
2. 34 cm
3. 8 cm
4. 11 cm

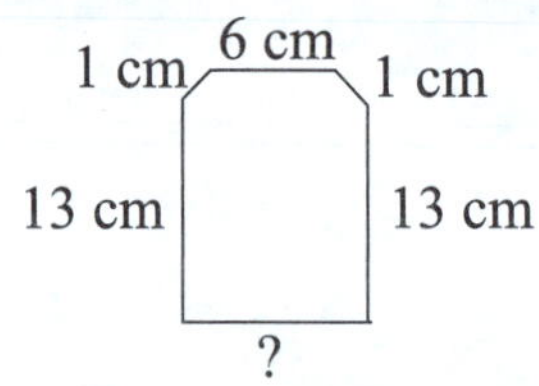

G. What is the area of the following object?

1. 23 sq. units
2. 18 sq. units
3. 13 sq. units
4. 34 sq. units

H. The perimeter of a tile having 5 equal sides is 410 cm. What is the length of each side?

1. 47 cm 2. 79 cm
3. 93 cm 4. 82 cm

I. Ravi cycles around a park shown below. How much distance will he cover if he goes around the park 3 times?

1. 4410 m
2. 1230 m
3. 5610 m
4. 5970 m

J. Harsha wanted to decorate his pillow with lace. If 1 m of lace costs ₹24, what is the total cost of the lace required?

1. ₹330
2. ₹240
3. ₹120
4. ₹450

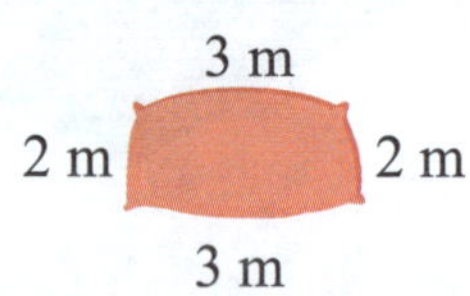

How many questions did you answer correctly? Score yourself.

easy ☐ average ☐ advanced ☐ remembering ☐ understanding ☐ applying ☐ analysing ☐ evaluating ☐ creating ☐

communication ☐ representation ☐ devising strategies ☐ mathematisation ☐ reasoning and argument ☐ using symbols ☐ using mathematical tools ☐ creativity ☐

PERIMETER

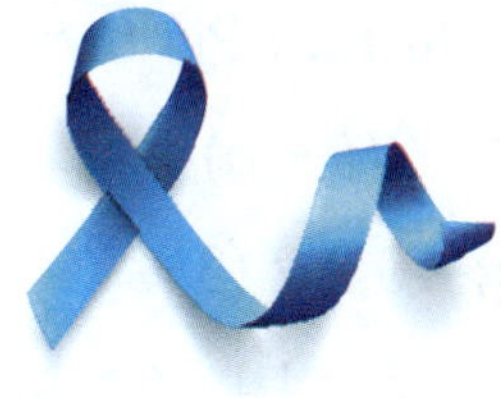

Raju wants to decorate the edges of a cardboard using satin ribbon. How much satin ribbon is required to decorate the cardboard?

We need to find the perimeter of the cardboard to find the required length of satin tape.

What is perimeter?

Perimeter is the distance covered along the boundary of a figure.

How to find the perimeter?

Perimeter is found by **adding the lengths of all the sides of a figure.**

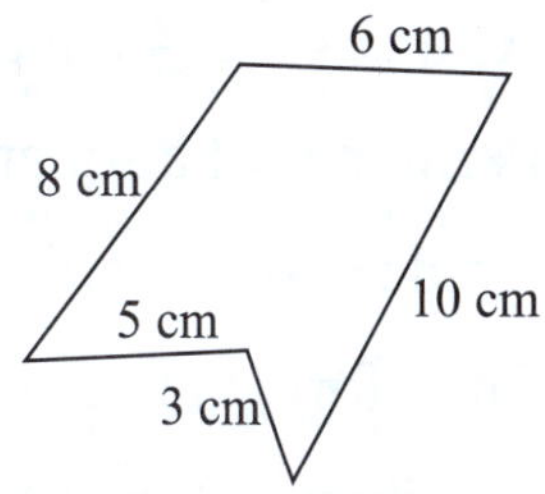

Let us find the perimeter of the given figure.

Perimeter is the sum of measurement of all the sides of the figure.

Perimeter = 8 cm + 6 cm + 10 cm + 3 cm + 5 cm

= 32 cm

Therefore, the perimeter of the figure is 32 cm.

> Walk along the boundary of your classroom until you reach the starting point. The distance covered by you is called the **perimeter** of your classroom.

Perimeter of a Rectangle

A rectangles has 4 sides. It has 2 equal lengths and 2 equal breadths.

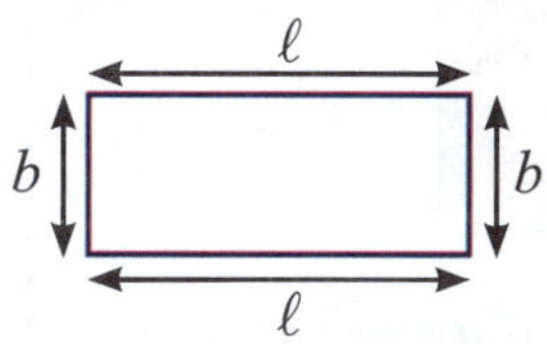

Perimeter of a rectangle

= length + breadth + length + breadth

= 2 times length + 2 times breadth

Therefore, the perimeter of a rectangle = 2 × (length + breadth)

> Let ℓ be the length of the rectangle and b be the breadth of the rectangle. Then, the perimeter of the rectangle is given by $P = 2(\ell + b)$.

Example 1: What is the perimeter of the given rectangle?

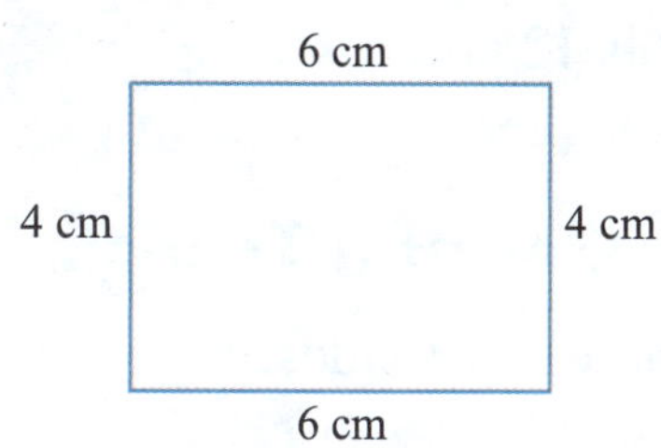

Solution: $\ell = 6$ cm and $b = 4$ cm

$P = 2(\ell + b)$

$\Rightarrow P = 2\,(6 + 4)$

$\Rightarrow P = 2 \times 10 = 20$

Therefore, the perimeter of the given rectangle is 20 cm.

Example 2: Find the breadth of the given rectangle.

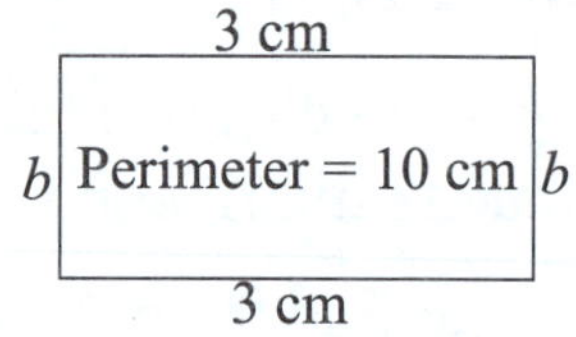

Solution: Perimeter = 10 cm, $\ell = 3$ cm, and $b = ?$

$P = 2(\ell + b)$

$\Rightarrow 10 = 2\,(3 + b)$

$\Rightarrow 2b = 10 - 6 = 4,\ b = 2$

Therefore, the breadth of the rectangle is 2 cm.

Perimeter of a Square

A square has 4 equal sides.

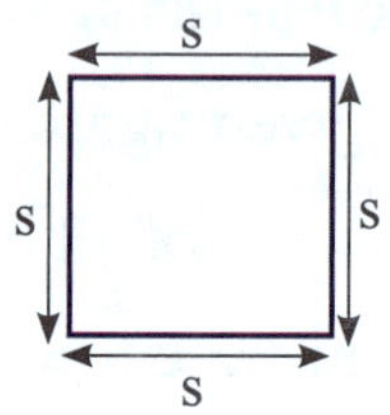

Perimeter of a square

= side + side + side + side

Therefore, the perimeter of a square

= 4 times side = 4 × (side)

Let s be the length of the square, then the perimeter of the square is given by $P = 4\,s$

Example 3: What is the perimeter of the given square?

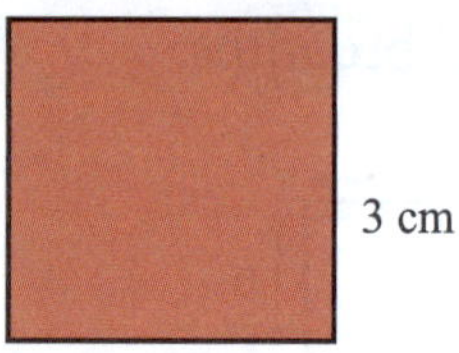

Solution: Side of a square = 3 cm

$P = 4 \times (\text{side})$

$\Rightarrow P = 4 \times 3 = 12$

Therefore, the perimeter of the given square is 12 cm.

Example 4: What is the measure of the side of the square if perimeter is 20 m?

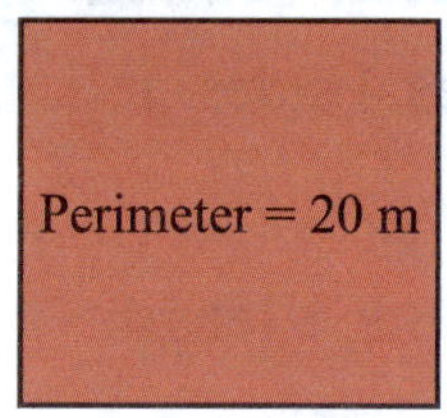

Solution: Perimeter = 20 m

$P = 4 \times (\text{side})$

$\Rightarrow 20 = 4\,s$

$\Rightarrow s = \dfrac{20}{4} = 5$ m

Therefore, each side of the given square is 5 m.

Perimeter of a Triangle

A triangle has 3 sides.

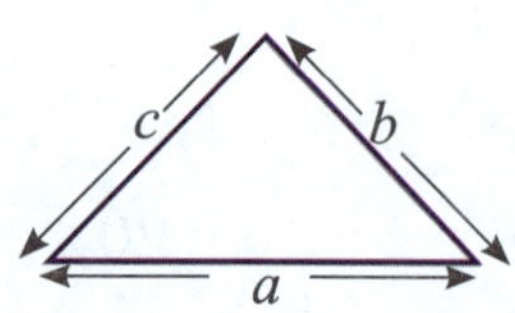

Perimeter of a triangle

= side 1 + side 2 + side 3

Therefore, the perimeter of a triangle = Sum of three sides

Let a, b and c be the length of the sides of the triangle, then the perimeter of the triangle is given by $P = a + b + c$.

Example 5: What is the perimeter of the given triangle?

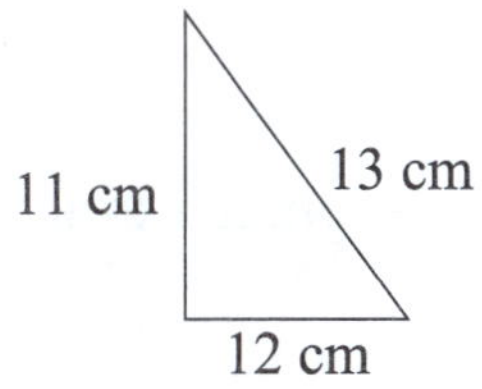

Solution: Length of 3 sides = 11 cm, 12 cm and 13 cm

$P = a + b + c$

$\Rightarrow P = 11 + 12 + 13 = 36$

Therefore, the perimeter of the given triangle is 36 cm.

Example 6: What is the length of the missing side of the triangle?

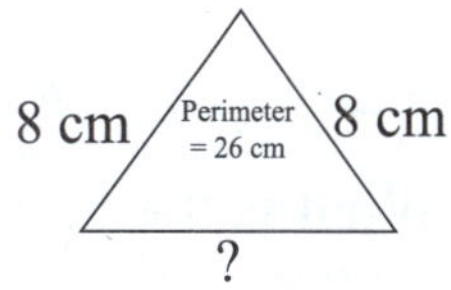

Solution: Length of 2 Sides = 8 cm, 8 cm, and perimeter = 26 cm

$P = a + b + c$

$\Rightarrow 26 = 8 + 8 + c$

$\Rightarrow c = 26 - 16 = 10$ cm

Therefore, the length of the missing side of the triangle is 10 cm.

WORD PROBLEMS ON PERIMETER OF RECTANGLE, SQUARE AND TRIANGLE

Example 7: Pramod has a small farm which is rectangular in shape. Its length is 20 m and breadth is 12 m. Find the perimeter of the farm and the cost of fencing the farm if it is ₹300 per metre.

Solution: $P = 2(\ell + b)$

Length (ℓ) of the farm = 20 m, breadth (b) of the farm = 12 m and the cost of fencing the farm per metre = ₹300

Perimeter of the farm

$= 2\ (\ell + b) = 2\ (20 + 12) = 2\ (32) = 64$ m

The cost of fencing the farm = Perimeter of the farm × Cost of fencing per metre = 64 × ₹300 = ₹19,200

Therefore, the perimeter of the rectangular farm is 64 m and the cost of fencing the farm is ₹19,200.

Example 8: Pradeep goes for a walk to a nearby park which is of square shape. The length of its side is 100 m. If he takes three rounds of the park, what is the distance covered by him?

Solution: $P = 4 \times$ side

The shape of the park is square, and its side is 100 m.

Pradeep walks 3 rounds.

Perimeter of the square park = 4 × s = 4 × 100 m = 400 m.

The distance covered by Pradeep is 3 times the perimeter of the park

$= 3 \times 400 \text{ m} = 1200 \text{ m}.$

Therefore, the distance covered by Pradeep is 1200 m.

Example 9: What is the total length of the beading of the triangular frame if each side measures 30 cm?

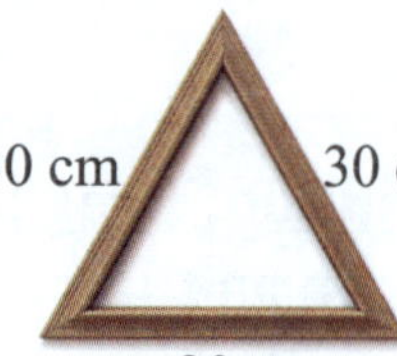

Solution: P = Sum of all 3 sides

Measure of each side = 30 cm

Perimeter of the triangular frame = 30 cm + 30 cm + 30 cm = 90 cm

Therefore, the total length of the beading of triangular frame is 90 cm.

Exercise 13.1

1. Find the perimeter of the following objects using formula.

a.

b.

c.

d.

e.
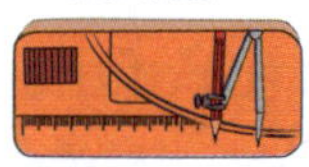

2. Find the missing sides in the following figure.

a. Perimeter = 48 cm

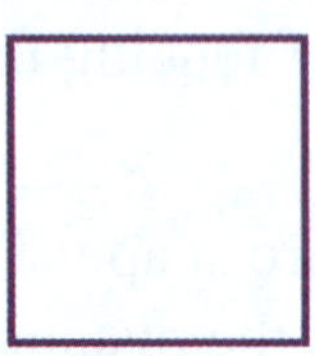

b. Perimeter = 30 cm

c. Perimeter = 32 cm

d. Perimeter = 80 cm

e. Perimeter = 150 cm

3. Find the perimeter of the following.

a.
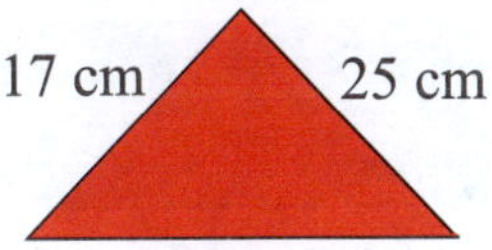

b.
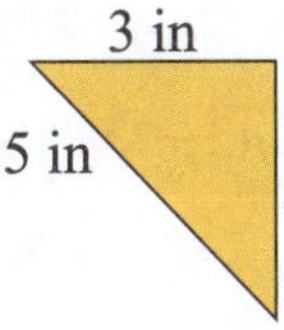

c.

d.
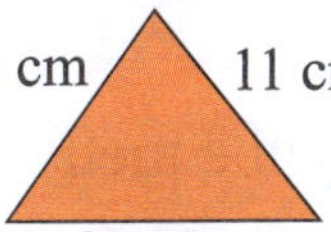

e.
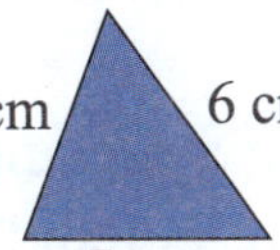

4. Solve the following problems.

a. Arvind bought a computer. The length and the breadth of the computer monitor are 30 inches and 20 inches, respectively. Find the perimeter of the computer monitor.

b. Hari bought a rectangular-shaped cake of length 30 cm and breadth 25 cm for his sister's birthday. He wants to decorate it by putting a ribbon along its edges. What is the length of the ribbon required by Hari?

c. Harshini has a triangular pillow, the sides measuring 50 cm, 60 cm and 60 cm respectively. She wants to put a lace border around it. What is the length of the lace required by her?

d. The perimeter of a hall is 88 m. If its length is 36 m, find its breadth.

e. A square field has a perimeter of 640 m. Find the length of its side.

AREA

Place different objects such as a book, paper, eraser, etc., on your bench. Each of them occupies a certain region on the bench.

The amount of surface or region covered by an object is called its **area**. The units of area are sq. cm (square centimetre), sq. m (square metre), etc., depending on the unit given in the question.

Drawing Room

Kitchen

Area of a Rectangle

In your previous classes, you have learnt how to find the area of certain figures by counting the number of unit squares they occupy.

Let us find the area of rectangles and squares by deriving the formulae.

Rakesh wants to tile the floors of different rooms in his house.

The floors of the rooms are shown.

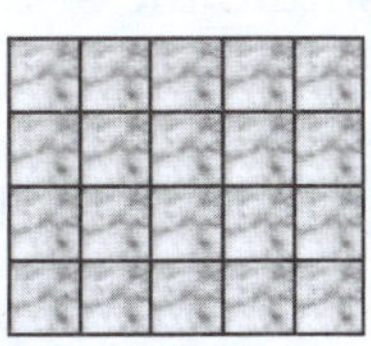

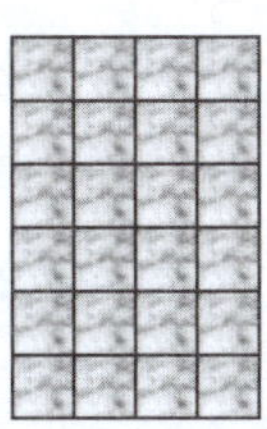

Find the length and the breadth of each floor and complete the table given below.

Room	Length (ℓ)	Breadth (b)	Area by counting squares	$\ell \times b$
Drawing Room	5	4	20	20
Kitchen	4	6	24	24

From the table, we can observe that the area of a rectangle obtained by the method of counting squares and by finding the product of its length and breadth are the same.

Area of the rectangle = length × breadth

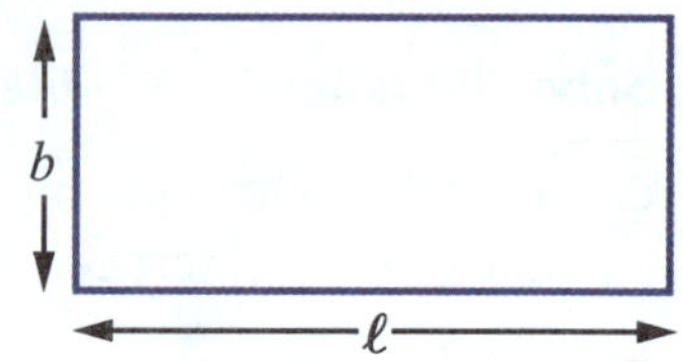

Let ℓ be the length and b be the breadth of the rectangle, then the area of the rectangle is given by $\mathbf{A = \ell \times b}$.

Example 10: Find the area of the given rectangle.

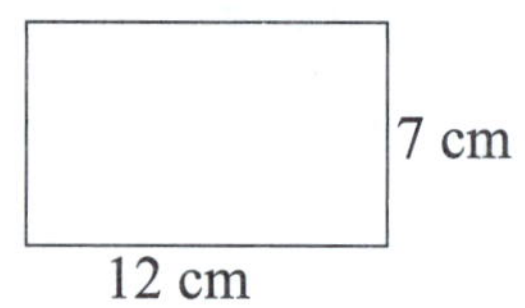

Solution: $\ell = 12$ cm and b = 7 cm

Area of rectangle = $\ell \times b$

A = 12 × 7 = 84 sq. cm.

Therefore, the area of the given rectangle is 84 sq. cm.

Example 11: Find the length of the given rectangle.

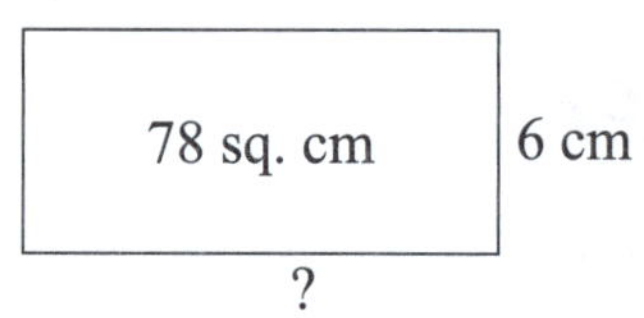

Solution: Area = 78 sq. cm and $b = 6$ cm

$A = \ell \times b$

$78 = \ell \times 6 \Rightarrow = \frac{78}{6} = 13$ cm.

Therefore, the length of the given rectangle is 13 cm.

Area of a Square

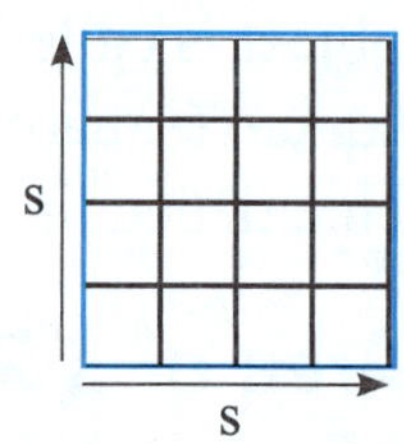

Area of the given square by counting number of small squares in the grid = 16 square units.

Can you find the area of a square using the formula?

We can find the area of square using the formula of finding the area of a rectangle.

Area of a rectangle = length × breadth

Let us substitute the sides of square in place of length and breadth of the rectangle with the sides of the square.

Therefore, the area of a square = side × side

Let s be the side of a square, then its area is given by $\mathbf{A = s \times s}$

Example 12: What is the area of the square with side 12 cm?

Solution: A = $s \times s$

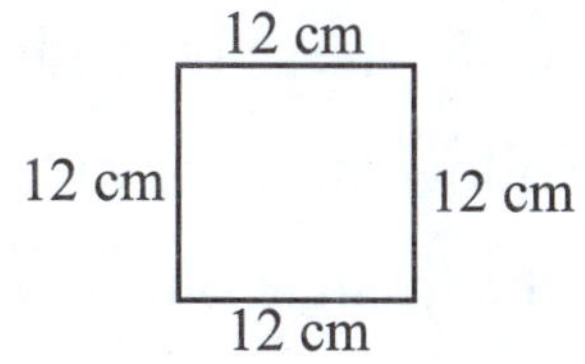

Each side of the given square is 12 cm.

The area of the given square = 12 cm × 12 cm

Therefore, the area of the given square is 144 sq. cm.

Example 13: Find the measurement of each side of the given square.

Solution: A = $s \times s$

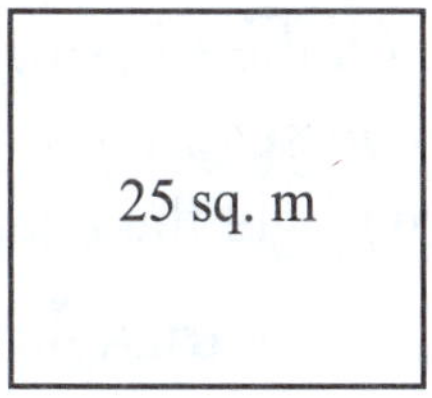

The area of the given square is 25 sq. m.

$25 = s \times s$

Identify the number that on being multiplied by itself is equal to the given area, that is 5 × 5 = 25.

Therefore, the measurement of each side of the given square is 5 m.

Area of a Triangle

You already know how to find the area of a rectangle if its length and breadth are known. We can use it to find the area of a triangle.

Complete the rectangle as shown in the following figure.

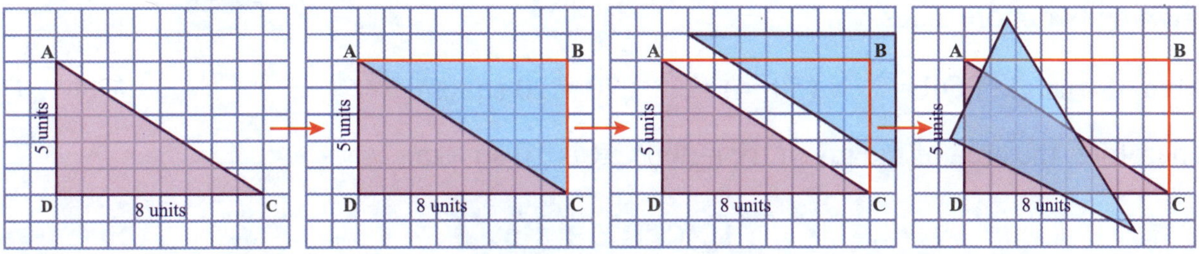

Trace this rectangle on a transparent sheet. Cut the two triangles. Place one triangle over the other. The two triangles overlap each other. So, they are of the same area and the sum of the areas of these two triangles is equal to the area of the rectangle.

Area of one triangle is half the area of the rectangle.

Area of triangle ADC = $\frac{1}{2}$ × area of the rectangle

Area of rectangle ABCD = (8 × 5) = 40 sq. units.

Area of triangle ADC = $\frac{1}{2} \times (8 \times 5)$ or $\frac{1}{2} \times 40$

= 20 sq. units

Therefore, area of triangle ADC = 20 sq. units.

Consider the triangle shown here.

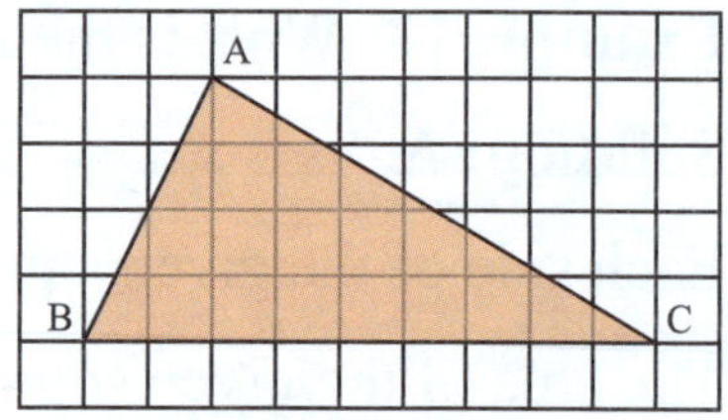

Can you use the same method to find the area of this triangle?

Yes. Follow the steps given below to find its area.

Trace the triangle on another sheet.

Divide the triangle into two triangles as shown in the figure and cut them.

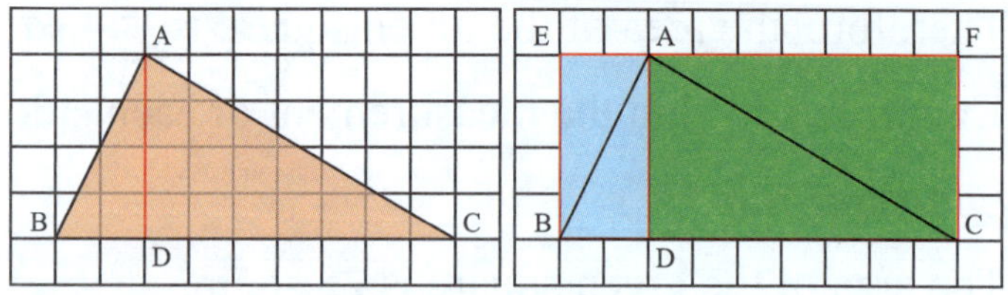

Then flip the two cut out parts and keep on the sides of the triangle in the reverse order as shown. Then you will get the nearest rectangle containing this triangle.

Area of the triangle ABC = Area of the triangle ABD + Area of the triangle ADC

Area of triangle ABD $= \frac{1}{2} \times (7 \times 4) = \frac{1}{2} \times 28 = 14$ sq. units

Area of triangle ADC $= \frac{1}{2} \times (2 \times 4) = \frac{1}{2} \times 8 = 4$ sq. units

Therefore, area of the triangle ABC = 14 + 4 = 18 sq. units.

Example 14: Find the area of the given triangle PQR.

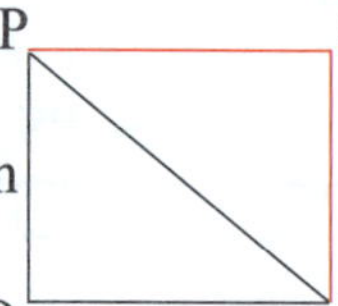

Solution: Make the given triangle PQR as rectangle PQRS by drawing two more sides.

Area of triangle PQR $= \frac{1}{2} \times (5 \times 4) = \frac{1}{2} \times 20 = 10$ sq. cm.

Therefore, the area of the given triangle PQR is 10 sq. cm.

Exercise 13.2

1. Find the area of the following objects using formula.

a. 25 in, 25 in

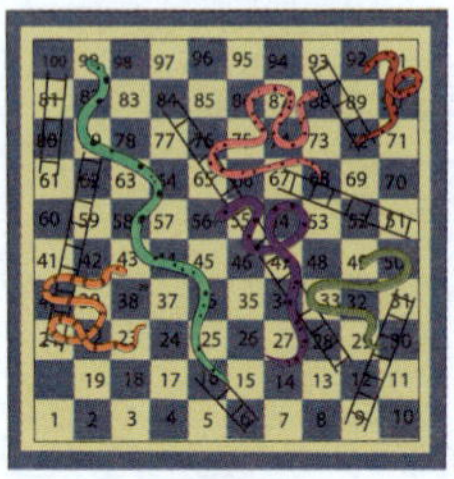

b. 2 cm, 2 cm

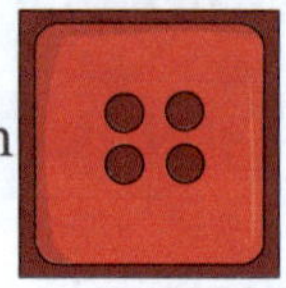

c. 50 cm, 30 cm

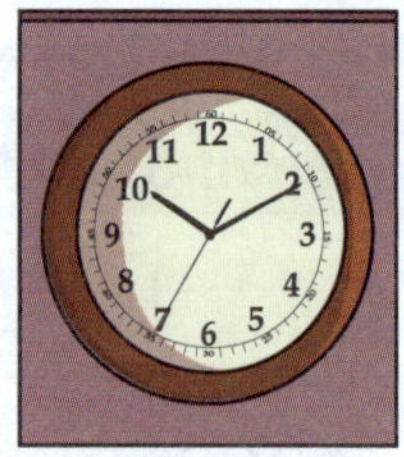

d. 12 cm, 8 cm

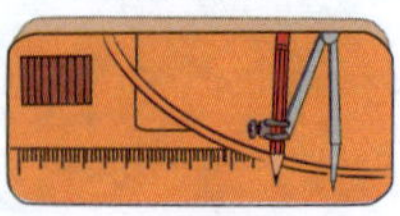

e. 10 cm, 6 cm

2. Find the area of the following if  **= 1 square unit.**

a. 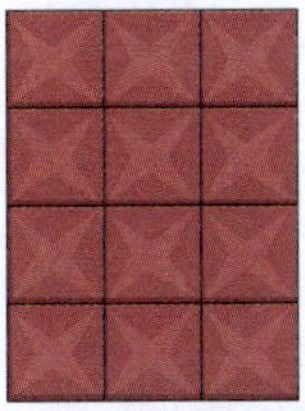

b. 

c. 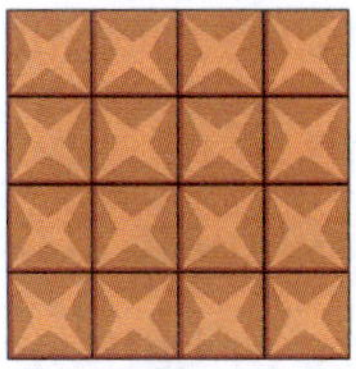

d. 

e. 

3. Find the missing sides in the following figures.

a. Area = 1500 sq. units

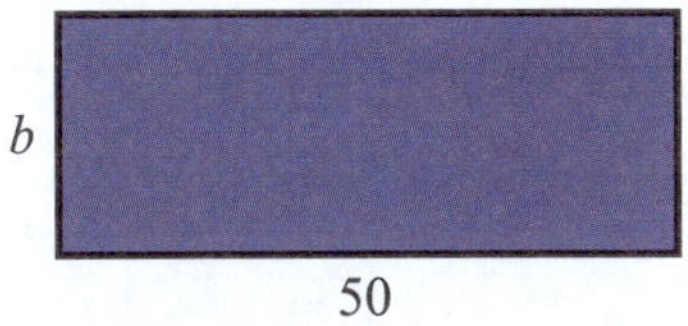

b. Area = 100 sq. units

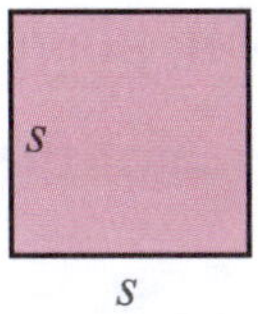

c. Area = 75 sq. units

d. Area = 152 sq. units

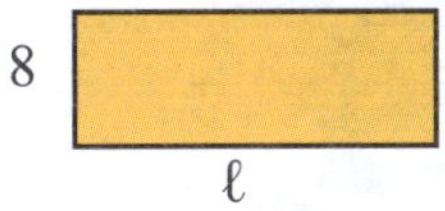

e. Area = 121 sq. units

4. Find the area of the following triangles without counting squares.

a. 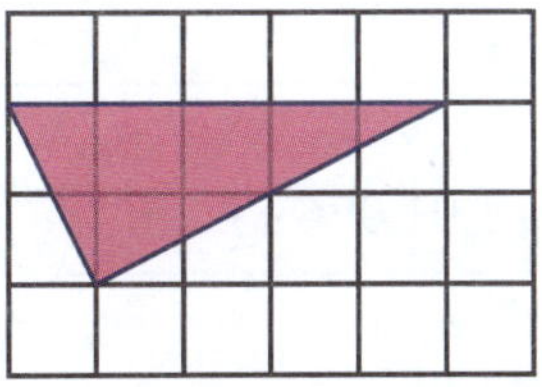

b. 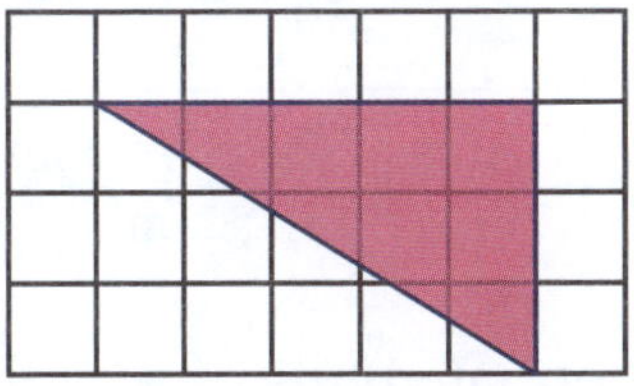

c. 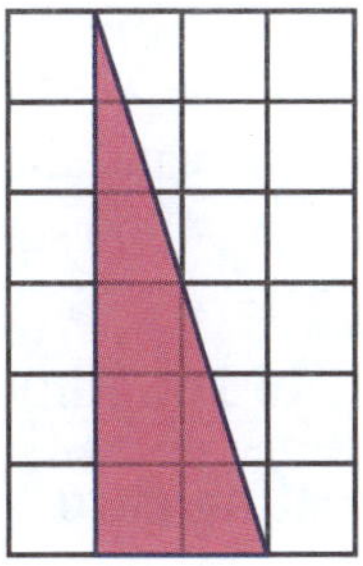

d. 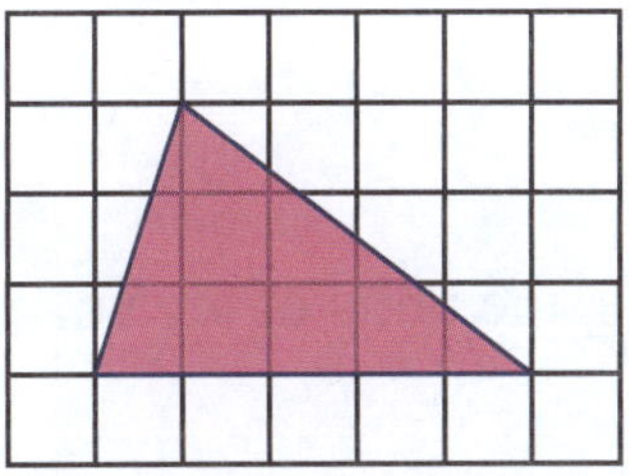

e 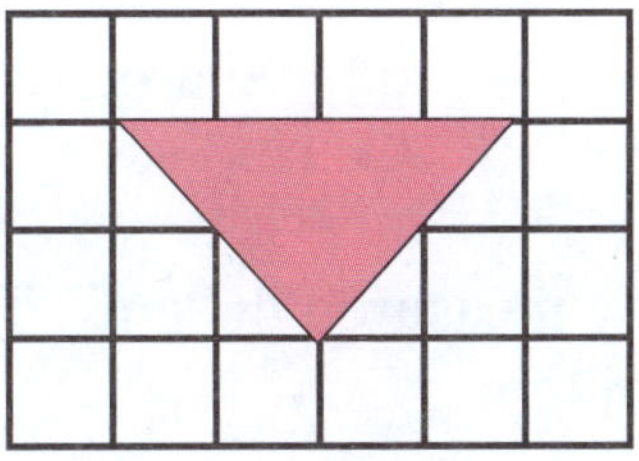

DIFFERENT UNITS OF AREA

Area is always measured in square units.

- The unit of the object can be mm, cm, m, km, miles, etc. The unit to be used depends on the size of the area that is being measured.
- The area of half of your eraser or half of a sim card can be of 1 sq. cm.
- The area of 25 textbooks, 3 newspaper sheets put adjacent to each other, or 1 single bed sheet can be of 1 sq. m.
- The area of 20 times of a school playground can be 1 sq. km.

Observe the areas of the following:

- Smaller areas of objects such as book, bench, etc., are measured in square centimetres.
- Areas of places such as classroom, playground, etc., are measured in square metres.
- Larger areas of places such as area of the town, state, etc., are measured in square kilometres.

Area of the book = 500 sq. cm

Area of the classroom = 150 sq. m

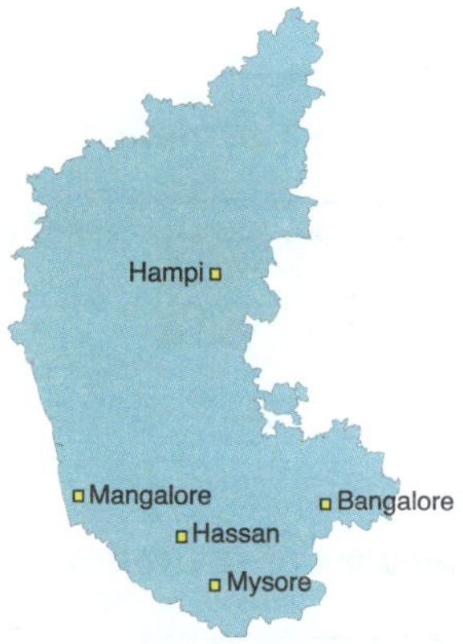

Area of Karnataka state = 1,91,976 sq. km

Example 16: Choose the appropriate units of area for the following.

a. Greeting card
b. Tablecloth
c. River
d. Sharpener

Solution:

a. Greeting card – It is usually measured in "cm". Therefore, the units of area of a greeting card is "square cm".

b. Tablecloth – It is usually measured in "m". Therefore, the units of area of a table cloth is "square m".

c. River – It is usually measured in "km". Therefore, the units of area of a river is "square km".

d. Sharpener – It is usually measured in "mm". Therefore, the units of area of a sharpener is "square mm".

WORD PROBLEMS ON AREA OF RECTANGLE, SQUARE AND TRIANGLE

Let's solve some word problems on area of rectangle, square and triangle.

Example 17: Shalini wants to decorate a wall of her reading room with square charts of side 2 m. The wall is 6 m in length and 4 m in height. How many charts are needed to completely cover the wall?

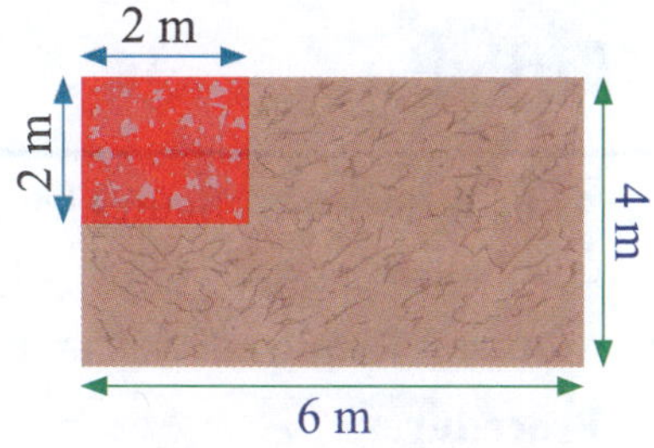

Solution: The length (ℓ) of the wall is 6 m and breadth (b) of the wall is 4 m.

The side (s) of a square chart is 2 m.

The area of the wall = $l \times b = 6 \times 4 = 24$ sq. m

The area of the chart = $s \times s = 2 \times 2 = 4$ sq. m

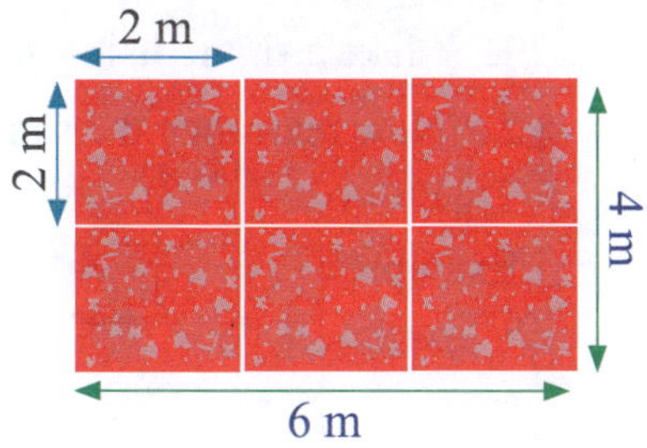

To find the number of charts required to completely cover the wall, we need to divide the area of the wall by the area of the chart.

Number of charts required

$$= \frac{\text{(area of the wall)}}{\text{(area of the chart)}} = \frac{24}{4} = 6.$$

Therefore, 6 charts are required to cover the complete wall.

Example 18: Rajesh wants to paint a wall of his son's room. The wall is in the shape of a square of side 8 m. The cost of painting the wall is ₹ 95 per sq. m. It includes the cost of the paint and the labour charges.

How much should Rajesh spend to paint his wall?

Solution: The wall is in the shape of a square and its side (s) is 8 m.

The cost of painting the wall is ₹95 per sq. m.

The area of the wall = $8 \times 8 = 64$ sq. m.

The total cost of painting the wall
= area of the wall × cost per sq. m. = 64×95

Therefore, the total cost of painting the wall is 64×95 = ₹6080.

Example 19: Find the height of the signboard, if its area is 120 sq. cm and the base is 10 cm.

Solution: Area of a triangular signboard = 120 sq. cm = $\frac{1}{2} \times (10 \times \text{height})$

$$120 = \frac{1}{\cancel{2}_1} \times \overset{5}{\cancel{10}} \times \text{height}$$

$$\text{Height} = \frac{120}{5} = 24 \text{ cm.}$$

Therefore, the height of the given signboard is 24 cm.

Activity

Aim: To infer that figures having different perimeter can have same area, similarly figures having different area can have same perimeter.

Material Required: Square tiles (area of each square tile should be 1 square unit)

Procedure:

1. Make a figure using square tiles and find its area and perimeter.
2. Now rearrange the same number of tiles tiles and find the area and perimeter of the figures formed.

Example:

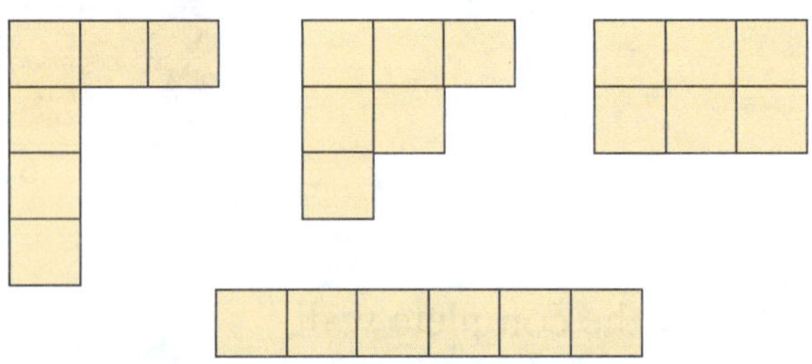

3. List the area and perimeters of figures in a table.
4. Now make another shape using different number of square tiles and find its area and perimeter.
5. Rearrange the shapes by adding or removing tiles in such a way that the perimeter remains the same.

Example:

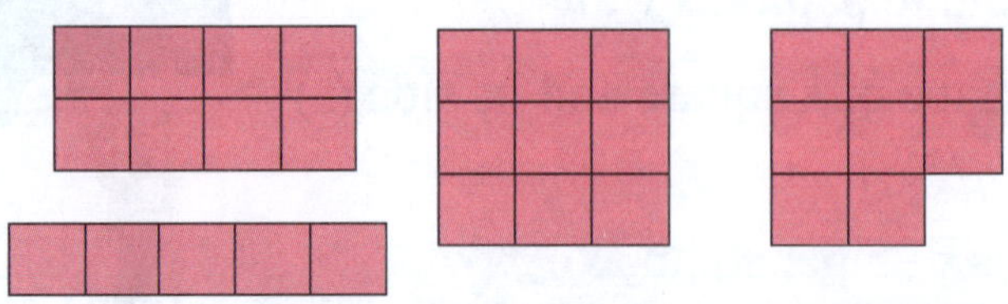

6. List the area and perimeter of the figures in a table and observe the data.

Conclusion: Figures with different perimeter can have same area and figures with different area can have the same perimeter

Exercise 13.3

Solve the following problems.

1. Murthy has a rectangular wooden box whose length is 7 m and breadth is 5 m. He wants to cover its top surface with a nice cloth. The cost of the cloth is ₹50 per sq. m. How much will it cost Murthy to cover the wooden box? (*Hint:* Find the area of the top surface of the box.)
2. In the middle of a rectangular field whose length is 25 metres and width is 15 metres, a house was built in the shape of a square whose side is 8 metres. What is the area of the garden around the house?

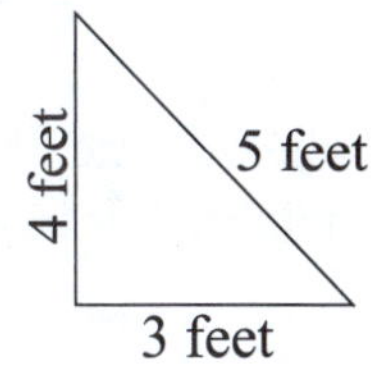

3. Tara cuts a cloth in the shape of a triangle measuring 4 ft by 3 ft by 5 ft as shown. What will be the area of the tablecloth required for her dining table?
4. The breadth of a rectangular field is 40 m. Its length is twice its breadth. Find the area of the field.
5. 150 bricks of length 10 cm and breadth 12 cm are used to tile a path of a garden. What is the area of the path?

VOLUME OF CUBES AND CUBOIDS

We have seen that standard units are required for measurement of perimeter and area.

For volume also, a standard unit is required.

A cube of side 1 unit – like, 1 mm, 1 cm or 1 m is used as the standard unit of volume.

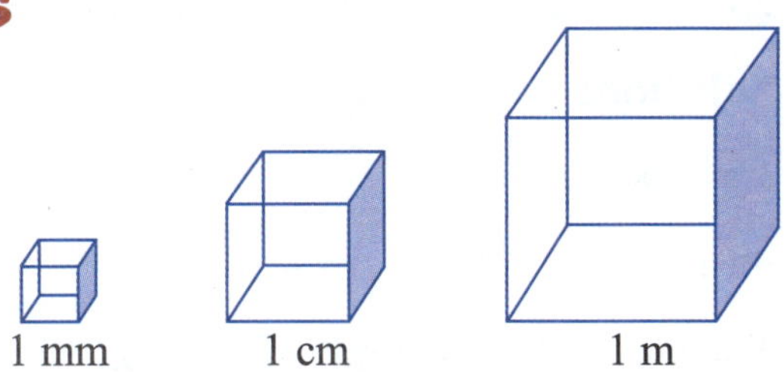

Observe the cubes of lengths 1 mm, 1 cm and 1 m. Their volumes are 1 cubic mm, 1 cubic cm and 1 cubic m, respectively.

The volume of a unit cube is 1 cubic unit.

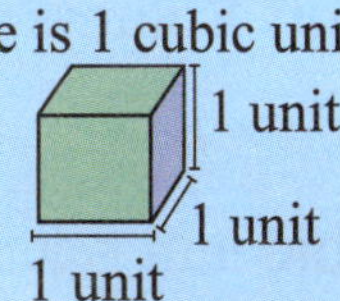

Volume is the amount of space occupied by an object. It is measured in **cubic units**.

In the previous class, you learned about how to find the volume of a box by counting the number of unit cubes it can hold.

Let us find the volume of this empty box.

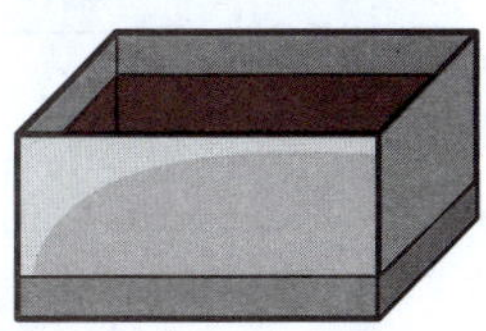

Fill the box completely with centimetre cubes and count the number of layers.

- The number of cubes in the first layer is $6 \times 5 = 30$.
- There are 3 layers.
- The total number of centimetre cubes filled in the box is $(6 \times 5) \times 3 = 90$.

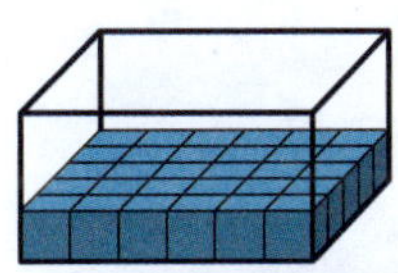

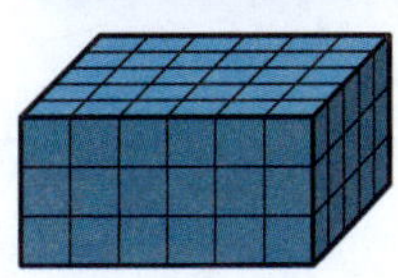

Therefore, the volume of this empty box is 90 cubic cm.

We can use a shortcut method to find the volume of any cuboid (as we did for finding the area of a rectangle). We need not count the number of unit cubes each time.

Volume of any cuboidal box = number of cubes per layer × number of layers

= number of cubes in each row × number of rows × number of layers

Length (ℓ) × Breadth (b) × Height (h)

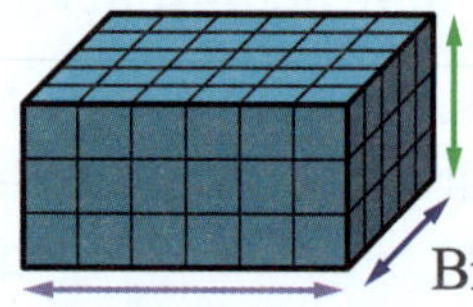

The volume of a cuboid whose length (ℓ), breadth (b) and height (h) is given by length × breadth × height, that is, $\mathbf{V = \ell \times b \times h}$

Example 20: What is the volume of the given wooden cube?

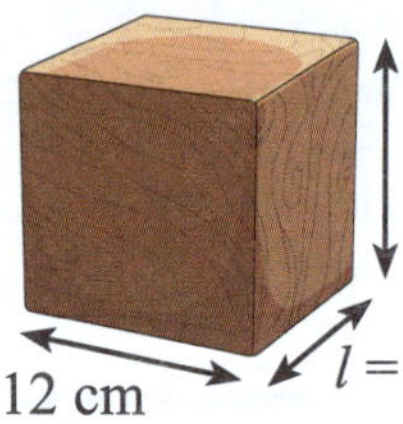

Solution: $\ell = 12$ cm, $b = 12$ cm and $h = 12$ cm

$V = \ell \times b \times h$

$\Rightarrow V = 12 \text{ cm} \times 12 \text{ cm} \times 12 \text{ cm} = 1728 \text{ cm}^3$

Therefore, the volume of the wooden cube is 1728 cu. cm.

Example 21: What is the volume of the box filled with rice?

Solution: $\ell = 30$ cm, $b = 45$ cm and $h = 60$ cm

$V = \ell \times b \times h$

$\Rightarrow V = 30 \text{ cm} \times 45 \text{ cm} \times 60 \text{ cm} = 81000$ cu. cm

Therefore, the volume of the box filled with rice is 81000 cubic cm.

Example 22: Find the length of a box, if its base is 5 mm, height is 10 mm and its volume is 400 cubic mm.

Solution: Volume = 400 cubic mm, $b = 5$ mm and $h = 10$ mm

$V = \ell \times b \times h$

400 cubic mm = length × 5 mm × 10 mm

$\Rightarrow \text{length} = \dfrac{400}{50} = 8 \text{ mm}$

Therefore, the length of the box is 8 mm.

Common Error

While writing the units of Area and Volume, choose the correct unit.

Area of a square of side 4 cm = 16 cu. cm.	✗	Area of a square of side 4 cm = 16 sq. cm.	✓
Volume of a cube of side 3 cm = 27 sq. cm.	✗	Volume of a square of side 3 cm = 27 cu. cm.	✓

Exercise 13.4

1. Find the volume by counting cubes. (volume of 1 cube = 1 cu. unit)

a. 

b. 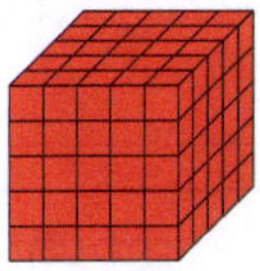

c. 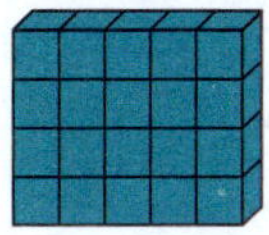

d. 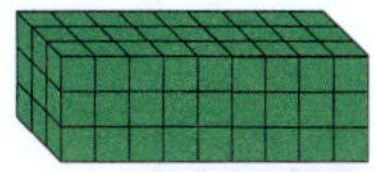

e. 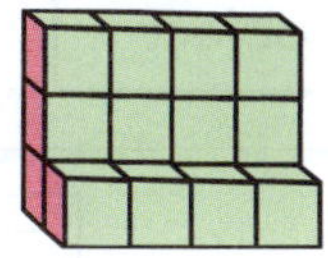

2. Calculate the volume by counting cubes. (volume of 1 cube = 1 cu. unit)

a. 

b. 

c. 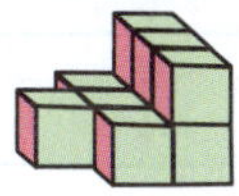

d. 

e. 

3. Find the volume of the following using formula.

a. 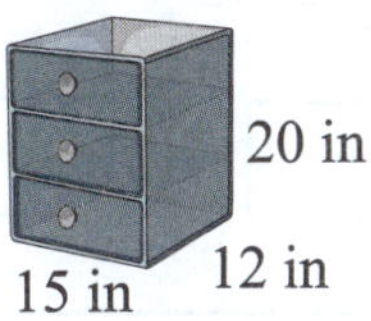

b. 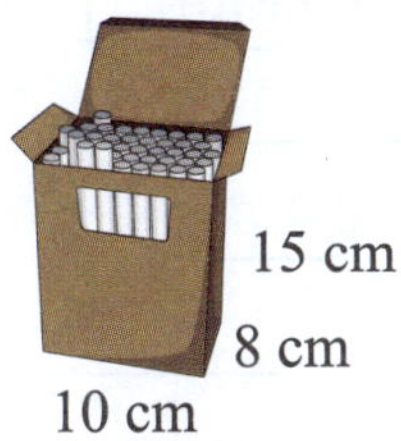

c. 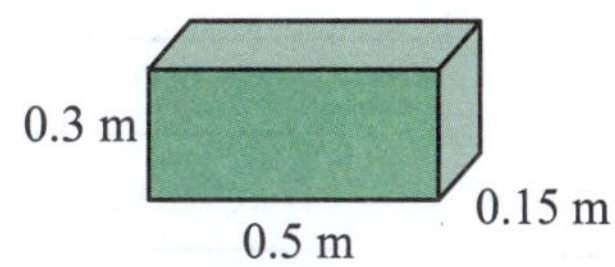

d. 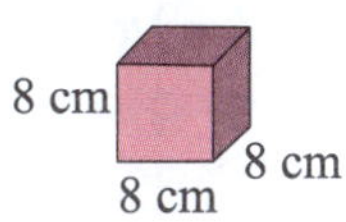

e. 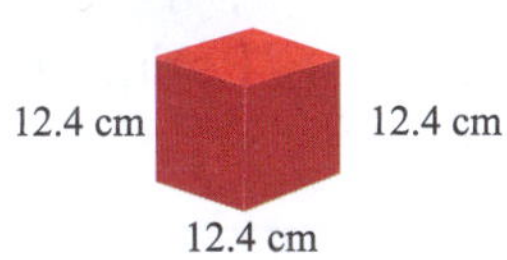

4. Solve the following problems.

a. A cuboid box of dimensions 30 cm × 20 cm × 6 cm has to be filled with matchboxes of dimensions 5 cm × 4 cm × 3 cm. Find the number of matchboxes it can hold. (*Hint:* Divide the volume of the cuboid box by the volume of a matchbox.)

b. A wooden piece which is in the shape of a cuboid has a length of 12 in, breadth of 8 in and thickness of 1 in. What will be the volume if 15 such wooden pieces are piled on top of each other?

c. A large container carrying bikes has the dimensions 20 ft × 10 ft × 8 ft. Find its volume.

d. A pond is 60 m long, 25 m wide and 2 m deep. Find the capacity of the pond in cu. m.

e. A rectangular container measures 15 cm by 10 cm by 3 cm. How many mℓ of water can it hold?

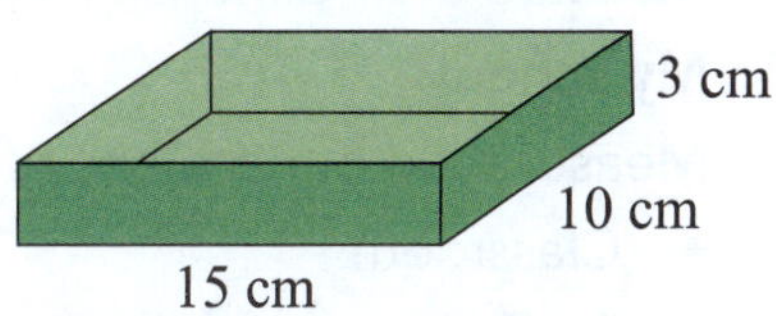

Concept Map

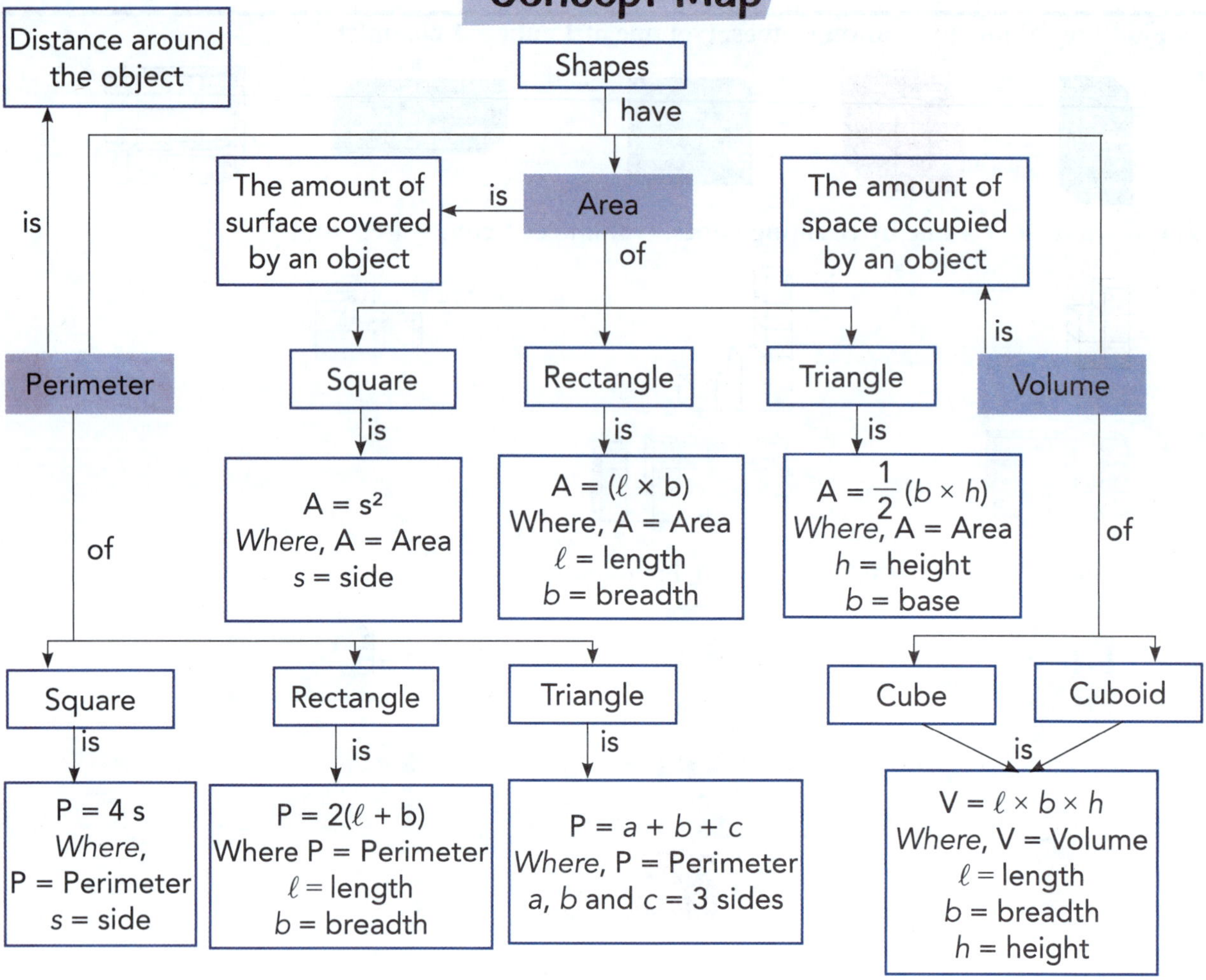

Projects

A. Clay models

Make models of cubes and cuboids using play dough.

Measure their dimensions and find their volume.

B. My school

Measure the dimensions of the following in your school.

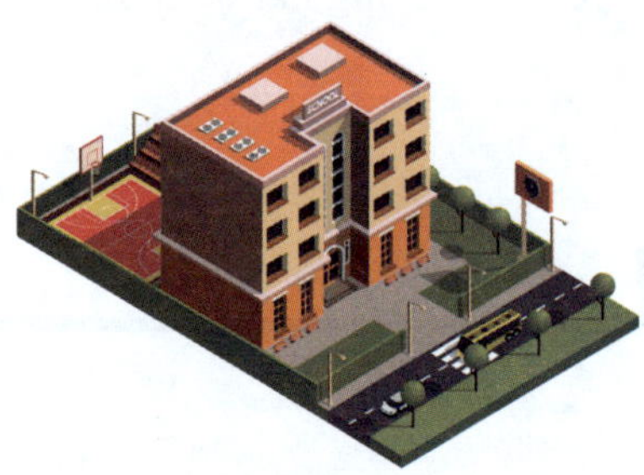

- Classroom
- Staff room
- Library
- Kindergarden play area

Find which of these is the smallest and which of these is the greatest in area.

Revision Exercise

A. Choose the correct option by finding the area of the following figures.

		a.	b.	c.	d.
1.	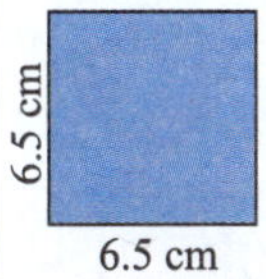	36.25 sq. cm	42 sq. cm	42.25 sq. cm	42.5 sq. cm
2.	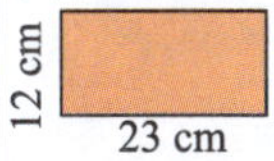	178 sq. cm	276 sq. cm	305 sq. cm	240 sq. cm
3.	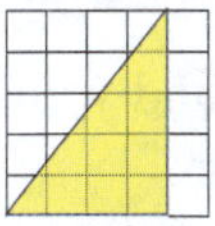	10 sq. units	20 sq. units	12 sq. units	9 sq. units
4.	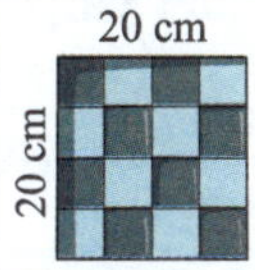	40 sq. cm	80 sq. cm	200 sq. cm	400 sq. cm
5.	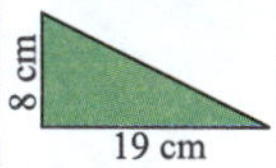	3000 sq. cm	344 sq. cm	76 sq. cm	461 sq. cm

B. Fill in the blanks. {by writing the appropriate units (sq. cm/sq. m/sq. km) for the area.}

1. Blackboard ________
2. Arabian Sea ________
3. TV screen ________
4. Lunch box ________
5. Cricket field ________

C. Match the following. (Find a volume with their dimensions)

1. $\ell = 7$ cm, $b = 5$ cm, $h = 2$ cm	a. 562500 cu. cm
2. $\ell = 3$ m, $b = 7$ m, $h = 4$ m	b. 2040 cu. m
3. $\ell = 3$ mm, $b = 2$ mm, $h = 5$ mm	c. 70 cu. cm
4. $\ell = 150$ cm, $b = 75$ cm, $h = 50$ cm	d. 84 cu. m
5. $\ell = 10$ m, $b = 17$ m, $h = 12$ m	e. 30 cu. mm

D. State whether the following are true or false.

1. Area is the amount of space occupied by an object.
2. The units of area are represented in sq. units.
3. If the length of the rectangle is ℓ and breadth is b, then its area is $\ell \times b$.
4. The area of a triangle is twice the area of a square.
5. The volume of the cuboid whose length is ℓ, breadth is b and height is h is given by $\ell + b + h$.

E. Find the volume of the following by counting the cubes. (volume of 1 cube = 1 cu. unit)

1. 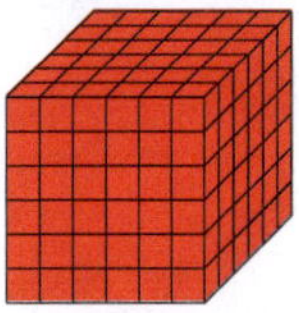
2. 
3. 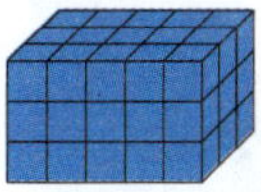
4. 
5. 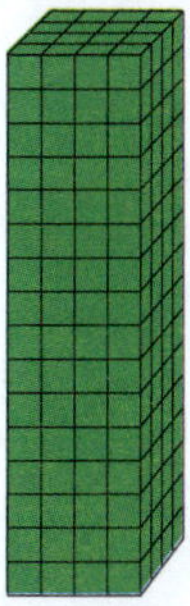

F. Find the volume of the following.

1. 

2.

3.

4.

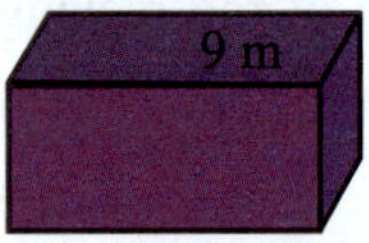

5.

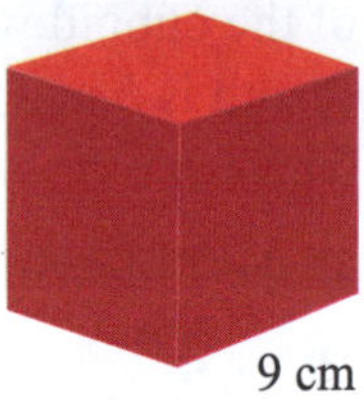

6.

7.

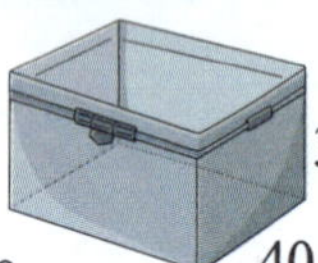

8.

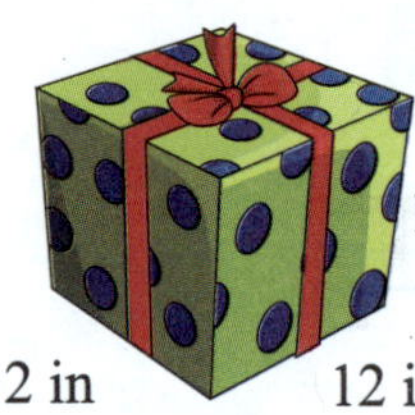

9.

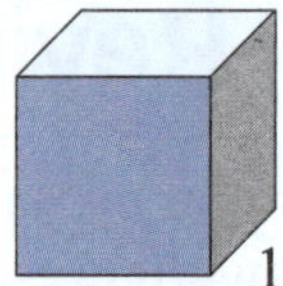

10.

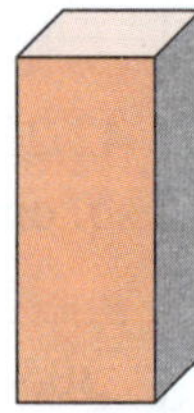

G. Application-based questions.

1. Find the area of a compound wall that is 100 m long and 7 m high.
2. The perimeter of a triangular carpet is 400 cm. If the two sides of the carpet measure 120 cm each, find the length of the third side.

3. What is the area of the floor which is 8 m in length and 4 m in breadth?
4. Find the volume of the cubical box whose side is 15 m.
5. Krishna wants to put a new carpet in his drawing room. He asks his father to buy a new carpet. If the dimensions of his room are 10 ft by 8 ft, what should be the area of the carpet required for Krishna's room?

Did You Master?

A. The amount of space occupied by an object is called ________.

1. volume
2. area
3. perimeter
4. dimension

B. The appropriate unit used for finding the area of a forest is _______.

1. sq. m
2. sq. mm
3. sq. cm
4. sq. km

C. The perimeter of the given figure is ______.

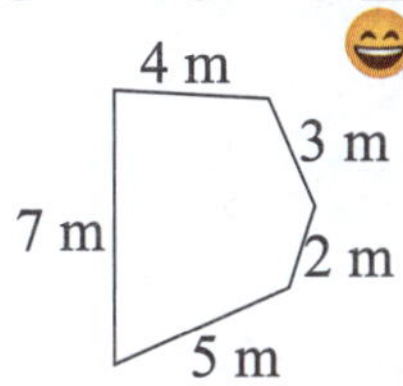

1. 25 m
2. 17 m
3. 21 m
4. 32 m

D. Find the length of the rectangle whose breadth is 30 m and perimeter is 160 m.

1. 50 m
2. 80 m
3. 130 m
4. 60 m

E. Find the area of the given triangle.

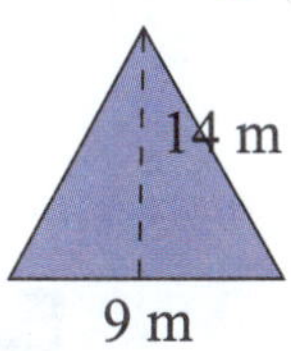

1. 63 sq. m
2. 126 sq. cm
3. 63 sq. cm
4. 123 sq. m

F. If 150 triangular tiles are laid in a dining room measuring 20 m long and 15 m wide, find the area of each triangular tile.

1. 1 sq. m
2. 2 sq. m
3. 15 sq. m
4. 30 sq. m

G. The volume of a cuboid whose length, breadth and height respectively are 35 cm, 27 cm and 11 cm is ______.

1. 1.0395 cu. m
2. 10395 cu. cm
3. 0.10395 cu. cm
4. 0.10395 cu. m

H. A tennis ball court along with its dimensions is shown.

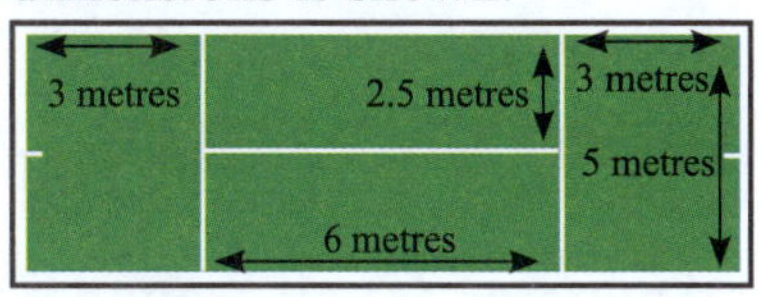

The area of the tennis court is _________ .

1. 18 sq. m
2. 7.5 sq. m
3. 60 sq. m
4. 120 sq. m

I. The capacity of a plastic container of dimensions 12 m × 6 m × 7 m is __________.

1. 504 sq. m
2. 504 sq. cm
3. 345 sq. m
4. 345 sq. cm

How many questions did you answer correctly.? Score yourself.

easy ☐ average ☐ advanced ☐ remembering ☐ understanding ☐ applying ☐ analysing ☐ evaluating ☐ creating ☐

communication ☐ representation ☐ devising strategies ☐ mathematisation ☐ reasoning and argument ☐ using symbols ☐ using mathematical tools ☐ creativity ☐

14 Nets, Symmetry and Patterns

Curricular Goals

- Understand numbers (counting numbers), discover and recognize patterns in number sequences (CG-1)
- Describe, recognize and create shapes that have symmetry (CG-2)

Competencies

- Discover, recognize, describe, and extend simple number patterns such as odd numbers, even numbers, square numbers, cubes and Virahanka–Fibonacci numbers (C-1.4)
- Recognize and create symmetry (reflection, rotation) in familiar 2D and 3D shapes (C-2.3)
- Discover, recognize, describe and extend patterns in 3D shapes (C-2.4)

Why This Topic?

Symmetry and patterns are all around us. Consider the following examples.

Flowers in a garden

Count the number of petals in these flowers.
Iris: 3 petals, Hibiscus: 5 petals, Marigold: 7 petals and Asters: 21 petals.
It is the number of petals within a flower that makes the pattern and symmetry of the flower.

Symmetry in monuments

The given picture is of the Sun temple at Konark. One half is a reflection of the other half. So, this structure is symmetrical along it's centre.

Can you think of any two buildings or structures that have symmetry in their structure?

Are You Ready?

A. What is the shape of the figure?

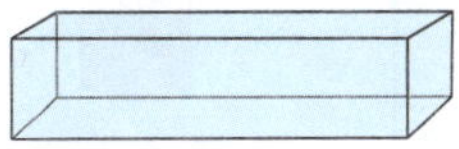

1. Cube
2. Cuboid
3. Cone
4. Cylinder

B. Which of the following solid shapes can be made using the given net?

1. Cube
2. Cuboid
3. Cone
4. Cylinder

C. The swimming pool is in the shape of a ________.

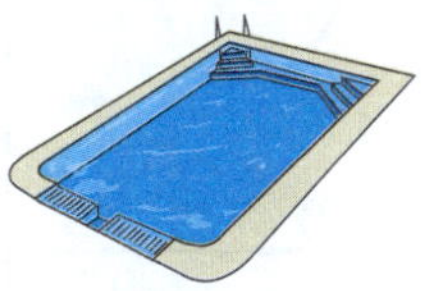

1. Cuboid
2. Cone
3. Sphere
4. Cone

D. How many squares is the net of a cube made up of?

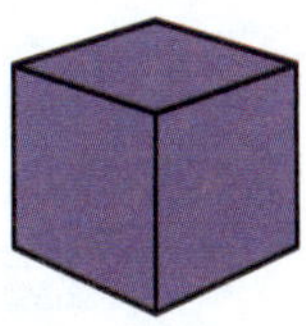

1. 8
2. 10
3. 4
4. 6

E. All these nets are of the same shape.

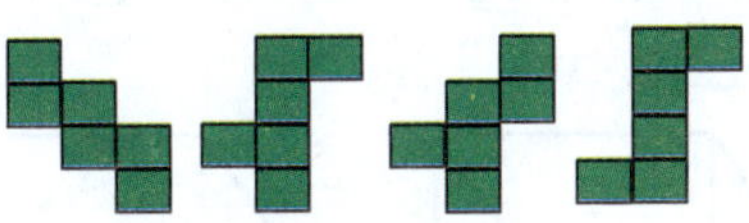

Which shape is it?

1. Cylinder
2. Cone
3. Cuboid
4. Cube

F. Does the given shape have lines of symmetry? If yes, how many?

1. Yes, 3 lines of symmetry
2. No lines of symmetry
3. Yes, 1 line of symmetry
4. Yes, 2 lines of symmetry

G. Which image do you obtain on reflecting the given image about the given line?

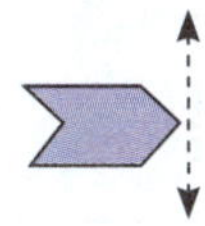

1. 
2. 
3. 
4. 

H. Which of the following is the net of the given octagonal box?

1. 
2. 
3. 
4. 

I. Observe the given number pattern and fill in the blanks.
95, 100, ____, 110, ____, 120

1. 105, 125
2. 105, 115
3. 115, 125
4. None of the above

J. Write the next three numbers in the given number pattern.
11, 14, 17, 20, ________, ________, ________

1. 23, 25, 27
2. 23, 26, 18
3. 23, 26, 29
4. 22, 26, 29

How many questions did you answer correctly? Score yourself.

easy ☐ average ☐ advanced ☐ remembering ☐ understanding ☐ applying ☐ analysing ☐ evaluating ☐ creating ☐

communication ☐ representation ☐ devising strategies ☐ mathematisation ☐ reasoning and argument ☐ using symbols ☐ using mathematical tools ☐ creativity ☐

NETS

In the previous grade, we studied about the nets of the following solid shapes.

Solid Shape	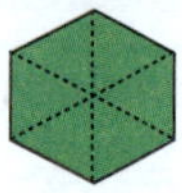 Cube	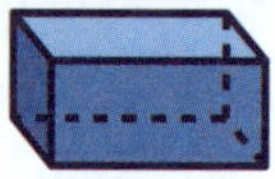 Cuboid	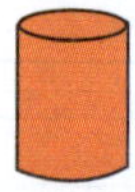 Cylinder	 Cone
Net	 It has 6 squares.	 It has 4 rectangles of one size and 2 rectangles of another size.	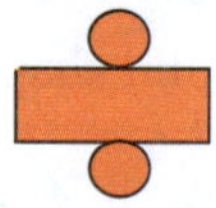 It has 1 rectangle and 2 circles.	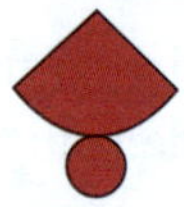 It has 1 complete circle and 1 section of another circle.

Let us look at the nets of some more solid shapes.

Solid Shape	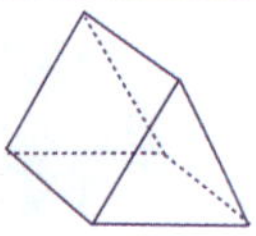 Triangular prism	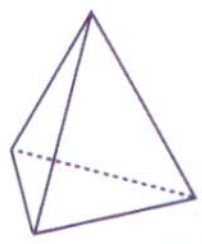 Triangular pyramid	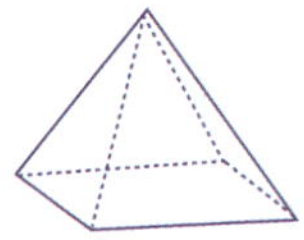 Square pyramid
Net	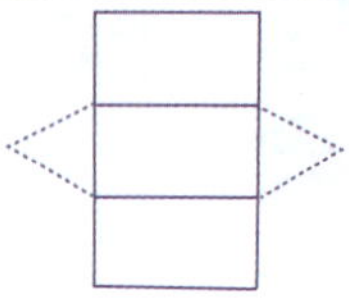 It has 3 rectangles and 2 triangles.	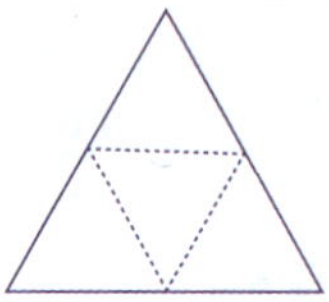 It has 3 triangles.	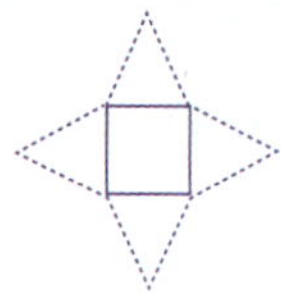 It has 1 square and 4 triangles.

DRAWING CUBES AND CUBOIDS

a

You might have seen many cubes and cuboids around you. Have you ever tried to draw them on a paper? Let us see the steps for drawing either of the two.

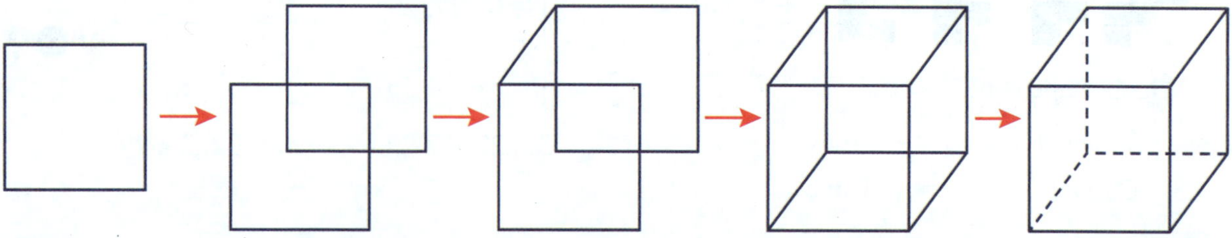

Draw a square | Draw another square on the top | Join the corresponding vertices using line segments.

There is a special dotted paper called the **isometric dot paper** which can be used to draw cubes and cuboids easily.

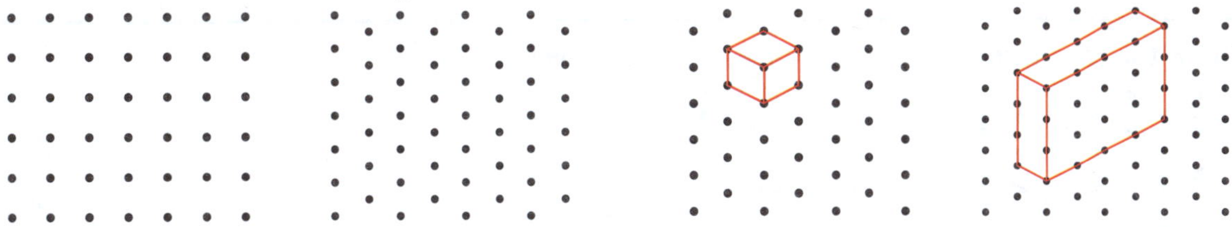

Dot paper | Isometric dot paper | Cube | Cuboid

DIFFERENT VIEWS OF SOLID SHAPES

Have you ever looked at your house from different angles? Does it look the same from all the angles? No, it looks different from the top, the front and the side. Following are these views.

Front view | Top view | Side view

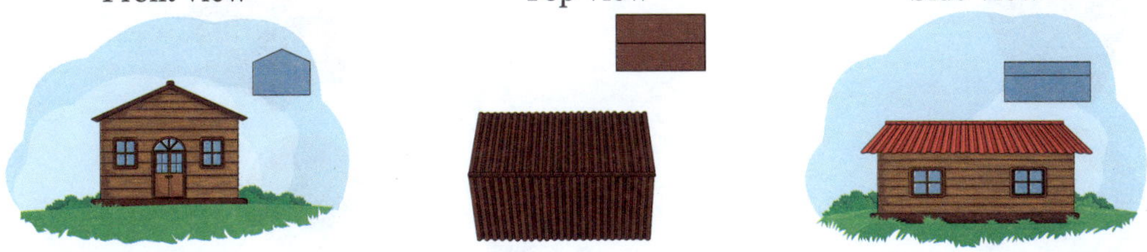

What are the different views of a bus? They are as shown here.

Front view | Side view | Top view

The different views of solid shapes are summarised here.

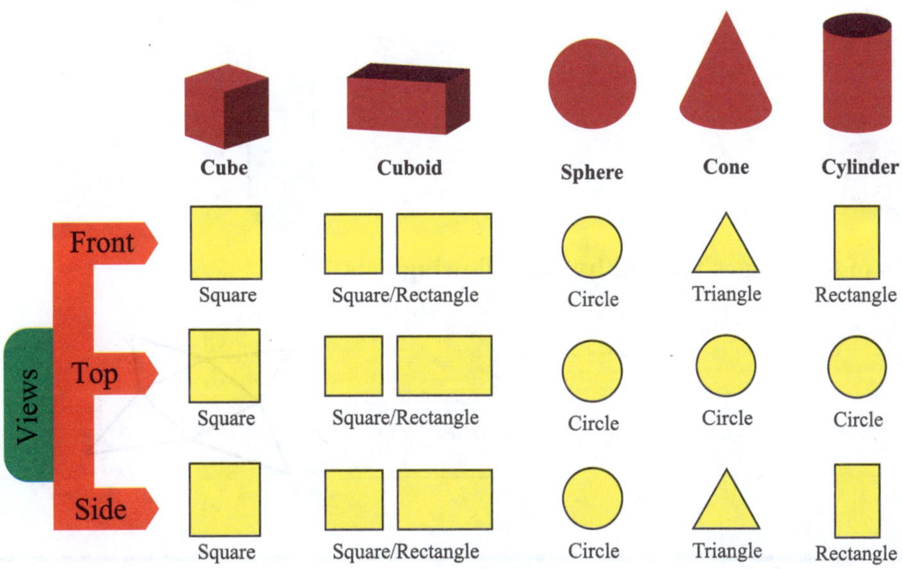

Exercise 14.1

1. Draw the remaining parts of the cubes and cuboids given here.

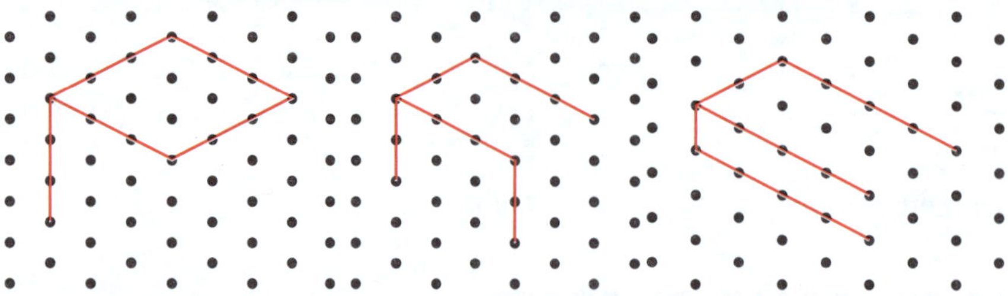

2. Match the side view of the objects to their top views.

Side View		Top View	
a.		i.	
b.		ii.	
c.		iii.	
d.		iv.	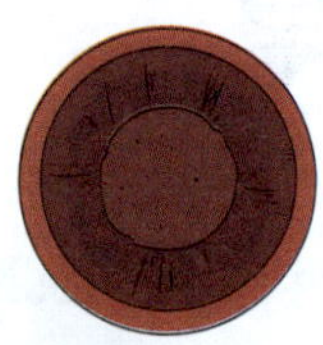
e.	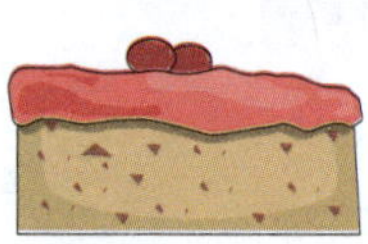	v.	

3. Write the names of the shapes formed by the following nets.

a. 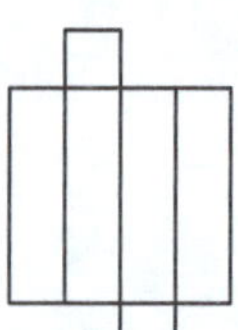 ____________

b. 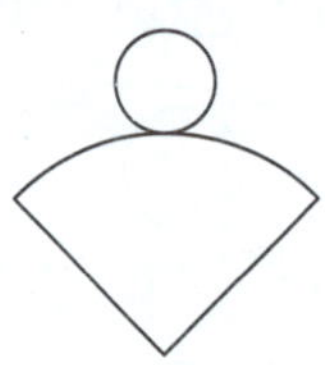 ____________

c. 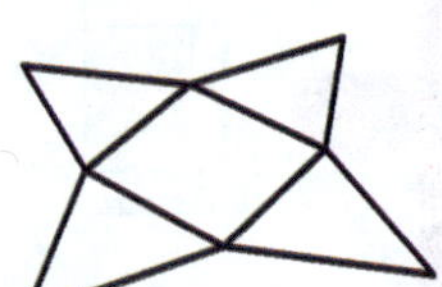 ____________

REFLECTION SYMMETRY

Look at the following buildings. Architects have used the concept of symmetry to construct these buildings. If you place a mirror along the dotted line in each of these figures, you can see that one-half is the mirror reflection of the other half. The line along which the mirror is placed is known as the **line of symmetry.**

Merchandise Mart – Famous Building in Chicago River Bank

Eiffel Tower – Paris

Leaning Tower of Pisa – Italy

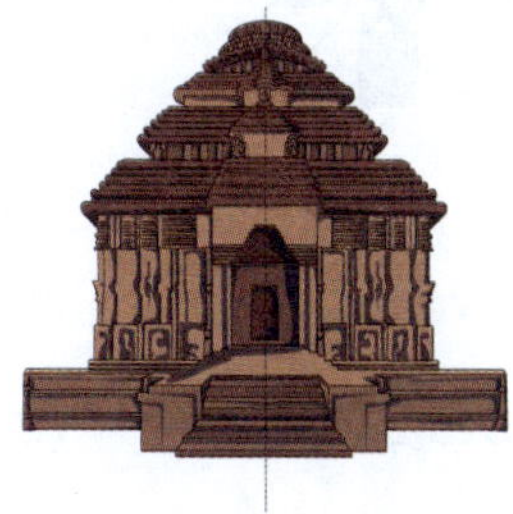

Sun Temple – Konark

A figure is said to have **reflection symmetry** if one half of it is the mirror image of the other half. If you fold the picture along the line of symmetry, each part exactly coincides with the other.

Note that all the above figures have only one line of symmetry. Can a figure have more than one line of symmetry?

Reflection symmetry is also known as line symmetry or mirror symmetry.

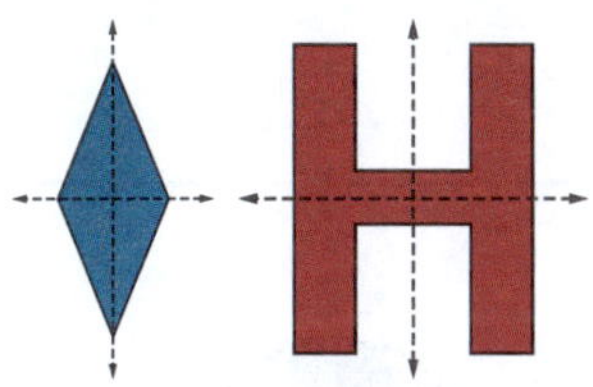

Figures with **two lines of symmetry**

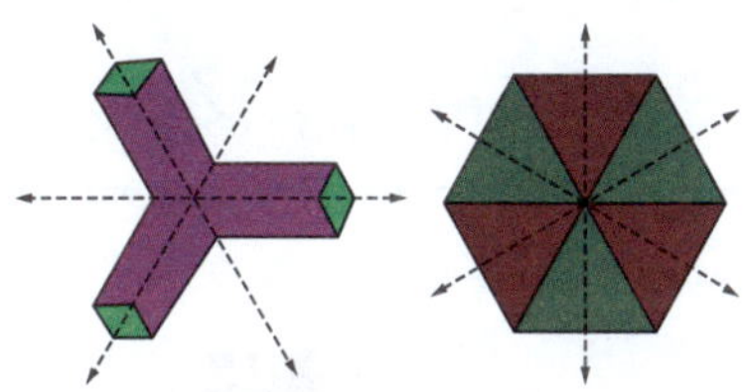

Figures with **three lines of symmetry**

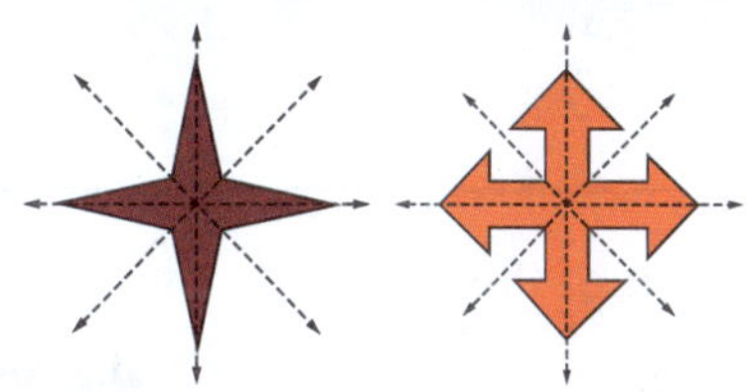

Figures with **four lines of symmetry**

Figures can have more than one line of symmetry.

Example 1: Are figure A and figure B symmetrical?

Solution: Figure A: Symmetrical, the dotted lines are the lines of symmetry

Figure B: Not symmetrical, the dotted lines are not the lines of symmetry.

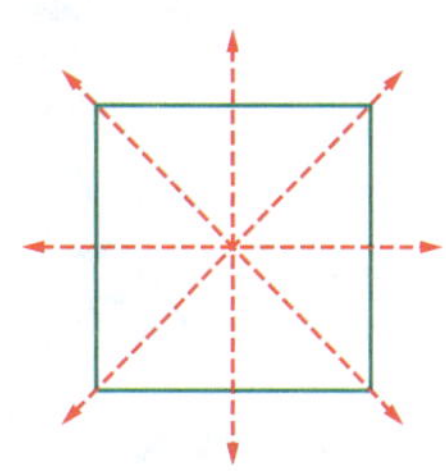

Figure A

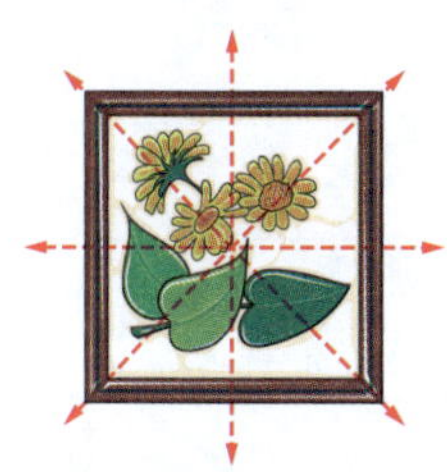

Figure B

Even though both the figures have the same square shape, figure B has a drawing inside which is not symmetrical and since we must consider not only the shape but also all parts of the figure, figure B is not symmetrical.

Reflection Symmetry in Symbols and Face Masks

The mathematical symbols +, –, ×, ÷, = also exhibit line symmetry as shown in the following image.

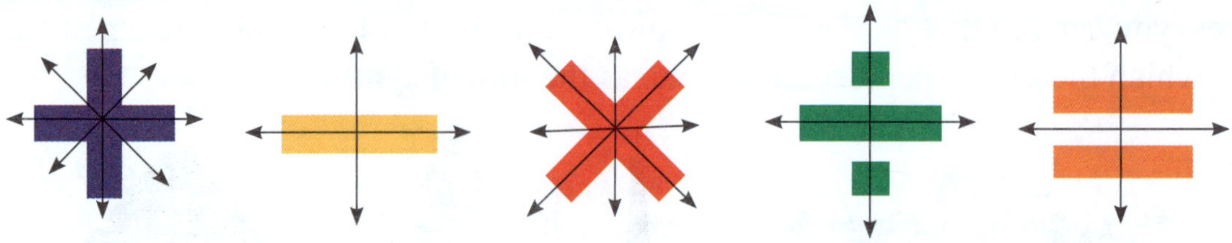

4 lines of symmetry | 2 lines of symmetry | 4 lines of symmetry | 2 lines of symmetry | 2 lines of symmetry

Example 2: Draw the lines of symmetry for the given face masks.

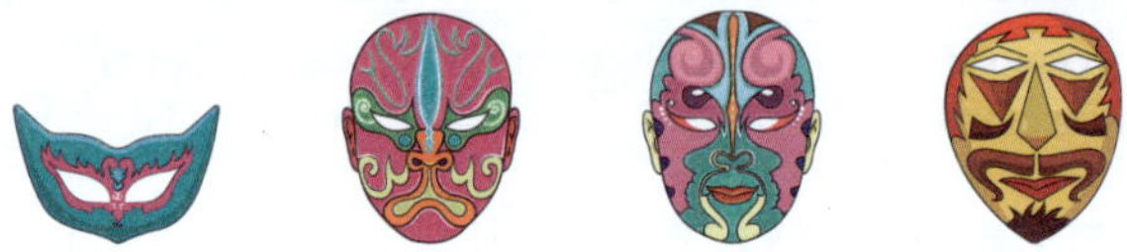

Solution: All the face masks have only one line of symmetry.

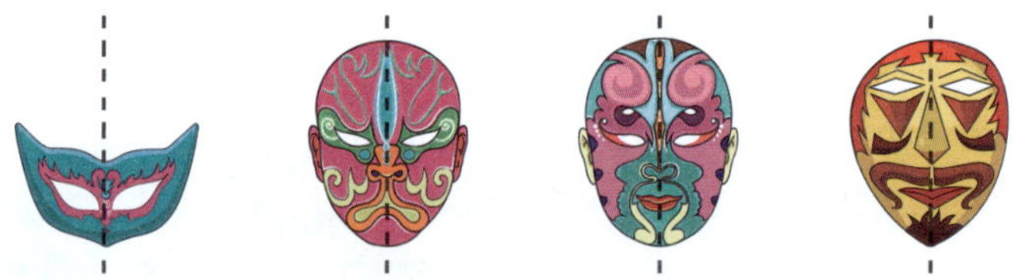

Exercise 14.2

1. Which of the following pictures is symmetrical?

a. 

b. 

c. 

d. 

e. 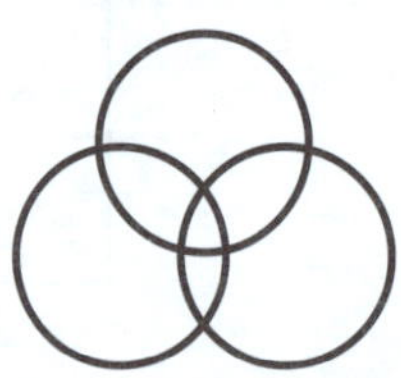

2. Draw the line(s) of symmetry for the following figures. Mention the number of lines of symmetry for each.

a. 

b. 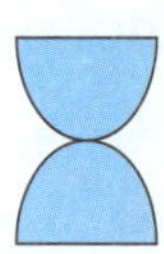

c. 

d. 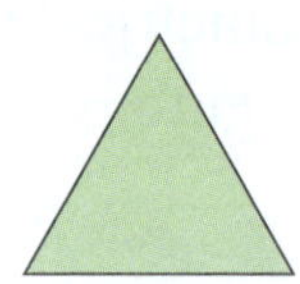

e. 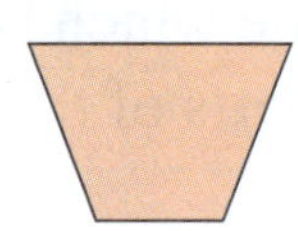

3. Which of the lines drawn are the line of symmetry for the given shape

a. 
b. 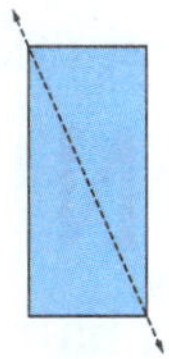
c. 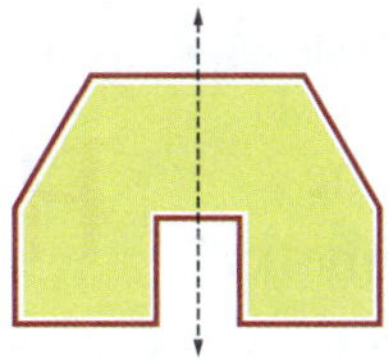
d. 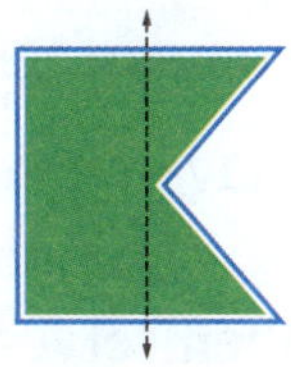
e. 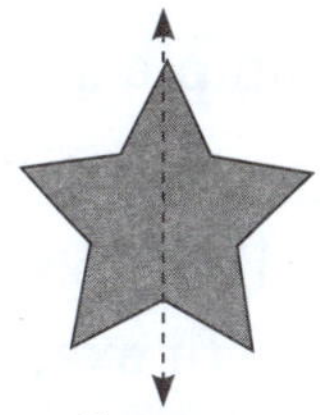

4. Place a mirror along the yellow line and draw the other half for each of the given figures.
(*Note: Use a transparent sheet, trace the figure, flip along the yellow dotted line and verify the figure you have drawn.*)

a. 
b. 
c. 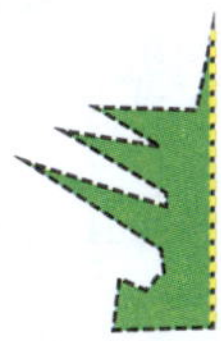
d. 
e. 

ROTATIONAL SYMMETRY

a

Look at the figure given here. It does not have any line of symmetry but still looks symmetrical.

This figure has rotational symmetry. A figure is said to have **rotational symmetry** if it fits exactly into itself when it is rotated by a certain number of turns, that is, the figure looks the same when it is rotated.

Turns

We have all seen a giant wheel during festival seasons when the entire city is beautifully decorated.

As a reference, consider the cabin of the giant wheel in which you are sitting, at the bottom. Once the giant wheel has been rotated and you've returned to where you started, you complete one full turn. When you are exactly in the opposite position, that is, at the topmost point of the giant wheel, then you complete a half turn. Similar explanation can be given for a quarter turn.

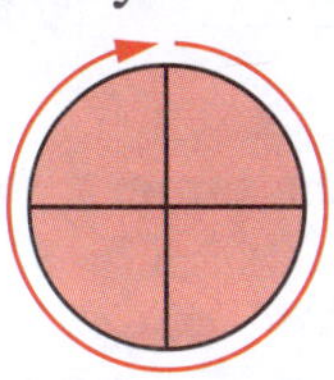

Full Turn

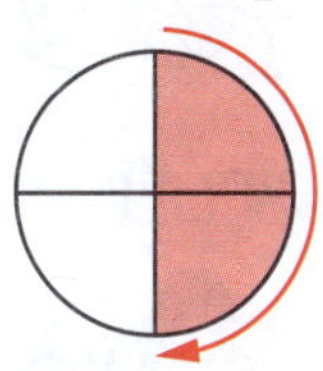

Half Turn or $\frac{1}{2}$ Turn

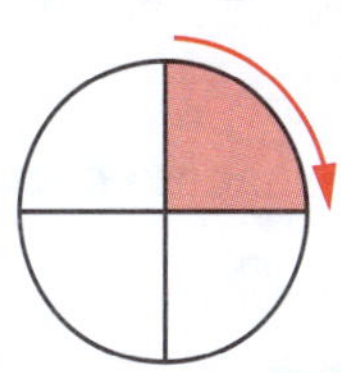

Quarter Turn or $\frac{1}{4}$ Turn

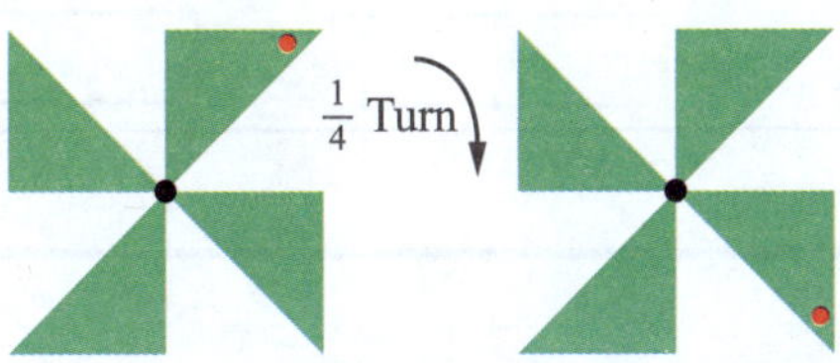

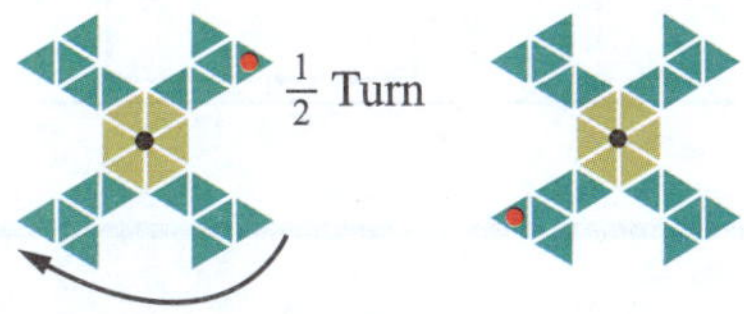

Rotational Symmetry in English Letters and Words

Example 3: Which letters of the English alphabet have rotational symmetry?

Solution: Only these seven letters of the English alphabet show rotational symmetry.

H I N O S X Z

They fit exactly into themselves when they are rotated by a half turn.

Example 4: Give some examples of symmetry in words.

Solution: Observe the words SIS and NOON. They look the same when rotated by a half turn.

SIS NOON

Example 5: Give a few examples of rotational symmetry in real life.

Solution: Out of many real-life examples which exhibit rotational symmetry, a few are shown below.

Windmill

Car wheel

Periwinkle flower

Giant wheel

Exercise 14.3

1. Tick (✓) the shapes that look the same after a quarter turn.

a. 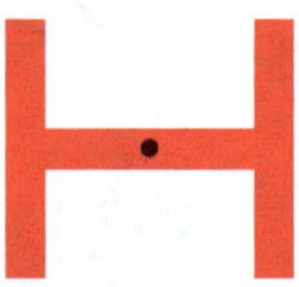

b. 

c. 

d. 

e. 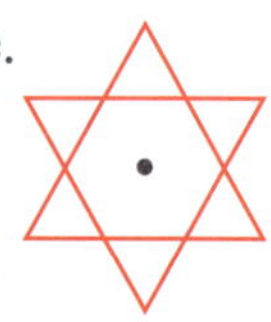

2. Tick (✓) the shapes that look the same after a half turn.

a. 

b. 

c. 

d. 

e. 

3. For the shapes shown below, specify the turn after which they will look the same.

a 

b. 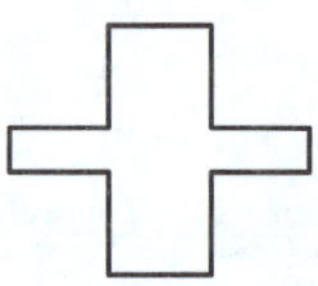

c. 

d. 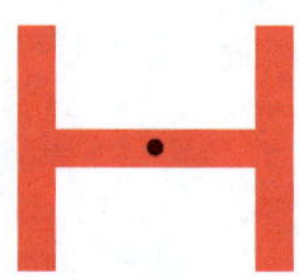

e. 

SHAPE PATTERNS

A shape pattern is a collection of shapes that follow a sequence. Following are some examples of 3D shape patterns.

- **Repeating pattern:** 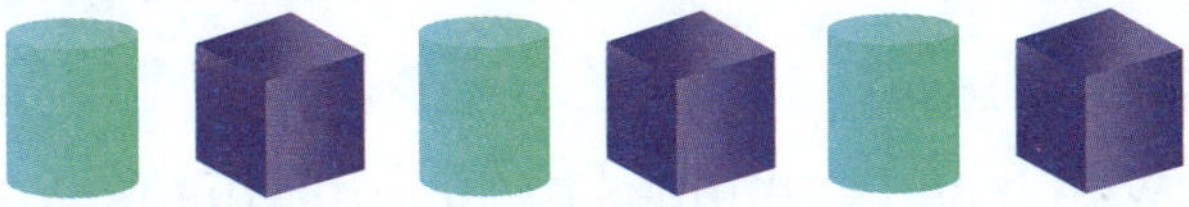

Here, cylinder and cube are repeated.

- **Increasing pattern:** 

Sphere Cone Cylinder Cube

We can have decreasing order of 3D shapes based on the number of faces they have.

The shapes are arranged in increasing order of the number of faces they have.

Example 6: Which shape will come next in the following pattern?

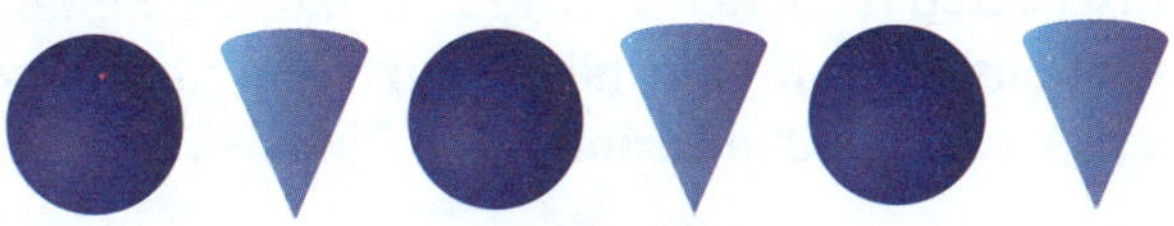

Solution: Here, sphere and cone are repeated alternatively.
Therefore, sphere comes next in the pattern.

NUMBER PATTERNS

Patterns can be seen in numbers too. Some of these patterns are summarised in the following table.

Odd numbers: If n is the starting number, the pattern continues with $n + 2$ each time, where n is an odd number. Example: 31, 33, 35, 37, 39,…	**Even numbers:** If n is the starting number, the pattern continues with $n + 2$ each time, where n is an even number. Example: 64, 66, 68, 70, 72, 74,…
Squares: If n is the starting number, the pattern continues with $n \times n$, $(n + 1) \times (n + 1)$, $(n + 2) \times (n + 2)$, $(n + 3) \times (n + 3)$ and so on. Example: 1, 4, 9, 16, 25, 36,…	**Cubes:** If n is the starting number, the pattern continues with $n \times n \times n$, $(n + 1) \times (n + 1) \times (n + 1)$, $(n + 2) \times (n + 2) \times (n + 2)$ and so on. Example: 1, 8, 27, 64, 125,…
Powers of 2: If n is the starting number, the pattern continues with $n \times 2$, $n \times 2 \times 2$, $n \times 2 \times 2 \times 2$, $n \times 2 \times 2 \times 2 \times 2$ and so on. Example: 2, 4, 8, 16, 32, 64,…	**Powers of 10:** If n is the starting number, the pattern continues with $n \times 10$, $n \times 10 \times 10$, $n \times 10 \times 10 \times 10$ and so on. Example: 10, 100, 1000, 10000,…

Example 7: Identify the rule and complete the missing numbers in the following patterns.

a. 26, 28, 30, ____, 34, 36

b. 4, 9, 16, 25, ____, 49

c. 6, 12, ____, 48, 96

d. 50, 500, ____, 50000

Solution:

a. The pattern starts with number 26 and the difference between the consecutive numbers is 2. So, the missing number is 32.

b. The pattern starts with 4 and they are squares of consecutive numbers.
So, the missing number is 36.

c. The pattern starts with 6 and continues by multiplying powers of 2.
So, the missing number is 24.

d. The pattern starts with 50 and continues by multiplying powers of 10.
So, the missing number is 5000.

Pingala (ancient Indian poet and mathematician) wrote the book Chandaḥśāstra, which had eight chapters. He discovered the series 0, 1, 1, 2, 3, 5, 8, 13, 21, 34, 55,… while working on the number of combinations of the **laghu** and the **guru** (possible patterns of syllables in Sanskrit poetry). This series was called **mātrāmeru** by Pingala (which later known as the **Fibonacci series**).

Virahanka (**ancient Indian poet and mathematician**) worked on the **Chhanda-sutras** of Pingala and was the first to describe Pingala's sutras. He established the Fibonacci series and the method to obtain them. Hence, the Fibonacci numbers are also known as the **Virahanka numbers.**

Exercise 14.4

1. Observe the following shape patterns and draw the next shape.

a.  ______

b. 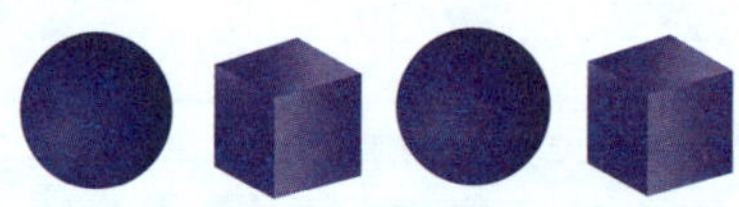 ______

c.  ______

d. 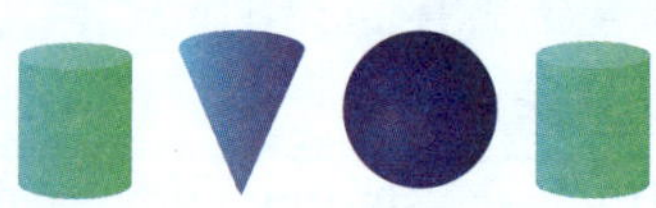 ______

e. 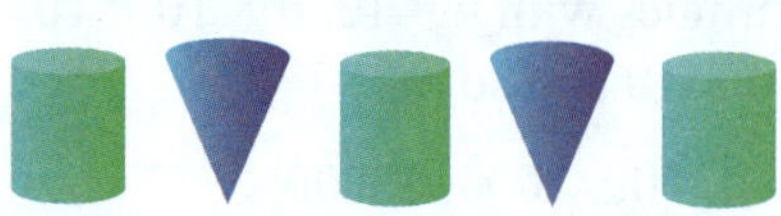 ______

2. Find the missing numbers in the following number patterns.

a. 17, 19, ___, 23, ____, 27, 29, ____

b. 25, 36, ____, 64, ____

c. 4, ___,16, ____,64

d. ____, 27, 64, ____, 216

e. 48, 50, ____, 54, ____, 58

Concept Map

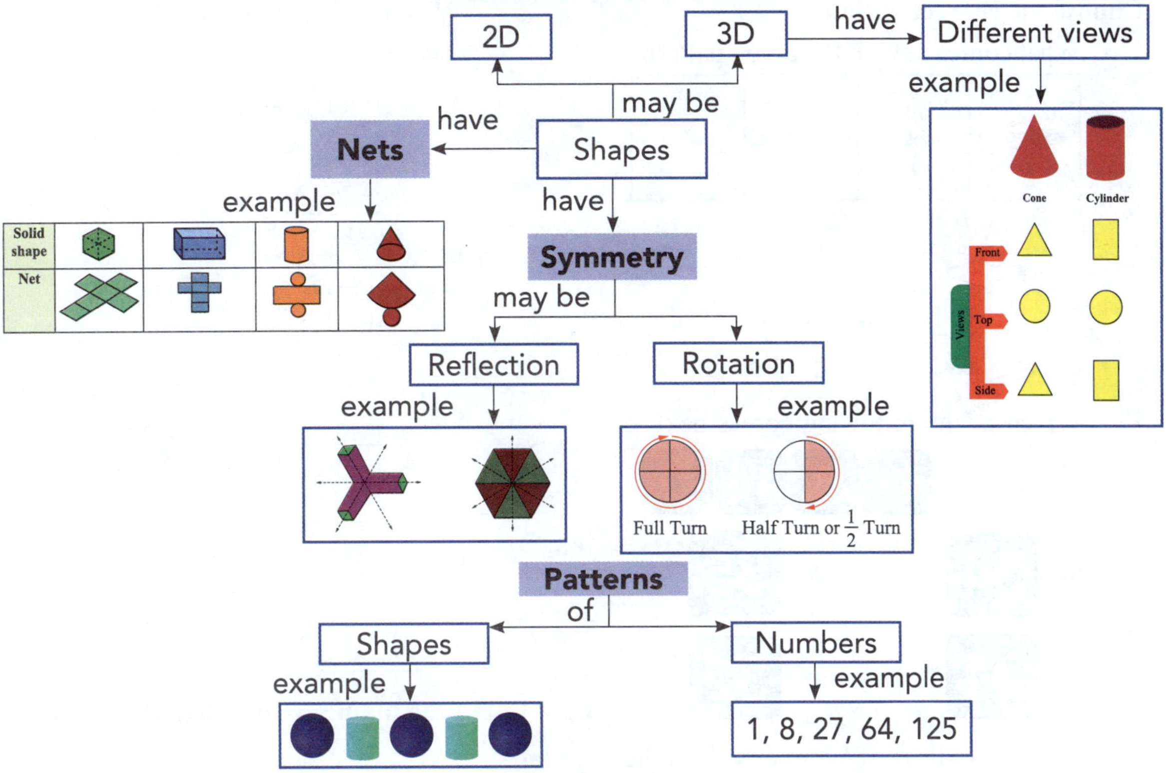

Projects

A. Golden Ratio and Fibonacci Sequence

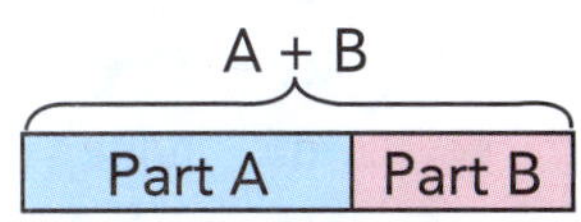

Take a paper strip and divide it into two unequal parts.
Label the longer part as A and the shorter part as B.
Find the ratios of A to B and (A + B) to A. What do you observe?

The ratio between the larger part to the smaller parts is the same as the ratio between the sum of the parts and the larger part.
This ratio is called the **golden ratio.**

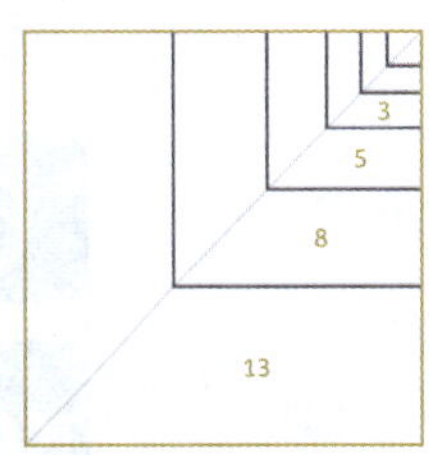

Virahanka-Fibonacci numbers are generated by adding the two preceding numbers starting from 0 and 1. That is,

0 1 1 2 3

0 + 1 = 1 1 + 1 = 2 1 + 2 = 3

1. Is there any relation between the Fibonacci sequence and the golden ratio? Explore.
2. The golden ratio is widely used in the field of architecture. Using the internet, find out the real-life application of the Fibonacci sequence and the golden ratio, prepare a chart on the same, and submit it to the class.

B. Road Signs

Collect 10 different road signs and find out which of them show line symmetry and rotational symmetry. A few signs are given alongside.

Revision Exercise

A. Choose the correct option.

1. What comes next in the given pattern?

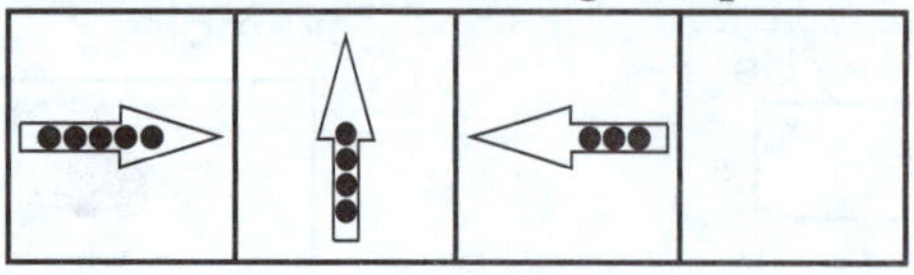

a.  b. 

c. 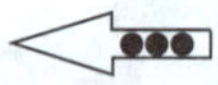 d. 

2. Which of the following comes next in this pattern? 4 | 8 | 16 | ___

a. 34 b. 35

c. 31 d. 32.

3. How many lines of symmetry does the given picture have?

a. 1
b. 2
c. 3
d. none

4. In which position will the given figure be after $\frac{1}{2}$ turn?

a. 

b. 

c. 

d. 

5. Which of these is the net of the given figure?

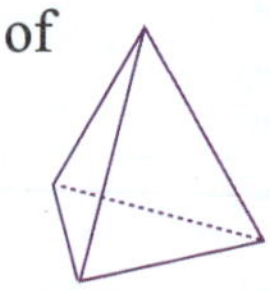

a. 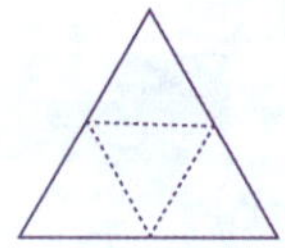

b. 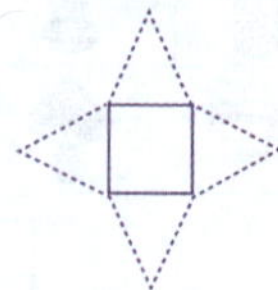

c. 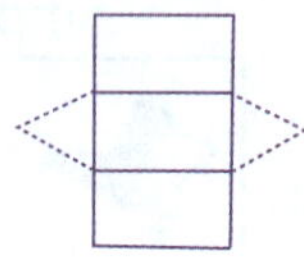

d. 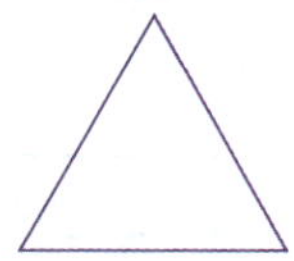

B. Fill in the blanks. (Complete the number pattern.)

1. 38, 40, 42 , _____
2. 20, 200, 2000, _____
3. 16, 25, 36, _____
4. 32, 64, 128, _____
5. 81, 100, 121, _____

C. Match the following.

1. 	a. The top and the front views are rectangles.
2. 	b. Two lines of symmetry
3. 	c. The top and the front views are circles.
4. 	d. Only one line of symmetry
5. 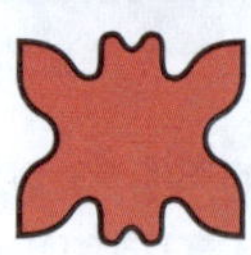	e. No line of symmetry

D. State whether the following are true (T) or false (F).

1. These letters have only one line of symmetry.

   A B C M

2. The side view of a cone is a triangle.
3. The number 0 has no lines of symmetry.
4. The view of a cube is same from all the angles.
5. An umbrella looks the same after 2 turns.

E. Draw the line(s) of symmetry for the following figures if they are symmetrical. Also, write the number of lines of symmetry.

1. 
2. 
3. 
4. 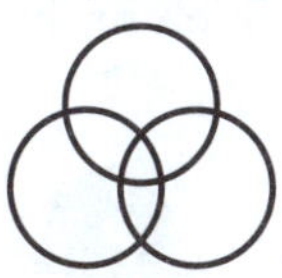
5. 

F. Write the number of turns needed for each of the following figures to come back to their original position.

1. 
2. 
3. 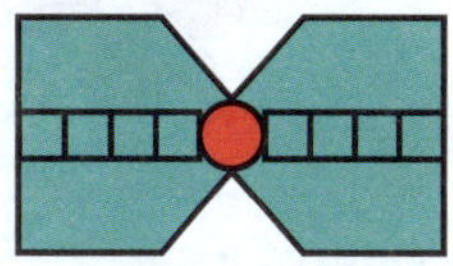
4. 
5. 

Space for rough work

Did You Master?

A. Choose the symmetrical half of the given picture. 

1. 
2. 
3. 
4. 

B. How many lines of symmetry does the picture have?

1. 3
2. 4
3. 6
4. 1

C. What is the top view of a cube?

1. 
Circle
2. 
Triangle
3. 
Rectangle
4. 
Square

D. Which of the following comes next in the pattern?

1. Cube
2. Sphere
3. Cone
4. Cylinder

E. After how many turns does the given shape look the same?

1. $\frac{1}{4}$ turn
2. $\frac{1}{2}$ turn
3. $\frac{3}{4}$ turn
4. 1 turn

F. The given picture represents the top view of which vehicle?

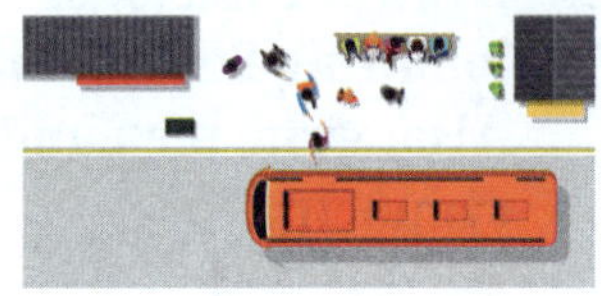

1. Train
2. Car
3. Bus
4. Lorry

G. What comes next in the pattern 49, 64, 81, ...?

1. 100
2. 121
3. 144
4. 140

H. Which of the following is not symmetrical?

1. 
2. 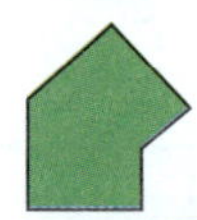
3. 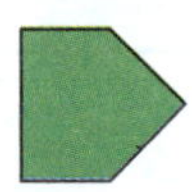
4. 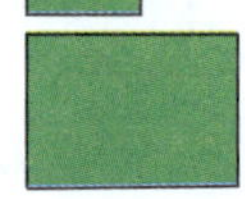

I. Which rule is followed in the pattern 25, 100, 175, 250?

1. +50
2. +70
3. +75
4. +55

J. Which number from 0 to 9 has only one line of symmetry?

1. 0
2. 6
3. 8
4. 3

How many questions did you answer correctly? Score yourself.

easy ☐ average ☐ advanced ☐ remembering ☐ understanding ☐ applying ☐ analysing ☐ evaluating ☐ creating ☐

communication ☐ representation ☐ devising strategies ☐ mathematisation ☐ reasoning and argument ☐ using symbols ☐ using mathematical tools ☐ creativity ☐

15 Data Handling

Curricular Goals

- Develop problem-solving skills with procedural fluency, to solve mathematical puzzles as well as daily life problems, and as a step towards developing computational thinking (CG-4)

Competencies

- Select appropriate methods and tools for computing with whole numbers, such as mental computation, estimation or paper and pencil calculation, in accordance with the context (C-4.3)

Why This Topic?

Graphs represent numbers and values that are otherwise difficult to visualise and understand.

Favourite sports of 60 students

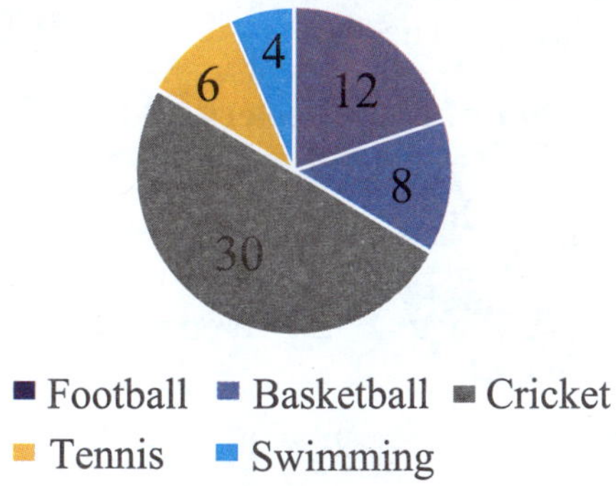

Best bicycle deal

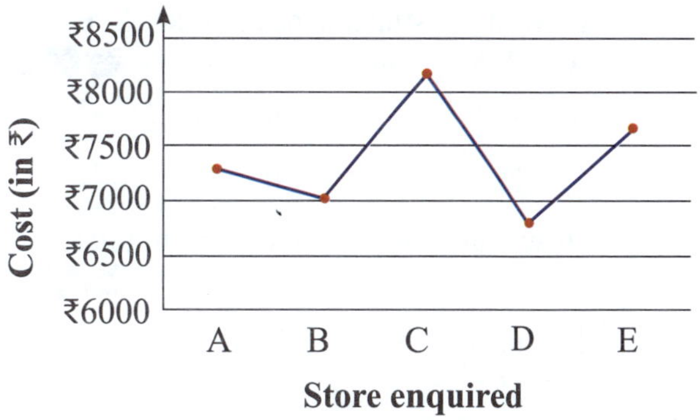

The favourite sports among a group of students can be represented using a circle graph.

A line graph can be used to compare the price of bicycles to find out the best deal.

Can you think of two examples from your daily life where you see the applications of bar graphs, pie charts and line graphs?

Are You Ready?

A. Read the given chart carefully and answer the questions that follow.

Number of students with different blood groups

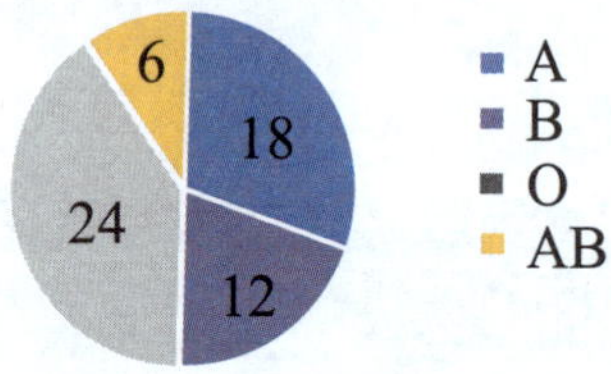

i. Which blood group is the most common?

1. A 2. B
3. O 4. AB

ii. Which blood group is the rarest?

1. A 2. B
3. O 4. AB

iii. How many students have B or O type blood group?

1. 32 2. 30
3. 36 4. 28

iv. How many students have either A, B and AB blood group?

1. 18 2. 30
3. 28 4. 36

v. How many students are there in total?

1. 60 2. 30
3. 44 4. 36

B. A doctor kept a log of the number of patients he saw in the past four days.

Log of patients

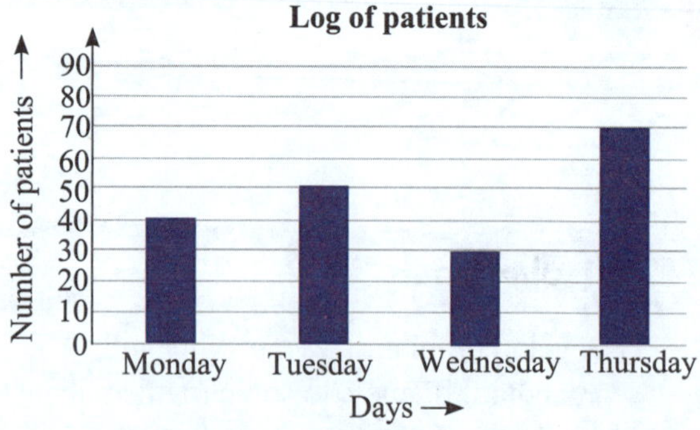

i. How many patients has the doctor seen in the last four days?

1. 120 2. 180
3. 190 4. 240

ii. How many patients has the doctor seen on Tuesday and Thursday?

1. 140 2. 130
3. 120 4. 110

C. From the given pie chart, what is the difference in the sale of two-wheelers on Sunday and Tuesday?

Number of two wheelers sold

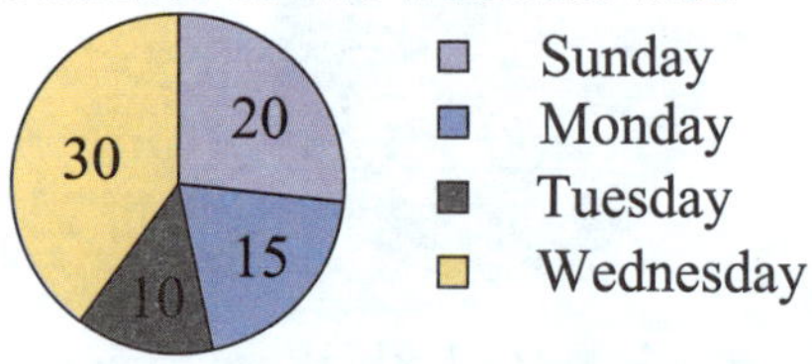

1. 40 2. 30
3. 20 4. 10

How many questions did you answer correctly? Score yourself.

easy, average, advanced, remembering, understanding, applying, analysing, evaluating, creating
communication, representation, devising strategies, mathematisation, reasoning and argument, using symbols, using mathematical tools, creativity

BAR GRAPHS

Let us do a quick recall of bar graphs, studied in the previous grade. A bar graph is a type of chart that uses bars to show and compare different pieces of information or data. It is a visual way to represent data and is easier to understand.

Example 1: The graph here shows the number of National Parks in eight states of India. Read the graph and answer the following questions.

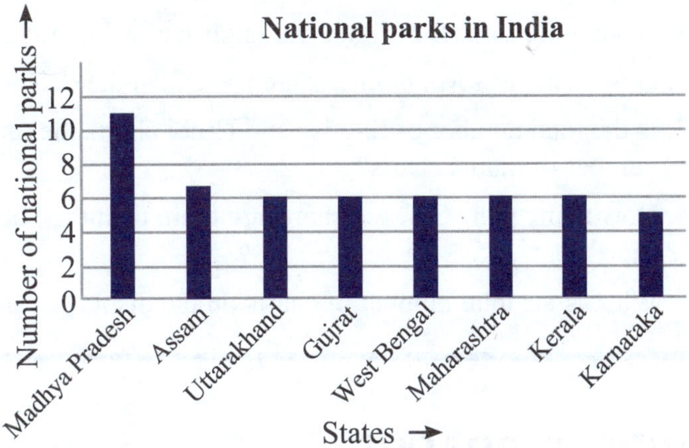

a. Which state has the highest number of national parks?

b. Which state has 5 national parks?

c. How many states have 6 national parks each?

d. How many national parks are there in Assam?

e. How many national parks does Maharashtra have?

Solution:

a. Madhya Pradesh, with 11 national parks, has the highest number of national parks.

b. Karnataka has 5 national parks.

c. There are 5 states that have 6 national parks.

d. Assam has 7 national parks.

e. Maharashtra has 6 national parks.

Example 2: A fertilizers store kept track of the number of bags of fertilizers sold in the past 4 days. The data is presented in the given bar-graph.

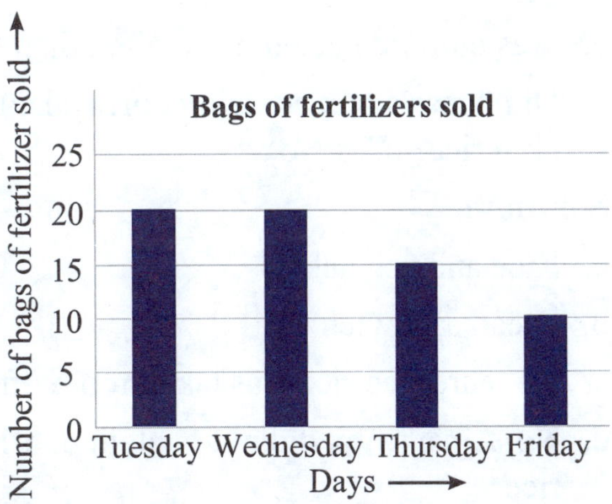

a. How many bags of fertilizers did the store sell on Friday?

b. How many bags of fertilizers did the store sell in all the 4 days?

c. How many bags of fertilizers did the store sell on Thursday?

Solution:

a. 10 bags of fertilizers were sold on Friday.

b. 65 bags of fertilizers were sold in all the 4 days.

c. 15 bags of fertilizers were sold on Thursday.

Exercise 15.1

The number of charts put up on the display board for Grade 5 is shown in the bar graph. Using this graph, answer the following questions.

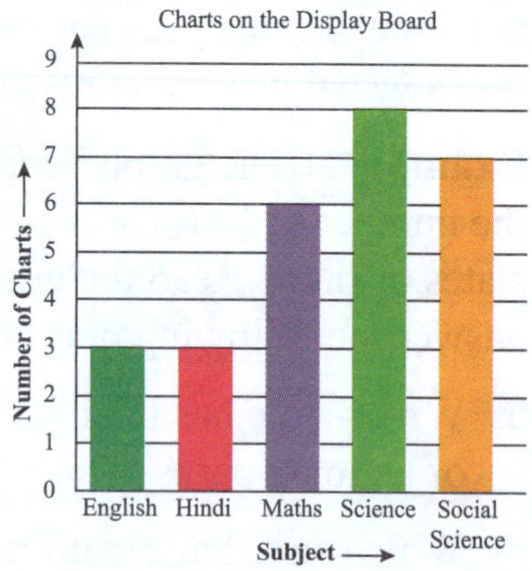

1. What is the number of Hindi and English charts on the display board?
2. How many less Maths charts are there than the Science charts?
3. Is the total number of English and Hindi charts the same as the number of Maths charts?
4. How many more Science charts are there than the Social Science charts?
5. What is the total number of charts on the display board?

CIRCLE GRAPHS

Circle graph is a circular chart divided into different sections. Different parts of information are represented by these sections. It shows how different parts of information are related to the whole and to each other.

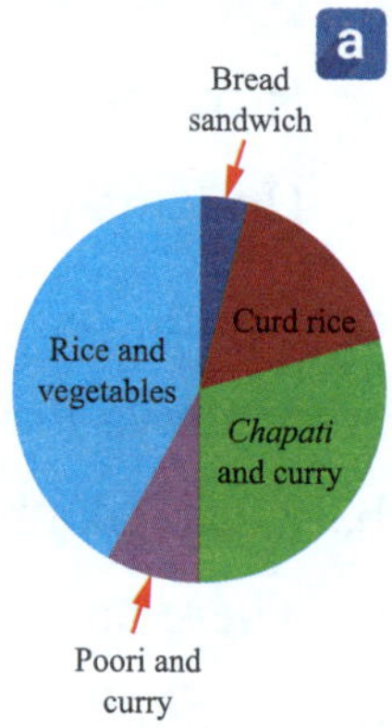

Example 3: The circle graph shown here represents information about different dishes in Amar's lunch box in a particular month.

a. Which dish did he take the maximum number of times in this month?

b. Which dish did he take the minimum number of times in this month?

c. Was curd rice taken more often than Chapati and curry? (Yes/No)

d. Did Amar's box contain poori and curry the same number of times as curd rice? (Yes/No)

Solution:

a. Rice and vegetables

b. Bread sandwich

c. No, curd rice rice was taken more often.

d. No, Amar's box did not contain poori and curry the same number of times as curd rice.

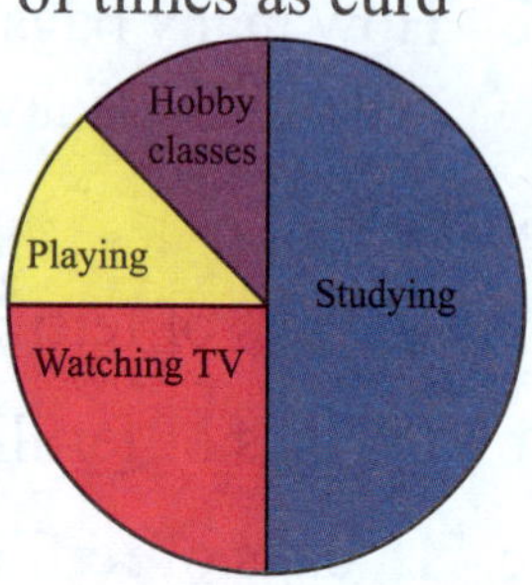

Example 4: The number of hours spent by Monica after school on different activities in a particular week is represented in the circle chart. The circle represents 16 hours.

Find the number of hours spent on each activity.

Solution:

Let us find the number of hours spent by Monica on each activity.

The total number of hours spent by Monica on these activities in that week was 16 hours since the circle represents 16 hours.

From the circle graph, we can find:

Time spent on studying is $\frac{1}{2}$ of the total hours $= \frac{1}{2} \times 16 = 8$ hours

Time spent on watching TV is $\frac{1}{4}$ of the total hours $= \frac{1}{4} \times 16 = 4$ hours

Time spent on playing is half of $\frac{1}{4}$ of the total hours $= \frac{1}{2}\left(\frac{1}{4}\right) \times 16 = \frac{1}{8} \times 16 = 2$ hours

Time spent on hobby classes is same as time spent on playing, i.e., 2 hours.

Activity	Number of hours
Studying	8
Watching TV	4
Playing	2
Hobby classes	2
Total	16

Exercise 15.2

1. The names of some Indian states and the number of world heritage sites identified by UNESCO in those states are listed below. The information is also represented in a circle chart. Complete labelling the circle graph by looking at the list.

State	Number of World Heritage Sites
Madhya Pradesh	3
Sikkim	1
Uttaranchal	1
Maharashtra	4
Karnataka	2
Rajasthan	2
Assam	2
Uttar Pradesh	3

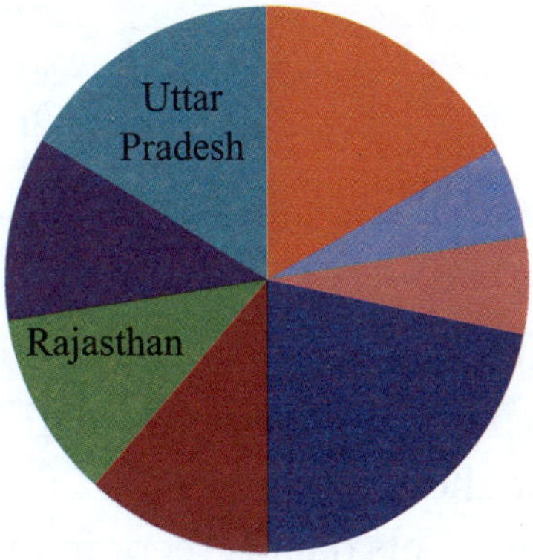

How many world heritage sites are there in these 8 states?

2. **The maths teacher made a list of all the reasons that the students gave for not being prepared for the test. She represented the reasons using a circle graph. The number of students in the class is 30. Complete the table by looking at the chart. Also, colour the different sections of the circle graph in different colours.**

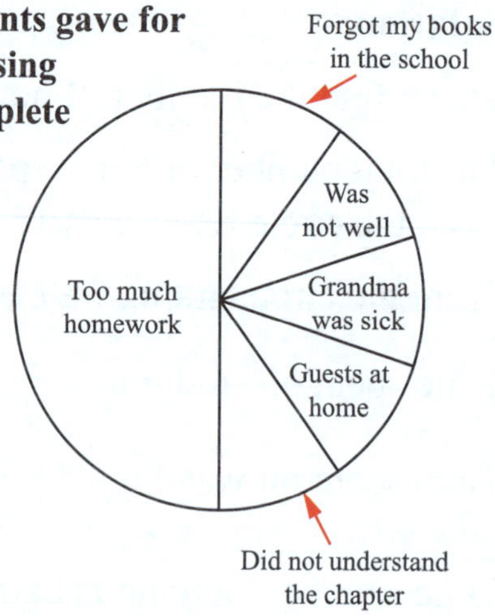

Reasons	Number of Students
Too much homework	15

LINE GRAPHS

Line graphs are used to display data. They consist of a series of data points that are connected by straight lines. Each point on a line graph represents a specific value of the data. Let us consider an example to see how these graphs are created.

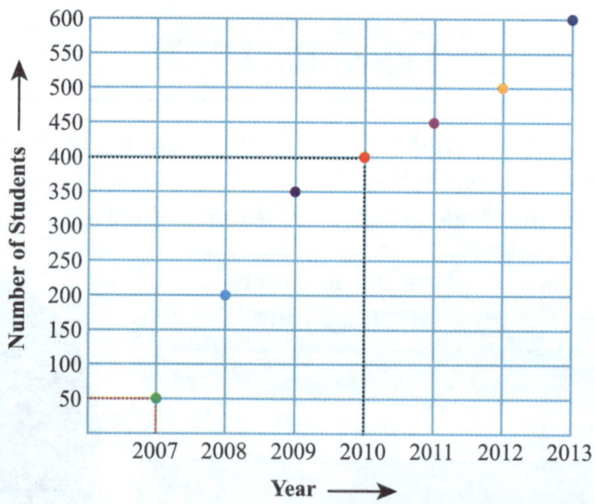

The number of students in different years since the school began in 2007 is listed below. This data is recorded in a line graph by putting a dot on the chart every year, after the admissions are completed.

Year	Number of Students
2007	50
2008	200
2009	350
2010	400
2011	450
2012	500
2013	600

Let us see how the dots have been placed.

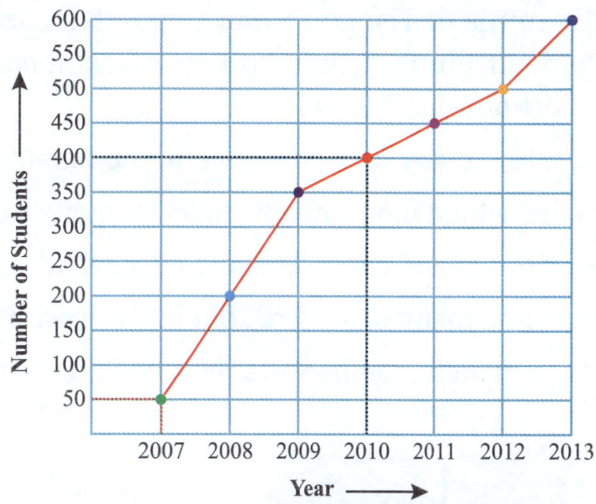

The red vertical line shows year 2007 and the red horizontal line shows 50 students. The green dot has been placed where the two red lines meet. It means that in the year 2007, when the school began, the number of students was 50.

The red dot is placed where the black vertical and horizontal lines meet. The red dot shows that in the year 2010, there were 400 students.

Similarly, find out what the other dots represent.

On joining the dots, you get a line graph.

Use a ruler to know exactly where the dots are placed.

Example 5: Based on the above graph, answer the following questions.

a. What was the number of students when the school began?

b. What was the number of students in the year 2012?

c. How many students joined in the year 2008?

d. In which year did the number of students reach 450?

e. How many more students are there in 2013 than in the year 2010?

Solution: From the line graph, we can observe the following.

a. The number of students when the school began in 2007 was 50.

b. The number of students in 2012 was 500.

c. Number of students in the year 2007 = 50

   Number of students in the year 2008 = 200

   Therefore, the number of students who joined in 2008 is 200 – 50 = 150.

d. In 2011, the number of students reached 450.

e. Number of students in 2013 = 600, number of students in 2010 = 400.

   Therefore, the number of students who joined in 2013 = 400 – 200 = 200.

   This means that 200 more students joined in the year 2013 as compared to 2010.

Example 6: The given line graph illustrates the monthly car sales over a period of 6 months from January to June of a company XYZ. Using the graph, answer the questions that follow.

a. How many cars were sold in the month of May?

b. In which month were the least number of cars sold?

c. How many cars were sold altogether?

d. How many cars were sold in the months of February and April?

e. In which months were the same number of cars sold?

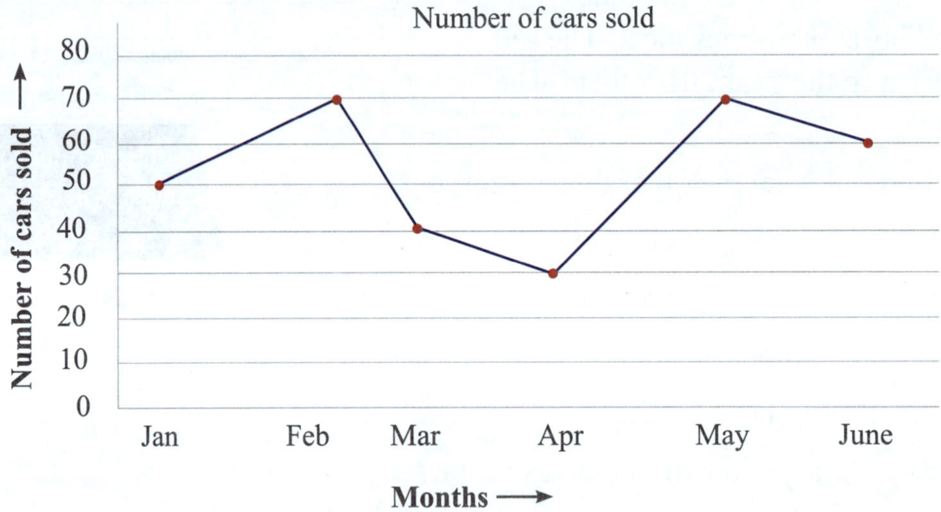

Solution: a. A total of 70 cars were sold in the month of May.

b. Car sales was the lowest in the month of April.

c. Total number of cars sold = sum of cars sold in each month

$$= 50 + 70 + 40 + 30 + 70 + 60 = 320$$

Therefore, a total of 320 cars were sold from January to June.

d. Number of cars sold in February and April = 70 + 30 = 100

e. The same number of cars were sold in the months of February and May (70 cars).

Exercise 15.3

1. **Omar was sitting in his balcony and watching the vehicles go by. He made a note of the number of vehicles that passed by after every 5 minutes for an hour. Based on the data, he made the following line graph. Observe the graph and answer the given questions.**

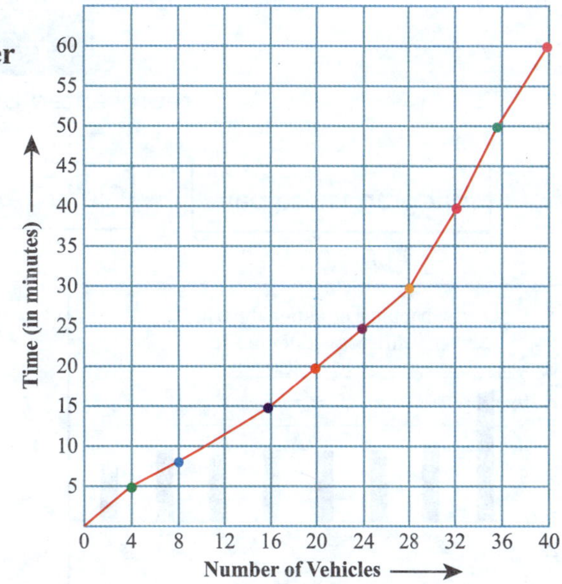

   a. When did 8 vehicles pass by?

   b. How many vehicles had passed by the end of 25 minutes?

   c. How many more vehicles had passed by the end of 30 minutes as compared to 15 minutes?

   d. When did 40 vehicles pass by?

   e. When did 32 vehicles pass by?

2. **The following line graph represents the average monthly temperature changes in Gangtok, Sikkim over a year. Read the graph and answer the following questions.**

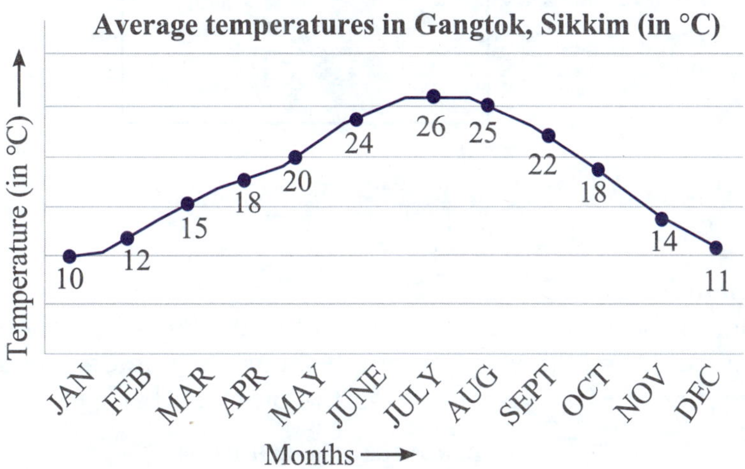

   a. Which month had an average temperature of 20°C?

   b. Which month had the highest average temperature?

   c. What is the difference in the temperatures between July and December?

   d. What is the difference in temperature between the month with the highest average temperature and the month with the lowest average temperature?

   e. Which month had the lowest average temperature?

Concept Map

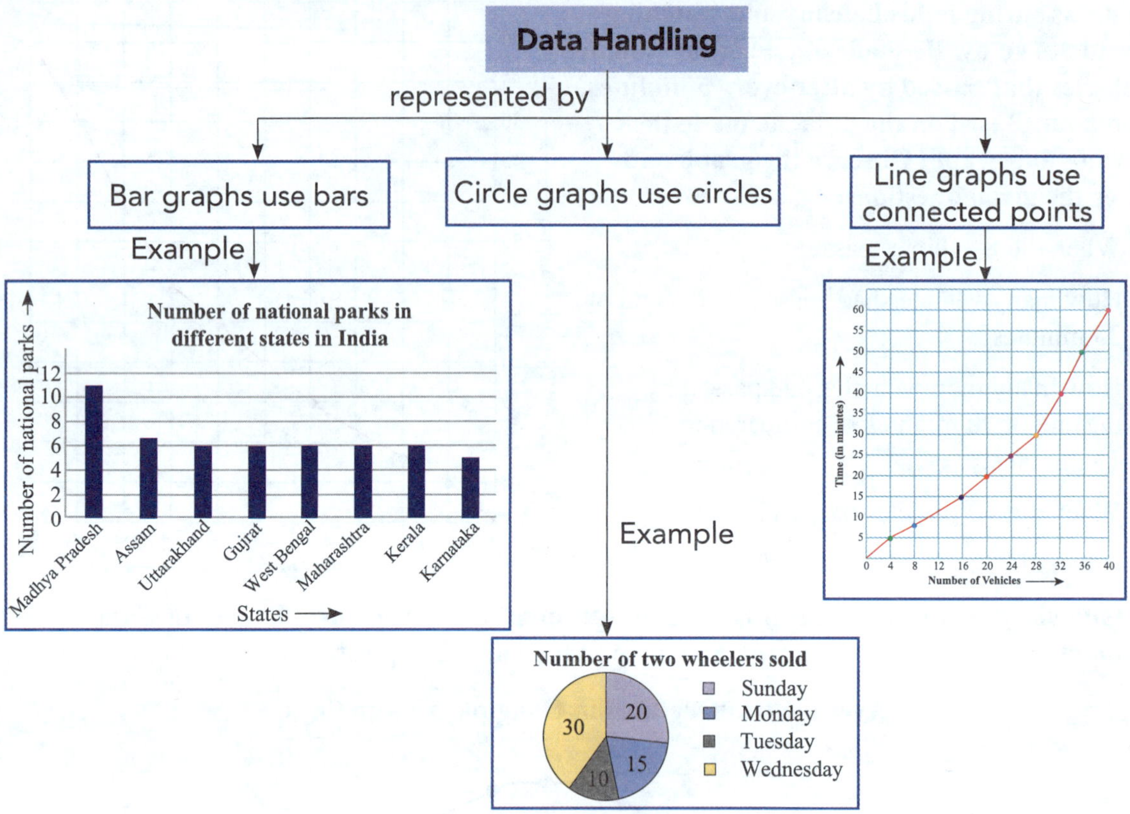

Project

Human Development Index (HDI)

HDI ranks the countries based on their performance in the key areas of health, education and access to resources. The following line graph shows the number of countries that fall into different categories of HDI levels. Interpret the graph and answer the questions.

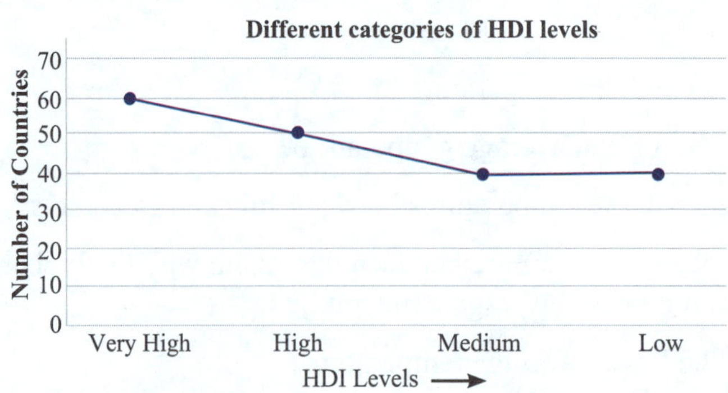

1. How many countries fall under low level of Human Development Index?
2. What are the reasons for low HDIs?
3. What do you think will help a country in improving its HDI?

Revision Exercise

A. Choose the correct option.
Mr. Madan owns a kitchen appliances store. He compared the sale of different items in his stores and recorded the data in a circle graph.

Kitchen appliances sold (Number of units)

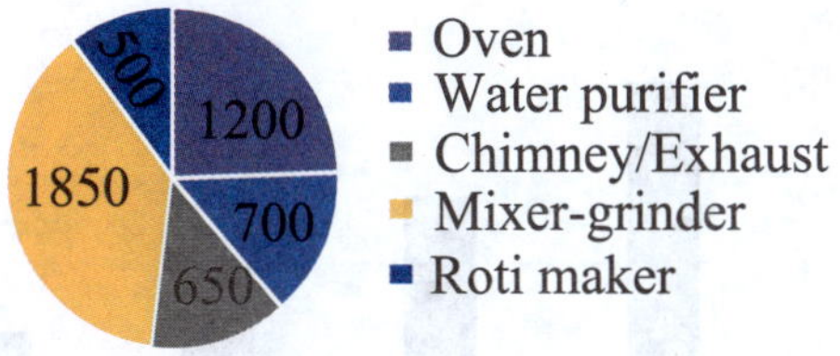

1. Which item was sold the most in his store?
   a. Oven
   b. Water purifier
   c. Mixer-grinder
   d. Roti maker
2. Which item was sold the least in the store?
   a. Oven
   b. Water purifier
   c. Mixer-grinder
   d. Roti maker
3. What is the difference in the number of ovens and mixer-grinders sold?
   a. 550
   b. 600
   c. 650
   d. 750
4. How many units of kitchen appliances were sold in all?
   a. 4900
   b. 4090
   c. 4990
   d. 4999
5. How many units of water purifier were sold?
   a. 500
   b. 700
   c. 650
   d. 1200

B. The line graph shows the number of workers in different departments of a steel factory. Read the graph and fill in the blanks.

Workers in different departments

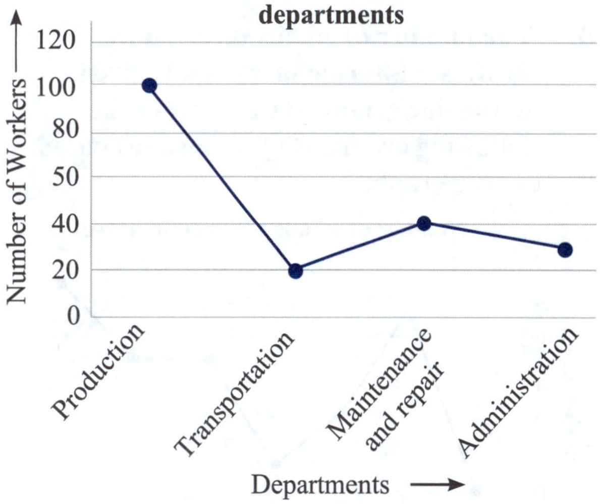

1. There are ________ workers in the transportation department.
2. There are a total of ________ workers in the steel factory.
3. There are a total of ________ workers when the departments of maintenance and repair and administration are put together.
4. There are ________ workers less in transportation as compared to production.
5. The ________ department has the highest number of workers in the steel factory.

C. Match the following.

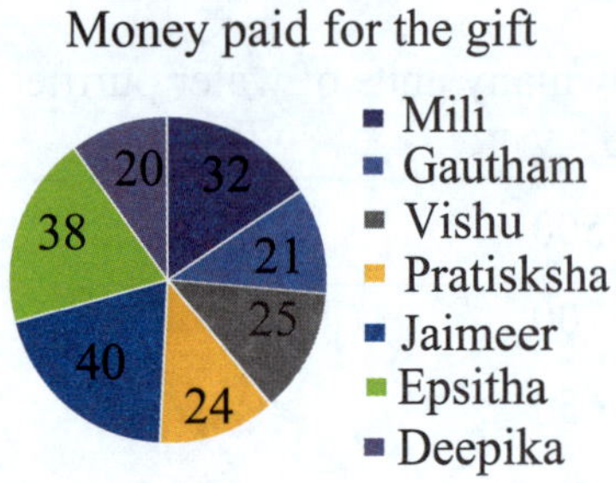

1.	Mili	a.	₹21
2.	Gautham	b.	₹24
3.	Jaimeer	c.	₹20
4.	Deepika	d.	₹32
5.	Pratiksha	e.	₹40

D. The number of emails received by Professor Sharma in a week is given in the line graph. State whether the following are true (T) or false (F) based on the graph.

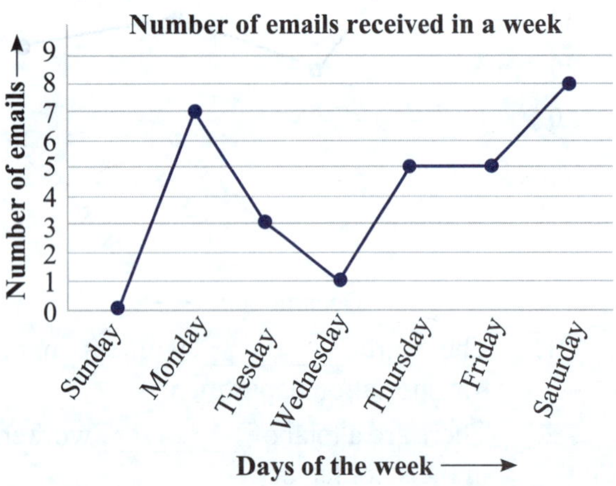

1. 7 is the highest number of emails that Professor Sharma received in one day.
2. 5 emails were received on Thursday and Friday each.
3. No email was received on Saturday.
4. There were total 3 emails on Sunday and Tuesday together.
5. The second highest number of emails were received on Monday.

E. Application-based questions.

A history teacher was teaching a class about the average life span of human beings in different periods of time with the help of the given bar graph. Read the graph and answer the questions that follow.

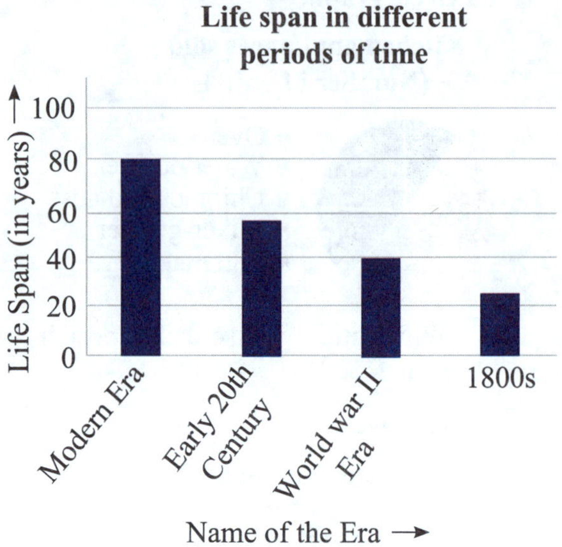

1. What was the life expectancy during the Modern Era?
2. What was the life Span during World War II Era?
3. What was the life expectancy during the 1800s?
4. What is the difference in life spans during the World War II Era and the Early 20th Century?
5. Which era has the highest life expectancy?

Did You Master?

A. A group of grade 5 students collected plastic bottles from their school ground and recorded their count.

Number of bottles collected

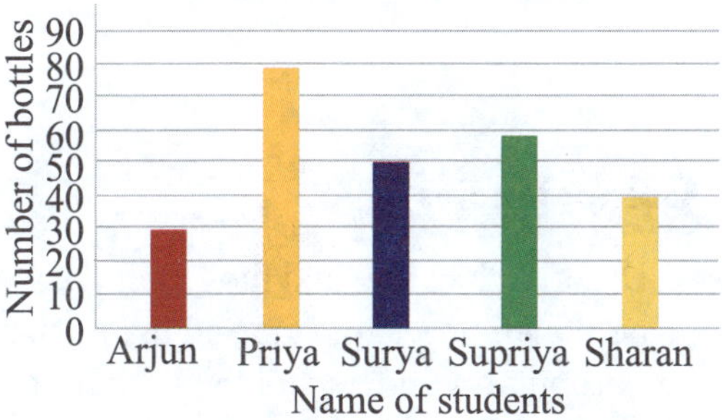

i. How many bottles did Arjun collect?

1. 30	2. 80
3. 50	4. 40

ii. How many bottles did Sharan collect?

1. 30	2. 80
3. 50	4. 40

iii. How many bottles did Surya and Supriya collect together?

1. 130	2. 120
3. 110	4. 100

B. The line graph shows the number of participants in an inter school competition from 2014 to 2023.

Participants in inter-school competiiton

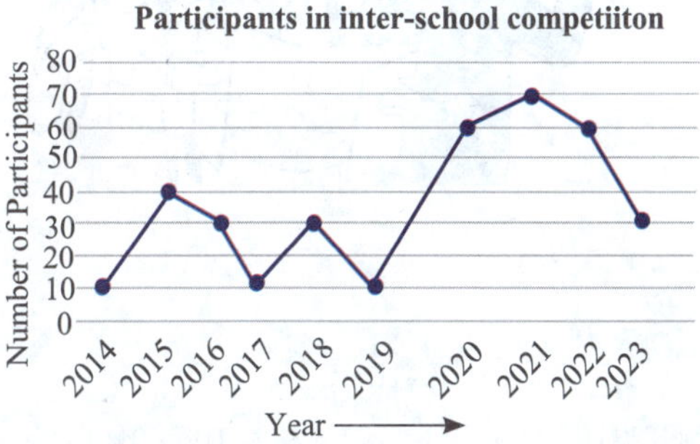

i. In which year did the inter school competition have 70 participants?

1. 2015	2. 2018
3. 2020	4. 2021

ii. In which year did the inter school competition have 40 participants?

1. 2015	2. 2018
3. 2020	4. 2021

iii. In which 3 years were there 30 participants each?

1. 2015, 2018, 2022
2. 2016, 2018, 2023
3. 2016, 2018, 2022
4. 2015, 2017, 2023

C. Six teams in a school raised ₹10,000 to buy sports equipment. They recorded their percentage of contribution in the following circle graph.

Money raised (in percentage)

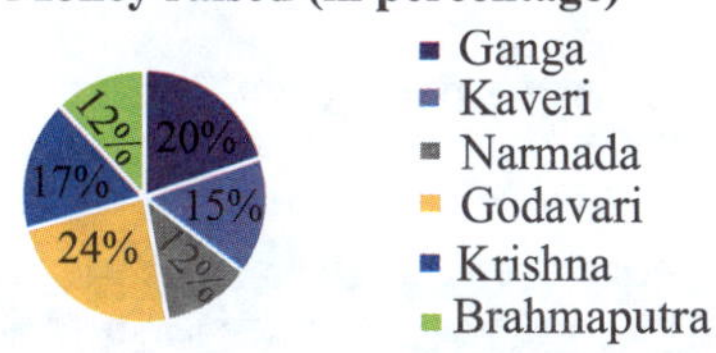

i. How much money did teams Narmada and Godavari raise together?

1. ₹3500	2. ₹3600
3. ₹3700	4. ₹3800

ii. How much money did teams Ganga, Krishna and Brahmaputra raise together?

1. ₹4600	2. ₹4700
3. ₹4900	4. ₹4800

How many questions did you answer correctly? Score yourself.

easy ☐ average ☐ advanced ☐ remembering ☐ understanding ☐ applying ☐ analysing ☐ evaluating ☐ creating ☐

communication ☐ representation ☐ devising strategies ☐ mathematisation ☐ reasoning and argument ☐ using symbols ☐ using mathematical tools ☐ creativity ☐

16 Mapping Skills

Curricular Goals

- Specify locations and describe spatial relationships (CG-2)

Competencies

- Describe location and movement using both common language and mathematical vocabulary; understand the notion of map (*najri naksha*) (C-2.2)

Why This Topic?

Maps are one of the most significant and crucial tools used by travellers, explorers and common people to know their location and to find their route from one place to another.

Google maps

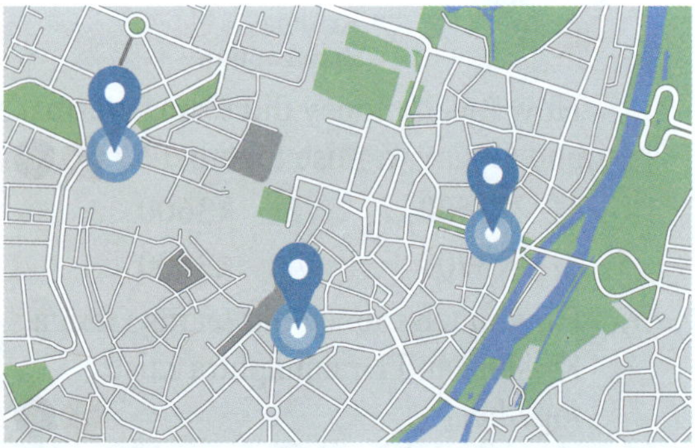

One of the most widely used location apps today is Google Maps. We can easily locate our house on it.

Giving directions

To give directions, like going straight from here, taking the second right turn, then taking a left turn and staying straight, it is necessary to know how to give directions.

Can you give two examples from your everyday life where you need to find the location of a place or search for routes?

Are You Ready?

A. The sun rises in the ______.

1. North 2. East
3. West 4. South

B. The sun sets in the ______.

1. North 2. East
3. West 4. South

C. Which way are you going if you are moving from point A to point B?

1. Going up
2. Coming down
3. Going to the right
4. Going to the left

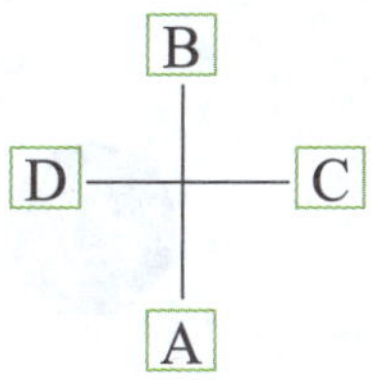

D. Which way are you going if you are moving from point C to point D?

1. Going up
2. Coming down
3. Going to the right
4. Going to the left

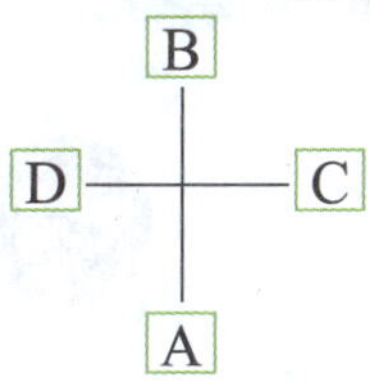

E. Karan is facing south and he turns 90 degrees clockwise, thrice. Which direction is Karan facing?

1. North 2. East
3. West 4. South

F. Which direction is to the left of South, when you are facing South?

1. North 2. East
3. West 4. South

G. What does this sign mean?

1. Go straight 2. Go left
3. Stop 4. Go right

H. What does this sign mean?

1. Turn right
2. Turn left
3. Do not turn right
4. Do not turn left

I. Following map shows the streets of a town. You are standing in Harbour Street.

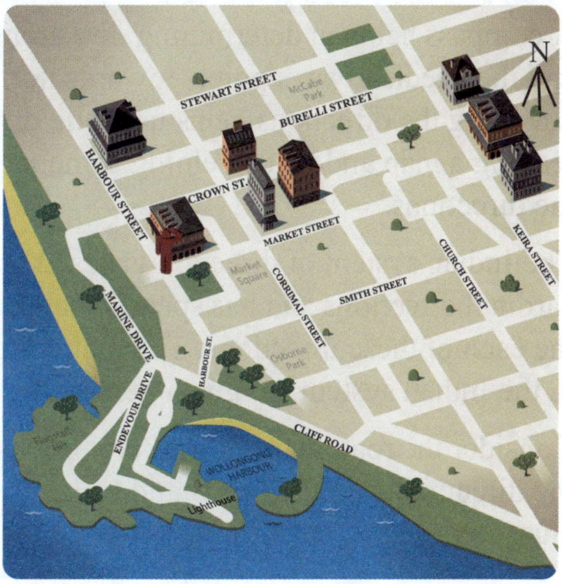

i. In which direction is Church Street located?

1. North 2. East
3. West 4. South

ii. In which direction is the lighthouse located?

1. North 2. East
3. West 4. South

How many questions did you answer correctly? Score yourself.

easy, average, advanced, remembering, understanding, applying, analysing, evaluating, creating

communication, representation, devising strategies, mathematisation, reasoning and argument, using symbols, using mathematical tools, creativity

MAP

A map is a drawing that shows the position of things such as countries, cities, towns, streets, rivers, mountains, etc. There are different kinds of maps which are meant for different purposes. The person who creates a map is called a cartographer.

Directions In A Map

We use directions to talk about the location of a place. There are four directions, namely **NORTH, EAST, SOUTH** and **WEST**.

A compass helps in determining directions and the needle always points towards north. Knowing the directions helps us while driving, reading a map and when helping somebody with the directions.

The Indian system of direction is based on the cardinal directions and has specific names for the each of these directions. The main directions in the Indian system are given here.

Consider the road map shown here. Let us mark the direction from the Bus Stand to Jai Niwas Guest House.

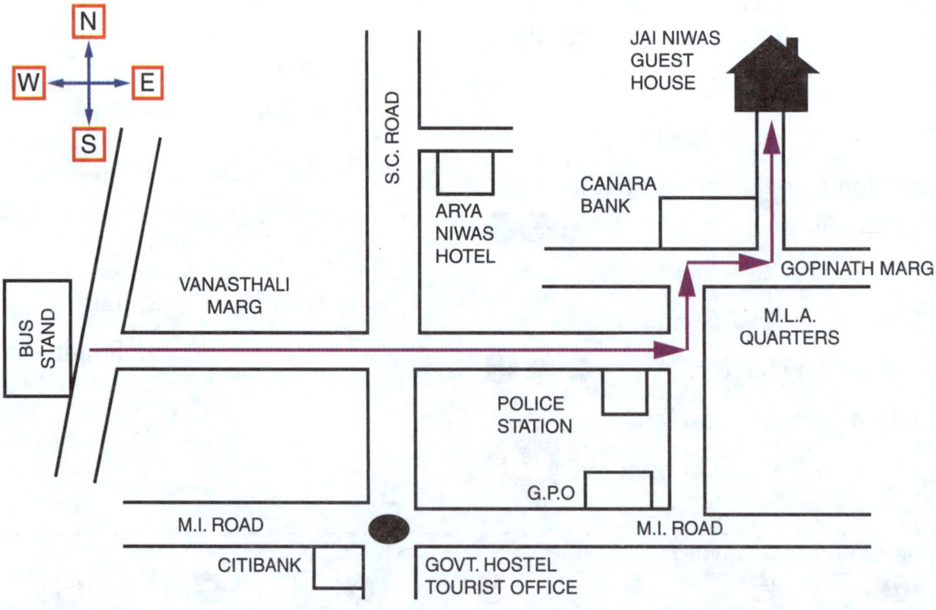

Move straight towards east and take the second left towards north till you reach Gopinath Marg. From there, take a right turn towards east and first left turn towards north to reach Jai Niwas Guest House.

Example 1: In the map given below, mark the directions from Sunflower School to The New Horizon High School. Explain the same in words.

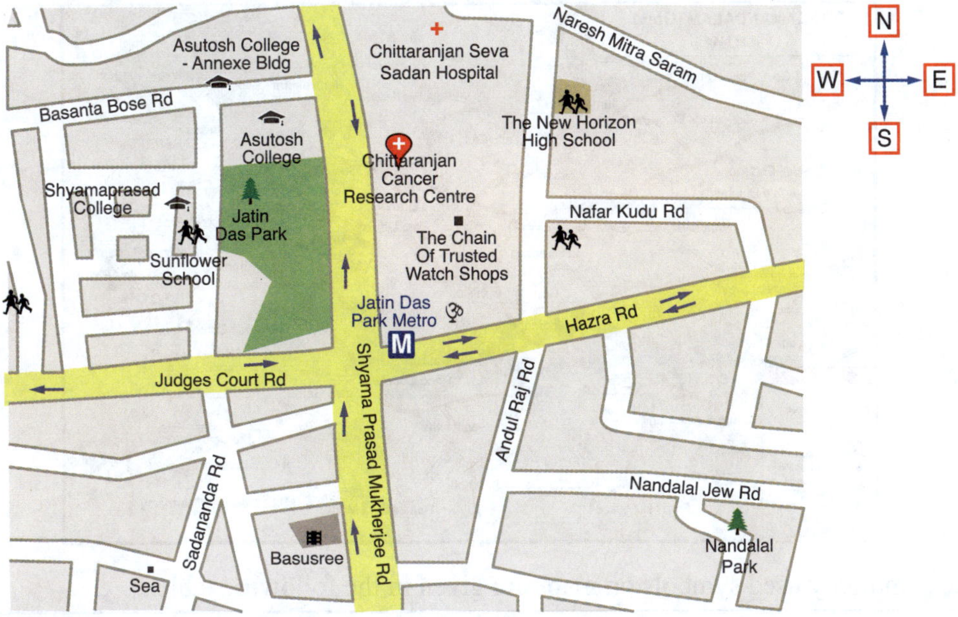

Solution: The directions to reach The New Horizon High School from Sunflower School are marked in the given map.

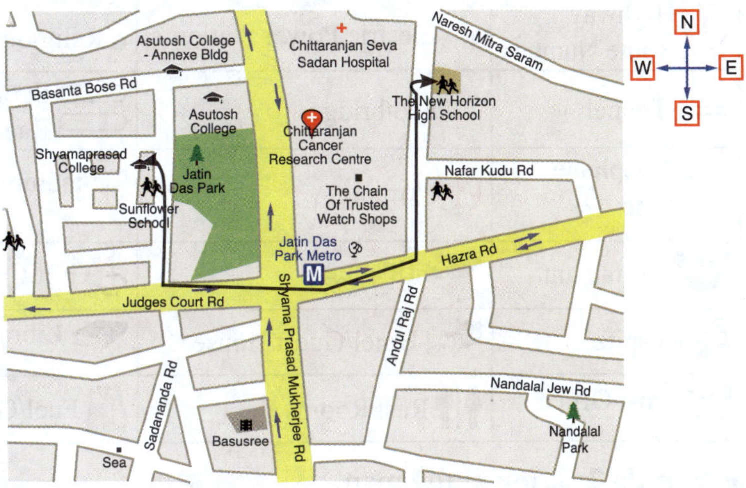

To go from Sunflower School to The New Horizon High School, walk south from Sunflower School till you reach Judges Court Road. Take a left and walk till you reach the junction of Hazra Road and Andul Raj Road. Take a left and walk till you find The New Horizon School on your right hand.

SYMBOLS AND LEGENDS ON A MAP

Symbols and legends are important elements of a map that provide key information in the map. These help the users in better understanding the contents and the features of a map.

Symbols are graphic representations used on a map to represent an object or a feature. They are also called **map legends.** A **key** or a **legend** is used at the end of the map to specify which symbol stands for what.

Look at the tourist map of Ooty shown here. There are some symbols used in the map which represent a specific location.

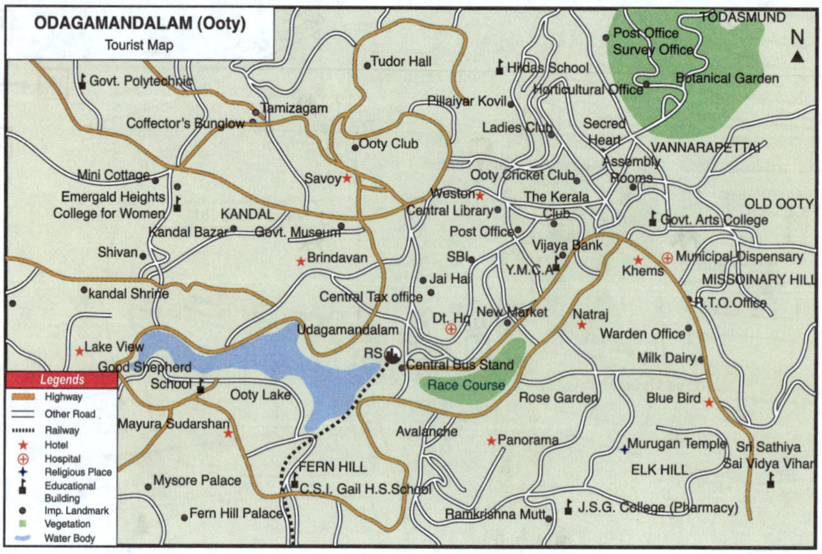

Some of the commonly used symbols on maps are given in the following table.

Bridge	Educational Building	Railway	Gate / Toll Gate
Highway Route Number	Electric Power Station	Religious Building	Fire Station
Tunnel	Footbridge	Sports Track/ Race Track	Electric Facility: large
Telephone Line	Airport	Stadium	Museum
Restaurant	Boating	Golf Course	Forest/Trees
Hospital	Hotel/Guest House	Library	Parking
Post Office	Rest Rooms	Fuel/Gas/Petrol	Telephone

Example 2: Look at the map shown here. There are some symbols used in the map which represent a specific location. How many schools are there?

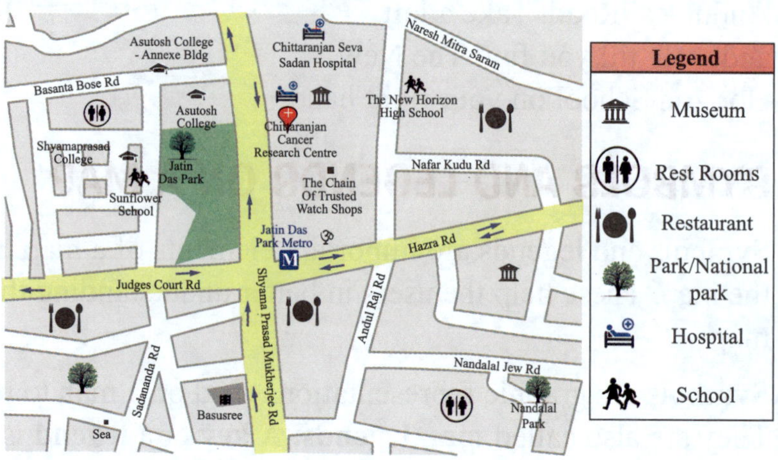

Solution: There are two schools in the given map: Sunflower School and The New Horizon High School.

SCALE IN A MAP

Look at the pictures of a bicycle, an elephant and a giraffe. Are these the original sizes of them? No, the sizes of the pictures have been reduced in some proportion in order to draw it in our books.

We use scale while drawing maps. The scale of a map is defined as the relation between the distance on the ground and the corresponding distance on the map.

Example 3: Look at the map of India shown here. One inch grid is used to draw the map. The scale used is 1 inch = 700 km.

What is the distance between Hyderabad and Bhubaneswar?

Solution: To find the distance between Hyderabad and Bhubaneswar, we first connect the two places using a line segment and measure its distance, which is 3.8 cm = 1.5 inches.

Actual distance between Hyderabad and Bhubaneswar

= 1.5 × 700 km = 1050 km

Therefore, the distance between Hyderabad and Bhubaneswar is 1050 km.

Example 4: Use the same map as in Example 3 to find the distance between Jaipur and Bangaluru?

Solution: Connect Jaipur and Bengaluru with a line segment and measure its distance, which is 7.18 cm = 2.83 inches.

Actual distance between Jaipur and Bangaluru = 2.83 × 700 km = 1981 km.

Therefore, the distance between Jaipur and Bangalore is 1981 km.

Exercise 16.1

1. Write appropriate directions for each of the following.

a. If you are facing west, which direction is to your right?

b. If you are facing south, which direction is to your left?

c. If you are facing north, which direction is behind you?

d. Which direction is halfway between east and south?

e. Which direction is exactly opposite to south-east?

2. Use the legend and count the number of features in the given map.

a. How many hospitals are there?

b. How many parks/national parks are there?

c. How many museums are there?

d. How many rest rooms are there?

e. How many restaurants are there?

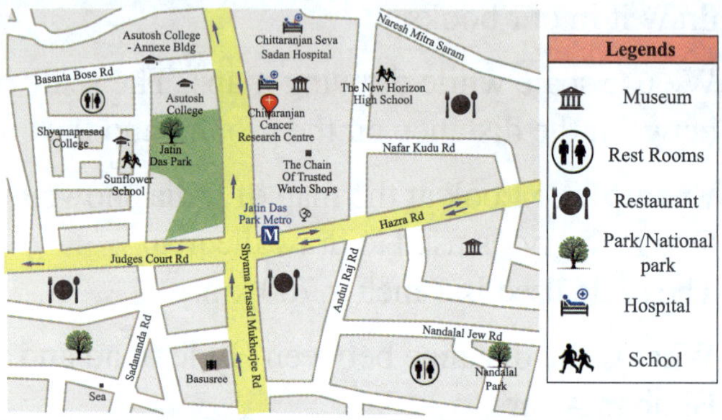

3. Observe the given map and find the actual distance of the following places, given that 1 inch = 700 km.

a. Raipur to Lucknow

b. Goa to Bhopal

c. Delhi to Thiruvananthapuram

d. Kolkata to Shimla

e. Mumbai to Chennai

Concept Map

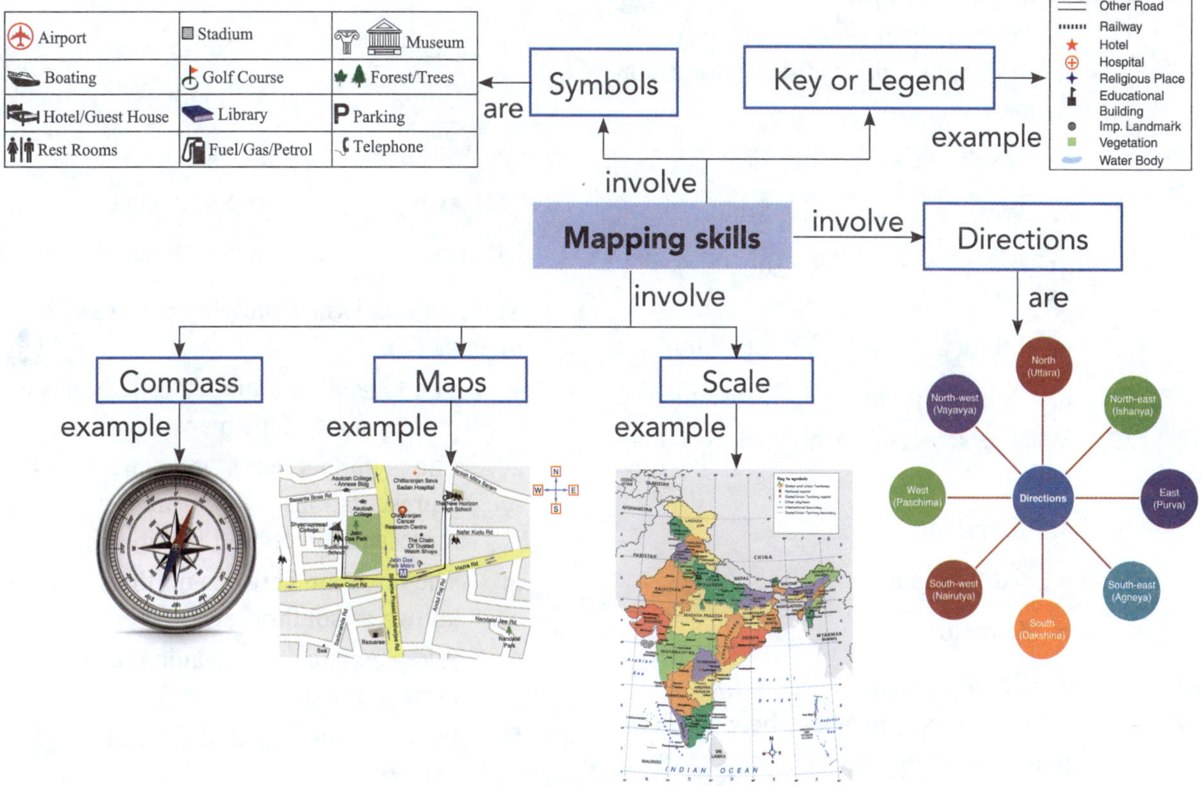

Projects

A. Make a route map!

Get into groups of two or three by selecting friends who live nearby your house. On a chart paper, make a route map from your house to their houses and your school. Mark the important features/buildings on the way to school and add it on your map. Display the chart in class.

Extension: You may check the correctness of each other's route map by taking the route map to reach your friends' houses. This must be done under teacher's/parent's supervision.

B. Puzzle your way!

A school bus is trying to reach school on time. The bus driver got a little mixed up with the route and cannot find the correct route to the school. Work in pairs and help the bus reach school on time.

Also, write in words the direction to the school.

Revision Exercise

A. Choose the correct option.

1. If you are facing south and turn 90° to your right, which direction are you facing?

   a. North b. East

   c. West d. South

2. What does the symbol  on a map indicate?

   a. Library b. Stadium

   c. Police Station d. Museum

3. What is a person who makes a map called?

   a. Map-maker

   b. Cartographer

   c. Director

   d. Photographer

4. What is the distance between two points 1 inch apart if the scale is 1 inch = 3000 m?

   a. 300 km b. 3000 km

   c. 30 km d. 3 km

5. What is the distance between two cities 7.25 inches apart if the scale is 1 inch = 1200 km?

   a. 8500 km b. 8600 km

   c. 8700 km d. 8800 km

B. Fill in the blanks.

1. A ___________ is used to tell direction.
2. We use directions to talk about ___________ of a place.
3. The distance between two points on a map is measured using a ___________.
4.  is the symbol used to indicate ___________ in a map.
5. Nairuthya means ___________ in the Indian system.

C. Match the following.

1. Dakshina	a. North-west
2. Ishanya	b. South
3. Agneya	c. East
4. Vayavya	d. South-east
5. Purva	e. North-east

D. State whether the following are true (T) or false (F).

1. The legend on a map is usually placed in the centre of the map.
2. The symbols on a map are graphic representations that are used to represent objects and features.
3. The direction between north and east is known as south-west.
4. A key explains the meaning of symbols used in a map.
5. Purva means East in the Indian System.

E. Application-based questions.

1. Mahesh walks 30 m south. He turns right and walks 50 m. He again turns right and walks 30 m. He turns right again. Which direction is he facing?
2. Kavya is facing south-east and turns 135° to the left. Which direction is she facing?
3. What is the distance between Thiruvananthapuram and Bangaluru if the distance on the map is 1.35 inch and the scale is 1 inch = 250 km?
4. A person is facing east. He turns 180° to the left and then turns 360° to the right. Which direction is he facing?
5. What is the distance between Delhi and Kolkata if the distance on the map is 7.5 inch and the scale is 1 inch = 185 km?

Did You Master?

A. Which direction does the needle on a a compass always points to?

1. North 2. East
3. West 4. South

B. Which of the following is NOT represented by a symbol on a map?

1. Road 2. Railway station
3. Hospital 4. Name of a city

C. What does the symbol  on a map indicate?

1. Hotel 2. Hospital
3. Hostel 4. Museum

D. Mayuri is facing east and turns 90° degrees to her left. In which direction is she facing now?

1. North 2. East
3. West 4. South

E. Jay is standing facing south-west and turns 180 degrees. Which direction is he facing now?

1. North-west
2. North-east
3. South-east
4. South-west

F. Swara is facing north-west and turns 180 degrees. Which direction is she facing?

1. North-west
2. North-east
3. South-east
4. South-west

G. Guneet wants to go to the library which is 400 m north and then 500 m east from where he is. In which direction should he walk to reach the library early?

1. North-west
2. South-west
3. South-east
4. North-east

H. After leaving the playground, Mehek rode her bicycle for 4 km south, 5 km west and 4 km north. In which direction should Mehek go to get back to the playground?

1. North 2. East
3. West 4. South

I. If two cities are 5.45 inches apart on a map and the scale is 1 inch = 130 km, what is the actual distance between the two cities?

1. 705.5 km
2. 706.5 km
3. 707.5 km
4. 708.5 km

J. Ashwin went to the railway station with his parents to welcome some relatives. He goes 3 km south, 4 km east, 4 km north and 3 km west from his house to reach the station. How many kilometres away is Ashwin from his home?

1. 1 km 2. 2 km
3. 3 km 4. 4 km

How many questions did you answer correctly? Score yourself.

easy ☐ average ☐ advanced ☐ remembering ☐ understanding ☐ applying ☐ analysing ☐ evaluating ☐ creating ☐

communication ☐ representation ☐ devising strategies ☐ mathematisation ☐ reasoning and argument ☐ using symbols ☐ using mathematical tools ☐ creativity ☐

Financial Literacy

SAVE MONEY SET GOALS

Saving money is like forming a good habit. You have to be consistent and disciplined. Think of ideas that can help you save money and make better choices with your spending. By doing these things, you can slowly build up your savings and feel better about your money.

One helpful thing is to set goals for yourself. These goals can be things you want to save money for. When you set goals, it helps you stay motivated and focused. It is even better if your goals are SMART, which means they are Specific, Measurable, Achievable, Relevant and Time-bound. This makes it easier to reach your goals and feel proud of what you have accomplished.

SMART goal elements

↓

S = Specific	M = Measurable	A = Attainable	R = Relevant	T = Time-bound

WHY IS SAVING SMART?

Suppose you have set a goal to save money without any plan. This goal is vague and there is no way to tell when success has been reached. Look what happens when you make the goal SMART.

A. Fill in the SMART table for Hazel. Her story is given here.

Romila and Ashish are back from Meghalaya. Before leaving, they invite Hazel to visit their city. Hazel decides to start saving money so that she can visit her friends during her vacation next year. She requests her parents and brother to contribute to her savings. Hazel starts saving ₹500 every month from her pocket money. Her mother gives her ₹1000 each month to save. Her father further contributes ₹2500 each month and her elder brother gives her ₹500 each month.

Related questions	Your SMART savings goal
What are you saving for?	
How much do you want to save?	
Is this realistic? It is doable?	
Is this worth saving for? Is this important for you?	
When will you meet the goal?	

B. Identify a short-term savings goal (something you had like to save for this year). Redraw the SMART table and fill in for your goal.

Pre-planning of Expenses

An important part of planning for your savings goals is **Pre-planning**. Without proper planning, your expenses can get messy and disorganised. You should always pre-plan your expenses to get an idea of how much you will end up saving. If you have a savings goal, then you may need to adjust your expenses so that you can meet your savings goal on time.

WAYS TO MAKE MONEY

Everybody wants to increase their savings. You can save more by either earning more, or by spending less. There are many ways in which you can also get some extra cash for your needs and wants.

- **Make your own items instead of buying them**

  For example, instead of spending time and money on expensive toys, there are hundreds of art and craft activities you can do with coloured paper and glue. These are known as **Do-It-Yourself (DIY)** projects. You can try making your own tie-dyed t-shirts, coloured pottery, soap making, knitting socks, bake cookies and so on.
- **Earn money by selling these DIY items**

  Start by selecting a DIY item that you enjoy creating and believe others would be interested in buying. It could be handmade jewellery, personalised greeting cards, painted pottery, knitted scarves or any other craft that you are skilled at making. ***You can organise a fair in your school and sell these items.***

DEMAND AND SUPPLY

The students of Class 5 love making DIY crafts. Each student has a special skill, such as painting, knitted items, making jewellery or creating unique decorations. They decide to have a mini market to sell their handmade DIY items. The mini market works on demand and supply.

Demand *is all about how much people want or desire something*. In this DIY market, some items are popular than others. Many people want to buy knitted socks because they find them attractive and unique. Knitted items are in high demand because lots of people want to buy them. On the other hand, only a few people are interested in buying bookmarks. These bookmarks are in low demand because not as many people want them.

Supply *refers to how much of something is available*. In the DIY market, each student has a limited number of items they have made. The student with the knitted items may have only a few pieces available because they take time and effort to create. The student with the bookmarks may have made a larger quantity because they are easier and quicker to make.

When the market opens, people start coming to buy the DIY items. They look at the knitted items and see that there are only a few available. Since the demand is high and the supply is limited, the student selling the knitted items can charge a higher price because many people want them. On the other hand, when people see the bookmarks, they notice there are many available. Since the demand is low and the supply is higher, the student selling the bookmarks may need to lower the price to attract buyers.

Understanding demand and supply can help us make better choices when buying or selling DIY items, as well as in other aspects of our lives.

Glossary

Chapter 1

Place value: The value of a digit according to its place

Face value: The actual value of a digit in a number

Rounding off: Writing a number nearest to its tens, hundreds, thousands, lakhs, ten-lakhs, crores or ten-crores

Chapter 2

Addition: The process of finding the sum of two or more numbers

Sum: The result of addition

Subtraction: The process of finding the difference between two numbers

Difference: The result of subtraction

Verification: The process of checking the answer

Chapter 3

Multiplication: The process of finding the product of two or more numbers

Product: The result of multiplication

Estimation: A rough calculation of a value

Division: Equal sharing or equal grouping

Dividend: The number that is divided

Divisor: The number which divides the dividend

Quotient: The answer obtained after division

Remainder: The number that is left over after division

Chapter 4

Factor: A number is said to be a factor of a given number if it divides the given number completely

Multiple: A number is said to be a multiple of a given number if it is divided by the given number completely

HCF: The highest common factor of two or more given numbers is the greatest number that completely divides each of the numbers

LCM: The least common multiple of two or more given numbers is the smallest of their common multiples

Prime number: A number that has only 1 and itself as its factors

Composite number: A number that has more than two factors

Twin prime numbers: Two prime numbers whose difference is 2

Co-prime numbers: Two numbers whose common factor is only 1

Prime factors: The factors of a number which are prime

Prime factorisation: The method of expressing a number as a product of its prime factors

Chapter 5

Numerator: Number of equal parts of a whole

Denominator: Total number of equal parts of a whole

Unlike fractions: Fractions having different denominators

Proper fractions: Fractions where the numerator is less than the denominator

Improper fractions: Fractions where the numerator is more than the denominator

Mixed fractions: A combination of a whole number and a proper fraction

Chapter 6

Like decimals: Decimals having the same number of decimal places

Unlike decimals: Decimals having different number of decimal places

Chapter 7

Percentage: A number expressed as a fraction of 100

Decimal point: A dot that separates the whole number and the decimal part

Tenth: First place after the decimal point that indicates a part of ten equal parts

Hundredth: Second place after the decimal point that indicates a part of hundred equal parts

Chapter 8

Measurement: The process of comparing an unknown quantity with a known standard to determine its size or amount

Length: The measure of distance from one point to another, usually measured in centimetres (cm), metres (m) or kilometres (km)

Mass: The measure of the amount of matter in an object, usually measured in grams (g) or kilograms (kg)

Capacity: The maximum amount that a container can have, usually measured in litres (ℓ) or millilitres (mℓ)

Conversion: The process of changing a measurement from one unit to another unit within the same measurement system

Weigh Scale: A device used to measure mass

Chapter 9

Time: The measurement of the duration of events, usually measured in seconds (s), minutes (min) or hours (h)

Duration: The length of time that something lasts or continues for

Elapsed time: The amount of time that has passed between the starting time and the ending time

A.M.: Abbreviation for "ante meridiem", indicates the time from midnight to noon

P.M.: Abbreviation for "post meridiem", indicates the time from noon to midnight

Temperature: A measure of the hotness or coldness of an object or environment, measured in degrees Celsius (°C) or degree Fahrenheit (°F)

Thermometer: A tool used to measure temperature

Chapter 10

Average: The value that is evenly distributed among a given number of quantities

Arithmetic mean or mean: Other names of average

Unitary method: The method of finding the value of one unit and then the value of the required number of units

Chapter 11

Profit: The extra amount earned by selling something

Gain: Another word for profit

Loss: The amount lost on selling or buying something

Cost price: The actual amount spent on making or manufacturing a product (C.P.)

Selling price: The amount that is fixed for selling a product (S.P.)

Overhead expenses: The extra charges, like transportation, repair, etc. paid on the product bought

Chapter 12

Ray: A part of a line

Intersecting lines: Pair of lines that cut or intersect each other at a point

Perpendicular lines: Pair of lines that intersect each other at 90°

Parallel lines: Pair of lines that do not intersect

Angle: The inclination of a ray with the other when they meet at a point

Protractor: A D-shaped instrument used to measure angles

Degree: A unit of measurement of an angle

Chapter 13

Perimeter: The distance around an object or a shape

Area: The amount of surface or region covered by an object

Volume: The amount of space occupied by an object

Chapter 14

Isometric dot paper: A special dotted paper used for drawing 3D objects

Symmetry: The property of a figure to keep its shape when reflected or rotated

Reflection symmetry: A figure is said to have reflection symmetry if its one half is the mirror image of the other half

Rotational symmetry: A figure is said to have rotational symmetry if it fits exactly into itself when rotated by a certain amount

Chapter 15

Data: Information or facts that are collected and used for analysis

Data Handling: The process of organising, collecting, analysing and interpreting data

Bar Graph: A graph that uses rectangular bars of different lengths to represent data

Circle Graph: A type of graph that uses a circle divided into sectors or slices to represent data, also known as pie chart

Line graph: A graph that uses points connected by lines to represent data

Chapter 16

Map: A visual representation of an area, showing its features, boundaries and relationships

Cardinal directions: The four main points on a compass: North, South, East and West

Compass: An instrument used to find directions

Legend/Key: An explanatory guide on a map that helps understand the symbols and other elements used to represent features or information on the map

Scale: A ratio or measurement on a map that relates the distance on the map to the actual distance on the Earth's surface

Route: The path or course taken from one place to another

Answer Keys

Chapter 1

Are You Ready?

A. 2 B. 3 C. 4 D. 2. E. 1
F. 1 G. 4 H. 2

Exercise 1.1

1.

	Number Name
a. 24,15,786	Twenty-four lakh fifteen thousand seven hundred eighty-six
b. 82,16,00,009	Eighty-two crore sixteen lakh nine
c. 1,24,36,205	One crore twenty-four lakh thirty-six thousand two hundred five
d. 5,80,42,513	Five crore eighty lakh forty-two thousand five hundred thirteen
e. 3,45,61,897	Three crore forty-five lakh sixty-one thousand eight hundred ninety-seven

2. a. 95,63,049 b. 10,00,20,091
   c. 7,00,00,201 d. 47,47,47,447
   e. 8,50,40,393
3. a. 8,00,00,000; 5,00,000; 2,000; 6
   b. 10,000; 900; 80; 2
   c. 7,00,00,000; 10,00,000; 5,000
   d. 87,05,06,405
   e. 1,00,00,001
4. a. 10; 100; 1,000 b. 10; 100; 1,000; 10,000
   c. 10; 100; 1,000; 10,000; 1,00,000
   d. 10; 100; 1,000; 10,000; 1,00,000; 10,00,000
   e. 100 1,000 10,000 1,00,000 10,00,000; 1,00,00,000

Exercise 1.2

1. Rajasthan, Karnataka, Tamil Nadu, West Bengal, Bihar
2. a. 2,78,56,145 < 27,84,05,614
   b. 7,89,999 = 7,89,999
   c. 10,02,540 < 60,02,504
   d. 10,00,001 < 1,00,00,001 e. 6,82,00,547 > 6,82,00,527

Exercise 1.3

1. a. 546,896,415
   b. 670,000,406
   c. 76,009,985
   d. Nine hundred million four hundred sixty-seven thousand nine hundred ninety-nine
   e. Seven hundred thirty-five million eighty-four thousand two hundred six
2. a. 1,24,054 < 21,40,589
   b. 2,44,56,122 < 3,45,47,892
   c. 90,00,001 > 90,00,000
   d. 57,89,456 < 5,08,91,243
   e. 5,22,14,561 < 76,87,41,321
3.

Number	Indian Place Value System	International Place Value System
a. 24587916	2,45,87,916	24,587,916
b. 312458	3,12,458	312,458
c. 748657136	74,86,57,136	748,657,136
d. 50060090	5,00,60,090	50,060,090
e. 9264906	92,64,906	9,264,906

4. a. 3,47,55,002
   b. 916,445,291
   c. 81,60,045
   d. 2,010,406
   e. 345,745,621
5. a. 45,00,000
   b. 2,80,00,000
   c. 78,60,000
   d. 54,30,00,000
   e. 7,08,000
6. There are 90,00,000 7-digit numbers. The largest 7-digit number is 99,99,999 and the smallest 7-digit number is 10,00,000. So, from largest to smallest 7-digit numbers, we count the how many numbers are there. There are 99,99,999-10,00,000+1=90,00,000 7-digit numbers. Similarly, we can say there are 9,00,00,000 8-digit numbers and 90,00,00,000 9-digit numbers.
7. 41,28,56,397, 43,28,56,197, 47,28,56,193, 47,28,56,391, 41,28,56,793, 43,28,56,791

Exercise 1.4

1. a. 34 b. 270 c. 1007 d. 790
   e. 55 f. 99 g. 521 h. 2151
   i. 1256 j. 2803 k. 145 l. 1785
   m. 1791 n. 1845
2. a. DCCCLXXXVIII
   b. CCCXLVIII
   c. DLXXVII
   d. DCCXCIX
   e. CDXXXIV
   f. CCLXXXVII
   g. MMDCCLXV
   h. MCDXLIX

Revision Exercise

A. 1. b 2. d 3. d 4. a 5. c

B. 1. 47,91,00,216,
2. lesser,
3. 30,24,969,
4. greater,
5. 8,00,75,156

C. 1. c, 2. d, 3. a, 4. e, 5. b

D. 1. true, 2. false, 3. true, 4. false, 5. false

E. 1. Indian system – 5,07,86,124, International system – 50,786,124
2. 4,00,00,000
3. 7,55,67,890, 7,55,76,890, 7,55,76,980,17,55,76,980
4. 86,00,000
5. CCXX

F. 1. ₹215, 2. Rekha, 3. 1 3, 4. May, 5. ₹ 85,00,326

Did You Master?

A. 1	B. 2	C. 4	D. 1	E. 3
F. 1	G. 4	H. 3	I. 1	J. 2

Chapter 2

Are You Ready?

A. 4	B. 3	C. 1	D. 3	E. 4
F. 1	G. 3	H. 2	I. 4	J. 1

Exercise 2.1

1. a. 861257877 D
b. 51546647 E
c. 974122279 L
d. 967122279 H
e. 646010669 I; DELHI
2. a. 38991757 M
b. 935444292 U
c. 38991757 M
d. 3678835 B
e. 12274181 A
f. 156940096 I; MUMBAI

Exercise 2.2

1. 13095091
2. 70052216
3. 528237344
4. 16296816
5. 106443008
6. 685375278

Exercise 2.3

1. a. 28,03,470 mobiles
b. 11,55,000 babies
c. 67,14,54,325 fans
d. 2,05,289 people
e. ₹7,33,78,565
f. 23,54,966 children
g. (Sample Answers) (i) Sum of 14,256 and 15,26,431
(ii) Sum of 1,26,348 and 14,14,339
h. (Sample answers) (i) Subtract 45,693 from 15,86,380
(ii) Subtract 7800 from 15,48,487
2. a. Rural places = 3,46,94,609
Female in rural places =1,68,95,450
Females in urban places = 1,20,52,982
b. Urban places = 2,36,25,962
Females in Rural places =1,85,39,981
Population = 6,10,95,297

Revision Exercise

A. 1. d	2. b	3. a	4. c	5. c
B. 1. + +	2. –	3. –	4. – +	5. + –
C. 1. c	2. d	3. e	4. a	5. b

D. 1. True
2. False
3. False
4. False
5. False

E. 1. 8212567
2. 2864793
3. 1647125
4. 71518050
5. 2374814

F. 1. 1104360 km
2. 77,65,060 children
3. 42415870 people
4. 71106050 buttons
5. 10924828 sofa sets

Did You Master?

A. 4	B. 3	C. 1	D. 3	E. 4
F. 2	G. 3	H. 4	I. 1	

Chapter 3

Are You Ready?

A. 2	B. 4	C. 3	D. 2	E. 4
F. 3	G. 2	H. 2	I. 2	

Exercise 3.1

1. a. True
b. False
c. True
d. False
e. False
2. a. 446208
b. 57024
c. 147906
d. 46655
e. 175338
3. a. 1739123
b. 836495
c. 3430420
d. 852996
e. 6063037
4. a. 13357310
b. 1223211
c. 14113320
d. 35555303
e. 5020041
5. a. 87,395
b. 61,491
c. 4,13,825
d. 5,54,040
e. 4,25,024
6. a. 16,60,695
b. 3,49,728
c. 42,17,265
d. 7,50,015
e. 3,44,756

7.

Number	Multiplied by 10	Multiplied by 100	Multiplied by 1000
a. 3459	34,590	3,45,900	34,59,000
b. 1600	16,000	1,60,000	16,00,000
c. 57,109	5,71,090	57,10,900	5,71,09,000
d. 49,287	4,92,870	49,28,700	4,92,87,000
e. 20,912	2,09,120	20,91,200	2,09,12,000

Exercise 3.2

1. 13,51,600 kg
2. ₹3,94,850
3. 5,44,000 kg
4. ₹16,65,640
5. ₹1,96,800

Exercise 3.3

1. a. 11379
   b. 4094
   c. 33771, remainder = 1
   d. 24396
   e. 8106, remainder = 1
2. a. 5442
   b. 1454, remainder = 8
   c. 3115, remainder = 12
   d. 2060, remainder = 10
   e. 2456
3. a. 94,555
   b. 2,85,823
   c. 1,97,403
   d. 33,792
   e. 20,020
4. a. 30,701
   b. 35,132
   c. 4572
   d. 44,206
   e. 17,450
   f. 4711
   g. 1542
   h. 1968
   i. 6166
   j. 39,782

Exercise 3.4

1. 1,606 students, yes
2. 13, 43
3. 3,247 bags, yes
4. 11,822 kg, 19 kg
5. 25,176 biscuits, 4,27,992 biscuits

Revision Exercise

A. 1. b 2. d 3. a 4. c 5. d

B. 1. 49852
   2. Quotient = 7 and Remainder = 65
   3. 1188000
   4. 153875
   5. Quotient = 45 and Remainder = 523

C. 1. d
   2. a
   3. e
   4. b
   5. c

D. 1. F
   2. T
   3. F
   4. F
   5. T

E. 1. 1254926
   2. 1318104
   3. 5407482
   4. 18046413
   5. 93395856

F. 1. Q = 845, R = 41
   2. Q = 2192
   3. Q = 33379
   4. Q = 127160, R = 3
   5. Q = 7461

G. 1. ₹2,02,640
   2. 45,012 kg
   3. ₹12,450
   4. 16
   5. ₹5847, ₹2859, Rice, ₹2988
   6. 666 tickets
   7. 2124 people

Did you master?

A. 2 B. 4 C. 3 D. 3 E. 4
F. 4 G. 2 H. 4

Chapter 4

Are You Ready?

A. 4 B. 3 C. 2 D. 4 E. 4
F. 2 G. 4 H. 3 I. 2 J. 4

Exercise 4.1

1.

Number	2	5	10	3	6	9
26352	yes	No	No	yes	yes	yes
36000	yes	yes	yes	yes	yes	yes
11011	No	No	No	No	No	No
3996	yes	No	No	yes	yes	yes
23484	yes	No	No	yes	yes	No

2. a. T
   b. F
   c. F
   d. T
   e. F
3. a. 2
   b. 3
   c. prime number, composite
   d. composite
   e. twin primes

4.

~~5~~									
5	~~15~~	~~14~~	17	~~28~~	~~27~~	71	41	~~46~~	~~81~~
~~99~~	~~60~~	29	~~49~~	~~51~~	~~63~~	~~93~~	~~86~~	37	~~10~~
3	1	13	~~22~~	~~39~~	~~45~~	~~20~~	67	~~91~~	43
31	47	~~77~~	~~50~~	~~69~~	~~30~~	~~87~~	~~56~~	~~76~~	23
~~32~~	11	~~38~~	~~42~~	~~46~~	~~98~~	19	~~26~~	~~30~~	~~12~~
~~90~~	~~21~~	37	61	~~4~~	~~33~~	~~18~~	~~92~~	~~95~~	~~25~~
59	~~88~~	5	~~24~~	~~35~~	~~20~~	~~44~~	~~66~~	~~16~~	~~58~~
73	~~18~~	79	7	~~52~~	~~55~~	~~75~~	~~14~~	~~28~~	~~40~~
~~93~~	~~34~~	~~40~~	~~64~~	~~80~~	~~70~~	37	~~9~~	53	~~36~~
~~62~~	23	~~57~~	2	89	~~25~~	~~78~~	~~44~~	~~85~~	~~72~~

Exercise 4.2

1. a. 2 × 2 × 5
   b. 2 × 2 × 3 × 3
   c. 3 × 5 ×5
   d. 2 × 2 × 2 × 3 × 5 × 5
   e. 3 × 7 × 7;
2. a. 2 × 2 × 2 × 5
   b. 2 × 2 × 2 × 3 × 3
   c. 2 × 5 ×5
   d. 3 × 3 × 3 × 3
   e. 2 × 2 × 2 × 2 × 3;
3. a.

2	56
2	28
2	14
7	7
	1

b.

3	27
3	9
3	3
	1

c.

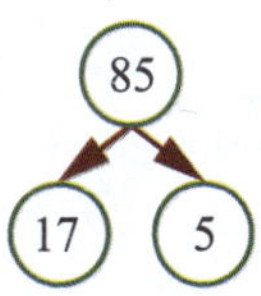

d.

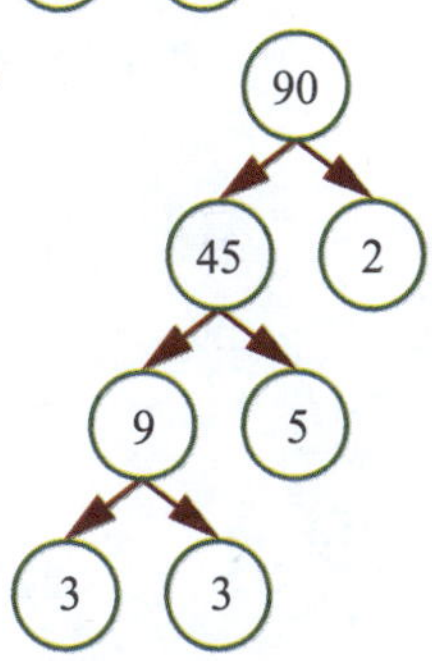

e.

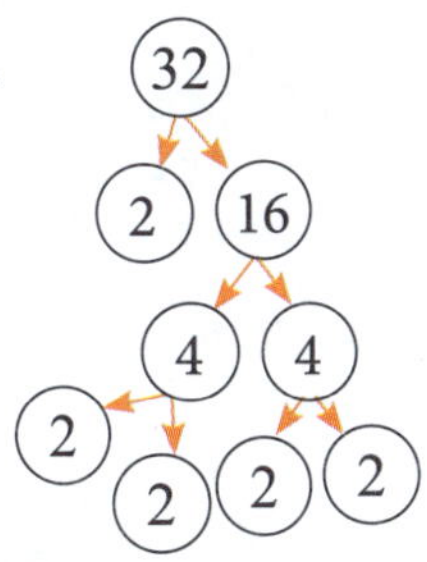

Exercise 4.3

1. a. 14	b. 9	c. 18	d. 15	e. 2
2. a. 14	b. 4	c. 5	d. 3	e. 9

Exercise 4.4

1. a. 72	b. 144	c. 336	d. 150	e. 60
2. a. 100	b. 120	c. 150	d. 255	e. 156

Exercise 4.5

1. 1   2. 54   3. 3   4. 30
5. 22; 132

Exercise 4.6

1. 6 books
2. 7:02;24 a.m.
3. 1008 seconds

Revision Exercise

A. 1. b	2. d	3. a	4. a	5. b
B. 1. 3	2. 35	3. 90	4. 24	5. 15
C. 1. b	2. c	3. e	4. a	5. d
D. 1. T	2. F	3. F	4. F	5. T

E. 1. 2 × 19
   2. 7×3×2×2
   3. 2 × 2 × 19
   4. 5 × 31
   5. 2 × 2 × 2 × 3 × 5

F. 1. 12, 24
   2. 6
   3. 7
   4. 64
   5. 25

G. 1. 12 fruits
   2. 30 students
   3. 2 days
   4. 6 cm
   5. 9 times

Did You Master?

A. 2 B. 3 C. 3 D. 1 E. 4
F. 3 G. 2 H. 4 I. 4 J. 3

Chapter 5

Are You Ready?

A. 3 B. 1 C. 4 D. 1 E. 1
F. 3 G. 4 H. 3 I. 2 J. 1

Exercise 5.1

1. a. < b. > c. = d. > e. <
2. a. < b. > c. > d. < e. =
3. a. $\frac{3}{8}, \frac{1}{2}, \frac{2}{3}, \frac{4}{5}$
   b. $\frac{5}{8}, \frac{3}{4}, \frac{5}{6}, \frac{5}{2}$
   c. $\frac{1}{3}, \frac{1}{2}, \frac{2}{3}, \frac{3}{4}$
   d. $\frac{16}{25}, \frac{4}{5}, \frac{13}{15}, \frac{9}{10}$
   e. $\frac{11}{21}, \frac{9}{14}, \frac{5}{6}, \frac{5}{2}$
4. a. $\frac{7}{8}, \frac{3}{4}, \frac{1}{2}, \frac{5}{12}$
   b. $\frac{2}{3}, \frac{2}{5}, \frac{1}{4}, \frac{1}{10}$
   c. $\frac{5}{2}, \frac{5}{3}, \frac{3}{2}, \frac{2}{5}$
   d. $\frac{4}{7}, \frac{1}{2}, \frac{2}{5}, \frac{3}{8}$
   e. $\frac{4}{9}, \frac{5}{12}, \frac{1}{3}, \frac{1}{6}$

Exercise 5.2

1. a. $\frac{8}{7}$ b. $\frac{12}{13}$
   c. $\frac{38}{27}$ d. $\frac{3}{2}$ or $1\frac{1}{2}$
   e. $\frac{13}{3}$ or $4\frac{1}{3}$ f. $\frac{24}{11}$ or $2\frac{2}{11}$
   g. $\frac{55}{23}$ or $2\frac{9}{23}$ h. $\frac{11}{10}$ or $1\frac{1}{10}$
   i. $\frac{23}{31}$ j. $\frac{32}{55}$
2. a. $\frac{13}{18}$ b. $\frac{47}{40}$ or $1\frac{7}{40}$
   c. $\frac{34}{35}$ d. $\frac{73}{80}$
   e. $\frac{41}{12}$ or $3\frac{5}{12}$ f. $\frac{92}{21}$ or $4\frac{8}{21}$
   g. $\frac{61}{18}$ or $3\frac{7}{18}$ h. $\frac{65}{12}$ or $5\frac{5}{12}$
   i. $\frac{101}{30}$ or $3\frac{11}{30}$ j. $\frac{9}{10}$
3. a. $5\frac{1}{3}$ b. $8\frac{9}{20}$ c. $5\frac{5}{6}$
   d. $3\frac{14}{15}$ e. $7\frac{33}{35}$ f. $8\frac{1}{28}$
   g. $7\frac{13}{21}$ h. $12\frac{5}{12}$ i. $3\frac{52}{63}$
   j. $9\frac{37}{40}$

Exercise 5.3

1. a. $\frac{4}{8}$ or $\frac{1}{2}$ b. $\frac{4}{11}$ c. $\frac{3}{19}$
   d. $\frac{13}{26}$ or $\frac{1}{2}$ e. $\frac{8}{7}$ f. $\frac{9}{15}$ or $\frac{3}{5}$
   g. $\frac{19}{30}$ h. $\frac{21}{19}$ i. $\frac{38}{22}$ or $\frac{19}{11}$
   j. $\frac{6}{10}$ or $\frac{3}{5}$
2. a. $\frac{25}{3}$ b. $\frac{17}{10}$ c. $\frac{7}{36}$
   d. $\frac{33}{20}$ e. $\frac{47}{5}$ f. $\frac{1}{20}$
   g. $\frac{61}{65}$ h. $\frac{57}{4}$ i. $\frac{6}{25}$
   j. $\frac{3}{20}$
3. a. $2\frac{1}{4}$ b. $7\frac{1}{3}$ c. $2\frac{5}{6}$
   d. $11\frac{4}{5}$ e. $2\frac{16}{21}$ f. $\frac{19}{20}$
   g. $9\frac{2}{9}$ h. $5\frac{1}{18}$ i. $4\frac{14}{15}$
   j. $4\frac{1}{5}$

Exercise 5.4

1. a. 10 b. 16 c. 20 d. $10\frac{2}{7}$ e. $17\frac{7}{8}$
2. a. $\frac{2}{30}$ or $\frac{1}{15}$ b. $\frac{8}{45}$ c. $\frac{3}{10}$ d. $\frac{4}{21}$ e. $\frac{1}{4}$
   f. $\frac{1}{48}$ g. 6 h. $\frac{2}{5}$ i. $\frac{5}{22}$ j. $\frac{1}{12}$

Exercise 5.5

1. a 25 b. $\frac{7}{30}$ c. 81 d. $\frac{2}{15}$ e. $\frac{2}{27}$
   f. $\frac{1}{24}$ g. 72 h. $\frac{1}{36}$ i. 81 j. $\frac{3}{28}$

2. a. $\frac{12}{13}$ b. $\frac{5}{14}$ c. $\frac{7}{12}$
d. $\frac{3}{25}$ e. $\frac{45}{88}$ f. $\frac{11}{24}$
g. $\frac{44}{5}$ h. $\frac{57}{8}$ i. $\frac{39}{10}$
j. $\frac{35}{22}$

Exercise 5.6

1. Vinay
2. 8 km
3. $\frac{2}{21}$ kg
4. 8 pencils
5. 96 pieces

Revision Exercise

A. 1. c 2. c 3. b 4. a 5. d
B. 1. < 2. $\frac{7}{20}$ 3. $\frac{3}{8}$ 4. 20 5. $\frac{3}{4}$
C. 1. e 2. c 3. a 4. b 5. d
D. 1. F 2. T 3. F 4. F 5. T
E. 1. $\frac{17}{40}$
2. $2\frac{10}{21}$ litres
3. 36 cookies
4. 30 pieces
5. ₹550
6. 200
7. ₹$81\frac{1}{4}$
8. $\frac{1}{6}$ litres
9. 25 pages
10. $9\frac{3}{4}$ kg

Did You Master?

A. 2 B. 1 C. 4 D. 3 E. 4
F. 1 G. 3 H. 3 I. 1 J. 2

Chapter 6

Are You Ready?

A. 3 B. 4 C. 2 D. 2 E. 3
F. 1 G. 1 H. 3 I. 4 J. 2

Exercise 6.1

1. a. like decimals
b. unlike decimals
c. like decimals
d. unlike decimals
e. unlike decimals
2. a. 0.4 b. 1.33 c. 0.14 d. 0.85 e. 0.48
3. a. $\frac{1}{2}$ b. $\frac{19}{10}$ c. $\frac{23}{20}$ d. $\frac{168}{125}$ e. $\frac{144}{25}$
4. a. < b. > c. > d. < e. >
5. a. 0.4, 0.462, 4.26, 4.62, 42, 46.2, 462
b. 0.5, 0.537, 3.57, 3.75, 35.7, 53.7, 357
c. 1.375, 5.75, 13.75, 15.73, 51.37, 137.5
d. 0.02, 0.088, 0.2, 0.211, 0.75, 1, 1.2
e. 1.009, 1.986, 11.209, 18.45, 19.01, 23.6, 29.4
6. a. 0.32, 0.302, 0.233, 0.102, 0.032
b. 14.99, 14.009, 4.9, 4.09
c. 111.1, 11.01, 1.001, 0.111, 0.11
d. 13.8, 3.9, 3.09, 3.009, 1.38
e. 1.2, 1.02, 0.12, 0.02, 0.002

Exercise 6.2

1. a. 99.01
b. 84.9
c. 72.05
d. 84.25
e. 149.1
2. a. 8.56
b. 36.73
c. 2.02
d. 69.31
e. 31.6
3. a. 57.5 km
b. 19.37 inches
c.14.33 cm
d. 1.2 kg
e. 16.1 km

Exercise 6.3

1.

	10	100	1000
a. 6.63	66.3	663	6630
b. 0.457	4.57	45.7	457
c. 9.91	99.1	991	9910
d. 3.456	34.56	345.6	3456
e. 456.7	4567	45670	456700

2. a. 256.8
b. 656.1
c. 1767.2
d. 388.8
e. 124580.9

Exercise 6.4

1. a. 0.3
b. 0.3
c. 1.729
d. 3.02
e. 0.0020
2.

	10	100	1000
a. 34.5	3.45	0.345	0.0345
b. 456.60	45.660	4.5660	0.45660
c. 34.9	3.49	0.349	0.0349
d. 11.289	1.1289	0.11289	0.011289
e. 0.08	0.008	0.0008	0.00008

Revision Exercise

A. 1. b 2. a 3. c 4. a 5. c
B. 1. > 2. < 3. < 4. < 5. >
C. 1. c 2. e 3. a 4. b 5. d
D. 1. F 2. T 3. T 4. F 5. T
E. 1. a. 3349.88
b. 67936.994
c. 6912.546
d. 4096.967
e. 83.185

2. a. 55.26
   b. 4.002
   c. 49.235
   d. 15.37
   e. 21.577
3. a. 21.6
   b. 1153.08
   c. 16.1
   d. 13.68
   e. 4.928
4. a. 0.235
   b. 4.3
   c. 7.105
   d. 0.08008
   e. 9.089

F. a. ₹356
   b. 39 km
   c. carrots, 0.25 kg
   d. 4.9 km
   e. ₹9.17

Did You Master?

A. 2	B. 2	C. 3	D. 4	E. 3
F. 4	G. 1	H. 3	I. 2	J. 4

Chapter 7

Are You Ready?

A. 3	B. 2	C. 4	D. 1	E. 4
F. 4	G. 2	H. 1	I. 4	J. 2

Exercise 7.1

1. a. 20%	b. 30%	c. 75%	d. 50%	e. 45%
2. a. $\frac{1}{25}$	b. $\frac{3}{4}$	c. $\frac{11}{100}$	d. $\frac{12}{25}$	e. $\frac{19}{50}$
3. a. 60%	b. 27%	c. 45%	d. 125%	e. 348%
4. a. 0.04	b. 1.12	c. 0.16	d. 0.24	e. 1.03

Mental maths

a. 10 b. 50 c. 50 d. 24

Exercise 7.2

1. a. 4.2 b. 468 c. 48 d. 28 e. 49
2. a. 72 b. 192 c. 16
   d. 36 apples, 24 oranges, e. 756 f. ₹55
   g. ₹133 h. 9 arrows I. 84 adults J. ₹124.46

Revision Exercise

A. 1. a	2. c	3. a	4. c	5. b
B. 1. $\frac{3}{25}$	2. 80%	3. 0.09	4. 80%	5. 160
C. 1. e	2. a	3. d	4. c	5. b
D. 1. T	2. F	3. F	4. T	5. T
E. 1. 400	2. 77	3. 20	4. 756	5. 432.16
F. 1. 24	2. 60%	3. 45%	4. ₹1,82,400	5. ₹351.75

Did You Master?

A. 4	B. 3	C. 2	D. 4	E. 1
F. 3	G. 1	H. 2	I. 4	J. 2

Chapter 8

Are You Ready?

A. 2	B. 4	C. 2	D. 4	E. 1
F. 1	G. 3	H. 1	I. 4	

Exercise 8.1

1. a. 285 mℓ
   b. 2750 mℓ
   c. 85 m
   d. 706 g
   e. 154 cm
   f. 3825 g
2. a. 20 km 80 m
   b. 16 ℓ 500 mℓ
   c. 2 kg 80 g
   d. 40 ℓ 6 mℓ
   e. 56 km 75 m
   f. 64 cm 1 mm
3. a. 0.67 ℓ
   b. 0.105 km
   c. 0.069 kg
   d. 2.87 kg
   e. 3.5 ℓ
   f. 4.06 km
4.

Measurement	In bigger unit	In smaller unit
5 m 40 cm	5.40 m	540 cm
4 m 27 cm	4.27 m	427 cm
16 m 5 cm	16.05 m	1605 cm
5 kg 350 g	5.350 kg	5350 g
7 kg 350 g	7.35 kg	7350 g
2 kg 595 g	2.595 kg	2595 g
1 ℓ 770 mℓ	1.770 ℓ	1770 mℓ
2 ℓ 725 mℓ	2.725 ℓ	2725 mℓ
7 ℓ 450 mℓ	7.45 ℓ	7450 mℓ

Exercise 8.2

1. a. 472.74 m
   b. 2153 cm or 21.53 m
   c. 259 ℓ 676 mℓ
   d. 13.132 ℓ
   e. 44.255 kg
   f. 287.706 km
2. a. 2 m 76 cm
   b. 80.11 m
   c. 13 kg 250 g
   d. 35220 mℓ
   e. 13.122 kg
   f. 608.25 kg
3. a. 7614.09 m
   b. 125.125 kg
   c. 190720 cm
   d. 1722.35 ℓ
   e. 152136 mℓ
   f. 1655.018 ℓ
4. a. 25.03 m
   b. 338.526 kg
   c. 6.6967 ℓ
   d. 3.03 ℓ
   e. 721 cm
   f. 6.125 ℓ

Exercise 8.3

1. a. 35 m 62 cm
   b. 154.975 kg
   c. 218.03 mℓ
   d. 707 g
   e. 72900 mℓ
2. a. ii b. i c. ii d. iii e. i

Revision Exercise

A. 1. b 2. d 3. b 4. c 5. d
B. 1. 7.7
   2. 2.1
   3. 1344
   4. 18.2
   5. 0.250
C. 1. d 2. e 3. a 4. c 5. b
D. 1. False 2. True 3. False 4. True 5. True
E. 1. 141.86 m
   2. 34.564 kg
   3. 1265 cm
   4. 116772 kg
F. 1. 195 kg
   2. 5400 m
   3. 21691.85 kg
   4. 13675 mℓ
   5. 185.4 kg
   6. Weighing strategy

Did You Master?

A. 2 B. 1 C. 2 D. 4 E. 3
F. 4 G. 3 H. 2 I. 3 J. 3

Chapter 9

Are You Ready?

A. 4 B. 2 C. 4 D. 2 E. 1
F. 3 G. 3 H. 3 I. 1 J. 4

Exercise 9.1

1. a. 450 minutes
   b. 84 hours
   c. 11520 minutes
   d. 72 hours
   e. 195 minutes
2. a. 6 h 30 min
   b. 2 min 4 sec
   c. 3 h 25 min
   d. 3 h 45 min
   e. 22 min

Exercise 9.2

1. 12:30 p.m.
2. 1:15 p.m.
3. 19th May
4. 10:20 a.m.
5. 74 days

Exercise 9.3

1. a. 36°C b. 19°C c. 41°C
   d. 35°F e. 13°F
2. a. 149°F b. 41°F c. 392°F
   d. 95°F e. 167°F
3. a. 20°C b. 40°C c. 230°C
   d. 25°C e. 80°C

Revision Exercise

A. 1. b 2. d 3. b 4. c 5. d
B. 1. 64.4 2. 80 3. 104 4. 35 5. 98.6
C. 1. d 2. e 3. a 4. b 5. c
D. 1. T 2. F 3. F 4. T 5. T
E. 1. 3:35 a.m.
   2. 11:00 p.m.
   3. 3:30 a.m.
   4. 1:10 a.m.
   5.1:40 a.m.
F. 1. 7:15 p.m.
   2. 1680 minutes
   3. 1 hour 25 minutes
   4. 235 degrees Celsius
   5. 35 degrees Celsius

Did You Master?

A. 4 B. 3 C. 2 D. 1 E. 3
F. 1 G. 4 H. 2 I. 2 J. 4

Chapter 10

Are You Ready?

A. 3 B. 1 C. 4 D. 3 E. 1
F. 4 G. 2 H. 4 I. 3 J. 3

Exercise 10.1

1. 5 2. 30 g
3. 7 4. 10 cm
5. 2.39 m 6. $\frac{1}{3}$
7. 3 cm 8. 2.0075
9. $\frac{11}{90}$ 10. 3 kg

Exercise 10.2

1. 34° Celsius
2. 14 m
3. 140 cm
4. 6
5. $\frac{11}{24}$

Exercise 10.3

1.

Items	Quantity	Price (₹)
Tea table	2	8000
Dining table	1	4000
Bean bags	3	6000
Garden chairs	12	9600
	Total	27600

2. Deenu deal is better deal: $\frac{17192}{7}$ = ₹2456 per bamboo
3. Buying the bag of 9 kg is profitable.
4. 330 plants
5. 36 km

Revision Exercise

A. 1. b 2. d 3. d 4. d 5. b
B. 1. $\frac{(a+b)}{2}$ 2. $\frac{9}{14}$ 3. 875 mℓ 4. ₹693 5. 240
C. 1. d 2. e 3. b 4. c 5. a
D. 1. F 2. T 3. F 4. T 5. F

E. 1. $\frac{7}{20}$ 2. 300 g 3. 22 4. 35 5. ₹25

F. 1. ₹259
   2. ₹56
   3. 64 minutes
   4. ₹5208
   5. 15 signboards

Did You Master?

A. 2 B. 3 C. 4 D. 2 E. 2
F. 4 G. 2 H. 4 I. 1 J. 3

Chapter 11

Are You Ready?

A. 1 B. 4 C. 3 D. 4 E. 2
F. 3 G. 1 H. 1 I. 3

Exercise 11.1

1. a.

S. No.	C.P.	S.P.	Profit/Loss	Profit/Loss Amount
1.	₹5630	₹5580	S.P. < C.P. then Loss	₹50
2.	₹10,475	₹10,754	S.P. > C.P. then profit	₹279
3.	₹22,958	₹22,589	S.P. < C.P. then Loss	₹369
4.	₹3650	₹3565	S.P. < C.P. then Loss	₹85
5.	₹12261	₹13126	S.P. > C.P. then profit	₹865

b.

S. No.	S.P.	Profit	Loss	C.P.
1.	₹1542	--	₹200	S.P. + Loss = ₹1542 + ₹200 = ₹1742
2.	₹55,761	₹1700	--	S.P. – Profit = ₹55,761 – ₹1700 = ₹54,061
3.	₹4500	₹344	--	S.P. – Profit = ₹4500 – ₹344 = ₹4156
4.	₹13,763	--	₹525	S.P. + Loss = ₹13,763 + ₹525 = ₹14,288
5.	₹15025	₹268	--	S.P. – Profit = ₹15,025 – ₹268 = ₹14,757

c.

S. No.	C.P.	Profit	Loss	S.P.
1.	₹8642	₹200	--	C.P. + Profit = ₹8642 + ₹200 = ₹8842
2.	₹4,050	--	₹300	C.P. – Loss = ₹4,050 – ₹300 = ₹3750
3.	₹1033	₹215	--	C.P. + Profit = ₹1033 + ₹215 = ₹1248
4.	₹12,377	--	₹650	C.P. – Loss = ₹12,377 – ₹650 = ₹11,727
5.	₹17456	₹345	--	C.P. + Profit = ₹17,456 + ₹345 = ₹17,801

2. Profit, ₹27
3. ₹4175
4. ₹398
5. ₹1920

Revision Exercise

A. 1. c 2. a 3. d 4. b 5. c

B. 1. loss
   2. profit
   3. cost price + profit
   4. selling price + loss
   5. profit of ₹1000

C. 1. Profit of ₹495
   2. Rohit: (CP) ₹8750 – (Loss) ₹250 = (SP) ₹8500 = CP for Karan
   3. ₹190 Profit

Did You Master?

A. 4 B. 1 C. 3 D. 2 E. 1
F. 4 G. 4 H. 3 I. 1 J. 3

Chapter 12

Are You Ready?

A. 3 B. 1 C. 2 D. 4 E. 4
F. 3 G. 1 H. 2 I. 2 J. 1

Exercise 12.1

1. a. ray
   b. line segment
   c. ray
   d. line
   e. line segment
2. Rays: $\overrightarrow{OS}$, $\overrightarrow{OR}$, $\overrightarrow{OP}$, $\overrightarrow{OW}$, $\overrightarrow{OV}$, $\overrightarrow{OU}$, $\overrightarrow{OQ}$, $\overrightarrow{OT}$

   Lines: $\overleftrightarrow{TP}$, $\overleftrightarrow{VR}$, $\overleftrightarrow{SW}$, $\overleftrightarrow{UQ}$
3. a. Perpendicular lines
   b. Parallel lines
   c. Intersecting lines
   d. Parallel lines
   e. Intersecting lines

Exercise 12.2

1. a. 

   b. 

   c. 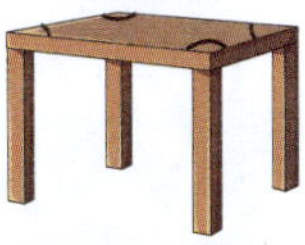

   d. 

   e. 

2. a. 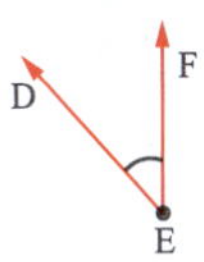

   b. 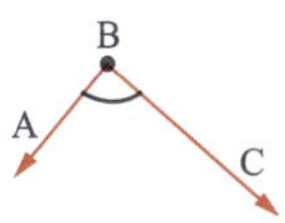

   c. 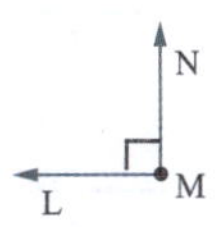

   d. 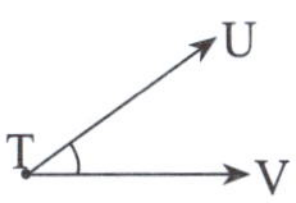

   e. 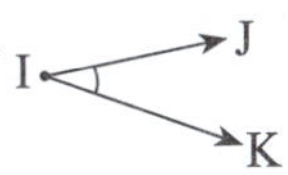

   a. ∠DEF, E, ED, EF
   b. ∠ABC, B, BA, BC
   c. ∠LMN, M, ML, MN
   d. ∠UTV, T, TU, TV
   e. ∠JIK, I, IJ, IK

Exercise 12.3

1. a. A b. O c. S d. R e. A
2. a. Right angle
   b. Acute angle
   c. Acute angle
   d. Right angle
   e. Obtuse angle
3. Right angles: ∠AOC, ∠COD, ∠FOD, ∠AOF
   Acute angles: ∠BOC, ∠BOA, ∠DOE, ∠FOE
   Obtuse angles: ∠BOD, ∠BOF, ∠COE , ∠AOE
   Straight angles: ∠BOE, ∠AOD, ∠COF
4. Acute angles: ∠GAB, ∠ABG, ∠AGB, ∠ECD, ∠DEC, ∠EDC, ∠GBF, ∠FGB, ∠CEF
   Obtuse angles: ∠GBC, ∠BCE, ∠AGF, ∠DEF
   Right angles: ∠GFB, ∠BFE, ∠FBC, ∠FBA
5. 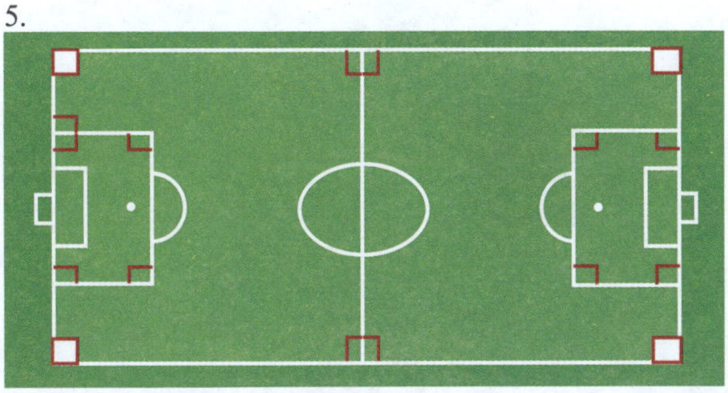

Exercise 12.4

1. a. 40° b. 90° c. 80° d. 50° e. 145°
2. Do it yourself.
3. Do it yourself.

Revision Exercise

A. 1. a 2. b 3. d 4. c 5. a

B. 1. 90°
   2. Acute angle
   3. Obtuse angle
   4. Right angle
   5. ∠IFG

C. 1. b 2. c 3. e 4. a 5. d

D. 1. true
   2. false
   3. true
   4. true
   5. false

E. 1. 90° Right angle
   2. 135° Obtuse angle
   3. 45° Acute angle
   4. 220° Obtuse angle
   5. 180° Straight angle

F. 1. Acute, Obtuse and Right angle
   2.

Parallel parking	Perpendicular parking	Parallel parking
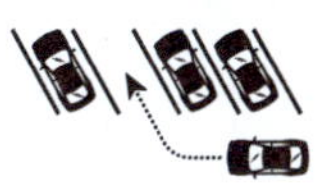	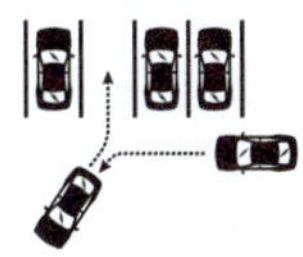	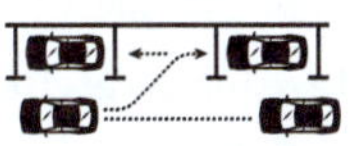

Did You Master?

A. 2 B. 3 C. 2 D. 1 E. 4
F. 2 G. 4 H. 4 I. 2 J. 4

Chapter 13

Are You Ready?

A. 3 B. 4 C. 2 D. 3 E. 4
F. 3 G. 2 H. 4 I. 1 J. 2

Exercise 13.1

1. a. 500 cm b. 60 cm c. 164 inches
   d. 40 inches e. 50 cm
2. a. 12 cm b. 12 cm c. 8 cm
   d. 30 cm e. 15 cm
3. a. 120 cm b. 12 inches c. 116 cm
   d. 33 cm e. 22 m
4. a. 100 inches b. 110 cm c. 170 cm
   d. 8 m e. 160 m

Exercise 13.2

1. a. 625 sq. cm b. 4 sq. cm c. 1500 sq. cm
   d. 96 sq. cm e. 60 sq. cm
2. a. 12 sq. units b. 24 sq. units c. 16 sq. units
   d. 14 sq. units e. 9 sq. units
3. a. 30 units b. 10 units c. 5 units
   d. 19 units e. 11 units
4. a. 5 sq. units b. $\frac{15}{2}$ sq. units c. 6 sq. units
   d. $\frac{15}{2}$ sq. units e. 4 sq. unit

Exercise 13.3

1. ₹ 1750
2. 311 sq. m
3. 6 sq. feet
4. 3200 sq. m
5. 18000 sq. cm

Exercise 13.4

1. a. 16 cu. units
   b. 125 cu. units
   c. 25 cu. units
   d. 81 cu. units
   e. 16 cu. units
2. a. 5 cu. units
   b. 9 cu. units
   c. 10 cu. units
   d. 11 cu. units
   e. 16 cu. units
3. a. 3600 cu. in
   b. 1200 cu. cm
   c. 0.0225 cu. m
   d. 512 cu. cm
   e. 1906.624 cu. cm
4. a. 60 matchboxes
   b. 1440 cu. in
   c. 1600 cu. ft
   d. 3000 cu. m
   e. 450 mℓ

Revision Exercise

A. 1. c 2. b 3. a 4. d 5. c

B. 1. sq. m
2. sq. km
3. sq. cm
4. sq. cm
5. sq. m

C. 1. c 2. d 3. e 4. a 5. b

D. 1. false 2. true 3. true 4. false 5. false

E. 1. 216 cu.units 2. 9 cu.units
3. 45 cu.units 4. 20 cu.units
5. 256 cu.units

F. 1. 1400 cu.cm 2. 2197 cu.cm
3. 300 cu.cm 4. 1323 cu.m
5. 729 cu. cm 6. 64 cu.in
7. 96000 cu.cm 8. 1728 cu.in
9. 3375 cu.cm 10. 1500 cu.cm

G. 1. 700 sq.m 2. 160 cm
3. 32 sq.m 4. 3375 cu.m
5. 80 sq.ft

Did You Master?

A. 1 B. 4 C. 3 D. 1 E. 1
F. 2 G. 2 H. 3 I. 1

Chapter 14

Are You Ready?

A. 2 B. 3 C. 1 D. 4 E. 4
F. 3 G. 1 H. 4 I. 2 J. 3

Exercise 14.1

1.

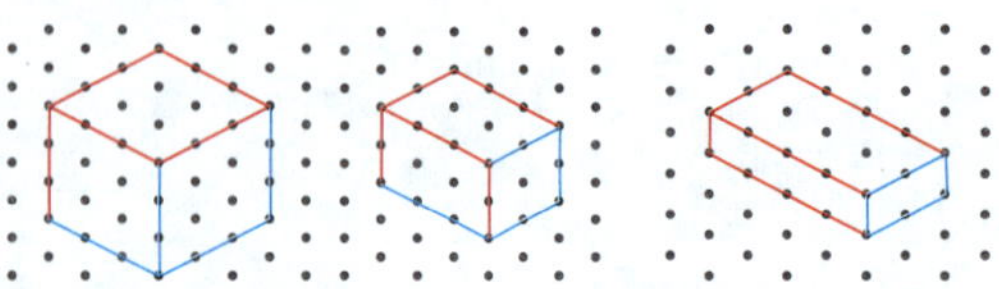

2. a. iv b. v c. i d. ii e. iii
3. a. cuboid
   b. cone
   c. square pyramid

Exercise 14.2

1. a, b, e
2. a. 1 line of symmetry
   b. 2 lines of symmetry
   c. 4 lines of symmetry
   d. 3 lines of symmetry
   e. 1 line of symmetry

a.

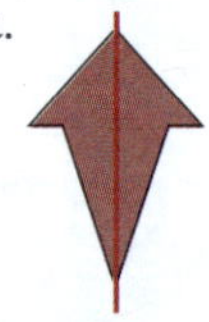

b.

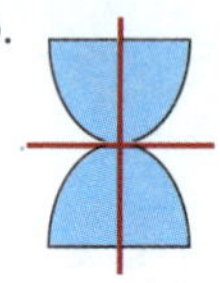

c.

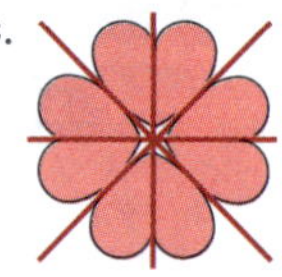

d.

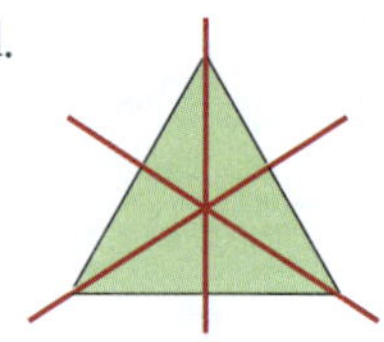

e.

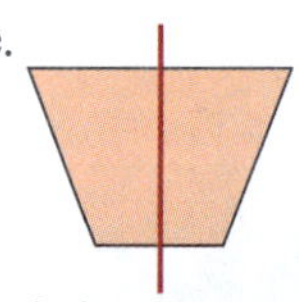

3. a, c, e
4. a.

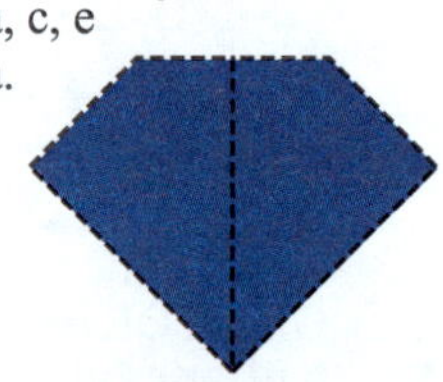

b.

c.

d.

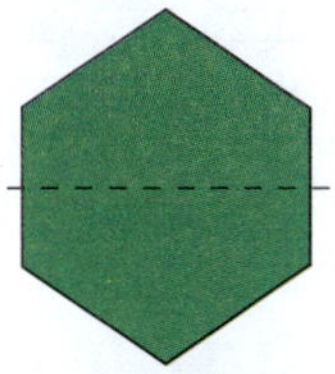

e.

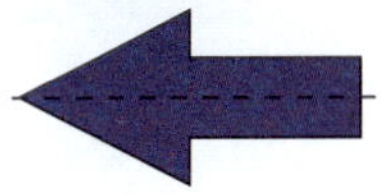

Exercise 14.3

1. b, c, d
2. a, b, d, e
3. a. $\frac{1}{4}$ turn

   b. $\frac{1}{2}$ turn

   c. $\frac{1}{4}$ turn

   d. $\frac{1}{2}$ turn

   e. $\frac{1}{4}$ turn

Exercise 14.4

1. a. cylinder
   b. sphere
   c. cube
   c. cone
   d. cone
2. a. 21, 25, 31
   b. 49, 81
   c. 8, 32
   d. 8, 125
   e. 52, 56

Revision Exercise

A. 1. b	2. d	3. a	4. d.	5. a
B. 1. 44	2. 20,000	3.49	4. 256	5. 144
C. 1. c	2. d	3. e	4. a	5. b
D. 1. T	2. T	3. F	4. T	5.F
E. 1. 1	2. 1	3. 6	4. 3	5. 1
F. 1. $\frac{1}{2}$	2. $\frac{1}{4}$	3. $\frac{1}{2}$	4. $\frac{1}{4}$	

5. 1 full turn

Did You Master?

A. 3	B. 2	C. 4	D. 1	E. 4
F. 3	G. 1	H. 2	I. 3	J. 4

Chapter 15

Are You Ready?

A. i. 3	ii. 4	iii. 3	iv. 4	v. 1
B. i. 3	ii. 2			
C. 4				

Exercise 15.1

1. 6
2. 2
3. yes
4. 1 more than social science
5. 27

Exercise 15.2

1.

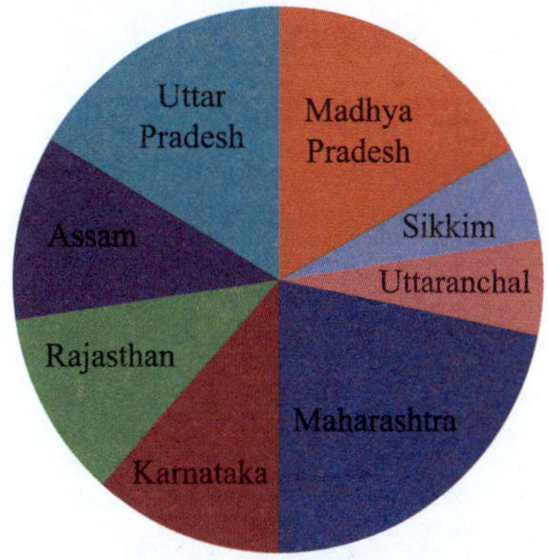

There are 18 world heritage sites in these 8 states.

2.

Reasons	Number of Students
Forgot my books in school	3
was not well	3
grandma was sick	3
Too much work	15
Guests at home	3
Did not understand the chapter	3

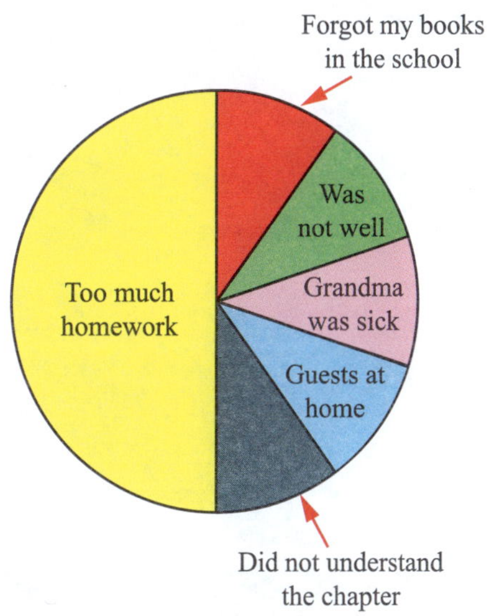

Exercise 15.3

1. a. between 5 and 10 minutes
   b. 24
   c. 12
   d. 60 minutes
   e. 40 minutes
2. a. May
   b. July
   c. 15-degree Celsius
   d. 16-degree Celsius
   e. January

Revision Exercise

A. 1. c	2. d	3. c	4. a	5. b
B. 1. 20	2. 190	3. 70	4. 80	

5. Production

C. 1. d 2. a 3. e 4. c 5. b

D. 1. False
2. True
3. False
4. True
5. True

E. 1. 80 years
2. 40 years
3. 25 years
4. 15 years
5. Modern

Did You Master?

A. i. 1 ii. 4 iii. 3
B. i. 4 ii. 1 iii. 2
C. i. 2 ii. 3

Chapter 16

Are You Ready?

A. 2 B. 3 C. 1 D. 4 E. 2
F. 2 G. 4 H. 3 I. i. 2 ii. 4

Exercise 16.1

1. a. North
b. East
c. South
d. South-east
e. North-west

2. a. 2 b. 3 c. 2 d. 2 e. 3

3. a. 413 km b. 686 km c. 1540 km
d. 959 km e. 714 km

Revision Exercise

A. 1. c 2. d 3. b 4. d 5. c

B. 1. compass
2. location
3. scale
4. rest rooms
5. South-west

C. 1. b 2. e 3. d 4. a 5. c

D. 1. False
2. True
3. False
4. True
5. True

E. 1. East
2. North
3. 337.5 km
4. West
5. 1387.5 km

Did You Master?

A. 1 B. 1 C. 2 D. 1 E. 2
F. 3 G. 4 H. 2 I 4 J. 1